LIBRARY OF HEBREW BIBLE/
OLD TESTAMENT STUDIES

496

Formerly Journal for the Study of the Old Testament Supplement Series

Editors
Claudia V. Camp, Texas Christian University
Andrew Mein, Westcott House, Cambridge

Founding Editors
David J. A. Clines, Philip R. Davies and David M. Gunn

Editorial Board
Richard J. Coggins, Alan Cooper, John Goldingay, Robert P. Gordon,
Norman K. Gottwald, Gina Hens-Piazza, John Jarick, Andrew D. H. Mayes,
Carol Meyers, Patrick D. Miller, Yvonne Sherwood

OBADIAH, JONAH, MICAH

A Theological Commentary

Philip Peter Jenson

t&t clark

NEW YORK • LONDON

Copyright © 2008 by Philip Peter Jenson

T & T Clark International, 80 Maiden Lane, New York, NY 10038

T & T Clark International, The Tower Building, 11 York Road, London SE1 7NX

T & T Clark International is a Continuum imprint.

Visit the T & T Clark blog at www.tandtclarkblog.com

Library of Congress Cataloging-in-Publication Data
Jenson, Philip Peter.
   Obadiah, Jonah, Micah : A theological commentary / Philip Peter Jenson.
      p. cm. -- (Library of Hebrew Bible/Old Testament studies ; 496)
   Includes bibliographical references and index.
   ISBN-13: 978-0-567-04222-4 (hardcover : alk. paper)
   ISBN-10: 0-567-04222-7 (hardcover : alk. paper) 1. Bible. O.T. Obadiah--Commentaries.
2. Bible. O.T. Jonah--Commentaries. 3. Bible. O.T. Micah--Commentaries. I. Title.
BS1595.53.J46 2008
224'.907--dc22
                              2008029752

06 07 08 09 10   10 9 8 7 6 5 4 3 2 1

CONTENTS

PREFACE

The three minor prophets discussed in this commentary display a remarkable variety. The 21 verses of Obadiah make it the shortest book of the Old Testament, but these provide the reader with plenty of questions that are far from being answered despite exhaustive discussion. The book of Jonah tells one of the best-known stories in the Old Testament, yet the more it is studied the more elusive becomes its message, or at least so I have found. Micah contains two of the best-known prophetic texts in the Old Testament (5:2[1]; 6:8), but also many passages that are extremely difficult to understand.

The frustrating task of a commentator faced with the vast amount written on even the shortest biblical text is what to leave out. Limited space inevitably means limited interaction with other scholarship. Instead I have seen it as my primary goal to explain the English text of these three books as best as I can, for the different translations often indicate the most significant interpretive challenges of the Hebrew text. Further it is how the vast majority of readers (even scholars) will encounter the Bible most of the time (Clines 1997a, 9). Of course, the ever-growing number of translations has made this an increasingly complex task. My starting point has been the New Revised Standard Version (NRSV), which often differs little from its predecessors, the Authorised Version (AV), the Revised Version (RV), the Revised Standard Version (RSV) and the more recent English Standard Version (ESV). However, other scholarly translations often adopt distinctive approaches to the text. The Revised English Bible (REB) is a British work that, following the lead of the New English Bible (NEB), tends to be bolder in its adoption of new solutions to problems in the text. The opposite policy is pursued by the New Jewish Publication Society translation (NJPS or Tanakh), a translation by Jewish scholars who see it as their task to translate the traditional Hebrew Masoretic text (MT), however persuasive the text critics might be in suggesting an alternative reading. The New Jerusalem Bible (NJB) represents Roman Catholic and continental scholarship. I have also occasionally referred to the Good News Bible (GNB) and the New Living Translation (NLT), which generally (though not always) represent an interpretive paraphrase rather than a more literal translation. One particularly difficult decision for translators is how to render the divine name (YHWH, generally LORD in English translations, though Yahweh in the NJB). For better of for worse I have used Yhwh, but readers are invited to follow the lead of the earliest translators and vocalize it in whatever way they find most fitting.

While my primary focus has been in explicating the plain sense of the text (Barton 2007), from time to time I have attempted to indicate how the text can be related to broader theological themes, including those taken up in the New Testament. Unapologetically I write as a Christian scholar whose main calling is to teach those called to study and preach the scriptures, although I trust much of what I have written will be valuable to others.

I am grateful to Professor Ronald Clements for his original invitation to contribute to the New Century Bible commentary on the three books. Since that series is no longer active, so I am extremely thankful to Andrew Mein for accepting it in the prestigious LHB/OTS series. Many have encouraged me during the long process of its writing, especially my colleagues and students at Trinity College Bristol and now Ridley Hall Cambridge. Of particular help has been David Clark, who carefully read through the text. Above all I am indebted to my wife, Ruth, whose support and encouragement continues to be the bedrock of my life and studies.

ABBREVIATIONS

ANET	*Ancient Near Eastern Texts Relating to the Old Testament*. Edited by J. B. Pritchard. 3d ed., with supplement. Princeton: Princeton University Press, 1969.
AV	Authorized Version
BDB	F. Brown, S. R. Driver and C. A. Briggs, *Hebrew and English Lexicon of the Old Testament*. Oxford: Clarendon, 1907.
BHS	*Biblia Hebraica Stuttgartensia*. Edited by K. Elliger and W. Rudolph. Stuttgart: Deutsche Bibelstiftung, 1977.
CAD	*The Assyrian Dictionary of the Oriental Institute of the University of Chicago*. Chicago, 1956–
DCH	*Dictionary of Classical Hebrew*. Edited by D. J. A. Clines. Sheffield, 1993–
ESV	English Standard Version
EVV	English versions
GKC	Gesenius' Hebrew Grammar, W. Gesenius. E. Kautzsch, translated by A. E. Cowley. 2nd ed. Oxford: OUP, 1910.
GNB	Good News Bible
HALOT	Koehler, L., W. Baumgartner, and J. J. Stamm, *The Hebrew and Aramaic Lexicon of the Old Testament*. Translated and edited under the supervision of M. E. J. Richardson. 4 vols. Leiden, 1994–99
JM	Joüon, P. and T. Muraoka. *A Grammar of Biblical Hebrew*. Subsidia Biblica 14. Rome, 1991.
KAI	*Kanaanäische und aramäische Inschriften*. H. Donner and W. Röllig. 2d ed. Wiesbaden, 1966–1969
LXX	Septuagint
mg.	Marginal reading
MT	Masoretic Text
NAB	New American Bible
NAC	New American Commentary
NIV	New International Version
NEB	New English Bible
NIDOTTE	*New International Dictionary of Old Testament Theology and Exegesis*. Edited by W. A. VanGemeren. 5 vols. Grand Rapids, 1997
NIV	New International Version
NJB	New Jerusalem Bible
NJPS	New Jewish Publication Society Version
NLT	New Living Translation
NRSV	New Revised Standard Version
REB	Revised English Bible
RSV	Revised Standard Version
Syr.	Syriac
Targ.	Targum
Vulg.	Vulgate

INTRODUCTION TO THE TWELVE

In the Hebrew Bible the twelve minor prophets are counted as one book (the Book of the Twelve) and complete the second subdivision (the latter prophets) of its second division (the prophets). The latter prophets comprise Isaiah, Jeremiah, Ezekiel, and the twelve. The earliest witness to the collection is Sir 49:10 ("May the bones of the Twelve Prophets send forth new life from where they lie"), whose author implies the existence of the collection even though he is referring to the individual prophets.

The first six of the twelve in the Hebrew Bible are Hosea, Joel, Amos, Obadiah, Jonah and Micah, and this is the order of the earliest texts we have (Fuller 1996) and the one followed by English Bibles. Most Greek manuscripts give the order of the first six books as Hosea, Amos, Micah, Joel, Obadiah and Jonah, but this is likely to be a later tradition. Several factors appear to be responsible for the order of books. There is a broad chronological movement from the eighth-century prophets (Hosea, Amos, Micah, Jonah), to the postexilic prophets (Haggai, Zechariah, Malachi). However, Joel is likely to be postexilic and Obadiah refers to the destruction of Jerusalem, so chronology cannot be the only guide. For the Septuagint length may be a factor, since the first five books are in order of decreasing size, yet Jonah is an awkward exception. Sweeney (2000, 57) suggests that there is a shift of focus from Israel (Hosea, Amos, Micah) to the nations (Joel, Obadiah, Jonah, Nahum).

The rabbinic explanation for the twelve being collected together was that this helped them from being lost (*b. B. Bat.* 14b), but recently there has been a strong move to argue that the twelve represent more than a pragmatic collection of individual prophecies (Redditt 2001). One proposal is that individual books are linked by catchwords, similar words or phrases found in two or more books. There are references to Edom in Amos 9:12 and Obadiah, and to God's gracious character in Jonah 4:2 and Mic 7:18. Both Micah and Nahum are concerned with the defeat of Assyria. But were these links already present in the original texts, or were they a product of a conscious redactional process? There have been detailed attempts to provide a history of the various stages of redaction that the twelve passed through (e.g. Nogalski 1993a; 1993b), although the lack of evidence makes certainty impossible (Schart 1996, 42–43).

A rather different approach was explored by House (1990), who argued that the twelve as a whole tell a story. There is a plot movement beginning with those prophets that emphasize sin (Hosea to Micah), to those that highlight punishment (Nahum to Zephaniah), to those that declare restoration (Haggai to Malachi). There are common themes (e.g. the day of Yhwh), common characters

(God, the prophet, Israel, the nations) and a common point of view (the implied author, the narrator, the implied audience). However, it can be pointed out that Obadiah, Jonah and Micah include a good deal on all aspects of the plot, and the rest of House's discussion remains at a very general level. Petersen (2000, 10) more cautiously speaks of a secondary level of redaction resulting in a "thematized anthology."

Ben Zvi (1996b) protests against this entire project, which he points out is a novel move that is not found in the earlier traditions of reading and inter-pretation. Implicit allusions to other books and the presence of common themes are not necessarily the result of deliberate shaping, but could be fortuitous. Moreover, the titles of the books strongly imply that they were regarded as separate prophetic books. Rather than looking at the author or redactor, he argues that the unity could derive from their primary intended readership, the educated postexilic community who would share a common language and worldview.

In practice, commentators have not found these larger perspectives very significant in explaining the details of the text. It is perhaps useful to point out parallels, but the primary context for determining meaning is the individual prophetic book. Many of the common themes can be regarded as aspects of a shared theology, rather than a distinctive emphasis of the twelve. The unity of the minor prophets lies not so much at the level of author or a readership, but in a common commitment to proclaiming a message from the God of Israel to a people who play a central role in the long and complex story to which the vari-ous biblical books bear witness.

OBADIAH

A. *Introduction*

At 21 verses the book of Obadiah is the shortest book in the Old Testament. It is unusual in being an oracle directed against a specific nation other than Israel, its neighbour to the south and east of the Dead Sea, Edom. Nahum and Jonah concentrate on one nation in a similar way, but most of the other prophets address several foreign nations in a block of oracles (e.g. Isa 13–23; Jer 46–51; Ezek 25–32; Amos 1–2; see Hayes 1968; Raabe 1995). Although it is possible that the focus on one nation in Obadiah is simply fortuitous, the frequent condemnation of Edom elsewhere (Ps 137:7; Isa 34:1–17; 63:1–6; Jer 49:7–22; Ezek 25:12–14; 35:1–15; Amos 9:11–12; Joel 4:19–21; Mal 1:2–5; Amos 4:21–22) suggests that it was especially singled out.

The reason for this special treatment is disputed (Dicou 1994, 182–97; Ben Zvi 1996a, 230–46). There was some history of dispute and enmity (1 Sam 14:47; 2 Sam 8:13–14; 1 Kgs 11:14–22; 2 Kgs 8:20–22; 14:7; 16:6), although this would be expected of any nation sharing a border, and Edom does not seem to be that different from any of Israel's other neighbours. During Judah's last days Edom appears to have planned rebellion against Babylon (Jer 27), but no overt moves were made and the nation escaped the destruction wrought on Jerusalem and Judah. Obadiah and other texts testify that the Edomites took advantage of the situation, but although this is the basis for the specific accusations, the vehemence of the language suggests an intensification due to another factor. From an Israelite perspective the distinctive identity of Edom was bound up with the close kinship ties of their founders. In Gen 25:30; 36:1, 8 the ancestors of the nations are twin brothers, the closest possible relationship. This was the basis for special treatment in the narratives (Num 20:14) and laws (Deut 23:7). It is a reason for judgment explicitly cited in several texts (Amos 1:11; Obad 10, 12; Mal 1:2). However this tradition developed (Bartlett 1969; 1977), it is the essential background for understanding the accusations of Obadiah.

Obadiah is first of all an oracle against a foreign nation, but there have been attempts to be more specific about its genre and setting. Wolff (1986, 19–21, 42–44) proposed that the author was a cultic prophet who answered the laments that were offered in exile (cf. Amos 4:21–22), possibly at services held in the ruined temple site (similarly Ogden 1982). The theory remains speculative, not just because of our ignorance of the time but also because the prophets often incorporated forms and language from elsewhere in their compositions. Niehaus

(1993, 495–96, 507) suggests that the book is a covenant lawsuit, but neither covenant nor lawsuit are particularly prominent themes.

There was no clear fulfilment of the prophecy of Edom's catastrophic demise. In the century following, the population and power of Edom waned and the area was increasingly under Arab influence (cf. Neh 2:19; 4:7; 6:1). Because of Edomite settlements in the Negev, to the south of Judah, this area became known by the related name of Idumea (1 Macc 4:29; 5:3; 1 Esd 4:50; Mark 3:8). The prophecies against Edom became another of the body of texts that were understood to refer to the last great day of judgment against all the nations.

B. *Date and Setting*

Obadiah has no specific references to kings or events that would specify its date and setting. The language and argument are general enough that it has been located in a number of different eras.

(1) The traditional rabbinic view identified Obadiah as Ahab's palace official (1 Kgs 18; i.e. c. 875–854 B.C.E.). He was given the gift of prophecy as a reward for his faithfulness (*b. Sanh.* 39b). The rabbinic arguments are a creative exercise in intertextuality, but Obadiah is a common name (there are twelve different Obadiahs in the Bible) and the lack of any link between this Obadiah and Edom makes this proposal unlikely.

(2) A slightly later ninth-century date is proposed by those who consider that Obadiah was a response to the Edomite revolt against Jehoram, king of Judah, which took place around 845 B.C.E. (2 Kgs 8:20–22; 2 Chr 21:8–17; Niehaus 1993, 501–2). However, there is no hint in the texts that the Edomites invaded Judah, as Obadiah implies.

(3) A number of scholars (Wellhausen 1892; Thompson 1956, 858) date the book to the fifth century B.C.E. on the understanding that Obad 2–9 describes a past event. Edom was eventually occupied by Nabatean Arabs, and Mal 1:3 (probably fifth century) portrays a devastated Edom. However, it is more likely that Obad 2–9 is predicting the future, and the placing of Obadiah in the first half of the Minor Prophets suggests that this dating is too late. Our lack of knowledge about these events (as for the first two theories) means that adopting this proposal leads to little interpretive gain.

(4) The most likely date is during the early exilic period, after the fall of Jerusalem in 587/586 B.C.E. Other exilic texts have similar criticisms of Edom's behaviour (Ps 137:7; Lam 4:18–22; Ezek 25:12–14; 35:1–14). The note in 1 Esd 4:45 that the Edomites burned the temple is doubtful, but reflects the same tradition.

(5) Ben Zvi (1996a) focuses attention on the way in which readers of the book would make sense of the final form of the text. The lack of clear historical references leaves open a range of possibilities, and we should be very conscious of the ambiguities of the book. This is a significant change of approach from the traditional historical-critical emphasis on the author and the earliest forms of the text.

(6) A similar move away from detailed discussion of historical development is evident among those concerned with the canonical book of Obadiah. Childs (1979, 414–15) emphasizes the shift in the book from a specific consideration of the historical acts of Edom to a more general portrayal of the day of Yhwh. In the light of this more universal perspective, Edom becomes less of a specific nation and more a representative of the wicked nations.

(7) In the commentary I adopt the view that the early exilic dating is both historically likely and fruitful for a richer interpretation. It allows our understanding of the text to be informed by what else we know of the exile. However, the historical perspective cannot be the only one if the book itself regards it of first importance that the specific acts of Edom have been set in a broader eschatological context. This emphasis on the canonical form of the book also raises wider ethical and theological issues that will be of interest to those reading it from the point of view of Jewish or Christian faith (see Section E, below).

C. *The Structure and Development of Obadiah*

Translations and commentaries show remarkably little agreement among about the structure and substructure of Obadiah (Fohrer 1966; Clark 1991). Difficulties arise mainly because there is an intricate web of linguistic and thematic connections between the verses (Wehrle 1987; Renkema 2003), and different scholars evaluate differently which feature indicates a significant structural division. The twofold analysis of Wolff (vv. 1–14/15b, 15a/16–21) is rather misleading, since in his opinion these sections are far from unified (see below). Seven distinct subsections are often detected (e.g. Ben Zvi 1996a; Wendland 1996), although Niehaus (1993) finds no fewer than ten. One uncertainty is whether v. 15 should be split up so that v. 15a completes vv. 1–14 and v. 15a opens vv. 16–21 (Wolff 1986; Barton 2001).

Fokkelman (2001) points out that most poems divide into larger units (stanzas or sections) and smaller units (strophes or subsections). Strophes are usually two to three verses, while stanzas contain several strophes and tend to be of a similar size. On the assumption that we should distinguish two levels of structure, Obadiah can be divided into three stanzas of about equal size, vv. 1–7, 8–15, 16–21. The same words recur towards the beginning and end of each section (Dick 1984, 17): "deceived" (vv. 3, 7), "day" (vv. 8, 15; also a keyword in this section), "mountain" (vv. 16, 21). The main actors in these sections are also distinctive: Edom (vv. 1–7), the brothers Edom and Jacob (vv. 8–15), and the nations Edom and Judah (vv. 16–21). Each section works out a different aspect of the primary theological message of the book, the justice of God, his punishment of the wicked (Edom) and vindication of the oppressed (Israel). The certainty of Edom's punishment is highlighted in vv. 1–7, the reasons in vv. 8–15 and the consequences for Edom and Judah in vv. 16–21.

The subsections (vv. 1a, 1b–4, 5–7, 8–9, 10–11, 12–15, 16–18, 19–21) are indicated in various ways (cf. Snyman 1989; Clark 1991). There is often a shift of subject matter or grammatical form, and at the beginning or end there can be a significant formula (e.g. "says Yhwh" closes vv. 1b–4 and opens vv. 8–9; a similar formula ends v. 18). Each subsection explores the theme of the section in different ways and often from different points of view. Bridge verses link the main sections: vv. 8–9 continue the theme of the punishment of Edom (vv. 1b–7), while v. 15a anticipates the more universal and eschatological tone of vv. 16–21.

The assumption made in this analysis is that the book can be read as a unified and coherent whole. Traditional historical-critical scholarship has expended a great deal of energy exploring the development of the prophetic books. It assumes that the final canonical form is the result of a long process of transmission, editing and redaction that can be discerned through the internal inconsistencies and differences in the text. There is nothing inherently unreasonable in this approach, but it remains speculative and people have recently become more aware of the difficulties in the project when applied to the biblical writings.

The divide among literary and historical scholars is sharply exposed when some surprise or difficulty in the text is encountered. Should it be taken as a sign of a different historical redaction or source, or is it a deliberate authorial device reflecting a rhetorical or theological rationale? For example, Wolff (1986, 21–22) regards vv. 1–14, 15b as a single unified discourse, which then became the basis for a number of additions (v. 15a and vv. 16–17, 18, 19, 20, 21). But is v. 15 the combination of an earlier, original oracle directed to Edom and a later universal oracle directed to all the nations? An alternative explanation is that prophetic theology regularly related the particular to the universal for good theological reasons. The unexpected order of v. 15a and 15b could be a deliberate inversion and a reflection of the theology of the author. This kind of surprise is characteristic of poetry and should not be reduced to the mundane (Robinson 1988). Very complex developmental theories (e.g. Weimar 1985) tend to underestimate the freedom of poetry.

The unity and coherence of vv. 16–21 have been questioned particularly sharply. Wolff (1986) distinguishes four different sources for vv. 18–21. Verses 19–21 is distinctive in that it is rhythmic prose rather than poetry (Barton 2001, 155). It makes use of *waw* imperfects and accusative particles, both of which are rare in poetry. The interpretation of the various places and peoples mentioned in this section are also disputed, and v. 20 appears to be textually corrupt. However, there are indications of careful structural composition, and many prophetic books include a mixture of prose and poetry. An interpretation that assumes the unity of this section seems as reasonable as an assumption of disunity.

D. *Obadiah Among the Prophets*

Obadiah has close links with a number of the other prophetic books. It is the fourth of the twelve minor prophets, which in the Jewish tradition were treated as one book. Chronology was one factor in the ordering of the twelve, though not the only one (see the Introduction to the Twelve). The relatively early placing of Obadiah makes a late date less likely, but more significant than chronology may be the thematic and linguistic links between the books (Nogalski 1993). In the final chapter of Amos we find an allusion to the restoration of the booth of David "that they may possess the remnant of Edom" (Amos 9:12), and this is the main subject of Obadiah. Other links are "the Day of Yhwh" (Obad 1; Amos 5:18–20; 5 times in Joel), and the use of "the Lord Yhwh" (Obad 1; 21 times in Amos). We may also note that various nations are addressed in these books (Theis 1977, 15): six in Amos (Amos 1–2; including Edom in 1:11–12), Edom in Obadiah and Assyria (Nineveh) in Jonah. However, the individual books have their own independent integrity, and the different order in the LXX suggests that early traditions did not recognize a strong redactional unity (Renkema 2003, 15–26).

There are a number of other allusions to passages in the twelve. There appears to be a quotation of Obad 17 in Joel 2:32, and several other close parallels (Obad 11//Joel 3:3[4:3]; 15//1:15; 16//3:17[4:17]; 18//2:5; 21//2:32[3:5]). The closest links, though, are between Obadiah and Jer 49 (Obad 1a//49:7; 1b–4//49:14–16; 5–6//49:9–10a; 8//49:7; 9//49:22; 16//49:12). Although some have thought that Obadiah influenced Jeremiah, most now consider that Obadiah had Jeremiah before him (Renkema 2003, 38). There might be a more complex relation to some other common text or tradition (Mason 1991, 90; Dicou 1994), but this does not seem necessary. Raabe (1996, 22–33) sums up the arguments for the priority of a pre-exilic Jeremiah oracle that was then adapted by Obadiah. Because the book of Obadiah has its own integrity, whatever the sources, a discussion of the relation of the parallels to Jer 49 will not play a large part in this commentary.

E. *The Message of Obadiah*

The primary message of Obadiah is that Yhwh's justice will be established. In vv. 1–15 this is worked out in relation to the Israel's specific historical experience of Edom's response to its defeat and exile. In vv. 16–21 this is caught up in a larger framework that includes all the nations (cf. v. 15a). God's justice includes not only punishment of the wicked, of whom Edom becomes a representative type, but also the vindication of Israel. The words of doom on Edom and the nations are first an implicit, then an explicit affirmation of God's good plans for Israel. Both negatively and positively the oracle provides hope and encouragement for God's people, for the underlying assumption is that the God of Israel is the sovereign Lord (vv. 1, 21) who makes use of the nations to punish both his own people (vv. 11–14) and those who took illicit advantage of their plight (v. 1)

One key principle that pervades how this justice is worked out is the law of equivalent retribution (*lex talionis*). The lawgivers of Israel began with the premise that the punishment should fit the crime, an eye for an eye and a tooth for a tooth (Exod 21:21–23; Lev 24:19–20; Deut 19:21). This principle of "poetic justice" is explicitly stated in Obad 15, but underlies the rest of the prophecy. It is applied especially to those who proudly consider that they, not God, control events (cf. Isa 10:5–16; 47:7–11). Those who seek in their pride to ascend to the heavens will be brought low (Obad 2–4). Those who mocked others will themselves be mocked (vv. 10, 13). Those who sought to possess the land of Israel will themselves be dispossessed (vv. 17–21). God reverses the intentions of the perpetrators with a corresponding punishment (Miller 1982, 130–31). Obadiah sees particular significance in this principle because, according to Israel's traditions, the ancestors of the two nations were the twin brothers Jacob and Esau (Gen 25–27; Obad 6, 10, 12). Obadiah extends the parallelism in a creative way by further portraying them as two "houses" (vv. 17, 18) and two mountains (vv. 9, 17, 19, 21).

The time framework for working out divine justice is undefined, as is often the case for the prophets. There is a move from the more specific historical references in vv. 1–14 to a future day of Yhwh in the indeterminate future. It is uncertain whether the day of Edom's punishment is identical to the universal day of Yhwh (Snyman 1992), or whether it anticipates it. The lack of immediate fulfilment encouraged a larger eschatological interpretation of these promises of judgment. On the day of Yhwh the wicked will be punished and the righteous vindicated (cf. Augustine 1972, chs. 18, 31).

For growing numbers of modern readers the asymmetric threats and promises of Obadiah raise acute issues of ethics and theology. The vivid depiction of Edom's coming downfall has been described as xenophobic (e.g. Wolff 1986, 22; Barton 2001, 124), a "'Damn-Edom' theology that represents a narrow nationalism" (Cresson 1972). However, it should be noted that the punishment of Edom is related to actions that would be widely condemned (pride, betrayal, greed). Obadiah is well aware of Judah's guilt that led to its judgment (vv. 12–14), and other prophets condemn Israel for similar faults (Mic 2–3). It is also necessary to acknowledge prophetic rhetoric and hyperbole. What is envisaged is not the annihilation of Edom, but the end of its independent rule (Renkema 2003, 40–44). It is easy to draw negative conclusions because of the brevity and silence of Obadiah, but a canonical approach requires a consideration of other scriptures. For example, it is possible to read Obadiah's words from the point of view of a chastened and penitent community, a righteous remnant (Allen 1976, 139; cf. Mic 4:6–7).

Thus the promises of salvation in Obadiah reflect the fundamental belief in Israel's election as the people of God and the choice of Zion as Yhwh's dwelling place on earth. Although he may have departed for a while, Obadiah looks forward to a time of renewed presence and protection for his people (Obad 15–21). The behaviour of Edom is condemned with such force not just because it contradicts general ethics, nor even because Edom and Israel are brother nations.

Even more significant is that Israel was the focus of Yhwh's purposes (Robinson 1988, 95). There is a canonical tension between the texts that regard the nations as subject to divine judgment and punishment (e.g. Obadiah), and those that look to some sort of sharing in Israel's blessing (e.g. Mic 4:1–5; 6:8). Jonah is one example of a sophisticated exploration of this tension. The New Testament resolves this tension primarily in terms of the mission of the church (e.g. Acts 1; Romans 1).

Christian interpreters can draw other lines of continuity between Obadiah and the New Testament (Bonnard 1972, 700; Lillie 1979). The coming of Christ is the divine judgment that brings the humiliation of the proud and the arrogant (Obad 3–4; Luke 1:52; 14:11) and demonstration of the folly of purely earthly wisdom (Obad 8; 1 Cor 1:17–2:16). Jesus turns Obadiah's portrait of brotherly enmity upside down in the parable of the Prodigal Son (Luke 15:11–32), in which Israel takes on the role of the elder brother. The motive of greed (Obad 13) is given a climactic exposition in the criticism of Rome and its commercialism (Rev 18). In this chapter Rome is named Babylon, reflecting the same universalizing of the "evil empire" that is evident in Obadiah's alignment of Edom with all the nations. Similar moves are evident in many of the great epics of the West, from Beowulf to Star Wars.

Obadiah's vision of salvation is also taken up in the New Testament, though transformed through meditation on the death and resurrection of Christ who drank the cup of God's wrath on behalf of all (Obad 16; Mark 14:36; Luke 22:20). The inheritance of the saints, the elect people of God, is a city (Obad 17, 21), but a future, heavenly one (Heb 11; Rev 21–22). Just as Obadiah encourages the people of God to await this future salvation with hope and patience, so the epistles know that faith, even to death, is the appropriate response to the apparent triumph of evil (1 Pet 1:3–9). For one day all inhabitants of the earth will come before the judgment seat of God to receive their due reward (Obad 15; Matt 25:31–46) and the kingdom shall be the Lord's (Obad 21; Mark 1:15; Rev 11:15).

F. *Outline Analysis of Obadiah*

Title	1a
Edom's downfall	1b–9
A Summons to War	1b
Pride Leads to a Fall	2–4
No Escape	5–7
A Shattered People	8–9
Edom's crimes against his brother nation	10–15
Edom and Israel on the Day of Yhwh	16–21

G. *Commentary on Obadiah*

Title (1a)

1a. "The vision of Obadiah." The briefest of titles matches the briefest of books. Obadiah is a common name meaning literally "the one who serves Yhwh" (see Section B, above). "Servant" was a common title for the prophets (e.g. 1 Kgs 14:18; 18:36), so some have proposed that it was a later general description of a model servant prophet (compare similar theories about Malachi, whose name means "my messenger"). However, the servant idea plays no part in the book. A symbolic name would also be better served by the fullest form of the name (see on Jonah 1:9), whereas here it is an abbreviated form (ending with *yâ* not *yāhû*). The lack of further information may instead indicate that the prophecy was written down soon after it was given, so no further definition of the identity of this Obadiah was deemed necessary (Wolff 1990, 44). Whoever the author, his name appropriately indicates a minor but significant contribution to the recorded inheritance of God's servants the prophets.

"vision" (*ḥāzôn*) occurs elsewhere to indicate a prophetic collection (Isa 1:1; Nah 1:1). Originally a visionary or seer was someone to whom God's will was revealed, especially in a vision of the night (2 Sam 7:14, 17). This specialized meaning continues (e.g. Dan 2:19; Mic 3:6), but was extended to became a more general term for prophetic revelation, and this broader sense is evident in translations such as "prophecy" (NJPS; cf. Targ.) or "revelation" (Allen 1976). Sight is a common metaphor for understanding, and in prophetic contexts it emphasizes the content rather than the means of revelation (1 Sam 3:1). We are told nothing about how the vision was communicated. The older theory of the ecstatic character of prophetic inspiration is too simplistic to account for the complexity of the prophetic books. Vision in the singular invites readers to interpret the entire book as a unified (albeit complex) whole, whether from a single author or as a redactional or canonical unity.

Edom's Downfall (1b–9)

A standard oracle of judgment sets out the reason for the crime, followed by the announcement of judgment, but this is occasionally reversed, as here. Obadiah 1b–9 is mainly a promise of punishment; vv. 10–15 is mainly the reason for it (Westermann 1967, 176–77). All means of escape from this punishment are successively eliminated: Edom's geographical advantage (v. 3), the limited aspirations of its enemies (v. 5), and help from its traditional allies (v. 7). The human resources of Edom are then surveyed, and these too prove broken reeds. Obadiah announces the wholesale destruction of Edom's political leadership (v. 8), military capability (v. 9a), and general population (v. 9b). Except for vv. 6, 8, Edom is addressed as a corporate body in the second person singular ("you"). However, although the Edomites are the apparent hearers, we need to be aware that the real readers are Israelites. The prophet expects them to work out the implications of the oracle, which become clearer and clearer as the oracle progresses.

A Summons to War (1b)

At this distance we cannot know the original setting of this initial oracle. It may have been a specific historical occasion (see Section A, above), perhaps some coalition of the Arab tribes against Edom (the possibility is suggested by passages such as Judg 6:1–6; 2 Chr 21:16; *ANET* 297–301; cf. Thompson 1956, 858). But it might also be an ideal portrayal of what will happen to an enemy of Israel. With poetic justice, Edom's fate is now Judah's, with former allies (v. 7) turning against her. Interpretation can acknowledge both since original readers gave way to later readers who read the oracle as a scripture addressing the world of their day.

1b. "Thus says the Lord Yhwh" is the standard prophetic messenger formula, here slightly expanded with "concerning Edom." We would normally expect it to be followed by a divine speech, as occurs in v. 2. Some scholars obligingly transfer the phrase there, but delayed speeches occur elsewhere (Jer 30:5–7) and its present place makes perfectly good sense from a rhetorical perspective. The phrase serves as a general title of this section (and also the entire book), allowing the reader to make sense of the following allusive verses ("Esau" is first named in v. 6). The purpose of the messenger formula was to indicate that the prophet was the authorized messenger of the sovereign God of Israel and spoke with his authority. It is elsewhere used of royal messengers (2 Kgs 18:28–29). Whereas "vision" highlights the eye, "says" draws attention to the ear. Together they stress the reality and immediacy of the divine communication that is being conveyed. The NRSV translates the verb as a present tense ("says"), but the verb is in the perfect form, usually indicating a completed action. It is likely that in these verses we have the so-called prophetic perfect, in which the divine word is so certain that the event is spoken of as already completed.

The main object of the divine communication is briefly summed up as "concerning Edom." The whole phrase can either be taken to refer to the first section, or to the whole of Obadiah. The latter is suggested by the parallel in Jer 49. The messenger formula is found in Jer 49:7, but the equivalent to Obad 2–4 only comes at Jer 49:15–16. The phrase can also be translated "to Edom" (Raabe 1996), but it is unlikely that this was meant to indicate that the oracle was delivered in Edom (Jonah is the exception that proves the rule). Rather, Israel through the prophet overhears the divine verdict on Edom. But is Edom only meant to be the specific nation to the southeast of Judah? The crucial role of the nations in the oracle invites a more representative reading, encouraging a generalization of the motifs directed to historical Edom.

The parallel to "We have heard" in Jer 49:14 is "I have heard" (so also Vulg., LXX), but the text in its present form also makes sense. The "We" is unlikely to refer to the members of the divine council (1 Kgs 22:19–22) or to a band of cultic prophets who have also received a word concerning Edom. The simplest explanation is that the prophet is identifying with the people of Israel, who are the beneficiaries of the oracle. There may also be a reference to other prophecies of the demise of Edom (especially in Jer 49), which Obadiah will now restate and expand.

The three phrases indicate the fact of a divine communication, its agency and scope, and its content. A double repetition of the same root highlights its urgency and importance. "A report we have heard" (*šᵉmûʿâ šāmaʿnw*) is revealed as a summons to rise up to war (*qûmû wᵉnāqûmâ*; cf. Josh 8:3). The report is conveyed by a messenger (*ṣîr*) or envoy (NJPS, NIV), a word that implies an official function. The leaders of the nations willingly take up the call to punish Edom at the command of Yhwh, who has sent the envoy (a passive verb often indicates divine action). The envoy could be heavenly (angelic) or earthly, but whichever it is the emphasis is on the stark difference of level and authority between the sovereign God of Israel and the kings of the earth who do his bidding. Although the battle might include Israel, the distinct treatment of the people of God in vv. 17–21 suggests that Israel merely looks on and does not need to undertake the risks of battle. The variable gender of nations in the Hebrew Bible is a common grammatical phenomenon. Edom is feminine here ("against her"), being envisaged as a land (feminine), but in vv. 2–16 is masculine because it can also be regarded as a (masculine) nation.

Pride Leads to a Fall (2–4)

The form of vv. 2–4 is an oracle of judgment, concluding with "says Yhwh," a phrase that often indicates the end or beginning of a section (cf. v. 8). The coming punishment is declared in v. 2, the reason for it given in v. 3, and confirmed in v. 4. Both the form and the imagery of the passage conveys a powerful message of the reversal of misplaced human confidence by divine decree. Verses 3–4 are interlocking and chiastic lines (Raabe 1996): heart/height ("clefts")/ heights/heart; bring down/height ("soar aloft")/height ("stars")/bring down. The chiastic form highlights the theme of reversal and just punishment. The outer lines indicate the movement from human pride to divine humiliation.

The imagery that unites this section is the vertical spatial dimension. This is particularly appropriate in Edom's case because of its natural geographical features. It can take refuge in mountainous regions (v. 3), and this becomes the source of the evocative metaphor of a high-flying eagle who fears no one (v. 4a). In turn this becomes the basis for an imaginative development with mythological overtones (v. 4b). But height is also a significant metaphor for pride (Job 41:34; Ps 138:6; Isa 2:12; Ezek 31:10). Edom thinks itself safe and unchallengeable, but the ultimate arbiter of high and low is the God of Israel (Gen 11:1–9; Isa 2:11–15). Edom has neglected to look up and so missed the real threat. It is Yhwh the God of Israel who is the most high (Amos 9:2) and who raises up and lays low cities and nations (Isa 26:5; Luke 1:52). Yhwh is enthroned above the heights (Ps 97:9[10]), and his sovereignty is asserted in every way, including the mythological. Any being or city or nation that makes divine claims will surely be brought low (cf. Isa 14:12; Ezek 28:17; Rev 18:21; Jerome [1994, 23 = Letter 22.4] applies this verse to Lucifer). But how could Edom know about the God of Israel's power? It is significant that the condemnation of Edom is from a universal moral perspective, and does not assume the special knowledge of the Torah that the prophets expect of Israel (cf. Amos 1–2; Barton 1980). All who are wise know that pride leads to a fall (Prov 16:18).

2. "I will surely make you least" is more literally "Behold, small have I appointed you." The NRSV has taken this as a prophetic perfect emphasizing the certainty of the event ("surely"). But the perfect verbs in this verse may be declarative, announcing the divine judgment anticipated in v. 1b ("I make you small," NAB). Though not yet evident, the sovereign power of Yhwh will soon make this declaration an earthly reality. Unfortunately the NRSV omits the introductory particle *hinnê* ("Behold," AV; "See," NAB, NIV; "Look," NEB). It adds weight to the declaration of judgment, but also indicates a change of point of view (Berlin 1983, 62–63). The nations eagerly look forward to the battle (v. 1b), but the result is already certain from the divine perspective. While the following words could be translated "small among the nations" (NIV), the construction is a standard way of expressing the superlative "least" (the corresponding element in the next phrase is also the totalizing "utterly"). Such hyperbole is characteristic of prophetic style, highlighting the devastating completeness of the divine judgment. Edom is about to be cut down to size (cf. NLT). "least" can refer both to population and to territory, since both are at stake in war. The personal and social implications for the Edomites are expounded in the next line, for they "shall be utterly despised" (*bzh*). The shame of reversal and defeat will be all the more keenly felt since some of these nations at least were formerly respected allies (v. 7; cf. Ps 41:9).

3. "Your proud heart" is more literally "The pride of your heart." "proud" (*zāḏôn*) can refer to a wilful arrogation of a right that is not legitimate, such as the right of the Egyptians (Exod 18:11) or Babylonians (Jer 50:29–34) to oppress Israel. If this overtone is present, then it would anticipate the more detailed accusation in vv. 10–14, where the disregard of a brother's rights is described. Since the offence is against the people of Yhwh, it is equivalent to acting presumptuously against the God of Israel. A personal response from Yhwh was therefore inevitable. "heart" (*lēḇ*) represents the core of the personality that guides behaviour (Barton 2001). Edom is deceived by an attitude that is described in the next two phrases and includes both thought and feeling, a rational calculation and its associated emotion. At the heart of Edom's deception was a false estimate of its geographical advantages. Approaching from the east there is a gentle rise from the North Arabian desert, but then the plateau falls sharply 4000–5000 feet into the Wadi Araba (for a description see Bartlett 1989, 33–54). From Judah's point of view, then, Edom did indeed have a "dwelling in the heights." The passes were easily fortified and in the last resort the Edomites could find safety in caves. "clefts of the rock" (Jer 49:16; Song 2:14) suggests inaccessible heights where only birds could easily live, thereby anticipating the eagle figure of the next verse. Unlike the other occurrences, "rock" (*sela*) is without an article, and so some have tried to identify a specific place called Sela (2 Kgs 14:7 = 2 Chr 25:12; possibly Isa 42:11). This may have been a rocky peak that overlooks modern Petra (the LXX translation, also meaning "rock"). The modern Sela (4 km from Buseira, the biblical Bozrah) is another candidate. However, the non-specific NRSV translation is supported by the parallelism, and we should not insist on grammatical precision in poetry. "Who will bring me down to the ground?" is a rhetorical question asked by Edom, which foolishly expects the answer "No one."

4. The first two lines set up the fall and highlight the ultimate power of Yhwh by extrapolating from Edom's boasts. Even if Edom were an eagle and could "soar aloft," it would not be out of reach. The next line ascends yet further, developing the vertical logic in a mythological direction. Even if the nests were out of reach of all earthly enemies and in the highest sphere of the cosmos (cf. Job 22:12), "set among the stars," this would not be high enough. There is a further progression from the majestic but contingent movement of an eagle in the air to the secure nesting among the stars (echoing the dwelling reference of v. 3). The eagle's nest was a secure mountain fortress that could not be assailed (Job 39:27–28) and could be used metaphorically of a nation (Num 24:21) or of the wicked (Hab 2:9). "soar aloft" is the usual translation, but the verb can mean "make high" as well as "go high," with the object of the next line (nest) also being intended here (cf. NJPS's "Should you nest as high as the eagle"). This is preferred by those who give significant weight to the parallel in Jer 49:16 where "nest" is clearly the object of the verb.

The image of the eagle has significant metaphorical overtones. Armies are frequently compared to an eagle, the king of the air (Ezek 1:10) and supreme airborne force of destruction (Job 9:26). The eagle's swiftness (2 Sam 1:23) and ability to swoop down on its pray unexpectedly were terrifying images of military might (Jer 4:13; 48:40; 49:22). But these nuances merely intensify the supreme power of Yhwh and the enormity of the reverse. The eagle comparison is also a striking contrast to the later verses (vv. 11–15), which portray Edom more as a vulture or a hyena, waiting to feast on the dead corpse of hapless Judah.

No Escape (5–7)
The images shift from heaven to earth. Two hypothetical events (robbery of a house, harvesting of a vineyard) emphasize through repetition and contrast the certainty and completeness of the coming divine punishment. Human undertakings are partial and incomplete for one reason or another, but God's judgment will not merely be inevitable (v. 4), it will be devastating in its comprehensiveness (v. 5). The plundering mocks the feelings of security implied in v. 3. The treachery of Edom's covenant partners (v. 7) is a just reversal of its own

opportunism towards its "brother" Judah (described in vv. 10–14). The passage is a succession of protases ("if"), apodoses ("would not") and exclamations ("how!"). The exclamations provide stylistic variety in both form and address (Edom is referred to in the third person rather than as "you"), and opens up space for readers to reflect on the implications of the judgment that is being declared.

5. In the first image thieves raid the wealthy house of Edom. The next phrase broadens the scope and intensifies the disaster. "plunderers" may suggest a surprise raid on a village, but it can also describe national enemies (Isa 16:4; 21:2; Jer 6:26). This ensures a ready application to the nation Edom of a metaphor that also evokes specific and personal associations. The target of the images comes to the fore in the anticipatory exclamation "how you have been destroyed." This is the kind of outburst that is known from funeral laments (2 Sam 1:19; Jer 9:19), but rather than striking a sympathetic note, here it takes on a savagely satirical context (compare the mock laments over the king of Babylon in Isa 14:4, 12). The interrupted grammar conveys the surprise and shock of the judgment, and might as well come from Obadiah himself as from a later redactor. The image of a raid at night further magnifies the terror, for in the dark plunderers are unseen and the victims defenceless. The main clause conveys the rest of the event, "would they not steal only what they wanted?" Criminal psychology makes this a more likely translation of the last few words (a noun, "their sufficiency"), than "no more than they needed" (NJPS).

The second image is that of harvesters gathering in the bunches of grapes. It may have been motivated by the good vineyards that could grow on the mountains of Edom (cf. Num 20:17). The grape-gatherers might be the people of the village, but the invaders of v. 5a could be those reaping the fruits of the hard work of the locals in growing the grapes (Isa 5:1–2). Whoever is in mind, they would invariably leave behind grapes that were unripe, rotten or too small. The practice of leaving gleanings was encouraged in the Torah, so that the poor would also be able to share in the harvest (Lev 19:10; Deut 24:21). However, impoverished Edom will not even have this consolation. While the first image conjures up the shock of sudden despoilment, the second is even more terrifying in its ordinariness. Edom's treasures will be systematically ransacked, all in a day's work for its ruthlessly efficient enemies.

6. The implicit message of v. 5 is here brought out into the open. The first line may be ambiguous, but the second clarifies the picture. Archaeologists are thankful that it was customary to hide valuables in time of war, perhaps in caves or underground (Prov 2:4; Job 3:21). Indeed the root of "treasures" means "to hide," but by metonymy it came to indicate valuables that might be hidden. Esau is represented by its treasures (cf. Matt 6:21). The root of "pillaged" is more accurately translated "searched out" (AV), but NRSV correctly interprets its use here as implying violent seizure ("ransacked," REB, NJPS, NIV; "looted," NJB). "searched out" is a rare verb but probably has a similar meaning. By divine directive (Isa 45:3; cf. Jer 49:10) Edom's enemies will not rest until the last remaining item of value has been uncovered. Edom is here called Esau, as also happens in the parallel (Jer 49:8, 10; cf. Deut 2:4–5; Josh 24:4). Genesis 25:30 gives the traditional explanation of the name in the context of the rivalry between the two brothers Esau and Jacob (cf. Gen 36; Mal 1:2–3). The use of "Esau" here deliberately sets up the motif of conflict between brothers that will be developed further in vv. 10–14. The punishment here is thus poetic justice for the looting that Edom carried out on Judah (v. 13).

7. The section ends with seven references to "you" or "your." Edom has been deceived about its physical security (v. 3), now it finds itself deceived (the same word) concerning its political security. The first three verbs are probably the prophetic perfect (cf. on v. 2), but the fourth is an imperfect. This may merely clarify the future implication of the perfects, and for consistency NRSV translates all in the past tense (and NIV all in the future!). Alternatively, it may imply that once the Edomites have been driven back, they are kept at bay by the setting of traps.

The difficulties of this verse may be illustrated by a more literal translation of the MT:

> To the border they have sent you—all the men of your covenant;
> they have deceived and prevailed against you—the men of your peace;
>   your bread (?) they make a snare under you;
>   there is no understanding in it/him.

NRSV has divided the first two lines differently, but in so doing has undermined the parallelism of "allies" and "confederates." These terms describe those with whom Edom had made an alliance or treaty, together with those who were on good terms with them (peace, *šālôm*, has here a political force; cf. Jer 38:22). The generality of the description does not allow us to identify these parties for sure. To what extent are these former allies the nations referred to in v. 1? Although they are enemies to Edom, non-military vocabulary is used, and the verbs ("deceived," "prevailed against," "set a trap") imply indirect actions rather than military battle. Edom took opportunities to plunder and harass Judah when it was in trouble. Now Edom suffers the same fate. The nations and Edom's former allies are agents of God's judgment in different ways.

"driven" has a wide semantic range and various scenarios have been suggested: (a) Edomite envoys seeking help are escorted back to the border after being refused any help; (b) Edomites are expelled from their cities and homes ("force you to the border," NIV; cf. REB, NJB; Gen 3:23; Jer 24:5); (c) most probably it refers to Edomite refugees who are refused asylum and sent back to the borders of Edom ("turned you back at the frontier," NJPS). This would be poetic justice in mirroring Edom's behaviour to Israelite refugees (v. 14).

"your bread" makes little sense, although some have conjectured it is a gloss on "men of your peace." In Ps 41:9[10] "man of peace" is interpreted as "the one who eats my bread." A small change in the vowels makes the noun into a verb meaning "to eat" (Prov 23:6) and is implied by several of the versions

(LXX, Vulg.). However, the "you" is a direct object and would suggest cannibalism! The difficulty is overcome by Davies (1977a), who proposes that the cognate verb has been accidentally omitted by a scribe transcribing one word instead of two (haplography). The original would then have read "those who ate your bread." There is evidence that covenants were made in conjunction with eating, both in Israel (Gen 31:34; Exod 24:11) and the rest of the ancient Near East. In their treachery, then (cf. Ps 55:20[21]), these allies "have set a trap for you," or more literally "under you." "trap" is a rare word, and unlikely to be related to the same word that elsewhere means sores or ulcer ("wound," AV; Jer 30:13; Hos 5:13). McCarter (1977) proposes "place of foreigners," but "trap" is supported by the versions (LXX, Vulg., Syr.), and the post-biblical meaning of the verb is "weave" or "twist," suggesting that some sort of rope trap or net may be meant here (Ps 140:5). It is difficult to imagine literal mantraps, so it may be a metaphor drawn from the realm of trapping animals or birds (Ps 69:22[23]; Keel 1978, 91).

NRSV interprets "there is no understanding of it" as a reference to the whole situation. From a human point of view such treachery is incomprehensible, but this highlights all the more the decisive role of the divine word (vv. 2–5). Others have interpreted "it" as the snare (NEB) or the land (McCarter 1977). The latter interpretation is close to taking the suffix as "him," and thus a comment on Edom's bewilderment ("he has quite lost his wits," NJB) or the nation's inability to detect such duplicity ("where is his wisdom now," REB). This would be an ironic comment on the traditional association of Edom with wisdom (cf. v. 8).

A Shattered People (8–9)
8. "On that day" refers to the great day of judgment against Edom, when Yhwh will "destroy the wise." It anticipates the universal judgment of v. 15. Edom and Teman were famed for their wisdom (Jer 49:7; Job 2:11), possibly as a by-product of being a trading centre and thus a recipient of the lore and knowledge of the East (Bar 3:23). Wisdom can refer to the general qualities of intelligence and skill that bring success in every area of life. Here, the repetition of "understanding" from the previous verse may suggest a particular focus on failure of political and diplomatic skills. "Mount Esau" is found only in Obadiah (vv. 8, 9, 19, 21). "Mount" represents the entire mountainous country, and "Esau" stands for Edom (as in v. 6). However, the primary motivation for this formulation is that it sets up the contrast with Mount Zion (vv. 17, 21; Ben Zvi 1996a, 121).

9. Wisdom is of value in warfare, but it is futile against Yhwh's wisdom (Isa 19:11–12; 31:1–2; 1 Cor 1:19). The warriors or "mighty men" (*gibbōrîm*) are not the rank and file, but the elite fighting forces and the generals (cf. 2 Sam 23:8–39). Without them the reserves who may have been called up have no chance. Bows can be literally shattered (Jer 51:56), but applied to soldiers it usually indicates a psychological rather than a physical brokenness ("terror-stricken," REB; "demoralised," NJB). It is often associated with fear (Josh 10:25). Teman is a name for the northern part of the country that included the capital

Bozrah (Amos 1:12; Ezek 25:13), and by extension (synecdoche) could also describe the whole country. NRSV has moved the final word of the MT ("for the slaughter") to the beginning of v. 10 (so also LXX, Syr., Vulg.). "Mount Esau" would then end v. 9b as well as v. 8b. However, the MT order also makes good sense. It specifies either the character of the cutting off ("by slaughter," RSV), or the reason ("because of slaughter"). If the former is meant, then the repetition of a similar word in the next verse would show (yet again) a correspondence between sin and punishment. Ben Zvi (1996a, 124–28) argues that here (and elsewhere) Obadiah is being deliberately ambiguous.

The conjunction translated "so that" usually indicates purpose, but can also indicate consequence (JM 169g; NJPS has a simple "and"). Once the army has been destroyed no further resistance can be offered and "everyone will be cut off." However, it is often difficult to distinguish purpose and consequence, for the final result (however reached) is also the will of Yhwh. The use of passive verbs is a common way to indicate the outworking of God's will, even if human forces are the immediate cause of events. "cut off" is often used for God's punishment of the wicked (Gen 9:11; Isa 14:20; 29:20), and Ezekiel uses it of Edom in particular (Ezek 25:13; 35:7).

Edom's Crimes Against His Brother Nation (10–15)

The next section continues the divine voice, which is clearly heard in v. 8 and probably also v. 13 ("my people"). The third person reference to Yhwh in v. 15 is not decisive. It is possible that the prophet takes over (e.g. in the rhetorical vv. 12–14), but there is no clear indication of any switch of speaker. In any case, the identity between prophet and Yhwh is such that the distinction is not necessarily significant (Ben Zvi 1996a, 172–74).

The distinctive emphasis of the section is that Yhwh's judgment is coming because of Edom's behaviour to his "brother," Israel. The accusations echo the punishments of earlier verses and, together with the specific statement of principle in v. 15b, assert that Edom's terrible fate is not arbitrary but reflects its actions against Judah. Following an introductory summary (v. 10; cf. v. 2), Edom is accused of inaction (v. 11a; cf. v. 7), plundering Jerusalem (v. 11b; cf. vv. 5–6), gloating over Judah's misfortune (v. 12; cf. v. 2) and helping to mop up survivors (v. 14; cf. v. 7). The crime is so serious because the identities of the two nations are bound up with their ancestors, the two brothers Jacob and Esau (vv. 10, 12).

Verses 12–14 comprise eight phrases with the same structure, each one combining a negative warning ("do not...," REB, NJB) with a reference to an aspect of Judah's calamity. Seven of these are "on the day of," the seventh occurrence being an exception. The construction (ʾal + jussive) normally refers to the present or future, but the oracle as a whole (and the bracketing verses vv. 11, 15b in particular) makes it clear that the disaster is past (hence NRSV's "you should not have..."). These lead up to the climactic clause giving the motive for heeding the warning in v. 15a, the judgment of God ("For the day of Yhwh is near"). The underlying principle that is the basis for judgment is stated in v. 15b, the well-known *lex talionis* (see Section E, above).

Taken at face value these verses are warning Edom not to undertake hostile actions against Jerusalem and Judah. However, the previous verses have made it clear that these events have already happened. It is most likely that the prophet is projecting himself back into the past and using a particularly dramatic device to further his critique. The extraordinary degree of repetition increases exponentially the reader's horror at the magnitude of Edom's crime on "the day of Jerusalem" (Ps 137:7). The pathos is increased by the reader's knowledge of the helplessness of the appeal, for we know that the warnings were in vain. Allen (1976, 156–58) compares a nightmare where the dreamer cannot affect the course of events, however much this is desired. The inexorable progression increases the feeling of horrible inevitability. Not content with evil thoughts and words (v. 12), the Edomites join Judah's enemies in their actions (v. 13) and then intensify the disaster and increase their guilt through actions taken on their own initiative (v. 14).

The verses in all likelihood refer to the fall of Jerusalem in 586 or 587 B.C.E. (see Section B, above), although the language remains general and not tied to any particular event. While the Babylonians were directly responsible for the invasion and destruction of city and the exile of its surviving inhabitants (2 Kgs 25), such was the reality of war in the ancient world. The treachery of a kin nation, however, burnt itself into Israel's memory as extraordinarily despicable. There are several parallels with Ezekiel's oracle against Mount Seir/Edom (Ezek 35). It is difficult to be sure about the historicity of more specific accusations, such as participation in the looting of Jerusalem. Stuart (1987, 418) suggests that the Babylonians would not allow such opportunism (though how do we know for sure?), so it might refer to the looting of towns ignored by the Babylonians. But prophetic rhetoric does not necessarily concern itself with accuracy in the minutiae. The continuity of purpose and attitude between conquerors and Edomites ("you too were like one of them," v. 11b) and the close identity between the people of Judah and their city could well have been sufficient reason to assimilate Edom to Babylon in an imaginary portrayal of Jerusalem's fall.

10. If the NRSV is right in linking "slaughter" to this verse, then the section begins with a dramatic double drumbeat (Rudolph 1971, 308) in giving the reason for the punishment. The two words might also be read as a single concept (hendiadys, cf. NEB, "murderous violence"). The flood (Gen 6:11, 13) is the paradigmatic example of divine judgment on violence, which can include many kinds of harmful activity. "violence" may refer to killing escapees (v. 14a), but this accusation is in some tension with the fact that it was the Babylonians who did most of the fighting. The specific accusations refer primarily to Edom's neutral stance or its supporting role. It is possible that the rhetoric of the prophet is condensing degrees of blame, so that Edom is charged with the crime that might otherwise have been averted if due brotherly support had been given. The mention of "your brother Jacob" alludes to the patriarch's rivalry with Esau (Gen 25:22–34; 27). The underlying understanding is that the relation between their original founders (the patriarchal ancestors) should guide the behaviour of the nations. Whatever the provocation, brother should refrain from harming brother. While antagonism between Judah and Edom was a constant in their history, the prophet argues that this should not have been a decisive factor in the crisis of the Babylonian invasion.

A clothing metaphor ("shame shall cover") describes Edom's state of mind, which is so overpowering that it is as clear and visible as a garment (Ps 89:45[46]) or a veil over a face (Ezek 7:18). This shame is Edom's realization of its own sin, guilt and folly. Nor is there any way back from this, for the next line states that Edom will be "cut off forever," indicating the permanent demise of Edom (thereby intensifying v. 9b). Once again this promise works out the *lex talionis*, for Edom has increased Judah's shame by gloating and completing its downfall (vv. 12–14; cf. Mic 7:10).

11. "Day" is a keyword in this section, occurring eleven times in vv. 11–15. The particular events of the fall of Jerusalem may well be in mind, but this is characteristically linked in v. 15a to the final day of Yhwh. In this way the particular crime of Edom is given an ultimate significance by being linked to the final judgment of the whole world. The order of events is unexpected, but makes good sense if the two pairs of lines each describe an earlier and a later event (ACBD; cf. Raabe 1996, 172). Edom (A) "stood aside," (C) "foreigners entered," (B) took the wealth, and then (D) "cast lots." By standing aside, Edom took the part of a hostile observer, rather than a brother and ally. Foreigners with no relation to Israel were then able to enter the city. "carried off "normally refers to taking people captive, so "wealth" (*ḥayil*) may include people as well as portable treasures (cf. 2 Kgs 24:13–16).

The division of spoils was often a disputed climax to the sack of a city, and the traditional way of resolving or avoiding argument would be to cast lots (cf. on Jonah 1:7). This would determine the fate of the people (cf. v. 14; Joel 3:3[4:3]) as well as goods (Ps 22:18[19]). The denial of brotherly duty leads to the climactic judgment that declares the effective end of Edom's special relationship with Israel, "you too were like one of them." The final comment gains additional force by being without a parallel half-line.

12. "But you should not have gloated" is more literally "do not look on," but the context here makes it clear that all the verbs are to be understood in the most vindictive way, implying triumph and scorn (Mic 7:10; Mesha inscription, *KAI* 181, 4). There is a stark contrast between the attitude of Edom and the situation of Judah. Edom gloated, rejoiced (i.e. cruel glee; cf. Ezek 35:15) and boasted (literally "make great the mouth"; cf. Ezek 35:13). Judah suffered misfortune, ruin and distress. The first line ends "on the day of your brother" (NRSV mg), but NRSV (also REB, NJB) omits the unique repeated "day." But first items in a list are often different from the rest and the double "day" may well pick up the similar double occurrence of day in v. 11a. It also gives prominence to the brother theme, which is integral to these verses (v. 10a).

13. Edom follows the lead of the foreigners in v. 11 who "entered the gate of my people" first. This enables Edom to pick over the goods of the city, completing the initial ransacking ("looted his goods"). The "brother denied" theme is invoked by "you should not have joined" (literally "do not, *you too*, look on his disaster," the same overtones of "see" as in v. 12b). After three different words for disaster in v. 12, the same word occurs three times, "calamity" (Ezek 35:5; used of Esau in Jer 49:8). The first occurrence, "their calamity" (*ʾêḏām*) invokes the similarly sounding Edom (*ʾĕḏôm*). "his goods" translates the same word as wealth (v. 11). "looted" is literally "to send forth [the hand]" (cf. vv. 5–6). "gate" is in the singular (contrast v. 11) but may be a collective ("gates," REB, NIV; cf. Gen 22:17; 24:60).

14. Scholarly ingenuity has multiplied possible scenarios for the first phrase, thanks to the ambiguity of the rare word for "crossings" (*pereq*). In Nah 3:2 the word means "booty," but this is inappropriate here and the cognate verb means "tear" or "rend," hence perhaps something divided. Are these the breaches in the wall of the city (LXX has "ways through"), the escape routes (Vulg. "exits"; Symm. "places of escape"), the "passes" into Edom (NJPS; Rudolph 1971, 304–5) or the forks in the road where deportees could escape (BDB; Wolff 1986, 55). Whatever the word means, it evokes the idea of fugitives nearly attaining escape and then being cruelly picked up by neighbours intending the total destruction of the nation.

"cut off" usually implies killing ("cut down"; "annihilate," NJB; cf. v. 11a), but this would make the next line anticlimactic, so others prefer "intercept" (Allen 1976). A fork in the road would allow more lines of escape to be covered, and the Edomites then "handed over his survivors" to the foreigners of v. 11 once more. The flight of King Zedekiah to Jericho (2 Kgs 25:4–5; Jer 39:4–5) illustrates the kind of situation envisaged. At various times Edom (along with other nations) is criticized for taking part in the slave trade (Amos 1:6, 9; 2 Chr 28:17). The use of "cut off" echoes its occurrence vv. 9 and 10, and is a further illustration of the *lex talionis* summed up in v. 15b.

15. The reason for the dire warnings of vv. 12–14 is finally stated, "the day of Yhwh." What might be surprising is the reference to "all the nations," since Edom is addressed again in the second person singular in v. 15b, like much of vv. 2–14. Many scholars (following Wellhausen 1892) wish to reverse the order of v. 15a and v. 15b, so that there is a neat progression, Edom in vv. 1–14, 15b; the nations in vv. 15a, 16. From a text-critical perspective, identical words occur in vv. 15b, 16a ("as"), so a scribe might have missed the first phrase accidentally, put it in the margin or between the lines, only for a later scribe to insert it in the wrong place. However, there is no support in the versions for this displacement theory and the pattern of command followed by reason ("for") is common (Jer 4:6; Amos 5:5; Prov 23:9; Ben Zvi 1996a, 140–41; Raabe 1996, 189–90). There is no need to treat the conjunction as an emphatic particle ("yea," NJPS; "certainly," Allen 1976, 161) or to omit it (REB, NIV).

We can also construct a good theological rationale for the present sequence. It relates the specific historical judgment of Edom closely to the universal eschatological judgment. The judgment of Edom gains validity from the general belief that Yhwh will judge all the nations (Watts 1981, 57). The move from the particular to the universal (and vice versa) is characteristic of prophetic theology and indeed the dynamic interplay between the two perspectives gives prophecy a great deal of its power and abiding relevance (Robinson 1988; Raabe 2002). Alter (1985, 146–62) has suggested that the move from the particular to the universal is a natural consequence of the progressive and intensifying character of prophetic poetry.

The evil that Edom has committed on Judah's "day" (vv. 11–14) becomes the reason for the reversal of roles on the day of Yhwh, the climactic act of God when the wicked will be punished and the righteous of Israel vindicated (Amos 5:18–20; Isa 13:6–13; Joel 1:15; 3:14; Zeph 1:7). This is the day already mentioned in v. 8, but now put in a larger context. It is not a literal day, but an era that may be flexibly interpreted. While the perspective of the first half of Obadiah is a close-up snapshot of a situation where Edom and the nations are related but distinct, the second part of Obadiah adopts a broader perspective. "all the nations" are one in their arrogance and wickedness. Edom represents them in its behaviour and anticipates in its own punishment the general day of judgment (v. 16). Edom's fate is a powerful proof and pledge that the ultimate day of doom is near.

The logic of the entire section is summed up in "As you have done, it shall be done to you," a statement that applies to Edom the classic *lex talionis* (see Section E, above). The double use of the same verb in complementary forms (active, then passive; Jer 50:29; Ezek 35:11) represents the logic of judgment through grammar as well as content. Edom is responsible for its actions, but must suffer the consequences. "be done" is an example of what is often called the divine passive (cf. Matt 7:2), since it subtly portrays both the indirectness and the inevitability of God's involvement in human affairs.

"deeds" ("conduct" NJPS) are ethically significant actions and this term is often used for the schemes of the nations (Ps 137:8). "head" stands by synecdoche (the part for the whole) for the whole person, especially as an ethically responsible agent (1 Kgs 2:33). As happens throughout Obadiah, Edom is personified and held responsible for its actions. The consequences of the deeds are metaphorically regarded as objects which are produced by Edom, only to be turned back ("return," *šûb*) to descend on Edom's head, just as a boomerang returns to the one who throws it. Edom is given no option but to receive its due deserts (cf. Joel 3[4]:4, 7).

Edom and Israel on the Day of Yhwh (16–21)

The theme of the day of Yhwh, introduced in v. 15, is given a more detailed exposition. The point of view shifts from earth (vv. 10–14) to heaven. There is a broad chiastic ordering of the material (ABCBA; Raabe 1996, 253): the destiny of Zion (vv. 16–17, 21) framing the repossession of the land (vv. 17b, 19–20), and in the centre the victory of the house of Jacob over the house of Esau (v. 18). The role of Israel as Yhwh's agent in the judgment of Edom (cf. Ezek 25:14) is in some tension with the nations functioning in that role in the first half of Obadiah (and a third perspective portrays Yhwh as the sole active agent and the "consuming fire," e.g. Isa 63:1–6). But both perspectives are at home in Israel's traditions and reflect equally valid theological convictions, for the God of Israel is both king of the nations and the one who has given Israel a special role in fulfilling his purposes. We might harmonize the texts by suggesting that the nations are involved in the destruction of Edom's military capability, thus allowing Israel to possess Edom's land and give the *coup de grâce* (Allen 1976, 168). But this may be seeking too much consistency. It is important to note that the participation of Israel in Edom's judgment is not presented as spiteful revenge, but the outworking of God's justice.

16. Drinking in this verse draws primarily on a well-known image of divine judgment. Being made to drink of the cup of divine wrath leads to effects similar to that of drunkenness: confusion, helplessness and disgrace (Isa 51:17–22; Jer 25:15–29; Matt 26:39; Rev 14:8–11; Raabe 1996, 206–42). If this is the sense of all three occurrences of the drink verb here (*šth*), then the first line refers to the people of Jerusalem, who in 587 B.C.E. suffered Yhwh's judgment in the destruction of "my holy mountain," a term describing the place of God's special presence (see on Mic 4:1). A more contextual interpretation (cf. v. 15) is that the "you" in the first line refers to the Edomites (as in Amos 4:21; Jer 49:12). Drinking then represents their feasting and celebration in the abandoned and conquered Jerusalem (Watts 1981, 57; Tanghe 1997). Although in Obadiah Edom is usually singular and "you" here is plural, this would continue the *lex talionis* theme. Their literal drinking will result in the opposite kind of metaphorical drinking ("the cup of punishment," Targ.). "gulp down" is as reasonable an interpretation of a rare Hebrew word as any. It is probably related to a noun meaning "throat" (Prov 23:2). Many emendations have been suggested (e.g. "stagger," RSV; "drink greedily," NJB; cf. *HALOT* 506). A homonym of the verb also means to "talk wildly" (Job 6:3; Prov 20:25), possibly evoking the idea of a tongue loosened by wine ("till their speech grows thick," NJB). The nations "around" reflects a common emendation, although it could also be applied to the action of "rounds" of drink ("in turn," REB). However, the word usually means "continually" (NIV, NEB, NJB), and the MT perhaps suggests the ongoing punishment of the nations in contrast to the temporary plight of Israel. "as though they had never been" (probably cited in Joel 2:32[3:5]) indicates that the nations are not only about to experience death and annihilation, but also that their identity and deeds will be forgotten, a particularly fearful punishment for the ancients (Ps 88:5).

17. "But" would emphasize the contrast between the fate of the nations (v. 16) and Yhwh's plans for his dwelling and his people. Alternatively, the Hebrew *waw* can be translated "and," thereby stressing that the vindication of Israel as well as the punishment of the nations both belong to the concept of the Day of Yhwh. "those that escape" are primarily all God's people who survive the judgment of the day of Yhwh. They are the remnant (REB's translation) who are qualified to dwell securely "on Mount Zion" (for the possibility of non-Israelites sharing in the promise, see on Mic 4:1–4). "it shall be holy" implies that the temple has been rebuilt, purified and consecrated, thus becoming once again a fit dwelling for God. The implication is drawn out in Joel 3:17[4:17]: "strangers shall never again pass through it." "Mount" and "holy" pick up "my holy mountain" of v. 16, so "holy" is unlikely to refer to the remnant, as REB, NJPS suppose.

The verbal root behind "take possession" can be translated as either "possess" or "dispossess." The object of the verb in the MT has the same root, "their own possessions" (RSV), but NRSV accepts a slight emendation so that the reference is to "those who dispossessed them" (REB, NJPS, LXX, Syr., Vulg., Targ.; Wadi Murabbaat 88). This thus continues the theme of judgment and makes a good transition to v. 18. It is another expression of God's justice in ensuring that roles of invader and invaded are reversed.

18. "Jacob" here might stand for the tribe of Judah and "Joseph" for the other ten tribes (as in Ps 77:15[16]; Zech 10:6; cf. Isa 8:14; 46:3). However, it is more likely that Jacob implies the whole people of God (cf. v. 17), while Joseph highlights that the promise also applies to the Northern tribes who were taken away by the Assyrians, never to return (2 Kgs 17). Hope for the return of the "lost tribes" and the reuniting of the two "houses" is found elsewhere in eschatological contexts (Isa 11:11–14; Jer 3:12–18; 30–31; Ezek 37:16). The metaphor is of a landowner (Yhwh) using fire and flame (the people of God) to burn the straw or stubble (the Edomites) in a land (Edom) that has been assigned for new growth (cf. v. 17b). The word translated "burn" may refer to the initial act ("set alight," REB, NJB; cf. *HALOT* 214), which is then followed by thorough burning. "consume" (generally "eat") captures well the range of the Hebrew word, which implies the complete consumption and disappearance of the object. The metaphor vividly portrays the destruction of the wicked who have aroused God's anger (Exod 15:7; Isa 5:24; Nah 1:10; cf. Matt 3:12; Luke 3:17). Neglectful of the divine factor, Edom's attempt to stamp out any survivors (v. 14) has resulted in the reverse of its intention, the survival of God's people and the sure promise that "there shall be no survivor (the same word as in v. 14) of the house of Esau." "the house of Esau" is a unique designation modelled after "the house of Jacob." Watts (1981, 61) notes that the sequence of early ascendancy by Esau followed by eventual religious and territorial dominance by Jacob is also found in the patriarchal narrative (Gen 25–36), and this may be one reason for the use of the patriarchal names. The closing quotation formula ("for Yhwh has spoken") emphasizes the authority of the word and the certainty of its fulfilment. It also closes this poetic section before the additional prose texts of vv. 19–21.

19. The NRSV (along with LXX, Vulg., Syr.) takes the Negeb, the Shephelah, and Benjamin as terms for the Israelites who live in these places (by metonymy, the place for the people). They then possess the territories of the other names, all of which have the object marker before them. An alternative explanation would be that the subject of v. 18 continues (i.e. "my people," REB) and all these names (NJPS), or all except Benjamin (REB), describe the lands that are being possessed. However, from the point of view of both syntax and meaning, NRSV makes good sense. The order of treatment is clockwise: South (Negeb), west (Philistines), north (Ephraim, Samaria) and east (Gilead). After the fall of Jerusalem the Edomites took over the Southern wilderness of the Negeb, and the Philistines expanded into the Western lowland (the Shephelah, from a root meaning low). Who precisely will possess these areas is not clear. "Benjamin" might suggest all the tribes are in mind (Judah for the south and west, the Northern tribes for the north). But although Benjamin had links with Gilead (e.g. 2 Sam 2), other Northern tribes possessed it officially (Num 32; Josh 18:11–28). It is more likely then the reference is to four parts of the tribe of Judah. This does, however, sit uncomfortably with the "all Israel" interpretation of v. 18, which is also suggested by the recurrence of "possess" through the section (vv. 17b, 19, 20; NRSV has added the third occurrence in v. 19 for the sake of sense; it also adds the first "possess" in v. 20). The verb is frequently found in the Pentateuchal promises of the land and the fulfilment sections of the conquest narratives. It picks up the ancient promises of God to the patriarchs and to the people of Israel (Gen 15:7; Deut 30:5; Josh 1:11). Galilee and Carmel are not specifically included (contrast Jer 50:19) and is one reason why Wolff (1986, 67) considers that the verse comes from an editor who wrote very soon after Obadiah.

20. Most agree that the first line has suffered an early textual corruption. Attempts to reconstruct the original are numerous and certainty is impossible. The most logical solution is to reconstruct a line that is parallel to the clearer v. 20b. The elements of this are a subject (the exiles), a location (in Sepharad), a verb ("possess"), and a territory (the towns of the Negeb). The NRSV finds a location in v. 20a with a widely accepted emendation to Halah, an Assyrian town where the exiles of the Northern Kingdom were sent in 721 B.C.E. (2 Kgs 17:6; 18:11; 1 Chr 5:26). However, the early versions take the word (*ḥēl*) to be a form of *ḥayil*. This can mean a "force" (NJPS) or "army" (NJB), but since the battle is already won, a non-military understanding such as "company" (NIV; e.g. 1 Kgs 10:2) would be more appropriate. Ben Zvi (1996a, 220–21) has recently argued for a meaning of "territory" (cf. 1 Kgs 21:23), where this form of the word occurs, albeit in the construct state. Another emendation provides an additional "possess" (identical to the verb in v. 20b). The object of the verb is "Canaanites" ("Canaan" REB; "the Canaanites' land," NJB), probably a reference to Phoenicia because of the link with Zarephath. This was on the northern frontier of historical Israel, between Tyre and Sidon and well known from the Elijah narratives (1 Kgs 17:9; cf. Luke 4:26). The people are usually called Sidonians (2 Kgs 16:31), but like Philistines (v. 19) the word is probably used to evoke the conquest and settlement of Israel (Josh 7:9).

The "exiles of Jerusalem" are those deported by the Babylonians in 587 B.C.E. (cf. Jer 40:1). The location of Sepharad is disputed. Suggestions include the Hesperides, near Benghazi (ancient Berenice) in North Africa (Gray 1953); Saparda in Southwest Media, known from various Persian cuneiform inscriptions; and Spain (Targ.; but Neiman 1963 argues that this is unlikely). The best suggestion is that it is Sardis (so GNB), the capital of Lydia in Asia Minor. Various Aramaic inscriptions indicate that there was a Jewish settlement there, at least by the time of the fifth century B.C.E. (Lipiński 1973). One inscription has even turned up the same spelling of the city (*sprd*, *KAI* 260; cf. Kornfeld 1957). While Mesopotamia is the best-known destination for exiles, Philistine and Phoenician groups took their share of Jewish slaves as opportunity offered (Obad 14), and these could be carried far afield through traders such as the Greeks (cf. Joel 3:1–8[4:1–8]).

21. The brevity and ambiguity of the verse provides the opportunity for very different interpretations. The NRSV has followed the versions (LXX, Aq., Th., Syr., Targ.) in translating a passive participle of the verb meaning "save." However, MT (also Symm., Vulg.) has an active participle, "saviours" (NRSV mg.) or "liberators" (NJPS) or the more general "victorious" (NJB). In Neh 9:27 the word describes the judges, and so Obadiah may again be invoking Israel's early traditions. The root of the "judge/rule" verb occurs frequently in the book of Judges (Raabe 1996, 269). The NRSV takes Mount Zion as the goal of the verb, "to go up" or "ascend." It is less likely to describe the location of the "saviours" (so REB: "Those who wield authority on Mount Zion") who then go up and rule Mount Esau (see on v. 9). Zion is the centre of government of both earthly and heavenly rule, even as it extends to Israel's enemies such as Mount Esau. "rule" (*špṭ*) has a range of meaning including rule and judge, and may be an act or a continuing function. Are at least some of those on Mount Esau included in the benefits of eschatological rule from Jerusalem (cf. Mic 4:1–4), or does this indicate a final act of just punishment ("wreak judgment," NJPS)? The latter is less likely because the focus is on the Israelites rather than the Edomites, who have been adequately dealt with in previous verses. It is perhaps best to acknowledge that we are asking questions that the author was not addressing. But from a broader biblical theological perspective, the positive scenario should not be excluded.

The final line is a fitting close and climax. As elsewhere in the Bible, we need to understand "kingdom" as active rule ("dominion," REB, NJPS; "sovereignty," NJB) rather than a realm (cf. 1 Kgs 2:15; Matt 12:28). The verse echoes v. 1 in its use of the divine name, Yhwh, and in the assertion of the sovereign will of God. As well as providing a stylistic *inclusio*, it sums up the implicit message of the entire book ("the theological value of this little book lies in seeing the whole as an exposition of its last line," Watts 1981, 66). The present earthly situation was that the kingdom appeared to belong to Babylonia and its gods (cf. the exilic laments of Ps 74:12; Amos 5:19), but the day of Yhwh will show who truly rules. Only this foundational doctrine provides the discouraged and defeated exiles with the courage to endure and a hope that could be expressed without the selfish vindictiveness and gloating that proved Edom's downfall.

JONAH

A. *Jonah: The Prophet and the Book*

There are few stories better known than that of Jonah, and even fewer that have been more intensely studied. Yet the history of interpretation reveals a remarkable diversity of opinion about its date, genre and message. Outside the book, Jonah only appears in the Old Testament in 2 Kgs 14:25, a summary of the reign of King Jeroboam II of Northern Israel (793–753 B.C.E.):

> [23] In the fifteenth year of King Amaziah son of Joash of Judah, King Jeroboam son of Joash of Israel began to reign in Samaria; he reigned forty-one years. [24] He did what was evil in the sight of the LORD; he did not depart from all the sins of Jeroboam son of Nebat, which he caused Israel to sin. [25] He restored the border of Israel from Lebo-hamath as far as the Sea of the Arabah, according to the word of the LORD, the God of Israel, which he spoke by his servant Jonah son of Amittai, the prophet, who was from Gath-hepher. [26] For the LORD saw that the distress of Israel was very bitter; there was no one left, bond or free, and no one to help Israel. [27] But the LORD had not said that he would blot out the name of Israel from under heaven, so he saved them by the hand of Jeroboam son of Joash.

Jonah is a paradoxical figure, an eighth-century prophet who announces not judgment but salvation to an evil king of Israel. This puzzling mismatch between calling and commission perhaps fits him for this strange story of a reluctant prophet being sent on a mission of mercy to Nineveh. Nineveh is the evil capital of the Assyrian nation, which will soon destroy the Northern Kingdom (2 Kgs 17). Jonah's solitary occurrence in 2 Kings also leaves his character as obscure as Melchizedek, a virtue for authors who wish to explore complex issues in a virtuosic way without constraint (Gen 14; Heb 7): "The less that was generally known about the prophet, the more freely the author could tell his story" (Wolff 1986, 98).

B. *The Date of Jonah*

Most scholars date Jonah much later than the eighth century. The individual arguments are not as conclusive as is sometimes thought, but the cumulative case is persuasive. The range of arguments includes the following, although a full discussion would also need to include the issues raised in other sections of this introduction.

(1) *Linguistic Arguments*. There are words that are influenced by the Imperial Aramaic that was common in the postexilic period. For example, *ṭaʿam* meaning "decree" (3:7) is found in the Biblical Aramaic sources, and the ascription "God

of heaven" (1:9) occurs mainly in postexilic and Biblical Aramaic sources
(except for Gen 24:3, 7). Admittedly it is difficult to be sure that a word we
know from later Aramaic sources was present in an earlier form of the language,
since the vocabulary of the Bible is so selective. Words that have been thought
late have appeared in earlier North Semitic dialects, such as that found at Ugarit
(Loretz 1960; Landes 1982). However, the number and distribution of such
words is reasonably persuasive.

(2) *Source-Critical Arguments*. Jonah would be late if it was quoting or
interacting with exilic and postexilic sources, such as Jer 1:8, 11; 26:3, 15 or
Joel 1:13; 2:13–14. Of course, the influence could be the other way round, or
these texts could be dependent on an older common tradition (see the cautions in
Magonet 1983, 65–87). Once again, any one case can be disputed, but the consensus appears to favour Jonah as the later book. However, great caution needs
to be exercised in building an argument on the assumption that Jonah is
interacting with a specific text.

(3) *Historical Arguments*. Are there hints in the book about which historical
era it comes from? The book itself is remarkably free of specific indications of
date, time and setting. Most modern scholars assume that Jonah is a fictional
account and the product of a later era. The challenge then becomes one of fitting
its purpose to a particular setting (see below). There are a number of conservative scholars who defend its historicity on various grounds. It is difficult to be
certain that there is no basis for the story in the eighth century, for the relationship between history, aesthetics and ideology is complex (Sternberg 1985; Long
1994). Clear-cut lines of distinction between history and fiction become blurred
when a narrator chooses to embellish, exaggerate, update and assimilate to a
different historical and cultural context. Nevertheless, the search for historical
evidence of Jonah and his mission outside the Bible has been largely futile. It
would make sense for a later author to choose a relatively obscure pre-exilic
prophet as the vehicle for a story with purposes other than the historiographic.
Linking the book closely to a particular setting seems to go against the way the
book avoids relating Jonah to any external political figures or historical events.
My own view is that the book of Jonah is likely to be postexilic, but it cannot be
dated more precisely than that.

C. *The Integrity and Unity of Jonah*

Earlier scholars suspected that the present book of Jonah had a complex pre-
history (Bewer 1911, 13–24). Various folktales or stories of storms and fishes
may have been adopted, adapted and edited by one or more storytellers (though
see Ben-Josef 1980). Awkward chronology may reflect the displacement of a
verse (e.g. 4:5). Repeated words or distinct linguistic usage might indicate
different sources (e.g. 1:3). Different sources have also been detected with the
help of distinct idioms and linguistic patterns. Schmidt (1905) used the different
names for God to detect strata, while Weimar (1982) considered that the verb +
cognate noun construction indicated a later redaction. Syllable counts led Houk

(1998) to reconstruct a complex history of the book. The psalm of Jonah has aroused widespread suspicion, both because of the appearance of poetry in a prose narrative, and also because of difficulties in making sense of its tone and content.

The whole enterprise raises formidable questions of approach and goal. Historical criticism is founded on a diachronic approach, in which the tracing of the development of a text through time is of primary interest. Others place more stress on a synchronic approach, attempting to make sense of the entire text (generally in its "final form") at a "snapshot" in time. The choice of approach influences how a commentator deals with difficulties and complexities in the text. It is usually possible (with sufficient ingenuity) to suggest synchronic and diachronic explanations of the same difficulty. For example, a contradiction between Jonah's actions in ch. 1 and his words in ch. 2 may indicate to dia-chronic critics that the psalm is from a different source, while a synchronic critic will find this to be a subtle indication of a complex character.

My starting point is to give priority to the synchronic approach. This is partly because many of the stricter criteria for detecting earlier sources are too sim-plistic: well-told stories display a sophisticated style (making significant use of repetition and variation) and portray characters whose complexity is suggested by surface contradictions. It is also partly because the present book of Jonah is the only text we have and the explanation of its present form (whatever its sources) is what I understand to be the primary goal of this commentary. Diachronic solutions should be a last resort once the best synchronic readings have been tried and found to be unsatisfactory. However, it is difficult to judge when this is ever the case in Jonah, where fine craftsmanship is so evident.

D. *The Genre of the Book*

Jonah has been assigned a bewildering number of different genres (see the surveys in Andrew 1967; Burrows 1970; Day 1990, 37–39; Salters 1994, 41–50). This in itself suggests that it is unique. Landes (1978, 146) comments, "the Book of Jonah as a work of literary art comes close to being *sui generis*." Nevertheless, a careful look at some of the categories suggested will provide a useful orientation to many of the interpretive issues raised by the book.

1. *Historical Narrative*
Some conservative scholars still defend the historicity of Jonah (e.g. Alexander 1985). They draw attention to various factors that might have predisposed the Ninevites to repent, such as invasion, a solar eclipse coupled with ominous omens, famine and disease, or a flood (Stuart 1987, 490). Wiseman (1979) sug-gests the king of Nineveh in question might have been the weak Ashurdan III (773–56 B.C.E.), and he cites examples of repentant behaviour in Assyria. On the other hand, those who regard Jonah as fiction frequently attempt the reverse, proving the impossibility of the book's historical character through inappro-priate and inaccurate details.

The swallowing of Jonah by the great fish is the most notorious issue. It is very doubtful whether unverified reports of similar swallowings contribute much to the discussion (Williams 1907; Davis 1991). This line of defence reflects a pseudo-scientific rationalism that is as dubious from a theological as from a historical point of view (Sherwood 2000: 42–48). It would be far simpler to assert that it was a miracle, unique and unrepeatable, but this would be to prejudge the issue of genre prematurely. The discussion of historicity is often inconclusive, since it is impossible to find any particular feature that will distinguish a well-told story that is based on a historical event (potentially including miracles) from one that is fictional.

Despite these cautions, it seems to me that a richer and more coherent interpretation of the book becomes possible if it is a basically imaginative work. The central figure of the book is indeed likely to be the one mentioned in 2 Kgs 14:25, but the world of the book of Jonah can hardly be more different from that of 2 Kings. A decision that the book was never intended to be read as historical narrative does not, or course, imply a low view of the value or authority of the book. The practical result of rejecting Jonah as a historical account is that the commentary will not discuss historical issues in detail.

2. *Imaginative Literature*

Jonah has been called many different kinds of imaginative literature, but few bear more than a passing resemblance to the book of Jonah. One way round this difficulty is to choose a genre, but admit that Jonah is an adaptation of that genre. Some of the suggestions are:

(1) *Allegory* (Ackroyd 1968, 245). It is possible to find theological or historical correspondences to many of the details in Jonah (e.g. Jonah the dove a is symbol for Israel, the fish is a symbol of exile). However, the equations are often arbitrary, with little corroborating support from the text. Most biblical allegories identify explicitly the correspondences, often in an explanatory appendix (Judg 9:8–20; Ezek 16; 37; Mark 4:1–20).

(2) *Parable* (Bewer 1911, 3–4; Allen 1976, 175–81) or *māšāl*, the nearest Hebrew equivalent (Landes 1978). Parables have a less direct correspondence to external realities than allegories. However, most parables are set within a larger narrative framework. They also have a simpler structure and characterization than we find in Jonah.

(3) *Legend* (Haller 1958; Keller 1982; Jepsen 1970). A legend can be defined as a story whose chief protagonist is a hero, although Jonah is more an anti-hero. It might be a story about a person who was historical but whose deeds have now been imaginatively embroidered. But this classification is too general to shed much light on the nature of the book.

(4) *Midrash*. A midrash is a commentary on a text. Unfortunately it is not clear which text Jonah is commenting upon. Budde (1892) suggested 2 Kgs 14:25, while others have proposed Jer 18:7–8. However, a midrash or a sermon (Andrew 1967, 82–85) normally interacts with a base text more explicitly. Further, it is often difficult to be sure whether Jonah quotes, echoes, deviates from or subverts any specific text.

One reason for the popularity of these genre proposals may be because they are more akin to fiction than to history. Yet, laying the primary stress on historicity (or the lack of it) probably reflects a modern rather than an ancient concern. In all of these suggestions the deviations of Jonah from standard exemplars of the genre appear to be more significant than the similarities. The more qualifications are required, the less useful the classification.

3. *Irony, Satire, Parody*

The presence of irony in Jonah has long been recognized. Irony can be defined as the implicit conflict between two different points of view. In the Bible it is an important theological category, for it enables an author to do justice both to God's sovereign will and the resistance to that will by human sinners. Jonah is a paradigmatic example of this kind of irony, for he succeeds dramatically in doing the opposite of what he wanted. He furthers God's will through his own freely chosen actions.

A recent trend has been to find in Jonah satire, a harsh form of irony designed to ridicule and deflate (Good 1981, 41) or "a caricature in words" (Burrows 1970, 96). The usual approach is to regard Jonah as the representative of a group of people whose behaviour and views the author of Jonah wishes to ridicule. Parody is very similar to satire, but subverts or ridicules a well-known genre. Miles (1974–75) suggests that different parts of the book parody well-known biblical genres: the call to prophecy, the prophetic critique of idolatry, the psalm of thanksgiving, the rejection of a prophet by the king and the prayer for death. Ackerman (1981) supports this approach by focusing on the dissonances between the psalm and its prose context. Rather than a temple, the entrails of a fish is the location for a song of thanksgiving, which in its first-person viewpoint suggests hypocrisy and self-delusion. Holbert (1981) seeks to show how Jonah fulfils five criteria for satire: (a) it is humour based on the fantastic, the gro-tesque, the absurd; (b) it has a definite target; (c) the attack of satire is indirect; (d) it pillories excessive behaviour (e.g. hypocrisy); (e) it is usually external in viewpoint. Orth (1990) suggests that Jonah parodies prophetic literature. Marcus (1995) probably gives the fullest list of potential examples of satire, parody, irony, the fantastic, the ridiculous, the exaggerated and the understated.

These authors display a lively ingenuity in maximizing the humour of the book, but there are some significant difficulties that they have to face. Berlin (1976) argued that many of the scenes that Miles (1974–75) had interpreted satirically could be read very differently. Because the clash of viewpoints is implicit, finding irony depends in large part on a wider frame of reference. The recent popularity of the approach may reveal more about the reading preferences of the late twentieth century. Humour is often culturally specific, and much depends on how we retell the story in the world of the reader (Carroll 1990). In addition, it is often hard to recognize satire and parody (Band 1990, 180), and, conversely, it is possible to find satire when it is not present. Satire is not so much a genre as a dominant mood or tone (Allen 1976, 176), and it requires a relatively slight shift of interpretation to find a basically serious story with some elements of compassionate irony (Simon 1999, xxi–xxii).

Another problem is that if Jonah is a parody or satire, then it is targeting a particular text or group that should be identifiable. But it has been difficult for scholars to settle on a specific target. Jonah has innumerable allusions and echoes of other biblical materials (see the references in the commentary). Jonah might represent people in general (Haller 1958, 35; Wolff 1975, 76), or Israel in general (Jeremias 1975, 99 refers to "Jona-Israel"). But he might also be a more specific representative of the nationalistic reform party of the fifth century, reflected in Ezra 9–10 and Neh 13 (Good 1981, 39). Burrows (1970, 105) discerned a conflict between the Jews returning from exile in Babylon and those who had remained in Palestine. Miles (1974–75, 170) identified a group among the returnees who took the national focus of the religious writings of Israel too seriously. Holbert (1981, 75) deduced an attack on Hebrew prophetic hypocrisy. Orth (1990, 274) found the target to be overrigid editors of the prophetic corpus. The underlying problem is that a narrative that is as open and complex as Jonah can be appropriated for any or all of these contexts.

Satire and parody also have serious implications for the characterization of Jonah, who usually becomes a flat and unlikeable character. He "was essentially self-centred, self-righteous, and self-willed" (Burrows 1970, 97); "He [the author] wants to teach the narrow, blind, prejudiced, fanatic Jews of which Jonah is but the type" (Bewer 1911, 64). This is in line with Christian readings of Jonah as the resistant Jew (Sherwood 2000, 21–42). However, the book itself contains contradictory signals. Jonah is both obedient and disobedient, orthodox and unorthodox. An alternative interpretation of contradictions like these is that is is being portrayed as a complex and ambiguous character, who responds in both honest and questionable ways to the situations in which finds himself.

To sum up, I do not think that Jonah is a sustained satire or parody. It is certainly full of irony and humour, but these enable the author to explore in a non-threatening way serious theological issues. It is possible to detect a web of allusions and citations of other texts (some ironic) in a book by an author who has inherited a rich literary and theological tradition, but this does not require it to be an all-out parody or satire (see further Jenson 2007).

4. *A Story*
Most recent commentators wisely leave the genre as general as possible. This can be achieved simply by calling it a short story ("Novella," Wolff 1975, 29–58; 1986, 82). Some have sought to specify the kind of story more precisely. Frequently this is done by emphasizing the close relation between Jonah and a group of texts known from elsewhere in the Bible. However, the number of such proposals tends to undermine the persuasiveness of any particular one.

(1) *A prophetic story.* The stories about prophets in Samuel and Kings also tell of dramatic miracles (e.g. 1 Kgs 18:30–39) and positive encounters with non-Israelites (e.g. 2 Kgs 5). But a more detailed look tends to highlight differences rather than similarities. Jonah's disobedience is unique and its open ending is very unusual. We can always suggest that the genre has been developed (Salters 1994, 48), but at the cost of reducing the value of the comparison.

(2) *A skeptical story*. Similar reservations can be expressed about those who highlight the similarities between Jonah and Wisdom Literature. In Proverbs we can find themes such as the fear of the Lord (Prov 1:7), judgment on evil (Prov 15:3), the power of the prayer of the righteous (Prov 15:29), and the significance of lot-casting (Prov 16:33). But none of these are specifically wisdom themes and their treatment in Jonah is distinctive (Landes 1967, 149–50). In a similar way it is possible to build up a list of parallels with Job—a legendary setting, the issue of theodicy, stylistic virtuosity, irony, the complaint against God, a closing divine revelation (Vawter 1983; Dell 1996). But God is much more concerned to reveal his will in Jonah than in Job.

(3) *A didactic story* (Feuillet 1947, 161). As for satiric interpretations, this classification requires the identification of the parties that are reflected in the various characters of the book and what they are being taught. A popular choice is the fifth-century background represented by the books of Ezra and Nehemiah. Jonah thus represents Jewish nationalists who wish nothing to do with gentiles and strive by all means at their disposal to preserve the purity of their Jewish heritage. In painting an unflattering portrait of Jonah, the author is protesting against particularism in favour of a more universalist perspective. The problems facing this (and other) proposals are many. It is simplistic and partial in its allegorical solution to the identification of the chief characters of Jonah (Clements 1974, 20). Jonah does not treat the burning questions of the fifth century (such as mixed marriages, the elimination of foreign influences from the returnees). It also tends to caricature the attitude to gentiles in Ezra and Nehemiah, where the open-handed generosity of Cyrus (Ezra 1), Darius (Ezra 6) and Artaxerxes (Neh 2) is welcomed, as much as the enmity of other parties is condemned. The difficulty in summing up the message of Jonah suggests that it is not a focused didactic story (Craig 1993, 159–60).

(4) *A proto-Christian story*. Christian interpreters have been tempted to identify Jonah with those advocating Jewish particularism, while the author of the book is a proto-Christian in his universalist faith. Once again this is a reductionistic strategy that forgets that the New Testament as well as Jonah reflects an inner-Jewish debate (Golka 1986). Both the Old and the New Testaments reflect various levels of openness to the nations around.

(5) *A multidimensional story*. Good stories are characteristically open, ambiguous and so multidimensional (Golka 1986). There are more questions in Jonah than answers (cf. Limburg 1993, 25–26). The interpretation of stories can be didactic, but this takes place within a broader theological framework and the specific cultural context of the interpreter. This may be seen in studies of the later interpretation of Jonah (Bickerman 1967; Sherwood 1997; 1998).

The main value of the "story" classification may simply be to prevent a reader being misled by interpreting it too narrowly as one of the genres discussed above. It also alerts us to the literary features of the book (Wolff 1975, 29–58; Magonet 1983; Trible 1994).

E. *The Message of Jonah*

The message of Jonah is notoriously difficult to identify. The main objections to
the standard proposals is that they do not do justice to all parts of the book, and
that the key to the meaning is imported from outside the story without sufficient
evidence. Key passages in the story can be interpreted in radically different
ways in order to support or undermine a particular reading. Attempts to narrow
the possibilities through locating a specific date, social setting or reference text
have by and large failed (see the previous section). The main suggestions for its
message are as follows, with the ones I consider least persuasive first.

(1) *Prophecy* (Emmerson 1976; Nielsen 1979). Jonah is upset at having his
status as a true prophet undermined by the failure of his prophecy (Num 23:19;
Deut 18:21–22). However, this seems a very unlikely attitude. A number of texts
make it very clear that the prophets and their hearers were well aware that the
fulfilment of their prophecies was dependent on how people responded (Jer
26:17–19).

(2) *Repentance* (Clements 1974). This is the traditional Jewish proposal,
reflected by the reading of the book during the afternoon service of the Day of
Atonement (*b. Meg.* 31a). Kaufmann (1960, 284–85) finds in Jonah a specific
rebuttal of the ancient idea that all sin had to be punished. This is very doubtful
from a historical point of view, and the theme of repentance is only prominent in
ch. 3.

(3) *Universalism* (Rowley 1945; von Rad 1965, 289–92). The condemnation
of a narrow nationalism or particularism, represented by Jonah, is a popular
Christian interpretation. Yet it is not at all certain that Jonah and Nineveh are
meant to be universalized in this way. Further, Jonah's complaint is primarily
about God's behaviour, not that of the gentiles.

(4) *Theodicy* (Fretheim 1977; 1978; Levine 1984; Simon 1999, xii–xiii). In
one version of this view Jonah is the proponent of strict justice, and concerned
that the exercise of God's mercy and compassion will undermine this. Yet if
Jonah is a general lesson in theodicy, it is strange that the lesson is taught far
away in Nineveh, rather than in Israel.

(5) *Sovereignty*. The elusive logic of ch. 4 has led to a number of scholars
suggesting that God's actions are inherently incomprehensible (Elata-Alster and
Salmon 1989), or that he is irrational (Bolin 1997, 183; Heschel 1962, 287).
There are a number of intriguing similarities between Jonah and Job (Dell 1996).
Yet, although there are hidden dimensions to the divine plan (Deut 29:29), the
Bible never sees this as a reason to give up exploring insights and perspectives.
God's sovereignty is hidden rather than irrational. Marcus (1995) gives up the
entire attempt to find a purpose and proposes that it is simply a satire on Jonah.
But this seems a council of despair, for there is a great deal that is said about
God and his purposes. The challenge is acknowledging the various facets of the
book in a way that is neither simplistic nor contradictory. The approach followed below organizes the discussion of the book's message by looking at the
main characters. A central feature of all narrative is the symbiotic relationship
between character, plot and theme.

Gentiles: Sailors and Ninevites

Many consider that Jonah teaches general lessons about the human condition. Human beings have both the capacity for evil (1:3) and for repentance and right behaviour (3:8). The sailors behave in an exemplary fashion from the beginning, while the Ninevites awake to their fate and change their lives. God has no particular quarrel with the sailors, but the evil behaviour of Nineveh emphasizes his passion for justice (3:4), longsuffering and the desire to exercise mercy (4:2).

These general truths are complicated by the Jewish character of the book. However far Jonah is told to travel, he is still a Jew, a member of a nation with a unique destiny, and he serves Yhwh, the God of Israel (1:9), who is unique and incomparable among the gods. Jonah's mission raises sharp questions about how Jews and gentiles are related to one another and to the God who both rules the world and reveals himself to Israel in a unique way.

The non-Israelites in Jonah represent two possibilities when a Jew meets gentiles. The sailors are ignorant idolaters, while the Ninevites are evil and violent. Ignorance is not the same as evil, and the sailors are earnest and scrupulously carry out their duties to the best of their abilities and knowledge. With the help of Jonah's testimony, they eventually come to a basic knowledge of Yhwh, the true God of Israel, and end up by sacrificing to him. The Ninevites begin in a far worse state, so evil that they are condemned to destruction. But when Jonah serves them notice of doom, they demonstrate (without much help from Jonah) a praiseworthy general moral and religious knowledge. Just as the commendable character of the sailors contrasts markedly with the sinfulness of Israel emphasized in its literature, so the piety and repentance of Nineveh's king is a striking contrast to the general run of Israel's kings. People and king recognize that their evil deeds were wrong and deserved punishment. They repent, change their ways and trust in God. Both sailors and Ninevites thus have an effective religious knowledge that enables them to pray wisely and act rightly.

The approach to non-Israelites is thus very positive, with conversion and repentance being fitting responses. Yet there remains a considerable inequality between them and Yhwh calls not one of Nineveh's prophets or priests to communicate his message, but Jonah. Without Jonah's active intervention the Ninevites would have been doomed and the sailors left in mortal ignorance. Despite the happy end of both stories, it is not clear how much theological movement there has been. The sailors' knowledge of Yhwh is limited to a brief experience of his power and mercy in saving them from death. The Ninevites experience his compassion, but postexilic readers would remember that it did not last long and the city will once again become the subject of God's judgment (Nahum). Jonah does not teach them Torah or introduce them to the finer points of Israel's understanding of Yhwh. It is going too far, then, to speak with some Christian interpreters of Jonah's mission to the gentiles to bring them to faith (Rowley 1945, 69). However, it should also be noted that the story is not inconsistent with this later interest (Bauckham 2003).

Jonah

The character and call of Jonah is evidently a central issue. Stuart (1987, 434) sums up the message simply as "Don't be like Jonah." But what is Jonah like? Early Jewish interpretation gave a positive evaluation of his motives, finding a man zealous on behalf of Israel. He is worried that if Nineveh heard the word of Yhwh and repented, it would show up Israel's rebellion and lack of repentance (Zlotowitz 1978, xxiii–xxix). His zeal is commendable even if it is misguided. Many recent interpreters see nothing at all commendable in Jonah, comparing him unfavourably with the non-Israelites he meets.

The challenge is not to let Jonah become a caricature, for this makes the book simplistic and God another superficial character. This is a major problem with many satirical readings, and also with those who regard him as a naïve national-ist who wants God to have nothing at all to do with heathens. God's persistence with Jonah only makes sense if there are substantive issues in conflict (cf. Job). There is little evidence that Jonah disliked the gentiles he met. His chief quarrel is with God, and that only in regard to a particular issue. Otherwise, Jonah's theology is orthodox (1:9), as is his thanksgiving on being saved from the fish in ch. 2.

Why, then, does Jonah not wish God to exercise mercy upon Nineveh? The simplest explanation is that he fears that Assyria will become the agent of God's punishment of Israel. God makes use of the nations in this way (Isa 10:5–6), and readers will know all too well the story of the destruction and exile of the ten Northern tribes (2 Kgs 17). Although this point is not explicit, other explana-tions stumble at why Nineveh and not some other city was chosen (contrast the non-Israelite setting of Job). The story shows that Jonah's attempt to thwart God's will was presumptuous. God's compassion and justice are fundamental aspects of his relationship to individuals, to Israel and to gentile nations. These people do not live in isolated worlds but they interact in the one world that God rules. Jonah's objection may be that compassion for Nineveh would have negative consequences for Israel. He thought he knew how God should organize the whole world. In the debate of ch. 4, God tries to reason with Jonah and show his inconsistency. Only God in his sovereignty can order events in Israel and in the nations. The call is to trust and obey him, even when this may lead to tragic consequences for Israel.

God's Agents in Creation

It is striking that the final phrase of the book includes a note of God's care for animals. This has sometimes felt to be so surprising and anticlimactic that it is interpreted as parody (Orth 1990, 272). However, a less intense "climbdown" is often found in biblical rhetorical structures (e.g. Job 31:38–40), and it is quite possible to read the final phrase in 4:11 as reinforcing the message of God's care for the city of Nineveh. Just as doom threatens animal as well as human when a city is about to be destroyed, so God's care extends to those caught up in the human bundle of life. The links with wisdom writings (see above) has suggested an important role for the doctrine of creation: "Creation theology—linking Jonah to Gen 1–11, the Psalms, and the Wisdom Literature—is what holds the book of Jonah together, without it being the main theme" (Golka 1998, 127).

In several other places non-human agents play a crucial role in furthering Yhwh's will. The prompt obedience of the great wind and the fish take forward the plot in ch. 1, as well as highlighting by way of contrast the disobedience of Jonah. The awesome force of the wind and the sea bring home to the sailors their helplessness and the greater fearfulness of the God who commands them (1:16). In ch. 4 the bush and the worm, the wind and the sun are all essential for the sharp lesson that God gives Jonah

On the one hand, these creatures have their valued place in the order of the world. In 4:10–11 God expresses concern for the animals of Nineveh, and by extension every living thing in the rest of his creation. At the same time, the story shows the priority of the human race, notwithstanding its sinfulness and disobedience (cf. Gen 1–3). Taking no part in the tragedy of sin or the comedy of being made in God's image, non-human creatures and plants have no option but to be mere agents, flat characters without depth and needing no redemption or judgment. As agents, they play their subordinate role in the story and provide living but limited illustrations of higher truths. The great fish saves Jonah, perhaps at the cost of some discomfort to itself, but there is no danger that it will complain to God as Jonah does. More poignantly, Jonah's theological lesson in ch. 4 necessitates the death of a harmless plant. But this willingness to risk inhabitants of the world he created for the sake of people is a feature of God's behaviour from the beginning.

God

The God of Jonah is evidently the key character in the book, initiating, speaking and acting to ensure his will is done. He is the authentic God of the Bible, one and sovereign, commanding and calling, just and merciful. The idolatry of the sailors is touched upon in passing (passages such as Isa 44 are much more heavy-handed), for their gods are only a foil for the portrayal of the living God of Jonah. The ineffective prayers of the sailors in the midst of the storm emphasizes that the God they do not know is sovereign over the forces of the universe. Only Jonah's confession (1:9) provides the name of the supreme God responsible. In ch. 3, idolatry is not at issue. The assumption is that the god of the Ninevites is the same as (or at least compatible with) the God whom Jonah serves. Whereas in ch. 1 the distinctiveness of Yhwh is emphasized, here his universality is assumed. It is sufficient for the Ninevites to know that there is a god who holds them to account for their behaviour.

In Jonah, God is more concerned about Nineveh's wickedness than its idolatry. He is the righteous judge of all the earth (Gen 18:25), and he does not condemn nations for what they do not know (a true knowledge of him), but for their failure to observe what is generally known about how to behave (Amos 1–2). But alongside this is the demonstration of God's mercy. God's violent response to Jonah's flight is paradoxically in order to open up the possibility of exercising mercy rather than punishment (Sternberg 1985, 318–20). His appointment of the worm and wind are for the sake of persuading Jonah to see things in the right way, not vindictive or sadistic ploys.

The precise reasons for providing Nineveh (and not some other city) with the opportunity for repentance are never given. Extensive sections of the prophetic books are devoted to the condemnation of sinful nations (e.g. Obadiah), but Jonah is sent only to Nineveh. God's sovereignty means that these reasons are ultimately hidden, but this is not the same as their being arbitrary or irrational. They are at the very least consistent with his passion for justice and mercy, and also his requirement for human beings to respond. His sovereign commands are worked out in dialogue with humans who are free to repent and change their ways (or not). In contrast with Sodom (Gen 18), the Ninevites changed their behaviour and God responded by changing his mind (Jonah 3:10). The situation is the reverse of that in Job. There the question is "Are God's actions in multi-plying undeserved suffering just?" Here it is "Is God's compassion towards Nineveh's deserved suffering just?"

The key texts about God's character are 4:2 and 4:10–11. The logic of both is difficult and requires us to guess the background. Jonah's complaint is framed as a traditional formulation of faith, except that the received tradition has "by no means clearing the guilty" (Exod 34:7) rather than "ready to relent from punish-ing" (Jonah 4:2). This is sometimes regarded as a new move (Freedman 1990). Israel can no longer depend on its keeping of the conditional Sinai covenant, for exile shows the bankruptcy of expecting Israel to obey. Israel must depend instead on something more basic, such as God's promises to Abraham (Isa 51:2) or his commitment to creation (Jer 31:35–37). However, this is an oversim-plification of the gracious character of God's covenant grace (Hillers 1969). The essential component of God's grace is also evident in the opening stories of Genesis, where there is an unavoidable tension between God's just condemna-tion of human rebellion and his willingness to continue interacting with those whom he has created.

This necessary element of grace in the equation of life is just as evident in the existence of Israel. "Ready to relent from punishing" (cf. Exod 32:14) may well represent reflection on the larger context of Exod 32–24 (Dozemann 1989). This section explores the sharp but essential tension between God's commitment to Israel and his just condemnation of sin. The significant difference in Jonah is that the subject of this traditional formulation is not Israel but Nineveh. The book can be regarded as an exploration of how the God of Jonah is both the one God of both Jew and gentile, and the unique covenant God of Israel, exhibiting in both modes his justice and compassion. Throughout the book the tension is maintained, and resolving the tension in favour of only one side is both prema-ture and simplistic.

F. *Outline Analysis of Jonah*

G. *Commentary on Jonah*

Jonah and the Sovereign God (1:1–16)

Setting: The Runaway (1:1–3)

The introduction to the book sets out the main characters (Yhwh, Jonah, Nineveh), some important keywords (rise, great, evil, proclaim), and an initial perspective on a major issue of the book (how does God relate to Jew and gentile?). The narrator's introduction (v. 1) is followed by the divine command to Jonah (v. 2), which triggers an unexpected and dramatic response: a prompt flight in the opposite direction (v. 3). As is common in the exposition of biblical stories, the pace is rapid as we move from Jonah's home town to Joppa and then out to sea. The description is objective and external, dealing with actions rather than motives or feelings. These are more than sufficient to set up the basic tensions that drive the initial plot. The geographical uncertainty is whether the journey will end up at God's or Jonah's preferred destination (Nineveh or Tarshish?). The theological and political uncertainty is whether Nineveh will have an opportunity to be warned about God's coming judgment, with all that might entail. From a personal point of view, we wonder what God will do to someone who so promptly disobeys him, and how far Jonah will change his ways.

The surprise and shock of the opening response by Jonah is magnified the more we are familiar with other prophetic narratives. Prophets may object to the divine commission, but only verbally and for a short while (Exod 3–4; Jer 1:6). They never coolly and comprehensively disobey like Jonah. Normally the divine word to a person elicits a verbal response, but we deduce that God never has a chance to persuade Jonah, for he acts instead of speaks. Jonah's silence is his first rebellion, and it is only in ch. 4 that we find a two-way conversation. The initial events begin the book's exploration of a classical theological tension, the apparent contradiction between divine sovereignty and human freedom. The opening verses portray a sovereign divine initiative, but God's word does not even manage to get a proper hearing from its first recipient.

The brevity of the account and the emphasis on action omit a great deal, particularly the content of the message Jonah is meant to proclaim (v. 2), and the motive for his flight (v. 3). The author does not set out all the relevant details immediately, because the emphasis in ch. 1 is on action, not motive. The discussion of inner motives is postponed until chs. 2 and 4 (Magonet 1983, 59). It is quite possible that we have an abbreviated speech (1 Kgs 2:30; Person 1996). Some of the gaps are filled in later (see further on 4:2), but the immediate result is that we are free to concentrate on the action of ch. 1, and the question of whether Jonah will escape from God or not.

How is a reader intended to respond to this chapter? A pious first-time reader might quickly judge Jonah as an anti-hero, for he has not only disobeyed Yhwh but also refused to announce judgment on a thoroughly evil nation. But a more theologically aware reader will know that prophetic oracles always have an implicit "get out of jail" card. Preaching to Nineveh will give them an opportunity to repent and be forgiven. Nineveh will then live on and be the cause of Northern Israel's demise (2 Kgs 17:5–6). Indeed, Nineveh's response will make all the more culpable Israel's continued evil in the face of a succession of prophets. Jonah may be in the wrong in disobeying God, but it is for reasons that are tied to a commitment to the value of election and the privileges of being the people of God. Jonah's behaviour thus raises important questions that we too wish to ask Yhwh. Jonah's chutzpah and his commitment to the people of God might then impress us, and all the more if we are aware of the readiness of God's servants to complain to him when he seems not to be acting as he should (Exod 5:22; Ps 80).

1:1. Now (*wayᵉhî*) introduces several books of the Bible (Joshua; Judges; 1 Samuel; Ezekiel; Ruth; Esther). Since it normally continues a narrative whose setting has been established beforehand, Sasson (1990) argues that the author is alluding to a number of stories about Jonah that were circulating. However, it can also be an indefinite opening without any particular connection to other events or texts (the "*waw* is virtually the equivalent of capitalization," Stuart 1987, 445). A prophetic tone is set by the entire phrase ("Now the word of Yhwh came to X…saying"), which comes frequently at the beginning of sections in Jeremiah and Ezekiel, while it tends to come in the middle of the story in earlier narratives (e.g. 1 Kgs 21:17, 28).

Jonah son of Amittai is the only personal name (apart from God's name, Yhwh) in the entire book. The full form of a name often occurs in the introduction of a story (e.g. Judg 4:4) and specifies this Jonah as the prophet of 2 Kgs 14:25 (see Section A, above), his only other occurrence in the Bible. There he is stated to come from Gath-hepher in the territory of Zebulun (Josh 19:13), about 15 miles west of the Sea of Galilee. Jonah is portrayed as an Israelite prophet of salvation to a sinful king, Jeroboam II (2 Kgs 14:24). Jonah thus becomes an ideal candidate for the author's exploration of themes of judgment and salvation, nationalism and universalism. But other than his name there is no further specification of date, place and political context (contrast Isa 1:1; Jer 1:1–2), probably hinting that this is not a standard prophetic book.

The most likely meaning of Jonah is "dove," a bird often associated with Jonah in Christian art. Allegorical interpreters enjoy exploring the image. The perverse action of Jonah in going in the wrong direction can reflect Israel's equally perverse disobedience of God: "Ephraim has become like a dove, silly and without sense; they call upon Egypt, they go to Assyria" (Hos 7:11). According to this reading, Jonah is a type of the people of Israel. Hauser (1985) suggests that Jonah is chosen because of the association of doves with flight (Ps 55:6[7]) and passivity (Nah 2:7), both features of Jonah's behaviour. However, the text provides no clear support for this, while the symbolism of doves is multivalent. They can also be associated with sacrifice, love, lament and dwelling among rocks (Lev 1:14; Song 1:15; Ezek 7:16; Jer 48:28; cf. Botterweck 1990). Similar caution needs to attend comments on the etymology of Amittai, "Yhwh is faithful," from the verbal root *ʾmn* (the root of "Amen") and related to *ʾemet* ("truth, faithfulness"). This could be irony, highlighting the contradictory understandings of Yhwh's faithfulness held by Jonah and by Yhwh himself in relation to Nineveh (Good 1981, 42). Yet this is never explicit, and all such proposals can only be speculative given that the primary source is probably Jonah's appearance in 2 Kgs 14:25.

1:2. The content of the word of Yhwh is a commission, one of the essential features in the initial call of a prophet (Isa 6:9; Amos 7:15). It echoes that of Elijah, the only other prophet to be sent to a foreign land (1 Kgs 17:9). Three imperatives ("arise, go...and cry," RSV) are followed by a reason ("for"). However, the instruction is brief and general. There is no messenger formula ("Thus says Yhwh ...") indicating the words to be delivered, nor are we told the substance of the proclamation. The words are the author's summary, and they conceal as much as they reveal. We do not know the purpose of the proclamation (presumably punishment, but a warning implies an alternative), and we do not know how faithfully Jonah will eventually communicate it (3:4).

The verb *qûm*, "arise" or "get up" (3:2 in the NRSV), is often an auxiliary verb in Hebrew. When it is attached to a second verb without "and," it shifts the emphasis onto the second verb (GKC §120g). Hence it can be omitted (REB, NIV) or the verb of motion reinforced ("set out for," Sasson 1990, 66; "go at once," NRSV). However, the descent motif in the first chapter (see on v. 3) suggests that something of the original spatial meaning should be retained. Jonah is instructed to arise, but we find him going down instead.

Nineveh was the infamous capital of the Assyrian empire in its last few decades and would have evoked bitter memories for Israelites. Sennacherib (704–681) made it his capital (cf. 2 Kgs 19:36) and it finally fell in 612 B.C.E. to the Medes and the Babylonians. It is the object of prophetic oracles of judgment in Zeph 2:13 and particularly Nahum (e.g. 3:7). It is "great" (*gādôl*), a keyword in Jonah, appearing 14 times with many different nuances. Here it can describe the size of the city ("vast" or "large" or "populous," 3:3; 4:11) or its political importance. It is also wicked (*rāʿâ*), another keyword (see on 4:1) and a characteristic that would be no surprise to readers of the book, especially with its echoes of sinful Sodom and Gomorrah (Gen 18:21; Jer 23:14). It is called great in Gen 10:11–12 before Israel comes on the scene, and as such could well be an archetype of any great city and a very appropriate choice for the application of God's justice.

Jonah is to "cry out against it." "cry out" (*qr*ᵓ) can refer to a positive or negative proclamation. Here the context clearly indicates that condemnation is in mind and the negative tone is reinforced by the use of the preposition ʿal ("against"). So we might interpret "denounce it" (REB) or "proclaim judgment upon it" (NJPS). The preposition can also mean "concerning," but there is no need to discern ambiguity here in the light of the later modification of the preposition (3:1) and Nineveh's subsequent repentance. We are not told the precise content or purpose of the message, which will be explored in chs. 3–4. What is clear is that Jonah is being commanded to do something unique. Others were called to prophecy against the nations (Jer 46–51; Ezek 25–32). Only Jonah had to travel physically to another country to deliver the message.

1:3. By using the same "arise" verb as in v. 2 the narrator records how Jonah immediately responds. A first-time reader might expect an obedient response such as "and Jonah arose and went" (cf. 1 Kgs 17:10), but the next word ("flee") shows that the opposite is the case. The deliberate and shocking opposition of Jonah to Yhwh's call is emphasized by the vocabulary, syntax and structure of the verse. A far lesser crime had deadly consequences in 1 Kgs 13:7–22, and Yhwh's lenient response suggests that the point at issue is not simply disobedience. The five active verbs (arose, went down, found, paid, went down) tell of Jonah's industrious application as he attempts to get as far away from Yhwh as possible. Hope for a successful flight is raised by the ease with which Jonah found a ship going to Tarshish. However, a good start is never the guarantee of a successful end (cf. Acts 27:13).

The sentence is complex because it has a concentric pattern (Lohfink 1961, 200–201; Trible 1994, 129):

> A   But Jonah arose to flee to **Tarshish** <u>from the presence of Yhwh</u>
>   B   and *he went down* to Joppa
>   C   and he found a ship
>   D   going to **Tarshish**
>   C′   and he paid his fare
>   B′   and *he went down* into it
> A′   to go with them to **Tarshish** <u>from the presence of Yhwh</u>

The threefold repetition of his destination, Tarshish, at the beginning, middle and end conveys the single-minded determination of Jonah in his flight to go as far in the opposite direction from Nineveh (located to the east of Israel) as he can. The identification of Tarshish is a matter as much for the imagination as for the atlas. It is as far to the east as fabled Sheba is to the west (Ps 72:10; Ezek 38:13). There is a cuneiform reference to "the kings [of the islands] in the midst of the sea, from Yadanana [Cyprus] and Yaman [Javan] as far as Tar-si-si [Tarshish], beneath my feet" (cf. Wolff 1986). In the Table of Nations (Gen 10:4–5), the coastland peoples spread from the sons of Javan, who are usually identified with eastern Mediterranean locations: Elishah (Cyprus or Crete?), Tarshish, Kittim (Cyprus?) and Rodanim (Rhodes?). These and other references do not help much to locate Tarshish specifically, and many identifications have been proposed. The most common is the Phoenician colony of Tartessos, on the Atlantic coast of southern Spain. However, it is also possible that there were several places called Tarshish (as was the case for several ancient cities, such as Carthage). Whatever the specific identification, the symbolic overtones of the name are primary. The ships of Tarshish are ocean-going vessels that can reach the farthest shore (Isa 60:9), may need to weather dangerous storms (Ps 48:7), and are the source of exotic rarities (1 Kgs 10:22). Tarshish represents the far side of the world, a place in the west beyond the bounds of sure geographical knowledge. There Jonah would be as far from any contact with the God of Israel as possible (Isa 66:19). It may be compared to similar places that are a coalescence of myth and geography (Timbuktu; El Dorado; Sasson 1990 cites equivalents known from cuneiform and Egyptian sources). The Talmud regards Tarshish as taking a year to reach (*b. B. Bat.* 38a, 39a), and Solomon's Tarshish fleet returns once in every three years (2 Chr 9:21). The ship is normally regarded as "going to Tarshish," but Sasson argues that in maritime contexts the verb should be translated "return from." In 2 Chr 9:21 the ships "go" and "return" (the verb used here). This nuance would highlight the urgency of Jonah, since the sailors would have had little time to recover from one voyage before setting out on another long trip. The same urgency is emphasized by the cost of the trip. While "his fare" is the normal translation, the suffix is feminine, and so Sasson (1990) suggests that the antecedent is ship (feminine in Hebrew) rather than Jonah. A better translation would then be "its hire" (the translation of the LXX and Vulg.). The cost of disobedience is high (contrast God's provision for Elijah in 1 Kgs 17:1–16), a point sharpened by Jewish commentators who suggested he had to buy the entire ship (*b. Ned.* 38a).

To find a Tarshish ship Jonah goes down to the port of Joppa (modern Jaffa) on the Palestinian coast. Many biblical (Josh 19:46; 2 Chr 2:15[16]; Ezra 3:7) and extra-biblical texts refer to Joppa, which became a Judean possession only in Maccabean times (c. 148 B.C.E.; 1 Macc 10:76). In c. 700 B.C.E. it belonged to King Sidqia of Ashkelon, but it was conquered by Sennacherib of Assyria in his campaign against Hezekiah and other rebellious states in the region (*ANET* 287). Since in Joppa Jonah is already in non-Israelite territory, it may appear that he is already on the way away "from the presence of Yhwh" (cf. Gen 4:16). The narrator here indirectly indicates the purpose of the flight, but it also highlights another theological tension: that between the universal and localized presence of Yhwh. It is a fundamental Israelite belief that there is no place where the creator God cannot be present (Ps 139:7–10; Jer 23:23–24). This includes the sea, as Jonah himself acknowledges (1:9), so why does he flee? Perhaps it was that "he might withdraw from the service of God" (Calvin 1979), making it physically impossible to reach Nineveh in time. It is less likely that he thought another prophet would be called to do the job (Stuart 1987). Simon (1999, 3) points out the strong correlation in the Bible between presence and obedience. Jonah disagrees with God by distancing himself, just as an obedient prophet presences himself with a "here I am" (Exod 3:4; Isa 6:6 cf. Gen 22:1). Simon (1999, 5) also suggests that Jonah has to do something because of the intensity of the divine injunction (Jer 20:9).

Twice the verb "go down" (*yrd*) is repeated, the first time referring to going down to Joppa, and second going on board (literally "he went down in it"). It is found again in 1:5, and for the fourth and final time in Jonah's prayer (2:6[7]). The descent imagery highlights Jonah's flight from God, since it contrasts with the traditional imagery for God's dwelling place in heaven (Gen 28:17; Ps 11:4). The depths are the location of the grave, the pit and the realm of death, so that Jonah's flight is almost suicidal in its direction (cf. Jonah 4:3). But it is also Israel's confession that God can come down and save those who are perishing in the deep waters of death (Pss 18:8–15[9–16]; 69:15[16]). Jonah can never descend far enough to be beyond the power and mercy of God.

No escape! (1:4–16)

The structure of this section has been the subject of extensive debate. Reading sequentially, we can find four scenes marked by the progress of the storm (Stuart 1987, 455): its beginning (vv. 4–5a), its continuation (vv. 5b–10), its worsening (vv. 11–15) and its cessation (v. 16). Others suggest elaborate chiastic structures (Lohfink 1961; Pesch 1966; Keller 1982; Landes 1967; Weimar 1982; Magonet 1983, 56–57; Christensen 1985; Simon 1999, xxviii). One of the simpler proposals is by Fretheim (1977, 73–74), who finds an outer narrative framework (vv. 4–5a/15–16), an intermediate request section (vv. 5b–6/13–14) and an inner dialogue (vv. 7–9/10–12). However, these schemes often involve the omission of significant features and the highlighting of certain aspects of the text at the expense of others (Trible 1994, 152–55). Chiastic analyses can helpfully indicate significant links, and it may well be significant that they suggest that the theological centre of the section is v. 9, Jonah's confession (there are 94 words before and after). But although this may be the theological climax, ordinary readers will regard the progression of the story as primary. In this the narrative climax is surely when Jonah is thrown overboard (v. 15). This is then followed by the calm denouement (v. 16) and a transition to the next section (v. 17[2:1]).

The tone of the chapter is an intriguing mix of violent or desperate action interspersed with dialogue that slows the action down and allows space for reflection. The initial action is the onslaught of the storm and the sailors' unsuccessful religious and physical attempts to deal with the danger (vv. 4–5). Their energetic response highlights Jonah's inactivity, and the captain's rebuke (v. 6) anticipates the later public recognition of Jonah's disobedience. The following pair of speeches by the sailors identifies the responsible party (vv. 7–8), and two further speeches (vv. 10–11) draw out the implications of Jonah's central opening confession (v. 9). After Jonah's reply (v. 12), the story could have moved directly to v. 15, but the author has heightened the tension by delaying the climax. The sailors make a final attempt to sail to land (v. 13), and then attempt to protect themselves from the consequences of their action by prayer (v. 14). Only when they finally overcome their scruples and cast Jonah into the depths does the storm cease (v. 15). A note of the sailors' pious response further conveys a sense of resolution and peace (v. 16).

The chapter develops not only through the events but also through the skilful repetition of keywords and phrases. In particular the phrase describing the fear of the sailors becomes longer and more emphatic each time it occurs (vv. 5, 10, 16; it is a "growing phrase" according to Magonet 1983, 31–33). How will the sailors and Jonah escape the unrelenting stormy sea (vv. 4, 11, 13), and more important, the God who caused it? Our curiosity is finally satisfied when we read of the quiet sea (v. 15) and rescued Jonah (1:17[2:1]). The removal of any cause for physical fear heightens even more the significance of the sailors' great fear of Yhwh (v. 16), which reflects a deep and lasting conversion. This is a fitting conclusion for these non-Israelite foreigners who from the start have demonstrated exemplary piety and energy in attempting to save their lives. Their eventual worship of Yhwh is from a moral point of view the fulfilment and completion of their honest and pious behaviour (albeit up to this point mis-directed to false gods). The repentance of evil Nineveh will provide a very different starting point in working out how God views the nations and Israel's relation to them.

From one point of view this section puts Jonah in a very bad light. Although he has the right theology, the sailors seem to be the ones with the right attitude in a time of trial, combining wholehearted endeavour and faithful prayer. But although being an Israelite was no guarantee of piety or virtue (Deut 9:5; Judg 19:12), dismissing Jonah's behaviour is too simplistic. His stubborn silence and preparedness to die emphasizes that his disagreement with Yhwh is more than merely personal. He may be profoundly in error, but he has a thought-out position and is able to explain calmly what is going on and how the situation can be remedied.

1:4. In the first episode (vv. 4–6) Yhwh hurls a storm at the ship (v. 4) and we are told the reactions of the sailors (v. 5a), Jonah (v. 5b) and the captain (v. 6). The sailors suffer their worst nightmare, an overwhelming, vindictive and unceasing storm (Ps 107:23–32; Ezek 27:25–28). It is supernatural in its intensity and hostility, but they (unlike our narrator) do not yet know who is behind it, why it has been sent, and how it can be stopped.

"But Yhwh hurled a great wind upon the sea." The English word order reflects the Hebrew, which varies the normal subject–verb pattern. A new scene and a new subject are thereby indicated. The emphasis this places on Yhwh is significant, for this is his response to Jonah's reaction (hence "but" for the and/but conjunction *waw*). Once Jonah is completely committed to his course, God too acts and makes the issue between him and Jonah a life or death matter in a way that is indirect yet inescapable. A remorseless chain of cause and effect links all the characters within two verses (God–wind–stormy sea–ship–sailors–captain–Jonah). "Hurled" (hiphil of *ṭwl*) is used of throwing a spear in 1 Sam 18:11 and for casting lots in Prov 16:33. It is a keyword in this chapter, coming four times and applied to three different objects: storm (v. 4), cargo (v. 5) and

Jonah (vv. 12, 15). The ship would set out in good weather, and the verb implies a sudden change soon after the journey began (Rudolph 1971). The wind is one of the weapons in God's heavenly arsenal (Jer 10:13), kept in reserve to effect his judgment (Jer 49:36). It could mean salvation for the righteous when it fell upon the wicked (Isa 41:16), but here it is intended to correct one of God's prophets. The "great wind" (glossed more terrifyingly as a hurricane by REB and NJB) is to whip up a "mighty storm" (the keyword "great" again). The storm is the rough sea with mighty waves that have been whipped up by the wind (Wolff 1986). It is also a sign of God's presence (Job 38:1; Ezek 1:4), particularly in the exercise of his wrath against the wickedness of the nations (Jer 23:19; Ps 83:15[16]). This is the first and shortest occurrence of the phrase.

Even at the start the storm is so furious that "the ship threatened to break up." Ezekiel 27 is an extended metaphor of "the good ship Tyre" (Limburg 1993, 49) and along the way sketches a typical sixth-century B.C.E. ship. It had fir planks, a cedar mast, a pine deck and was powered by oak oars and linen sails. It was steered by pilots and maintained by skilled artisans. The heavy cargo would be presided over by merchants, and the whole commanded by an experienced captain. However, in Jonah, as in the Bible generally, only two parties are ever involved in dialogue (in this chapter, Jonah and either the sailors or the captain). "Break up" describes the shipwreck of Tarshish ships in 1 Kgs 22:19 (cf. Ezek 27:34). However, "threatened" is always used of human reckoning or thinking. Emendations are unnecessary, since there is no reason why we should not see here a lively personification (as in Isa 23:1), especially since this leads to assonance (*ḥiššᵉbâ lᵉhiššābēr*). Sasson (1990) even finds this onomatopoeic, evoking the sound of planks cracking from the force of the waters. According to the ship's opinion (and who would know better!) the storm will soon overwhelm it. No wonder the sailors are terrified (v. 5).

1:5. This verse is divided into two sentences each describing three actions, first of the sailors (v. 5a) and then of Jonah (v. 5b). The correspondence heightens the contrasting behaviour. "Then the mariners were afraid," although they do not yet fear greatly (vv. 10, 16), for they are not yet aware of what the reader knows. The mariners or sailors are *mallāḥîm*, which in earlier works was related to *melaḥ*, "salt" (cf. "old salts"). However, it ultimately goes back to a Sumerian word referring to the handling of a ship, hence Akkadian *malāḥu* and cognates in other Semitic languages meaning sailor. In Ezek 27:29 they are a special part of the crew, but in Jonah such fine distinctions are besides the point and the reference is to all the sailors. They still believe something can be done, and strive to do it with all their might, using all their religious and material resources. "Each cried (cf. 3:6) to his god." It is also possible to translate plural "gods," suggesting that the sailors prayed to as many gods as they could, both the god(s) of the sea and wind, and their own personal or national gods. The reference to the cry of each individual person may suggest a single god, as might the contrast with Jonah's service of Yhwh (v. 9). "(Men) of the seventy languages were there on the ship, and each one had his god in his hand" (*Pirke de Rabbi Eliezer*, cited in Limburg 1993, 105). But however many gods are called upon, and however many are doing the praying, none of these "SOS prayers" (Allen 1976, 207) made any difference. Thus, the second step taken is physical: "They threw the cargo that was in the ship into the sea." The verb for threw is the same as in v. 4, but the sailors have not yet discovered the right object to throw into the sea and the relief is at best temporary. "cargo" is a general term that can refer to any kind of container (Beyse 1995, 170). In a specialized sense it can refer to baggage (Jer 46:19; Ezek 12:3–4) and here it no doubt refers to the ship's cargo (cf. Ezek 27:12–27; Acts 27:18), as well as all kinds of other strictly unnecessary items: provisions, furniture, baggage, weapons, tools, even spare spars and rigging. The purpose is to lighten the ship, reducing the possibility of it being swamped by waves or sunk by the water already shipped.

"Jonah, meanwhile" indicates an interruption of the sequential narrative mode of the three verbs in v. 5a (cf. v. 4a). The subject changes from the sailors to Jonah, but even more striking is the contrast of behaviour. When does Jonah go down? Most find here a flashback technique to describe what Jonah had done ("had gone down") soon after he entered the ship, the result of the psychological strain of attempting to thwart God, or the physical exhaustion of a rapid flight. However, it is also possible that Jonah's behaviour is a reaction to God's message in the storm (so Sasson 1990). Jonah is no longer able to flee spatially, so he withdraws in the only way open to him, through sleep, a form of passive resistance. The verb also activates some of the basic themes of the chapter: the descent of Jonah to the gates of death ("gone down," as in 1:3; 2:6), his preference for death rather than active obedience ("lain down"), and his deliberate non-attentiveness to God's call ("was fast asleep"). The word for ship here (*sᵉpînâ*) is different from the one used in v. 3 (*ʾānîâ*). It is derived from a verb meaning "to cover," so may indicate a boat with a covered lower deck that would provide some protection from the elements and hold perhaps a mat to sleep on. "Hold" translates a word that is often found in the dual form (*yarkāṯāyim*), suggesting the meeting of two angles or "sides" (so ʌv). From the perspective of someone at an entrance, this meeting point may be quite distant, and so we find it used in references to the innermost parts of a cave (1 Sam 24:3), or the farthest parts of the earth (Jer 6:22). On the mundane level it could refer here to deepest part of the ship where the two sides of the ship join (hence "hold"). A more ominous reading is suggested by Isa 14:15, where the word describes the depths of the pit and is parallel to Sheol (cf. Ezek 32:23). The impression of a suicidal tendency is confirmed by the next verb, "lain down," which is used of death in the same contexts (Isa 14:18; Ezek 32:19, 21, 27, 28). "fast asleep" translates a verb suggesting a deep sleep that is oblivious even to major surgery (the cognate noun occurs in Gen 2:21) or grave danger (Judg 4:21). There is an ironic contrast between the praiseworthy activity of the sailors, who are in fact ignorant and helpless, and the passivity of Jonah, who knows what is going on and is the only one who can save the ship. Sasson's suggestion that this marks a turning-point in Jonah's flight and marks his readiness to receive the divine message (Dan 8:18; 10:9) is unlikely—Jonah descent is not yet finished.

1:6. Dialogue marks a move away from the action, slowing the pace so that we reflect on the theological implications of the events until action resumes in v. 13. We follow the steps by which the captain and the sailors learn what is really going on. Perhaps they had already begun to wonder whether their mysterious passenger was responsible for the storm. Their captain represents them all when he berates the one person who has not yet called upon his god(s).

"captain" is literally "the chief of the rope." "Chief" is a title found elsewhere for the person in command of a group of people (e.g. captain of the bodyguard, Jer 39:9–10; cf. the Akkadian "chief of the sailors," *CAD* M I, 152). This would suggest that "rope" is a collective for sailors, by metonymy from the ropes they would manipulate to sail the ship. However, rope is singular and an alternative reference would be to the rope by which the helmsman steered the boat ("the officer in charge at the prow," LXX; "helmsman," Vulg.). The storm is not able to draw near Jonah in his secluded spot, but the captain is able to come, and wakes him with an exclamation, a command and a wish. "What are you doing sound asleep" (the same word as in v. 5) again highlights the contrast between the frantic yet fruitless efforts of the sailors and Jonah. Even though the captain remains ignorant of the cause of the storm, he becomes Yhwh's mouthpiece when he tells Jonah to "get up" (*qûm*) from his sleeping position and call on God for help (Jonah 1:14; 3:8; cf. 1 Kgs 17:20–21). These verbs echo God's original commands to Jonah to arise and cry out (v. 2). "Jonah must have thought he was having a nightmare" (Allen 1976, 207). The article used with the title ("the god") refers back to "your god" of the previous phrase (GKC §126d), but the third person comment also makes it clear that the sailors are ignorant of Jonah's god. The captain's words contribute to the subplot, tracing the sailors' progress from pagan piety, commendable but useless, to a saving commitment to Yhwh by the end of the chapter (v. 16). "spare a thought" only occurs here and the cognate languages suggest a meaning of "consider, think of." The versions often prefer to specify this as a favourable remembrance (LXX has "save"; Targ. has "have mercy on"), making the prayer more demanding and specific. Are we to see here a good or a bad model of prayer? Some (e.g. Calvin 1979) find ignorance of the true God and a utilitarian motivation. In a polytheistic context "perhaps" could be a pragmatic realization that Jonah's god may or may not be the one responsible, or a doubt whether, even if he were, he would spare a thought. Prayer could remind a forgetful or reluctant god to do something, but not always (1 Kgs 18:26–29; contrast Ps 121:3–4). A successful prayer might prompt the god to forgive, or intercede with the god who was responsible. However, the generally favourable presentation of the sailors suggests a positive interpretation. Israel's great men of prayer often called upon their God to remember his people (Exod 32:13; Isa 38:3), and similar saving intercession could be hinted at here. The initial "perhaps" acknowledges the tension between insistent petition and trusting submission to God's sovereign freedom (see similarly 3:9). This combination of boldness and humility is the mark of Israel's best prayers (Gen 18:24; Exod 32:30; Zeph 2:3). The captain needs to be enlightened about the identity of the true God, not corrected in his theology of prayer. "so that we do not perish" makes explicit the immediate motivation of the sailors, as of the people of Nineveh (3:9). Fear as well as delight may lead to faith. In extreme danger only the intervention (or not) of the god in charge will make a difference between life and death (cf. Heb 2:14–15).

1:7. We may assume that Jonah took as little notice of the captain's words as of God's, remaining silent or giving an evasive answer. In the absence of decisive proof of responsibility, the sailors decide to cast lots. If the storm is caused by divine wrath, as all in the story assume, lots are the standard means by which the responsible person can be identified (Josh 7:10–18; 1 Sam 14:40–42). This is true even in Israel, where other means of divination were prohibited. Indeed, the high priest himself was responsible for the Urim and the Thummim, a form of lots that may have comprised two stones with dark and light sides (Exod 28:30). Their combined score allowed a yes/no/neutral decision (1 Sam 28:6). In the storyworld of Jonah all correctly assume that there is a divine hand behind the storm, that the divinity has been offended by a guilty person and that casting lots can determine who it is.

"Cast" here translates the literal "cause to fall," with the result that the lot fell on Jonah. Elsewhere lots are thrown (Josh 18:8, 10), but the verb here was probably used to describe any manipulation of bones, stones, pieces of wood and so on ("draw lots," NJB, GNB). The supposed Urim and Thummim method would no doubt be too time-consuming for Jonah's shipmates. Sasson suggests that the quickest method would be to inscribe names on shards and pick one. Whatever the method, it is the result that is the primary concern of both sailors and readers. The threefold repetition of the word for lots indicates the seriousness of the measure, which was necessary if the sailors were going to understand what was going on and take the necessary measures to survive. The inevitable result merely reinforces the chapter's demonstration that God's call and the long reach of his arm are inescapable.

1:8. The sailors round on Jonah and fire a salvo of rapid questions at him, reflecting the urgency of the situation but probably also a pent-up anger that Jonah has been slow in revealing his role. However, they remain reasonably restrained and do not ask directly what he and his god are quarrelling about. "why this calamity (*rāʿâ* again) has come upon us" has been regarded as a later gloss (Bewer 1911, 37; Wolff 1986, 107; cf. NJB, NEB) on the grounds that it is superfluous after lot-casting. But although it is omitted in some LXX manuscripts, this could have been a transmission error, with the scribes skipping from one "us" to the next (homoioteleuton). "why" translates a rare and ambiguous phrase (perhaps "inasmuch to whom"). It has been interpreted as introducing an object clause specifying Jonah as the guilty party: "you who are responsible for this calamity" (Sasson 1990, 107; cf. NJPS). But most commentators take it as a request to name the God responsible for the storm: "on whose account" (so RSV; *DCH* 1:432; NRSV's "why" is more general). This would fit a chiastic structure in vv. 8–9. The sailors ask first about the god responsible (v. 8a, question 1) and then Jonah's identity (v. 8b, questions 2–5). Jonah answers in reverse order by affirming that he is a Hebrew (v. 9a) and that he fears Yhwh (v. 9b). Both "Hebrew" and "LORD" are in the emphatic first position in their phrase.

Four questions about Jonah's identity all begin with the same letter in Hebrew. The first is "What is your occupation?" In Ps 107:23 this word describes the business of traders endangered by the sea. Sasson (1990) argues for a more specific question "What is your mission?" since by now the sailors surely regard Jonah as more than an ordinary trader. Our sailors are faced with the additional complication that the businessman is out of favour with his deity. The following three questions seek to locate Jonah not just geographically ("Where do you come from? What is your country?") and ethnically ("And of what people are you?"), but also religiously. In the ancient world divinities (even with cosmic and international powers) were based in specific places and linked to a particular people. It is not just the reason for the calamity that is important, but also the character and interests of the god responsible that will help the sailors understand what has happened and what they might do about it.

1:9. Jonah's answer is an orthodox confession of faith echoing praises of the Psalms (Ps 95:5). It opens the first recorded conversation in the book and its significance is highlighted by its placing at the centre of vv. 4–16. His first reply is to the final question, while his second illuminates question 1 (on the interpretation adopted above). What about the other three questions? The flashback in the next verse implies that we are meant to understand that it is only an extract from the dialogue (as in the speeches of Acts) and much of what we know has been omitted—that Jonah is a prophet fleeing from his god's command, and that Hebrews live in Canaan. A more negative evaluation of Jonah's character would be that he gave a devious answer, refusing to mention what his business was. Perhaps he simply informs the sailors about the most crucial factors in the situation. Knowing in detail about his business will not change the basic situation.

"I am a Hebrew" answers the fourth question about his people, and "Hebrew" is the usual way in which foreigners refer to Israelites (Gen 39:14; Exod 1:19; 1 Sam 4:6). The note of distinctiveness and claim to belong to Israel's God, Yhwh, might be a reason for pride on Jonah's behalf. However, an ironic reader might think that Jonah's real distinctiveness lay in his disobedience and refusal to call upon his God.

Reference to Yhwh emphasizes the agency of the specific God of the Israelites (Exod 3:13–15; 6:1–8). In the second part of the verse Jonah describes him as "the God of heaven." This appears mostly in texts of the Persian period (2 Chr 36:23; Neh 1:4; Dan 2:18), but it is also found in earlier texts (Gen 24:3, 7). As with "Hebrew," Jonah may be using an earlier title that could easily be understood by a pagan audience. Normally Yhwh is praised as the one who makes (Gen 2:4) or creates (Gen 14:19) "heaven and earth," a pairing of opposites that indicates the whole (merismus). However, a third term, "sea," can also be added in a tripartite definition of the totality of existence (Gen 1:26, 28;

Ps 135:6; cf. Hag 2:6). Here the selection of sea and dry land makes it crystal clear that Jonah's God is responsible for the storm. "dry land" rather than "earth" highlights the principal quality of the land that the sailors are trying to reach. The phrasing confirms that the sailors have uncovered not just the right man but also the right god. Yhwh's power is frequently praised through affirming that he makes the waters and the dry land (Gen 1:9–10; Ps 95:5). Using a conflict metaphor, he may be praised for his victory or rule over the sea (Ps 89:9) and the floods (Gen 9:11; Ps 29:10). These two terms often appear in Exodus contexts describing God's saving power (Exod 14:16, 22; 15:19; Ps 66:6; Neh 9:11). At this stage of the story, however, the sailors are only informed of Yhwh's competence, rather than his will to save (Wolff 1986). Ironically, Jonah, the one who reveals and confesses Yhwh, will deliberately put himself in the place of the Egyptians who are immersed in the waters of the sea, while the pagans will emerge to praise Yhwh as saviour (v. 16).

"I worship Yhwh" is more literally "I fear (*yārēʾ*) Yhwh." The NRSV unfortunately conceals the link with the other three uses of the word in vv. 5, 10, 16. It is a weak interpretation to regard this "fear" as merely a technical term for religious affiliation (so Wolff 1986). The use of the same word for Jonah's fear and that of the sailors points to a sophisticated play on the range of nuances associated with a central concept in Israel's theology. As the chapter proceeds the physical fear that the sailors feel before the danger of the storm shades into the godly fear that acknowledges the dangerous power (for good or ill) that attends an encounter with the holy and fearful God (Exod 3:6; 15:11). Israel knew that trusting and humble acknowledgment of this fear was the surest mark of true loyalty to the covenant God (Deut 5:29; Fuhs 1990, 306–308). The consequent worship, obedience and service becomes the deepest and most secure basis for the life and joy that is associated with the knowledge and presence of Yhwh (Deut 6:24; Ps 40:3[4]). This is what the sailors finally discover and celebrate. Some draw a strong ironical contrast between the apparent implications of Jonah's words and knowledge and his own behaviour. "Jonah's fear is a feeble thing, for all its orthodoxy, compared with the numinous awe of the seamen" (Allen 1976, 209). However, Jonah's calmness comes from his knowledge of God's power and control. The violence of the storm is not unexpected, and his willingness to suffer the consequences emphasizes the intensity of the disagreement between him and God.

1:10. The note of fear in v. 5 is repeated, but it is now heightened by the increased knowledge that the sailors now have of both the human and the divine causes of the storm. A common Hebrew idiom (found frequently in Jonah) is used to convey this growing fear, and the verb is followed by the noun formed from that verb, literally "and the men feared a great fear." The NRSV captures both the increased intensity of the emotion and its progressive character in translating "the men were even more afraid." They respond with an exclamation of shock or horror, "What is this that you have done!" This is followed by three further phrases introducing a flashback. As is the case elsewhere (1:3, 16; 4:2),

the author has taken events out of chronological order. Jonah did say more
("because he had told them so") but the previous verse has set out the central
issue, while in this verse we already know the details and abbreviating the dialogue allows us to focus on the horror of the sailors as they realize the implications of Jonah's action. It is more likely that the note refers to the interrogation
in the previous verse than what Jonah said at Joppa. Omitting it allows the
confession in v. 9 to be felt with its full force, while the note here gives us a
short space to appreciate the feelings of the crew.

1:11. "With this seventh question from the sailors, the interrogation is complete"
(Limburg 1993, 55). The sailors have asked and Jonah has revealed why the
storm began; now they must ask him what they need to do to him ("must"
according to REB; NJPS; JM 113m). Perhaps the sailors recognize that Jonah is
not prepared to do anything that will lead to the storm ceasing, and so take on
this responsibility as well. Their goal from the beginning has been "that the sea
may quiet down for us," and now they are close to achieving it. Apart from here
and v. 12, "quiet" (*štq*) is only found in Prov 26:10 (of a quarrel ceasing) and in
Ps 107:30, which describes a storm quietened after an answer to prayer. The
urgency of their question is reinforced by a note of the sea's growing violence:
"For the sea was growing more and more tempestuous." This is literally "for the
sea [was/is] going and storming." "going" is an auxiliary verb indicating a
continuing process of the second verb (e.g. Josh 6:13; GKC §113u), but the verb
can also suggest growing intensity, as here (cf. Exod 19:19; 2 Sam 3:1).

1:12. As was the case earlier, Jonah may refuse to obey, but he is not refusing to
tell the truth, so he tells them that they have to pick him up and throw him into
the sea. For "Pick me up" NJPS has the lively "heave me overboard," but the
verb (*nś'*) has a clear nuance of lifting up. Jonah has been going down, and may
appear at first to suggest that this be reversed, but it is only a temporary measure
in order to effect an even deeper descent, to Sheol itself. "throw" is the verb
used in vv. 4 and 5. Throwing the cargo overboard has not succeeded, for the
right action had not been united with the right object, but throwing Jonah
overboard will work. Disobedience leads to divine wrath and the sentence of
death (Deut 30:15–20), so when Jonah drowns the cause of the storm will be
removed and the sea will quiet down. Why does Jonah not cast himself overboard? It may be due to the strong prohibition of suicide, which in the Old
Testament is only ever sought in a passive way (Judg 9:54; 1 Sam 31:4), but it
also allows the worthy character of the sailors to be further illuminated as they
overcome yet another hurdle.

The main question is how we are to interpret Jonah's intention and mood.
Does the instruction reflect compassion for the seamen, for Jonah knows that
God is compassionate (4:2)? "The piety of the seamen has evidently banished
his nonchalant indifference and touched his conscience" (Allen 1976, 210–11).
A note of repentance and regret can be read into the partial confession "for I
know it is because of me (cf. v. 7) that this great storm has come upon you." But

Jonah's behaviour is all stubbornness. Jonah progressively attempts physical flight in the boat, psychological flight in deep sleep and now absolute flight in death (Trible 1996). Jonah is quite prepared to die for his beliefs or prejudices (4:3, 8) and perhaps his death will thwart God's plans. In fact, Jonah's solution serves both to save the sailors and further his own goals. Being thrown overboard breaks the physical link between him and the sailors, so there is no need for the storm to continue. Ironically, the result will confirm the faith of the sailors in Jonah's God and bond them to Jonah in an even deeper way.

1:13. As before, the action is described before the explanation (v. 14). Instead of obeying Jonah, the men rowed hard. Normally the open sea is safer that the treacherous reefs and shallows off a coastline. Perhaps they reasoned that if Jonah's God wanted him to resume his mission, then he would be satisfied if they bring the ship back to land. The word for row describes digging down (to Sheol in Amos 9:2) or piercing through (a wall in Ezek 8:8). The sailors attempt to dig the oars into the sea so that they can bore through the waves. But as they probably expected, they could not make any headway ("and they got nowhere," GNB). Our author explains by repeating the phrase about the sea that we have met before (vv. 4, 11), now intensified by an additional "against them."

1:14. Prayer is once again the sailors' pious response (cf. v. 4). This time however "they cried out to Yhwh," the first mention of the specific name of Israel's God on the lips of the sailors and a mark of true conversion (2 Kgs 5:17). That which Jonah refused to do ("cried" is the same word as vv. 2, 6) the author has the sailors do in an exemplary manner, combining desperation and humility. Their short prayer displays in brief the classic structure of a communal prayer of complaint (Pss 44; 74; 79–80): address, plea and motivation. The address to Yhwh is preceded by an initial particle of entreaty ("Please," cf. 4:2) and followed by another similar one ("we pray"), the doubled emphasis being typical for situations of life and death (Gen 50:17; 2 Kgs 20:3). "do not let us perish on account of this man's life" is explained more specifically: "do not make us guilty of innocent blood." "do not make us guilty" is literally "and do not lay upon us." The shedding of innocent blood results (metaphorically) in a heavy burden of guilt that will be laid upon those responsible (Deut 19:10; 21:8).

Why do the sailors need to pray this if Jonah has admitted his guilt? (1) One possibility is that the sailors were still uncertain about Jonah's guilt and wanted to allow for making a mistake. In this case the calming of the storm is necessary as the final proof. However, the prayer to Yhwh must assume the trustworthiness of Jonah and it makes no sense to qualify their action with this kind of doubt. (2) Perhaps the sailors were worried about applying the wrong sort of punishment (Wolff 1986), but again the sailors always regard Jonah as truthful. (3) The issue may be the lack of proper procedures in arriving at the punishment. All life belongs to God. He alone can take it, but he may delegate the responsibility to a court of law. Here there has been no opportunity to follow the approved legal procedures (Allen 1976), and so the sailors acknowledge their part in anomalous and possibly guilty behaviour. However, this seems a rather fussy concern in the circumstances. (4) The best solution may be that, though strictly unnecessary, it is a further reflection of the sailors' piety, now directed towards Yhwh. The phrase is also found in Jer 26:15, where Jeremiah warns the people against shedding his innocent blood. Ironically, the sailors are concerned about shedding even the blood of a guilty man.

The final part of the prayer is an acknowledgment of what the sailors have learnt about Jonah's God. "for you, O LORD, have done as it pleased you" is an acknowledgment of his absolute sovereignty (Ps 115:3) and the necessity for mortals to act accordingly (Eccl 8:3). Events have shown that nothing can prevent Yhwh from fulfilling his will, whether it be the ignorant evil of Nineveh, the active hostility of Jonah, or the utmost effort of innocent sailors.

1:15. With verbal echoes of v. 12 the narrator underlines the reluctant obedience of the sailors: "they picked Jonah up and threw him into the sea." When the sea ceased from its raging, it is evident that their prayer had been heard. The sea, like the ship in v. 4, is probably personified, since raging is a quality applied elsewhere not to inanimate objects but to God (Isa 30:30; Mic 7:9) and kings (Prov 19:12). The sea registers in an observable way both the wrath of Yhwh and his satisfaction when his will is done. The midrash expands this brief statement into a mini-drama through taking "lifted up" as referring to "from the sea": "R. Shimon said: ...They cast him in as far as his ankles and the sea stopped raging. They lifted him back to them and the sea was wracked by storm. They cast him in as far as his navel and the sea stopped raging. They lifted him back to them and the sea was wracked by storm. They cast him in as far as his neck and the sea stopped raging. Again they lifted him back to them and the sea was wracked by storm against them. They cast him in all the way and at once the sea stopped raging" (cited by Simon 1999, 15).

1:16. The final response of the sailors is noted, but silence about Jonah's fate suggests that his story is "to be continued" (Limburg 1993, 58). The satisfactory denouement of the action is calmly conveyed by a unique triple use of a verb with its cognate accusative (Golka 1988). Literally, the sailors feared a great fear (the climax of the growing phrase in vv. 5, 10 and Jonah's words in v. 9), they sacrificed a sacrifice and vowed vows. The English translations vary the style, but at the expense of removing the repetition, which is probably meant to indicate closure and completion. Sacrifice on board the ship might be implied, but these could hardly be those properly offered in the temple, and so the Targum inserts a future tense: "they promised to present sacrifices before Yhwh." A traditional Christian solution is to regard the sacrifice as a spiritual matter (Jerome; see Sasson 1990). A more straightforward interpretation is that they immediately offered a single corporate sacrifice. Sasson quotes references that show sacrifices on ships were reasonably common. Ships on a long voyage typically carried livestock, and a simple sacrifice on a small scale would be possible (assuming the animals had not been thrown over the side). Such a sacrifice could well represent more substantial sacrifices that the sailors would individually offer when they reached dry land. For a Jewish reader this would need to be in Jerusalem, but the emphasis is on the fitting response of the sailors rather than their conformity to Jewish law.

The vows would probably have included a promise of further sacrifices. In Israel, the vow or votive offering (Lev 7:16; 22:18) is a type of peace offering that was the appropriate object of a vow. It is likely that it would have been accompanied by a testimony to the way in which God had answered the one who had made the vow (Ps 22:22–25[23–26]). Even though the sailors are not Jews, it is likely that we are to think of some combination of sacrifice and testimony. This would confirm the thoroughgoing conversion of the sailors. Yhwh would not only be their help in times of crisis, but would be their God from now on (Gen 28:20). While faith in Yhwh might still be worked out in a polytheistic framework (Trible 1996) the sailors have experienced some of the essential characteristics of Israel's God. They have had decisive proof of his power over the sea and the heavens, they have experienced his mercy in sparing the innocent and they have seen his fearful punishment on those who resist his will. As such, their faith is consistent with the Israelites' faith in a God who made sea and earth, who saved them from death in Egypt, who controlled the waters of the Red Sea, and whose judgment fell on those who disobeyed him.

Thanksgiving for Deliverance from Death (1:17–2:10[2:1–11])

This poem of thanksgiving has played a central role in the debate about the composition, structure and meaning of the book as a whole. Following the action-packed first chapter, the contrast in form, mood, language and attitude is striking. The natural instinct for traditional historical critics has been to question its authenticity. Many regard it as having been added later, possibly to correct the rest of the book's view of Jonah (e.g. Simon 1999, 16). The theology of the psalm can be considered entirely separate from the rest of the book (Walsh 1982). Why, then, was it inserted? Some recent writers have considered the insertion of the poem as a deliberate ploy by the author or redactor in order to satirize Jonah (see Section D, above). However, an examination of the arguments against the poem's integration with the rest of the book shows that they are not as conclusive as at first appears.

(1) We expect a psalm of lament or complaint rather than of thanksgiving, since Jonah has not yet been delivered onto land, or we would expect the thanksgiving to come after 2:10[11]. But elsewhere in the Bible a full answer to prayer is not needed before thanksgiving can take place (1 Sam 2; Isa 38; Dan 2). Jonah's closest encounter with death was not in the fish's belly, but in the water as he drowns. Being swallowed was a spectacular and unexpected rescue, and more than sufficient assurance that God would bring him eventually to dry land.

(2) The portrait of a pious Jonah contradicts the rebellious Jonah of the prose. Yet we are about to see in ch. 3 Jonah fulfilling at least the letter of Yhwh's

initial command. The thankfulness communicated in the Psalm is a good explanation for his change of attitude. Jonah's faith is never in question in the book,
only how it applies to Nineveh. The poem is an orthodox expression of thanksgiving, just as Jonah's confession of faith in 1:9 is orthodox. If Jonah were fully
realigned to God's will, then we would expect a confession of sin. The absence
of any such element can be interpreted to indicate that there is a disjunction
between his actions and his will. It is this contradiction that sets up the attempt
by God to persuade him in ch. 4.

(3) The poem uses different vocabulary from that of the prose. "Cast" in v.
3[4] is different from the "throw" of ch. 1, and the keyword "great" does not
occur in the poem at all. However, genre and situation are crucial in determining
vocabulary. Hebrew poetry has a somewhat different vocabulary from that of
prose, and adjectives (such as "great") are usually avoided. Poetry is less tied to
particular historical circumstances, and other poems inserted into narratives
have relatively little explicit connection to the specific context (1 Sam 2:1–10;
Isa 38:9–20). There are, though, broader thematic links, in particular the
depth/height language that both fits the story and is characteristic of many songs
of thanksgiving.

(4) The text makes good sense if the poem is excised. However, showing that
it is possible to cut out a part of a text while retaining a logical storyline does not
prove that this is probable or even desirable. Authors are rarely minimalists,
interested only in the progress of a basic plot. Delaying the progress of the
action allows space for reflection upon the significance of an event (Bar-Efrat
1989, 35, 161). At a structural level there are suggestive parallels with both chs.
1 and 4. In chs. 1 and 2 there is a crisis situation (storm/drowning), followed by
response (prayer of sailors/prayer of Jonah), Yhwh's reaction (deliverance) and
a concluding response of worship (sacrifice, vows). Chapters 2 and 4 both provide pause for reflection following eventful narration (chs. 1 and 3). In terms of
content, ch. 4 both continues and builds upon the basic theme of ch. 2, the mercy
of Yhwh who saves those who cry to him. Above all, the poem can provide an
insight into the inner motives and thoughts of Jonah The author has deliberately
suppressed these in ch. 1. Without the poem we would not know whether Jonah
was unconscious for the three days and nights, or suffering in agony (Stuart
1987). More detailed parallels between poetry and prose have been suggested
(Landes 1967, 16–17; Magonet 1983, 60–63; Stuart 1987, 471–72), although
these can downplay the differences between the chapters.

(5) The poem consists of a pastiche of quotations from other psalms and
texts. However, this is typical of Hebrew poetry and Landes (1967) and
Magonet (1983, 40–44) argue that it demonstrates features that make it a unique
creation and specifically appropriate for the book of Jonah. Several keywords
from ch. 1 and the prose introduction recur ("call," "go down," "sacrifice").
Sherwood (2000, 257–58) highlights the unique demythologizing character of
the psalm: metaphorical water references found elsewhere here describe a literal
drowning. This makes it less likely that it was simply taken from the available
pool of thanksgivings and inserted.

No single argument is decisive, and much depends on an initial decision on whether we expect to find disunity and disjunction, or unity and complex harmony (Trible 1994, 161). Since there is no textual evidence that the poem was ever omitted, and we are ultimately ignorant of the conventions and expectations of ancient authors, the onus of proof lies on critics of the poem's authenticity (Golka 1988, 90). If the poem is to be read as part of the story, then various interpretive strategies are possible. Some traditional readings were hagiographic, maximizing the piety of Jonah, at least eventually (see the midrash cited in the comments on v. 1[2]). Recent satirical readings tend to make him a thoroughly unlikable character, full of self-delusion and egoism. Magonet (1983, 178) argues that the stress on the first person reflects Jonah's stubborn refusal to accept God's dismissal, so that God continues to let him drown until he acknowledges God. Similarly Trible (1996: 508) finds boastful egoism. However, the first person is characteristic of all laments and the criticism of Jonah's self-centredness may be anachronistic.

Both extreme piety and extreme impiety are, I suggest, caricatures that do not do justice to the contradictions between the poetry and the narrative, which imply a more complex and rounded interpretation of Jonah's character. Jonah has been doing his utmost to distance himself from any speech with God up to this point, but now he reopens communication with God. The imminent danger of death finally turns him to prayer, and the answer to that prayer leads to a genuine appreciation of the power and mercy of God. But the continuing story shows that deliverance has not fully transformed his deep disagreement with God's call. The poem is to be taken at face value as representing a paradigmatic deliverance (2:9[10]), but this does not mean that this is the full truth or that elsewhere Jonah's motives and actions are blameless. Jonah's attitude to God is ambivalent (Landes 1967; Alexander 1998, 66–67). Drowning has broken through Jonah's apathy and unwillingness and implicit in the decision to pray is the decision to fulfil God's original commission, even though he continues to disagree (as ch. 4 will emphasize). This prayer is a graphic sign of Jonah's basic (though not full) reversal of attitude. There are ironic contrasts between one stage of the story and another, but these are gentle ironies that reflect sympathy for Jonah and his reasons for rebellion.

The poem is enclosed within a prose introduction (1:17[2:1]), describing the beginning and middle of Jonah's fishy experience, and a prose conclusion (2:10[11]) relating the nauseous end of his unique sojourn. The poem is basically a psalm of thanksgiving with numerous echoes of language and motifs that are found elsewhere, particularly in Psalms, Job and Lamentations. However, it is also (in my reading) a poem through which the author gives us access to one moment in Jonah's consciousness. Where and when do we locate the psalm in terms of the story? Many consider that the distress referred to is Jonah's tomb-like sojourn in the belly of the whale (see the more specific suggestion of the Jewish midrash quoted below). However, it makes much more sense if we regard it as being prayed in the fish but referring to the events already described in 1:15, 17, that is, being thrown overboard, almost being drowned and then being rescued by God through the fish. A fish's belly may be dark, dank and uncomfortable, but precisely because of its similarity to the grave Jonah is reminded that he has been saved from a fate far worse. Whatever the conditions, he is safe, saved from drowning in one of God's creatures that is swimming purposefully on its way. Jonah will no doubt have worked out that God is taking him back towards Nineveh. He realizes he has no choice but to obey—at least outwardly, for the next chapters will amply qualify this assent by noting behaviour and words that signify reluctance and strong disapproval. But that is to come. The present chapter is a reflection on God's undeserved rescue of Jonah. It is a psalm of thanksgiving, reflecting Jonah's overall decision (however qualified in practice) to open up communication with God and walk the path of obedience. In the fish Jonah realizes that he can never escape God's call.

The psalm has a non-chronological structure worked out in five strophes (Simon 1999, 17) that overlap with one another in a complex way. The second and third strophes refer to the basic plight of the drowning Jonah, leading to the turning point, the prayer described in the fourth strophe. The first and fifth strophes provide the calm framework, the acknowledgment of the God who saves. In more detail: the first strophe (2:2[3]) presents the basic salvation schema of the psalmist's cry (in a situation of threat) and God's answer (assuring salvation). The second announces the plight, being cast into the deep (v. 3[4]), together with the psalmist's despairing response (v. 4[5]). The third strophe expounds the psalmist's watery plight (2:5–6a[6–7a]) but also announces God's salvation (2:6b[7b]). The fourth highlights the psalmist's prayer in response to death (v. 7[8]). The fifth strophe generalizes the lesson and includes a testimony that only the true God can save (v. 8[9]), along with a vow of sacrifice to Yhwh (v. 9b[10]. The final phrase echoes the opening summary verse and declares for the last time the central message of deliverance (2:9[10]). The detailed poetry shows high art at the level of sound, and the shift in verbal form (perfect/imperfect/*waw* consecutive) is also significant (Walsh 1982; Watts 1993). A number of discussion have attempted to apply a theory of Hebrew poetry to the poem, whether in terms of syllable counting (Christensen 1986), a pattern of longer and shorter phrases (Cross 1983) or stresses. However, none of these have proved fully persuasive, and it is doubtful that a more original version of the psalm should be reconstructed on the basis of such theories.

Many significant links can be made between the psalm and the framing story, yet there are also significant elements in the psalm that we would not deduce from the story, and aspects of the story that are not mentioned in the psalm. The comments below refer at times to the psalmist (acknowledging that the poem cannot be reduced simply to Jonah's experiences) and to Jonah (because the psalm now invites us to read it in the light of his particular story).

1:17[2:1]. The previous section ended by carrying on the story of the sailors to its logical conclusion. The next section returns to Jonah out of strict chronological sequence, so that we could translate in the pluperfect (NLT, AV) that Yhwh *had* provided a large fish to swallow up Jonah (cf. AV). The initiative remains with Yhwh, whether in wrath to cause a deadly storm or in mercy to save a wretch. "Appointed" (RSV) or "ordained" (REB, NJB) is probably better than "provided," since the verb (*mnh*) describes not just the means of rescue from a watery death, but the way in which a king uses those at his command to fulfil his purposes (Dan 1:5, 11). As is true of other significant animals in the Bible (Num 22:22–35; 1 Kgs 17:1–6; cf. Sasson 1990), the fish is a perfectly obedient agent of Yhwh of the sea and dry land (cf. 1:9). It mediates God's grace, further highlights the contrary behaviour of Jonah and makes a substantial contribution to his journey. Elsewhere in the Bible comparison with animals is used to intensify the shame of Israel's disobedience (Isa 1:3; Jer 8:7).

Our author tells us nothing about the identity of the large fish (better "great fish"—the keyword again). Our ignorance has stimulated artists and interpreters down the ages to feats of imaginative portrayal and scientific ingenuity that are both marvelous and unnecessary (Sherwood 2000). The LXX *kētos* was used for the most impressive cosmic and mythological sea monsters (Gen 1:21; Hebrew *tannîn*), including Rahab (Job 26:12) and Leviathan (Job 3:8). More mundane suggestions, often motivated by a desire to prove the historicity of the incident, include a large shark or sea dog (Keil 1871). The traditional "whale" derives from English translations of the Hebrew and the Greek. *kētos* might be used of seals (Homer) but eventually became a technical term for whales (Aristotle, Pliny). The more specific identification of the sperm whale derived from the practical consideration that this species can swallow men (and even horses) whole.

The time that Jonah was in the belly of the fish (three days and three nights) is also an index of distance. Perhaps we should imagine that the fish journeys to a shore near to Nineveh, making up for the time and distance lost while Jonah travelled in the opposite direction. Depending on context, three days can be a loose approximation for a relatively short or long period of time, but here the addition of three nights suggests a substantial period of time (Bauer 1958; cf. 1 Sam 30:12, the other Old Testament occurrence of the full phrase). It may imply that Jonah stayed awake for the whole time and so emphasize the slow passage of time and the opportunity for him to reflect (Job 7:3), a dramatic contrast to his previous deep sleep in the ship (1:5). There is also mention of three days and three nights in *Inanna's Descent to the Underworld* (*ANET* 55, l. 169) and so some have thought that Jonah was in a "precarious transitory state of his existence, hovering between life and death, with only a very tenuous possibility of survival" (Landes 1967, 447). Landes suggested that three days is a significant time for the death of a person to be fully sealed (cf. John 11:39). However, it was argued above that Jonah's near-death experience was drowning rather than incarceration in the fish. In Matt 12:40, Jesus compares his future stay in the tomb to Jonah's fishy sojourn. Although Jesus' actual time of burial was shorter, we should not require an inappropriate precision either of the author of Jonah or of Jesus quoting him. "belly" (*mēʿeh*; plural in the Hebrew) refers loosely to any internal organ. An imaginative poem by Aldous Huxley (cited in

Limburg 1993, 63) suggests he was "Seated upon the convex mound/Of one vast kidney." No doubt much less comfortable than the ship's hold (1:5), Jonah's refuge now serves God's purposes and not his.

2:1[2]. "Then" interprets the ambivalent Hebrew *waw* ("and/but/then"). It might suggest Jonah prayed at the conclusion of the three days (see the midrash below), but the timing could be undefined. Whenever the prayer was composed and uttered (in the storyworld of the book), it refers back (according to the interpretation followed above) to Jonah's traumatic time in the water before being swallowed. The specific formulation "the LORD his God" often indicates a special close relation between Yhwh and the one praying (e.g. Moses in Exod 32:11; David in 1 Sam 30:6; 2 Kgs 16:2; the nation in Ps 33:12). The combination occurs again in v. 6[7], the heart of the psalm.

It is puzzling that fish here is feminine (*dāgâ*), but masculine (*dāg*) in 1:17[2:1]. There is no evidence of textual corruption and no simple explanation. Sasson (1990) suggests that the storyteller is employing stylistic variation, since both masculine and feminine forms were available and the sex of the creature was not significant. Sex is, however, crucial for the imaginative midrash (cited Simon 1999, 19): "Jonah was in the belly of the [masculine] fish for three days and didn't pray. The Holy One, Blessed be He, said: 'I made him a spacious place in the belly of the fish so that he would not be in pain, but he still will not pray to me! I shall prepare for him a pregnant fish carrying 365,000 fry, so that he will be in pain and pray to me." On a symbolic level, Trible (1994, 158–59) speculates that the feminine form activates feminine imagery of the belly, so that this becomes a womb, reflecting Jonah's move from death to life.

2:2[3]. The two halves of this verse comprise a double summary of the basic experience of salvation (cf. Ps 120:1). From a situation of need Jonah prays to God who then saves. The two lines display complementary parallelism, beginning with the human cry and moving to the corresponding divine response. There is also chiasm, the structure being: call–need–need–call. The first line exhibits specification ("distress" is further defined as "the belly of Sheol"), while the second moves backwards in time, since hearing precedes answering, and so prepares for the flashback in the next verse. Chapter 1 locates the "distress" as the violent storm, where being thrown into the middle of a raging sea is as sure a death sentence as could be imagined. But the word used (*ṣārâ*) often has overtones of narrowness or restriction, which is very appropriate for Sheol, the unique Hebrew term for the barred world of the dead (Johnston 2002, 79). It is the dull place to which one descends when dead (Gen 37:35), where the praise of God that defines life in all its fullness is excluded (Ps 6:5[6]). Its parallels include the pit (cf. v. 6[7]; Isa 14:15) and the grave (Ps 49:14[15]). Sheol can be portrayed both as a beast that devours the living (Isa 5:14) and a prison from which escape is impossible (v. 6[7]). Death is so certain for Jonah that he can already be considered as in the "belly of Sheol." "belly" (*beṭen*) is a different word from that used in v. 1[2] and may describe either the stomach or the womb

(Freedman and Lundbom 1977, 95). Only Yhwh can raise up those who have descended there (1 Sam 2:6; Ps 30:3[4]). Walsh (1982) interprets the poem in isolation and regards the distress as being Yhwh's doing and the speaker's anguish is partly due to there being no evident reason for his plight (as is the case in Ps 18:4–5, cf. v. 20). However, reading it in the context of Jonah indicates a clear religious reason, for Jonah has disobeyed God and is one with the wicked who are destined in a special way for Sheol (Pss 9:17[18]; 31:17[18]). Yet God's mercy is all the greater for being imparted to an unfaithful servant who decides to pray only at the last moment. Jonah's salvation (cf. v. 10) is assured by the prayer being answered, for God's word is effective (Isa 55:11). Logically we would expect hearing before answer, but parts of the poem may well be telling the story back to front. The next verses will describe the situation of distress that evoked the prayer in the first place. As with other poems (e.g. 1 Sam 2:2) there is a switch from testimony to what God has done in the third person ("he"), to direct thanksgiving to him in the second person ("you"). There is a similar switch in v. 9[10])

2:3[4]. vv. 3–6[4–7] describe Jonah's plight in three progressive phrases ending with him sinking beneath the waves. The psalm uses no less than seven watery terms (Barré 1991, 241 n. 22) that spell distress and death for Jonah. These occur elsewhere in the psalms (Pss 69:2[3], 15; 88:7[8]), but there they usually comprise a limited metaphorical exposition of the psalmist's plight. Nowhere else is the motif exploited with such consistency ("this short psalm unleashes a veritable flood of water imagery," Miles 1990, 174). The sea is both deep and far from land or home, and the poem combines in a masterly fashion the vertical and the horizontal. "cast," "surrounded" and "the heart of the seas" can include both dimensions, but the initial "the deep" and the final "over me" emphasizes the vertical, whereas the next verse stresses the horizontal. "cast" (cf. Ps 102:10[11]) is different from "hurl" in ch. 1. Although Jonah has had himself thrown into the sea, here it is Yhwh who is responsible. The difference can be resolved by presuming that Jonah acknowledges that his death is God's righteous judgment on him. In the deep, as in the heart of the seas, there is no land or sky visible. In such a place people are as far from their natural environment as possible, and Yhwh's judgment is absolute and inescapable (Exod 15:8; Ezek 27:27).

The aquatic imagery gains additional force if watery mythological associations are activated, although they do well enough as a hyperbolic description of the terrors of literal drowning. In the ancient Near East God establishes the world by subduing the forces of water (often represented by sea monsters) that sought to overwhelm the dry land. The motif was used to emphasize God's role in judging his enemies (especially when the Egyptians were drowned in the Red Sea, Exod 15), or in rescuing those who call to him. Both associations are relevant here. Some have thought that "the deep" (*mᵉṣûlâ*; cf. Exod 15:5; Ps 69:2[3]) is a gloss because the phrase is rather long and the word is without the expected preposition "into." However, there is no textual evidence for its omission and poetry is often elliptic. "the flood" (*nāhār*) usually means "river" and so may refer to marine currents (Simon 1999). In the plural it can refer to "the underground rivers of chaos and death which belong to the underworld (Isa 44:27; Ps 24:2; 93:3)" (Wolff 1986, 134). The second half of the verse is a verbatim repetition of a phrase from Ps 42:8 (cf. 1 Sam 22:5; Ps 88:7[8]). REB's "surging waves" takes the two words for wave ("all your waves and your billows) as hendiadys. "Breakers and rollers" would be an alternative translation that retains the basic meaning of the underlying verbs. The psalms frequently praise the God who rules over the waves (Ps 93:4) and the billows (Pss 89:9[10]; 107:25, 29), but here they engulf Jonah and lead him to despair.

2:4[5]. The translation and interpretation of this verse is difficult. In Ps 31:22[23] it is enemies that drive the psalmist from God's presence, but in Jonah the banishment must be due to God's punishment (Ps 88:7[8]). If vv. 3–7[4–8] reflects a chronological progression, then NRSV is right to translate "Then I said." Half-way down, let us say, Jonah begins to reflect on why he has come to this point and begins to desire to live and worship again. The renewed description in the next verses heightens the suspense by literally deepening Jonah's plight, but God has heard the implicit plea and hastens to answer.

However, this is just one interpretation of the Hebrew *waw*, and the traditional ambiguous "and" opens up other possibilities. If chronological progression is not significant, as is the case with many psalms and poems, then this may be an alternative perspective on the experience of v. 3[4]. The description so far has been in terms of the externals. Here the emphatic first person pronoun is used ("and as for me, I said") to suggest the internal thought of Jonah that was evoked by the watery threat around (thus "I thought" in REB, NJPS). Like Adam (Gen 3:24; 4:14), Jonah has sinned and been banished from the presence of God. He laments, "I am driven away from your sight." He may have started by fleeing on his own account, but now he recognizes he has no control over his destiny and is driven by divine agents of judgment that he cannot command (cf. Isa 57:20; Amos 8:8). "your sight" is literally "your eyes," but the biblical writers characteristically use parts of God's body to refer metaphorically to attitudes and ideas. So, while in an absolute sense it is impossible to evade God (Amos 9:3; Jer 16:17), here it indicates the loss of an intimate and right relationship between Jonah and God. When the psalmist looks on God (or at least his temple), he may be sure of his blessing and help (Ps 34:15–16[16–17]).

The next half of the verse reflects more specifically on the idea that the presence of God, represented by the temple, is the necessary condition for life. As Jonah draws near to his watery death, the NRSV has him ask "How shall I look again upon your holy temple?" "How" assumes a minor emendation (so Theod.), but it could also be taken as a restrictive particle ("nevertheless"; "yet I will…," NIV; Ps 31:22[23]). If this expresses too much confidence, then the imperfect might reflect a rhetorical wish (GKC §107n), perhaps along the lines of "yet I would look again upon your holy temple." Jonah has been going downwards, but here begins to look back towards the source of life, God in his holy temple. The location of the temple is firstly Jerusalem (Ps 79:1; Wolff 1986, 135). However, Yhwh's dwelling place is also in heaven (Mic 1:2; Ps 11:4). By virtue of the one who dwells in it, the temple is the highest of all dwellings (on a mountain in Ezek 40:2; 48:1–2[2–3]) and the centre of the cosmos (Ezek 5:5). It is there that Yhwh hears his prayer (v. 7[8]), and from where he can come down and bring Jonah up from the depths (Ps 18:1–16[2–17]). When Jonah speaks of being far away and drowning in the depths, he powerfully expresses the utmost distance from God (Ps 139:8[9]).

2:5[6]. From the second half the vocabulary becomes unique to Jonah, suggesting to Magonet (1983, 49) that "the sudden change from familiar to unfamiliar language takes one into the depths of a frightening new world, far from God." First "the waters closed in over me." "closed" is a rare verb and has the snares of death as its subject in Pss 18:4[5] and 116:3. "over me" is literally "as far as the *nepeš*," which is often translated "soul" (AV), but here might be "neck" (REB, NJB; Ps 69:1[2]) or even "throat" ("choked me," GNB; see further on 2:7[8]). Breathing becomes impossible and drowning begins. Second, "the deep (*tᵉhôm*) surrounded me" or, even stronger, "engulfed me" (NJPS). "the deep" can describe the primeval masses of water that were separated from the land at creation (Gen 1:2). It was the ultimate origin of underground sources of water (Gen 49:25; Ezek 31:4) and was located beneath the earth, ever ready to threaten its existence through a destructive flood (Gen 7:11). In going down Jonah enters this terrifying and limitless body of water, and is well on his way to the only deeper place, Sheol (Ezek 31:15). "abyss" (LXX *Abussos*, Vulg. *Abyssus*) perhaps captures some of its horror. However, the deep is still in God's control (Ps 135:6) and Jonah, like God's people at other times (Ps 106:9; Isa 51:10), will find that God is sovereign even there. Third, "weeds were wrapped around my head," just like a turban (Exod 29:9; Lev 8:13). Perhaps we are to imagine Jonah reaching the seabed and becoming entangled by the tall seaweed (REB, NJB) or kelp (Sasson 1990). They prevent Jonah's escape and so become the equivalent of cords of death (Ps 18:4–5[5–6]). The three phrases build up an overpowering feeling of entrapment and restriction, a sure pledge of imminent death (contrast Ps 18:19[20]; 118:5).

2:6[7]. NRSV, following *BHS*, joins the first phrase of this verse to the last one, so that the seaweed is "at the roots of the mountains." However, the preposition (*l*) suggests "to" rather than "at," and we would expect a directional preposition or suffix for "to the land" if it was related to "went down." If we retain the received punctuation, the two phrases describe in parallelism the place that Jonah has reached. "land" is the subject defined by the following phrase (*casus pendens*; Golka 1988). Literally we might translate: "to the roots of the mountains I went down; as for the land, its bars [are] around me for ever."

"went down" is the third and final occurrence of *yrd*, the completion of Jonah's personal flight down and away from his God (Jonah 1:3, 5). Here it has overtones of drowning (Exod 15:5) and descent into the realm of the dead (Ezek

31:14; Ps 49:17[18]). By degrees the slippery slope (Allen 1976) of his disobedience has reached its nadir. Jonah is at rock-bottom (Golka 1988) and has even passed through death's door. "roots" (*qeṣeb*) is a rare word found in this context only in Sir 49:15, where it is parallel to "the foundations of the world" (Deut 32:22; Job 28:9; 1QH 3:31). The meaning of this phrase is uncertain, since geographical, mythological and metaphorical ideas cross and coalesce in ways that are not entirely consistent (Keel 1978, 56–57). For example, the mountains could be regarded as the world axis that unites the three elements of the cosmos: the heavens, the earth, and the underworld (Talmon 1978, 439). Geographically, the seabed could be regarded as the lowest point of the mountains, since originally even the mountains were covered by the primal sea before they withdrew (Gen 8:2–3; Ps 104:6–8). The context makes it clear that "land" is here the "underworld" (so NJB; "land of the dead," NLT; Isa 26:19; Jer 17:12–13; Sir 51:19). It is portrayed as a city entered through gates with bars (Deut 3:5; Ps 107:16; cf. the gates of Sheol in Isa 38:10), for it is an inescapable prison. It is less likely that the bars are the weight of the water that presses down upon Jonah and prevents him rising up (Keil 1871). "closed upon me" has the NRSV adding an appropriate verb, for the preposition is often found with verbs of shutting (BDB 126; Gen 7:16; Judg 9:51). The NIV ingeniously makes the noun into a verb with "barred me in." The geographical extreme of the underworld is matched by the chronological extreme of "forever." The finality of these assertions is literally false, but the hyperbole effectively communicates Jonah's absolute despair. It also serves to underline the power of the forces that must be overcome, thereby magnifying the even greater power of Yhwh who can alone rescue from such straits (2 Cor 1:8–10). The turning-point has now been reached now that Jonah can go no deeper, and thus the note of amazement and gratitude in "yet you brought up my life from the Pit, O LORD my God." Pit (*šaḥat*) is yet another term for the grave, or the abode of the dead, being also dark, deep and inescapable (see on 2:2[3]). The inconsistency with the previous watery metaphors matters not at all. Parallels for Pit include Sheol (Ps 16:10) and the heart of the seas (Ezek 28:8; cf. also Ps 30:3[4], 9[10]). Now, though, the realm of death is left behind in the triumphant announcement of God's reversal of Jonah's descent. Characteristically the poetry has little interest in the precise mechanism of the rescue, and all mediating agents (such as a fish) are subsumed to the praise of the object of Jonah's prayer. "O LORD my God" at last specifically acknowledges the only one who can save from death. The double mention of Yhwh here and in the next verse implies that this is the centre and pivot of the poem.

2:7[8]. The path to salvation is summarized. The first phrase sums up his plight: "As my life was ebbing away." The verb (hithpael of *ʿṭp*) indicates a feebleness or faintness arising either from physical deprivation (hunger in Amos 2:12; Ps 107:5) or when a person's spirit is overwhelmed by trouble or discouragement (Pss 77:3[4]; 142:3[4]). "life" is *nepeš* was originally the word for "throat," the source of a person's breath and basic appetites. By extension it came to stand for the person's life itself. The traditional "soul" (cf. NJB) too strongly implies a distinction between body and spirit that is foreign to Semitic thought. Wolff (1974, 25) suggests that *nepeš* pre-eminently points to "needy man." Several of these nuances are appropriate here. Water is the immediate physical danger for Jonah's breathing (cf. v. 3[4]), but the ultimate reason for Jonah's plight is his disobedient relationship with God, the only source of satisfaction. It is the change in this that changes everything, and so Jonah confesses, "I remembered Yhwh." This is by no means mere intellectual realization of his error, but entails a turning and a commitment to doing God's will (Ps 19:7[8]). This is the presupposition for effective prayer, and Jonah was able to testify that "my prayer came to you into your holy temple." The content of the prayer is not specified, but the context indicates it is a prayer to be saved from drowning and death. Jonah's prayer is here regarded as a concrete message that becomes effective when it reaches God in his holy temple (Ps 18:6[7]; Isa 37:14–17), where God hears and acts (1 Kgs 8:45; Neh 1:11). This assurance, celebrated in thanksgivings such as this, is held in tension with complaints that God has not heard (Pss 88:2[3]; 102:1[2]). This is never due to God's absence or his hardness of hearing, but is related to the mystery of divine freedom, an aspect of God that is acknowledged in other prayers in Jonah (1:6; 3:9).

2:8[9]. "Those who worship" translates a unique piel form of a Hebrew verb that usually means "keep" or "hold" (*šmr*). Whether in the piel or emended to the qal, this probably means "hold to," suggesting a regular, habitual attitude of trust and reliance ("pay regard," RSV; "cling to," NIV, REB, NJPS), and so is broader than what is usually implied by "worship." Hosea 4:10 and Ps 31:6[7] draw a similar contrast between idolatry and allegiance to the true God. "vain idols" translates two words in a construct chain. The first is the "vapour" or "vanity" of Eccl 1:2 (*hebel*), but in the plural it usually refers to idols (Jer 8:19), empty nothings (Deut 32:21). The second word also suggests emptiness, so that together the basic idea of "empty folly" (NJPS) is strongly emphasized. Understood concretely, the phrase would have as its target humanly constructed idols understood as "false gods" (REB, NJB; cf. Isa 44:9–20). The living testimony to the power of the saving God entails a contemptuous or a triumphant dismissal of all the great powers of the ancient world (cf. Jonah 1:5).

These people "forsake their true loyalty," but it is not clear who is forsaking what or whom. "true loyalty" translates *hesed*, one of the great theological words of the Old Testament. It can describe acts of kindness to other members of the covenant community, but devotion to God appears to be the meaning here. In the larger context of Jonah it could be a comment on the way the sailors learnt how to abandon loyalty to their false gods (Alexander 1998). This would then be ironic, since it is Jonah who seems to have abandoned his loyalty to God (Golka 1988; Trible 1996). However, the Psalm tells not their story but that of the Israelite speaker, so it is more likely to refer to apostates than pagans. Most references to *hesed* are to the loving kindness or steadfast love that the God of Israel shows to his people ("the grace that could be theirs," NIV). However, the verse has an antithetic chiastic structure: A ("who worship") B ("vain idols") B′ ("their *ḥeseḏ*") A′ ("forsake"). This may imply a more direct contrast between the God of Israel and idols. By metonymy, the attribute of *ḥeseḏ* can stand for the God who supremely manifests it (Ps 144:1[2]; cf. Jonah 4:2), as is implied by the NRSV translation. If this is so, then Jonah is making a general negative point in order to highlight the loving kindness that he has experienced as deliverance. Jonah's disagreement with God is from within this basic commitment, however he behaves.

2:9[10]. "But I" translates an independent pronoun that provides an emphatic contrast with those mentioned in the previous verse (cf. v. 5[6]). "sacrifice" and "pay" employ a verbal form (the cohortative) that expresses Jonah's declared intent. Someone in trouble would vow to commit something to Yhwh if he would help (see on 1:16). This could be a thanksgiving sacrifice (*tôḏâ*, Lev 7:15, the same word as "thanksgiving" here). Since this is a form of peace offering, where the meat would be shared with others, it is an effective public witness to someone's thankfulness. A sacrifice could have been the content of the vow mentioned in the next line, although vows could include other commitments as well. Again the congregation at worship is the most appropriate context for the fulfilment of such vows, and both sacrifice and vows are linked in Ps 116:17–18 (cf. 22:25[26]). The congregation needs to hear and learn from his experience of salvation. Rather than "pay," "fulfil" (REB, NJB) or "perform" (NJPS) would be preferable for the verb used here (piel of *šlm*), although such sacrifices would of course cost a great deal.

"Deliverance belongs to Yhwh" is an appropriate doxological summary and generalization of God's will to save, seen by the sailors in ch. 1 and now confirmed by Jonah (cf. 2:2[3]). A similar doxology is found in Ps 3:8[9] (except the words are reversed) as the conclusion of a similar pattern of distress, cry and divine answer. Deliverance or salvation (*yᵉšûʿāṯâ*) is a central Israelite affirmation about the character of God and his ability and desire to save his people (Exod 15:2; Isa 43:11). It is at the root of the name of Jesus ("Yah saves," Matt 1:21) and is one of the ways the New Testament expresses the significance of the work of Christ (John 3:16; Acts 4:12; Romans 5:9–10; Rev 7:10). It stands alongside the equally fundamental affirmation of Yhwh as creator (Jonah 1:9; Col 1:15; Rev 3:14; Westermann 1982).

2:10[11]. The psalm has taken place during a time of reflection that suspends the movement of the story. The prose of this verse indicates the closing of the poem in form as well as content, and sets Jonah on to the road to Nineveh again. Yhwh speaks to the fish which, like the storm, is Yhwh's obedient servant (cf. Ps 104:26), and responsive to his command (cf. LXX *prosetagē*, "commanded"). "spewed" (*qyʾ*) is too polite according to Sasson (1990). Vomiting is the correlate of the swallowing of 1:17[2:1] (cf. Job 20:15), and is usually the response to too much rich food or strong drink (Prov 25:16; Jer 25:27). Satirical interpreters make much more of the vomiting, seeing it as the fish's response to the disgusting self-righteousness of the prayer (Holbert 1981). The milder view of Wolff's (1986, 139) is that it is "slyly absurd rather than bitter," the storyteller's ironic comment on someone who thinks he can escape God. Others see it merely as the necessary reversal of the initial swallowing (Simon 1999), although other words could have been used. Perhaps the indignity of the journey with its ignoble end is an implicit reminder of God's displeasure and the need for obedience. The contrast between the fine sentiments of the poem and the prosaic reality are typical of the tension between the poetic ideal vision and the more mundane accounts in prose (compare the victory song of Judg 5, or David's lament in 2 Sam 1 with the preceding prose accounts). But whether expressed in poetry or prose, Jonah's experiential knowledge of his God's command of sea and dry land (1:9) is now complete. He is ready to do what God wants. We are not told the location of the dry land. The strong echoes of 1:1–2 in 3:1–3 may suggest that it was near his starting point (Joppa), emphasizing the radical shift in Jonah's attitude.

A Fresh Start (3:1–10)

Many commentators find the main structural division in this chapter at v. 3b, where the focus moves from the shoreline (vv. 1–3a) to Nineveh (vv. 4–10). But this puts too much weight on the circumstantial clause of v. 3b (informing us about Nineveh) and disturbs the pattern of command (vv. 1–2) and response (vv. 3–4). The first part of the chapter describes Jonah's actions and words (vv. 1–4), followed by those of the inhabitants of Nineveh (vv. 5–10). There are teasing echoes of ch. 1 throughout ch. 3 (Trible 1994, 110–20): a divine commission, Jonah's witness to God, a praiseworthy response by pagans (particularly as represented by an unnamed leader) and a disaster averted.

The Fruits of Jonah's Conversion (3:1–4)

The impression is that the renewed call comes immediately. Enough time has been lost already. Some Jewish commentators inserted a trip to Jerusalem for Jonah to pay the vows made in ch. 2, but this downplays the urgency of the commission. There was no restriction to when vows were fulfilled, so long as this happened eventually. Magonet (1983, 179) makes the more imaginative suggestion that Jonah wished to escape his commission by fleeing to Jerusalem to pay his vows. The repeated command is needed to prevent this evasion.

There are a number of differences between the two similar introductions to chs. 1 and 3, but both focus on the outward action. Because of this it is difficult to be certain about Jonah's own thoughts and attitudes. Did he go resisting inwardly (Trible 1996), reluctantly (Fretheim 1977, 108–9), resigned to his charge or eagerly (like Noah in Gen 6:22 or Abraham in Gen 12:4)? How far should the text be examined for subtle indications of the author's purpose? And how far does an interpretation contribute to an overall portrait of Jonah's character? I have argued that the story makes the most sense if Jonah emerges grateful but with a continuing ambivalent attitude to his commission. His silence, together with hints provided by the narrator, indicates that he has been subdued but not persuaded (Simon 1999). But whatever his attitude, the most important point in these verses is that he did obey, whereas in ch. 1 he disobeyed. The letter of the command is fulfilled, whatever the spirit in which this was done (Golka 1988).

3:1. The opening words are the same as 1:1 except "a second time" replaces the unnecessary "son of Amittai." Jonah is unique in being given his assignment twice. The possibility of a second chance is in itself surprising, for those closest to God (such as prophets and priests) are judged most strictly (Ezek 9:6; 1 Pet 4:17), and disobedience usually leads to death (1 Kgs 13). However, the theme of mercy and God's willingness to persevere is prominent in Jonah. God is also longsuffering, not wishing anyone to die. So he listens carefully to Abraham's plea for Sodom (Gen 18), bears patiently Moses' excuses (Exod 3–4), forgives David (2 Sam 12) and Jesus gives Peter a second chance (John 21:19). The verbal repetition highlights on the one hand the power of God's irresistible will and his irrevocable word (Isa 55:11), and on the other the very different reaction of Jonah (Cohn 1969, 50). The author does not have God restate the obvious, that Jonah's flight was all along misguided and futile.

3:2. The first half of the verse exactly repeats 1:2. It might even take place in more or less the same location (see on 2:10[11]). "proclaim to it" now replaces "cry out against it" (1:2), reflecting the same verb (*qrʾ*) but a change in the preposition (*ʾel* rather than *ʾal*). This is often found in neutral rather than adversarial contexts, but is this merely stylistic variation? REB's "denounce it" assumes there is no difference (LXX and Vulg. also have identical wording). But the versions may reflect a later stage of the language when the distinction between the prepositions had become blurred (Bolin 1997, 124). The case for a more positive shift in meaning is strengthened by the other subtle changes. The reason for the denouncement, the evil of Nineveh (1:2), is omitted. Again, this might be because we already know about it, but it still gives the verse a more positive feel. Instead, Jonah is given a specific "message," a noun derived from the same verb (*qᵉrîʾâ*), so a more literal translation would be "proclaim to it the proclamation." "tell" is a participle (*dōḇēr*; "which I am speaking to you"), and may refer to the past, present or future, depending on context (GK 116m-p). The LXX looks to the past ("according to the former proclamation") as does GNB ("I have given you"). A future nuance ("as I shall tell you," NJB) would presumably refer to divine inspiration in Nineveh, but the present tense is probably best, emphasizing the necessity for Jonah to obey rather than the content of the message.

Has the message changed since ch. 1? From an objective point of view the answer is probably "no." It is unlikely that the delay (if any) due to Jonah's flight had made much difference to the behaviour of the people of Nineveh. It is even less likely that the behaviour of Jonah or the sailors has changed anything significantly. Yet from another point of view the phrasing may well have been adapted so that it prepares for the eventual happy conclusion. The theological issues remain whatever the wording or the nuance. A clear statement of judgment in the prophets is never unqualified because of the complex relation between God, his people and history (Jenson 1995). Although the rhetoric of the moment may suggest that there is no alternative, the "perhaps" of the sailors (1:6) and the "may" of the king of Nineveh (3:9) is an authentic reaction to a God whom Israel knows is both sovereign and holy, merciful and compassionate, free to work in surprising ways.

3:3. The exact obedience of Jonah is emphasized by the repetition of words from the previous verse, "set out" ("get up"), "went" ("go") and "word" (*dābār*, from the same root as "tell"). By varying the language most of the translations fail to convey this characteristically subtle communication of content through form (REB, NIV and GNB prosaically spell out that "Jonah obeyed"). "according to the word of Yhwh" comes in the reference to Jonah in 2 Kgs 14:25 and is used elsewhere in Kings (e.g. of Elijah's obedience in 1 Kgs 17:5). At last Jonah is beginning to act like a biblical prophet, if only for this verse. Details of the journey and the time it took are omitted as being of no significance for plot and character, although the reader may imagine a growing intensity of mixed emotions as the goal of the journey draws ever closer.

A circumstantial clause (introduced by a simple *waw*) interrupts the sequence of story-telling verbs (*waw* imperfects) in order to give the reader the important background information about Nineveh's size (cf. Gen 10:12). "exceedingly large" is literally "great to God/the gods" (*lēʾlōhîm*). The plural form is used both for pagan gods and for the God of Israel, where it is probably understood as a plural of majesty (GK 124g-i). Beginning with those I judge to be the least persuasive or interesting interpretations, the phrase could mean: (1) "great to the gods." Some find a reference to the Mesopotamian divinities, since Nineveh contained many shrines and was a great religious centre (Wiseman 1979, 36). Yet, it is unlikely that our author refers to pagan gods, for they play no part in the story elsewhere. (2) "important to God." Stuart (1987) suggests that "great" indicates importance or significance (BDB 153; *HALOT* 170), perhaps because of its size or population (4:11), perhaps because it is the epitome of wickedness (2:3). Yet "great Gibeon" (Josh 10:2) refers to size rather than significance (Sasson 1990). (3) "belonging to God." Sasson suggests that the preposition indicates ownership (*DCH* 1:283), reminding us that the whole earth is the object of God's sovereign disposal and care (cf. 1:9; 4:11). (4) "vast" (REB) or "beyond compare" (NJB). The NRSV and most others interpret the phrase as a form of the superlative (Thomas 1953). However, we would expect "city of God" (cf. "cedars of God," Ps 80:10[11]) or "city before God" (cf. "hunter before God," Gen 10:9) rather than the simple "to God." Nor do the early translations understand it this way. Nevertheless, this explanation provides a good transition to the second phrase, which provides a more specific definition of Nineveh's size. (5) "great [even] for God" (Bewer 1911). Nineveh is so great that God can be used as a yardstick. On a literal reading this would undermine the incomparability of the God of Israel, but there could be an ironic nuance. Nineveh may be divinely great from a human point of view, but for the God of Jonah the main issue was its evil ways (1:2; 3:8, 10; cf. the similar ironic contrast in Gen 11:5).

The note that it is "a three days' walk across" (literally "a walk of three days") is even harder to interpret. It might refer to: (1) "requiring a three-day visit" (Stuart 1987), based on diplomatic protocol in Assyrian texts. This is attractive for those wishing to read Jonah historically and realistically. Even so, Jonah's visit is hardly diplomatic, and the description is general not specific. (2) The time taken to traverse the greater Nineveh territory. But there is no evidence for such a district and v. 4 clearly implies a walled city. (3) The time taken to go through all the streets. However, v. 4 clearly indicates that the diameter is meant (earlier commentators also took it as a measure of circumference, but this does not increase the distance significantly). (4) An idiom for a long time (Bauer 1958). However, it still seems too long a time for a city journey. (5) A storyteller's exaggeration. "The reader is not supposed to do arithmetic. He is supposed to be lost in astonishment" (Wolff 1986, 148). This is the most enjoyable solution, although we might then also expect an exaggerated number of citizens in 4:11 (see the discussion there). The implication is that the prophet's task is overwhelming, and the success of his half-hearted proclamation even more amazing (Good 1981, 48).

Both phrases seem to emphasize Nineveh's physical size and importance, though from a human rather than a divine perspective. The archaeologists provide various comparative figures: Gibeon was 1 hectare; Jerusalem grew from 4 hectares (David's time) to 16 (eighth century) to 60 (seventh century); the Athens of Themistocles was 220 hectares; Babylon covered 100 hectares (3200 according to Herodotus, *Histories* 1.178). Nineveh in comparison covered 740 hectares, was at most 5 km wide, and had a circumference of 12 km. The Greek historian Diodorus Siculus (2:3; cited by Bewer 1911, 51), dependent on an earlier source, gave it more mythic proportions, writing that "it was well-walled, of unequal lengths. Each of the longer sides was 150 stadia; each of the shorter 90. The whole circuit then being 480 stadia [about 88 km] the hope of the founder was not disappointed. For no one afterward built a city of such compass, and with walls so magnificent."

"was" need not be taken as a reference to a situation that was in the past but no longer pertained. Nineveh may well have been destroyed by the time of the writing of Jonah, but the clause is intended to help us appreciate the city that Jonah encounters, not to provide a later historical perspective.

3:4. "Jonah began to go into the city, going a day's walk": It is possible that "began" governs both the next phrases. Sasson (1990) translates: "Hardly had Jonah gone into town a day's journey." Yet why specify the "day's walk," since this would then be superfluous? It seems preferable to keep to the traditional understanding of the syntax, so that "began" governs only "go into" ("Jonah began by going a day's journey," REB). He therefore starts preaching early the second day. But why only a day's walk? A positive interpretation of Jonah's prophetic behaviour can point to the way that "he cried out" uses the same verb that appeared in the divine command in 3:2. Perhaps he eagerly did the three-day walk in one or preached while he walked so that only one day was needed. However, a less positive interpretation is more likely. On a diameter under-standing of three days, "a day's walk" would not be the heart of the city (Bewer 1911), but in the middle of nowhere. Then there is the strange brevity of the oracle, a mere five words in Hebrew. There is no messenger formula, no accusa-tion, nor any reason given (Trible 1996, 511–12). Admittedly biblical speech can be selective and the audience might be expected to fill out the details from their knowledge of the rest of Jonah and other prophetic oracles of judgment (Person 1996, 75–76). However, speech is an important means for communi-cating character, and the author may well be portraying the resistant attitude of Jonah by means of the minimal length of the oracle. What results is like a spoilt child who cannot avoid doing something, but will do his best to sabotage the deed through the spirit of the performance (Rudolph 1971). The reluctance that will clearly emerge in ch. 4 wins out over any good intention stemming from the experience of ch. 2. To reluctance Allen (1976, 222) adds incompetence and despair: "lost like a needle in a haystack inside this gigantic Vanity Fair, this Sodom of a city, the tiny figure feels he can go no further." How did Jonah communicate? Did he use Aramaic (unlikely to be understood by the populace) or a translator (Gen 42:23)? But few biblical narratives are concerned about how foreigners converse with Hebrews (Ezek 3:4–7; Isa 36:4–11 are exceptions) and this is a question that only a mundane literalist will need to answer.

Forty days is a round number for a substantial length of time. It may be a *terminus ad quem*, by which time Nineveh *is* overthrown (the participle here has an undefined time reference; cf. "tell" in v. 2). Most take the participle as refer-ring to a subsequent future event (Targ. adds "at the end of"). But more appro-priate for an urgent prophetic oracle is three days, which is the reading of LXX and Old Latin. Moberly (2003) proposes that Jonah uses forty in order to decrease the urgency of the message and reduce the Ninevites' inclination to repent immediately, or ever. This is consistent with other indications of the text. Yet Jonah still obeys, even if minimally, and so opens a space for action. Jonah's proclamation may be inadequate, but it is sufficient to convey the main points at issue: divine judgment on evil behaviour. In the world of the narrative the Ninevites know enough about what this means to respond. Nineveh will be overthrown, but in what way? The evident reference is to destruction, and the verb is used to describe God's overthrew of Sodom and Gomorrah (Gen 19:21, 25, 29; Deut 29:23[22]; Amos 4:6, 11). But the phrase also has a potential ambiguity, for the verb can also express a radical overthrow of a person's life in other ways: "God's intervention to transform an individual's life, resulting in a "change of heart'" (Seybold 1978, 426; cf. 1 Sam 10:9; Hos 11:8). Sasson (1990) argues that the ambiguity guards against a notion of a capricious or erratic deity, as well as being predictive. However, it is likely that all prophecy had an implicit contingency. God's actions were open to how people responded. It is important to give priority to the observable repentance of Nineveh (v. 10) rather than any Delphic ambiguity in the words. We as readers may enjoy the narrator's hints about what will happen, but this is on a different level from those involved in the action.

The Fruits of Nineveh's Conversion (3:5–10)

The story now divides (as at 1:15) and we leave Jonah until 4:1. We may imagine him quickly retreating from the city, his job done, and sitting down outside to see what happens. Meanwhile the response of the people is summarized in v. 5 before being illustrated, focused and intensified by the response of the king in vv. 6–9. The section concludes by the all-knowing narrator recording the response of God (v. 10). The pattern of threat–repentance–divine reprieve is found elsewhere, for God is both just and merciful (1 Sam 7:3–14; Ezra 8:21–23; Jer 36:3; Joel 2:11–29; Stuart 1987). The heart of the section is the king's speech (vv. 7–9). This has an introduction (v. 7a, defining the scope of the decree and its authorization), a balanced set of three negative and three positive instructions (vv. 7b–8, with a note of addressees repeated before each set), and a conclusion providing a rationale (v. 9; Trible 1994, 184). We have seen the turning round of Jonah in the first two chapters; this section describes the turning round of Nineveh and of God (Wolff 1975, 103–15).

The language of these verses echoes various biblical texts. One of the most significant is Jer 18:7–8, the only example where the same pattern is applied generally to other nations. Even there, though, it is intended as a lesson for Israel, and there is a range of possible ways in which the words of Jonah to Nineveh can be related to the nations and Israel. (1) Jonah stands for Israel and Nineveh for the nations. The message of the text is that they are all on the same level. God cares for the nations as much as for Israel and desires to have mercy on all who repent. He is also equally judge, for Nineveh as well as Israel will be punished for their wickedness. (2) Israel, represented by Jonah, is at a lower level than Nineveh. The behaviour of the king of Nineveh is an object lesson for those such as King Jehoiachim (Jer 36), who refused to listen to God. That which is possible for Nineveh is impossible for Israel. (3) Israel, represented by Jonah, encounters a specific city that illustrates a remarkable piety. Israel is at a higher level in regard to knowledge, but at a lower level in respect of behaviour. The author implicitly summons his hearers to exhibit both faith and knowledge (cf. 2 Pet 1:5–7) through ironically setting one against another. (4) Both Jonah and Nineveh are unique, and the story is an opportunity to explore some of the paradoxes of divine judgment and mercy that affect both Israelites and pagans in different ways at different times (see Section E, above). The particularity of the story qualifies any generalization that makes too absolute a claim.

3:5. The narrator indicates a comprehensive commitment to mourning and penitence through the three verbs describing the response to Jonah's words and the inclusive reference to "everyone, great and small" (cf. Joel 2:16). The sailors came to know of Jonah's God through fear of his present power. The people of Nineveh believed God even though their doom was in the future and merely announced. They trusted him without seeing (Ps 78:22; 2 Cor 5:7) and so showed saving faith (Gen 15:6; contrast Isa 7:9). The use of the general word "God" rather than the Israelite name Yhwh is appropriate, for Jonah's minimalist proclamation made even a cursory knowledge of his distinctive character impossible for the Ninevites.

The inward attitude of faith ("believed," the hiphil of *ʾmn*) is expressed and mirrored by a double outward action. First, they proclaimed a fast. "proclaimed" (*qrʾ* as in v. 4) is a verbal indication of obedience. Jonah's proclamation led to a domino effect to which all willingly contributed. A public fast was a national response to actual (Joel 1:14; 2:15) or threatened disaster (Jer 36:9; 2 Chr 20:3), often in response to sin (1 Sam 7:6) and undertaken in hope of an answer from God (Dan 9:3). It included abstinence from food and other practices of self-denial (Lev 16:29; Isa 58:3, 5). Along with other mourning customs (cf. v. 6), this is the reverse of life-enhancing behaviour. It reflected and intensified the depth of humiliation and repentance of the participants, who aligned themselves with the sphere of death that they thereby acknowledge is deserved and expected. God's righteous judgment is embraced and anticipated in the hope that the forgiveness and mercy of God would prevail. Sackcloth was the opposite of the fine clothes fit for festivals (Ps 30:12), being a rough, course-woven garment worn most uncomfortably next to the skin as a hair shirt. It was usually made of goat's hair, and so would have been almost black (Isa 50:3; Kronholm 2004, 185). "everyone, great and small" is literally "from great to small', an indication of the entire class through means of its extremes (merismus). Although theoretically it could refer to height (tall and short) or age (old and young; cf. Gen 19:4), it is most likely to refer to social class (nobles and slaves), with its associated attributes of wealth (rich and poor) and power (powerful and powerless). The mention of "great" prepares the way for the description of the "greatest" in the next verse, the king.

From a historical point of view the conversion is implausible (see Section D, above), but traditional Jewish commentators have suggested various reasons for the behaviour. The Ninevites had listened to the witness of the sailors, or they were persuaded by Jonah's repulsive appearance from the fish's gastric juices, or they paid attention to any god that came along. However, in the story the immediate response emphasizes all the more the faith and repentance of the people. The exaggerated portrayal of their piety is caught well by Luther's "none but saints inhabited the city" (cited by Wolff 1986, 151). More to the point may be the contrast with other biblical towns. God could not even find a minimum number of righteous people in Sodom (Gen 18–19). The kings of Israel were unrepentant when similarly warned by the prophets (Jer 36). Trible (1994, 182) suggests that different kinds of response by the sailors (gradual illumination) and the Ninevites (immediate faith) warn us against stereotypes of the foreigner or non-believer. Even pagan cities can express corporate repentance, to the dismay of cynics and exclusivists.

3:6. "news" is the normal noun for "word" (*dābār*). It can sometimes means "event" (*DCH* 2:399), but the other occurrences in Jonah (1:1; 3:1, 2) suggest that the content of Jonah's oracle was passed on to the king of Nineveh. He is as nameless as the captain of the sailors (1:6) and as the Pharaoh of Egypt (Exod 1:19), indicating a typological rather than a historical treatment. The usual title is king of Assyria (22 times in 2 Kings alone), and this unique occurrence may hint at a typical and folkloric style similar to that in Exod 1–15. Some see here a flashback: "the saying had (meanwhile) reached the king of Nineveh" (Wolff 1986, 143), but the form of the initial verb (a *waw* consecutive) normally indicates sequential narrative. Jonah did not reach the centre of the city. His message spread like wildfire among the citizens, eventually reaching the king who we may imagine to be the very last to hear the bad news.

Once the word reaches him, the king rapidly carried out four actions in exemplary fashion (cf. 2 Kgs 19:1–2; Ezek 26:16). The first two distance him from his normal royal status, while the third and fourth make him one with the people as a mourner and penitent. The actions have a chiastic rhythm, since the first and last refer to his location and the middle two relate to his clothing. The king "rose from his throne," not to flee (1:3) but to show that in the light of the coming judgment there is no distinction between king and commoner, for all are threatened with death. The same point is emphasized by the next two actions. He exchanges his robe for sackcloth, the garment the people have already put on (v. 5). Finally, "he sat in ashes," often associated with sackcloth in mourning and bitter lamentation (Jer 6:26). "ashes" (*ʾēper*) is better dirt or loose soil (Sasson 1990), since most occurrences do not suggest sacrifice and burning. It is a synonym of dust (Job 42:6; Sir 40:3; cf. Isa 47:1) and is found primarily in contexts of death and mourning (Job 2:8; Esth 4:3). The connotation if not the referent of ashes is thus appropriate. The movement from throne to ashes is a downward movement towards the grave but, unlike Jonah's downward movement in ch. 1, is carried out voluntarily and from the best of motives. "He has 'overturned' in dwelling, dress, and dignity" (Trible 1994, 184). Whatever Jonah may or may not have said, the king shows a proper fear and faith in the divinity. Only God can replace sackcloth with a garland of joy (Ps 30:11[12]), raise the needy from the dust (1 Sam 2:8) and deliver those about to die (Ps 56:13[14]; Isa 26:19; Dan 12:2).

3:7. Though clothed in sackcloth, the king is still king, just as the high priest remains a unique representative when wearing simple garments on the Day of Atonement (Lev 16:4). The corporate repentance of the city would not be complete without a proclamation, setting the official seal on the spontaneous personal reaction by people and king. "had a proclamation made" (hiphil of *zʿq*) is a different verb from the keyword *qrʾ* and was used in 1:5 to describe the sailors' cry to God for help. Here it was probably chosen to convey the similar tone of the king's decree ("he had the word cried," NJPS). Elsewhere the verb can means summons (e.g. Judg 4:10, 13), and an alternative implication would be that the king summoned before him the officials who will enforce his words or the herald who will announce it (Lux 1994, 135).

There is uncertainty about where the actual content of the proclamation begins. (1) "In Nineveh..." (Sasson 1990). The first two words in the Hebrew translate as "And he had it cried out and he said." "And he said" often introduces direct speech (1:6; 2:2[3]). "In Nineveh" would then be part of the decree, defining its scope. (2) "No human being..." (1:11; 3:1; AV; NJB; Wolff 1986; cf. LXX, Vulg.). This follows a word omitted by the NRSV ("saying") that usually introduces direct speech. However, it would be appropriate for the decree to include a statement about the authority behind it. (3) "By the decree..." The MT has a minor pause after "Nineveh," and most translations and commentators agree that there is no strong reason to follow the alternatives.

"decree" (*ṭaʿam*) often means "taste," with the nuance of discernment in a political context (Job 12:20; cf. "good taste"). In Aramaic the related word means decree (Dan 3:29; Ezra 4:19; 6:14), so that many see this as an aramaism and so evidence of a late date. However, the word is more likely to have been motivated by the wordplay with the cognate taste verb later in the sentence. Nowhere in Israel or Assyria do we know of a decree issued by the king and his nobles (literally "great ones"—the keyword yet again; cf. v. 5), although such a practice is found in Persian records (Ezra 7:14; Herodotus, *Histories* 3.31, 84, 118). Whatever the historical background, the form of words in the story further emphasizes the comprehensive and united front presented by the city.

The recipients are first given three negative commands (in the jussive), followed by three positive ones (v. 8). A literal translation would be: "human beings and animals, herd and flock: let them not taste anything, let them not feed, and water let them not drink." The two pairs of living beings is another example of *merismus*, indicating totality (cf. v. 5). Herd and flock are the two main classes of domestic animals that would be under the control of the Ninevites. They are the sacrificial animals (Num 22:40) that are closest of all to human beings (Lev 27:32). The instruction not to drink intensifies the fast to an extreme, for this would lead to death after two or three days (Esth 4:16). The verb for "feed" (*rʿh*; "graze," NJB, NJPS) has the same consonants as the keyword evil/calamity, another example of the author's delight in wordplay.

3:8. Human beings and animals are again the recipients of the three positive commands. The people are already wearing sackcloth, the king has just changed his clothes and now the animals are to join in. Commentators have variously regarded this inclusion of animals as a sign of inexcusable cruelty, high comedy or deep seriousness. The first response may be illustrated by a rabbinic interpretation: "Rabbi Shimon ben Levi said: The repentance of the Ninevites was fraudulent. What did they do? Rabbi Honeh in the name of Rabbi Simon ben Halafta: They put calves inside and their mothers outside; foals inside, and their mothers outside; and these bellowed from here, and those from there. They said: 'If you do not have mercy on us, we will not have mercy on them'" (*j. Taʿanit* 2a cited by Simon 1999, 31). A humorous interpretation has been related to the various wordplays that the passage contains. The king has the good taste to ensure that no-one tastes anything. The animals may not have contributed to the evil of the city but can refrain from grazing (the same consonants as "evil"). A pompous king would reinforce this tone. If he was the last to know and react, does he look around to find some way to make his mark? His eye fixes on the animals who are as yet untouched by the situation, so he commands them (several times) to share the fasting and to be covered with sackcloth.

On the other hand, ironic touches and wordplay can coexist with deep seriousness. The modern interpreters who favour humorous interpretation may underestimate the close links between humans and animals that are found in traditional societies. From the perspective of Nineveh, there could be no half-measures, and in many societies animals are involved in customs (such as mourning) that we tend to think as being strictly human affairs. In Genesis, animals and people are created on the same day (Gen 1:24–31), an ox may receive the human death penalty for murder (Exod 21:28) and cultic and prophetic imagery included mixed human and animal creatures (Ezek 1:10; 10:14). The phenomenon of sacrifice presupposes some sort of identity between people and animals (Lev 1:4; 16:21), and God's concern for the animals is found in many places, including Jonah 4:11. The involvement of animals in various mourning customs is found in Greek and Roman texts (Herodotus, *Histories* 9.24; Plutarch, *Alexander* 72), but their value is limited since the differences are as significant as the parallels (Mulzer 2002). In various poetic passages they are portrayed as crying out to God (Joel 1:18, 20). Perhaps we should again distinguish between the levels of artistry we as readers may enjoy, and the deadly seriousness of the Ninevites as they await the divine judgment. This text was no doubt the source for the similar behaviour described in Judith 4:10.

The second instruction includes the key word "cry" or "call" (*qr*) again, completing a full circle: God tells Jonah to cry out to Nineveh; Jonah cries out to Nineveh; the king tells Nineveh (including its animals) to cry out to God. Sackcloth is a conventional and external symbol. "mightily" (more literally "with strength") intensifies the note of fervent prayer in a personal and individual way. The final command to turn from evil highlights the moral demands of God, indicating that the Ninevites understood well enough why the word of judgment had come. "All shall turn from their evil ways" echoes similar injunctions to Israel in Jeremiah (18:11; 36:3, 7; cf. Ezek 13:22), except there they come from an unsuccessful prophet appealing to a hard-hearted people rather than a king exhorting a people who have already repented. "turn" (*šûb*) has a physical spatial basis, but often describes a radical moral or religious reversal or repentance. The spatial metaphor is continued in "ways," which is a comprehensive term for a lifestyle ("wicked behaviour," GNB; Ps 1:1, 6; Acts 9:2). The NRSV's inclusive language misses the combination of general appeal (the plural verb) with a focus on individual response. A literal translation would be: "let them turn every one (*ʾîš*) from his evil way" (AV). On the journey of life Nineveh has been heading in the wrong direction. Now the king commands the people to turn and begin walking in the ways of righteousness and peace. The final clause appeals for the Ninevites to turn "from the violence that is in their hands." "violence" (*ḥāmās*) is a general term for sin, oppression and exploitation, often expressed in violent and murderous ways (Haag 1980, 478–87). "in their hands" might be weapons used for violent bloodshed and murder (Ezek 7:23). Although the formulation is extreme, the rhetoric is intended to include every sort of ill feeling towards a neighbour (Matt 5:21–22), as is often the case in prophetic denunciation or liturgical confession. The requirement for all nations (not just Israel) to restrain violence was assumed by the biblical writers and prophets. Violence was the cause of the flood (Gen 6:11, 13), and the prophetic oracles of judgment against the nations contain accusations of violence (Obad 10; Ezek 28:16; Assyria is targeted in Isa 10:13–14; Nah 2:10–12; 3:1). The Ninevites are not accused of idolatry, for they have not had the opportunity to come to know the true God of Israel, but they are responsible for maintaining basic universal ethical standards.

3:9. Elsewhere "Who knows" might express sceptical resignation in the face of a situation that cannot be changed (Prov 24:22; Eccl 6:12), but here it reflects a similar theology to the "perhaps" of the captain (1:6). The door is open for a potential divine response to those who fast (2 Sam 12:22) and dare to take decisive action (Esth 4:14; Crenshaw 1986). Its function is to underline trust and total dependence, and to negate any notion of manipulation, guarantee or bargain. Yet the vocabulary makes it clear that the king does hope for a commensurate response from God. The turning of the Ninevites (*šûb*) from their violence (v. 8) will hopefully result in a turning of God from his destructive judgment (cf. Zech 1:3; Mal 3:7). First "God may relent (*šûb*) and change his mind" (niphal of *nḥm*), and as a result "he may turn (*šûb*) from his fierce anger." The root *nḥm* has a range of meanings relating to attitude (negative: "be sorry," "regret"; positive: "have compassion") and action ("relent," "repent," "change one's mind"). Here the focus is on the second nuance, although it depends on a prior change of attitude in response to changed circumstances. The first two phrases come in Joel 2:14, except that Yhwh appeals to his people (for a discussion of the difficult question of how these verses relate, see Magonet 1983, 77–79). A literal translation of "his fierce anger" would be "the heat of his nostril," reflecting two common metaphors of wrath. An angry person becomes physically hot ("burning," Zeph 3:8), and a similar physiological basis for the second may be the phenomenon of snorting with anger (Exod 15:8; Job 4:9; Johnson 1974, 351; Sauer 1997, 168). The vivid metaphors remain transparent behind the conventional phrase, but the biblical language for God reflects a robust anthropomorphism. The only way for God to turn from such fierce anger is either for judgment to take place (Josh 7:26; Jer 30:24) or for him to change his mind in response to intercession (Exod 32:12) or a change of behaviour (2 Chr 29:10). The king knows the choice that is before him. Nineveh's wickedness has kindled God's wrath, which will result in death. Yet it may not be too late, and the king's edict is intended to turn Nineveh from its wickedness and thereby God from his original intentions. The ultimate purpose is "that we do not perish." The king, and the nation with him, put their trust in a righteous and merciful God who is able to grant life as well as death. The same hope appeared in 1:6. There the subsequent events testified to the power of the God of Jonah, here his mercy and forgiveness, but in both cases the result is life and joy.

3:10. God saw a changed lifestyle. "No fire and brimstone fell on this latter-day Sodom after all" (Allen 1976, 226). There is no explicit recognition of the fasting, prayers and other penitential rites, for these are worthless apart from deeds of righteousness (Isa 58:1–10). "When God saw" is more literally "and God saw" (a *waw* consecutive). The uninterrupted flow of the narrative suggests that God's change of mind immediately followed the repentance of the Ninevites (Bewer 1911, 55). Did the Ninevites have to wait beyond forty days to know of this? We are not told, for (as in 1:16) the interest is about to shift to Jonah and his reaction. "how they turned" (*šûb* once again) emphasizes the content of what God saw and caused him to turn. "how" could also be translated "for," emphasizing that righteous deeds were the result of repentance.

The strong link between cause (the change in the Ninevites) and effect (the change in God's mind) is also conveyed by the repetition of the same words as in the king's speech. The imperative of v. 8 has become an indicative ("they turned"), as has the hope of v. 9 ("God changed his mind"). The turning of God is also portrayed by the chiastic structure of the sentence (Magonet 1983, 22–23):

A	what they did	literally "their deeds" (from the ʿāśâ root)
B	their evil ways	literally "their way of evil (rāʿâ)"
B′	calamity	punishment (rāʿâ)
A′	bring upon them	literally "to do to them" (the ʿāśâ verb)

The third and fourth elements are an almost exact repetition of Exod 32:14, except that "God" is used instead "Yhwh," and "upon them" instead of "upon his people." "What Israel in her early days experienced then, Nineveh—hitherto so brutal—experiences now" (Wolff 1986, 155). The vocabulary also appears several times in Jeremiah (8:6; 26:13, 19), especially in the classic statement of the relation between deed and consequence in Jer 18:7–10. However, the context and the alignment with "their evil ways" suggests that "punishment" (REB, NJPS) is preferable to the morally neutral calamity (see further on 4:1). "said" in context may have the nuance "threatened" (REB, NJB) or "promised" (BDB 161, 6) or "planned" (NRSV on Exod 32:14). The fifth and final phrase "and he did not do it" (again the ʿāśâ root) is only two words in the Hebrew and echoes the similarly short final phrase in the previous verse ("so that we do not perish").

Jonah and His God (4:1–10)

Now that Nineveh is sorted out, attention turns to the character who has proved most difficult to deal with—Jonah. In this chapter God seeks to persuade him rather than to overwhelm him (ch. 1) or to force him to reluctant assent (ch. 3). There is little agreement about the internal structure of the chapter. Magonet (1983, 57) advocates an elaborate chiastic structure, centring on vv. 7–8a, but there are asymmetries that weaken its persuasiveness (see the comments on similar suggestions for ch. 1). It does emphasize that speech dominates both the beginning and end of the chapter. Jonah has the most say in the first half, but

God has the last word in the final two verses (both have 39 words). In the middle there are various moves and countermoves without speech (vv. 5–8a).

A decision about subdivisions depends on a judgment about which are the most important features of the chapter:

    (1) 4:1–3/4–11 (Limburg 1993). God takes the initiative in v. 4, to which Jonah can be understood to respond. The MT has a significant division at this point (a *setumah*).

    (2) 4:1–4/5–11 (REB, NJB, NJPS; Wolff 1986). This is the view followed here. The scene changes in v. 5 from within the city to outside it (see below), and there is a shift from speech to action.

    (3) 4:1–5/6–11 (NRSV; Simon 1999). Jonah takes the primary initiative to v. 5, after which God initiates events.

    (4) 4:1–6/7–11 (Sasson 1990). The mood changes in v. 7 from anger to despair.

Verse 5 is at the heart of much controversy. Structurally it may be regarded as a transition (Trible 1994, 196), but it can also be regarded as the opening of the second section. The main question raised by v. 5 is the timing of the various acts in chs. 3–4. There are two main proposals:

(1) The sequence in the text is not the chronological order, which in fact is: 3:1–4 → 4:5 → 3:5–10 → 4:1–4 → 4:6–10. After the sermon (3:1–4), Jonah immediately leaves the city (4:5) and waits to see what will happen. After forty days, God forgives Nineveh (3:10) and Jonah complains (4:1–4, 6–10). A text-critical explanation would be that v. 5 was a later gloss, or that it had originally been after 3:4, but there is no manuscript support for this and it is difficult to see a scribe confusing the order so radically. A traditional grammatical solution has been to understand 4:5 as being in the pluperfect tense ("Now Jonah had left the city," NJPS; Ibn Ezra, Kimchi). Van der Woude (1983, 267–72) has alternatively suggested that all of 4:5–9 belongs before 4:4. Stylistic support for this flashback technique would be the author's habit of describing the character's reaction to an event, before filling in the background (Rudolph 1971). But there is no sign of interruption to the narrative flow. The *waw* consecutives continue, and we would have expected a change in the syntax to indicate this (Gibson 1994, 65, 166–67). Elsewhere the author indicates a disruption of chronological time through specific techniques ("for" in 1:10 refers back to the past; in 1:17[2:1]; 3:1 there is a change of venue and character).

(2) The text gives the chronological order of events (3:1–4 → 3:5–10 → 4:1–4 → 4:5–10). This is the more likely, once it is accepted that 4:1–4 takes place inside the city. Jonah comes to know about God's change of mind soon after the king's edict, rather than after forty days. Perhaps he became aware of it as soon as the Ninevites started to repent, or perhaps God made his change of mind known to him in some way. Whatever his source of knowledge, it evokes Jonah's first complaint and plea from within the city. God's response then drives him outside, just as God's first word to him (in 1:2) drove him to flee. This time it is not possible for Jonah to influence events, so the only way to resolve

matters without giving up his principles is to die. Suicide, though, is never an acceptable option in the Bible, so he prays for God to take his life. Why does this happen before the forty days are over? If the Ninevites begin to sin again within the forty days, God might change his mind again. I take it that Jonah recognized the whole-hearted response of the Ninevites and knows that their repentance will last. He waits outside the city in a continuing expression of disagreement with God's action, out of stubbornness rather than with any clear expectation that matters will change.

Jonah's Complaint and Yhwh's Response (4:1–4)

In the first section the narrator's introduction (v. 1) leads to a complaint by Jonah (vv. 2–3) and a response by Yhwh (v. 4). The main question raised by the section is why Jonah became displeased and so angry that he wanted to die. The answer given is crucial for an interpretation of the entire book.

(1) The midrash supplies a straight-forward physical answer, as unlikely as it is amusing: "Because of the great heat in the belly of the pregnant fish, Jonah's clothing, his jacket, and his hair were burned up, and flies, mosquitoes, ants, and fleas settled on him and made him so miserable that he wished he were dead" (*Midrash Jonah*, cited in Limburg 1993, 112).

(2) Jonah was upset that he had to travel all the way to Nineveh when he (and God) knew perfectly well that God would forgive the people of Nineveh. Yet the biblical authors are well aware that people are needed to carry out God's plans. Indeed, it is precisely for this reason that Jonah flees (Rudolph 1971, 365).

(3) Jonah is personally affronted that he is regarded by the people of Nineveh as a false prophet whose predictions do not come true (Deut 18:21–22; cf. 1 Kgs 22:28). A variation on this theory is that Jonah was upset because he was not told to announce the forgiveness and so prove himself a prophet (Sasson 1990, 295–97). But the prophets clearly recognized that God's words are open to changing circumstances and that he does change his mind (2 Kgs 20:1–6). Paradoxically the successful prophet is one whose predictions of judgment are wrong (cf. Mic 3:12).

(4) Keller (1982) suggests that Jonah originally fled to escape having to announce judgment on Nineveh due to his belief in God's compassion. After being persuaded that God is vindictive, God's mercy so confuses him that he knows no longer what to believe about God. With his honour as man and prophet lost, only death remains. However, such an extreme view is simplistic and unlikely.

(5) Jonah is an advocate of Israel's unique status as Yhwh's elect people. Several variations of this are possible. (a) An extreme negative reading of Jonah's character is that he is a narrow, vindictive nationalist who does not want another nation than Israel to experience God's compassion. The author condemns the kinds of attitude reflected in Nehemiah and Ezra. Jonah is furious that God forgave non-Israelites in the same way he forgave Israel (Exod 32). But this kind of reading is not just simplistic, it is in danger of reading back into the text later anti-Jewish sentiments (Lux 1993, 197–98). (b) A more historically

nuanced reading recalls that Nineveh is not just any foreign nation. Assyria is the source of the terrible destruction and exile that Northern Israel will suffer. "The prophet knows…that the penitence of the Gentiles would be disaster for the Jews" (Jerome, cited by Wolff 1986, 168). Their repentance would spare them so that in the future they will be able to act as agents of God's punishment. (c) Jonah's complaint is that God's even-handed compassion on Nineveh eliminates any difference between Israel and the nations. If God takes the side of Israel's enemies, is it pointless to serve him (Wolff 1986, 168; cf. Mal 3:14)? However, this oversimplifies the consistent asymmetry between the God of Israel and the idols of the nations, both in Jonah and elsewhere (Jonah 1:5, 9; Ps 115).

(6) Jonah complains that the exercise of mercy undermines the clear exposition of divine justice. "Divine compassion is perceived not only as unnecessary but as actually harmful, because mercy undermines the force of justice by detracting from the certainty of punishment and obscures the clarity of judgment by adding a factor that cannot be calculated in advance" (Simon 1999, 35). The difficulty with this view is that it seems strange that the arena for exploring the issue is a notoriously evil pagan city.

(7) My own tentative suggestion is that Jonah recognizes that God is both compassionate and just. The disagreement is how this works out in particular cases. Why is Jonah sent to Nineveh, and not to another evil city in Israel or elsewhere? It is the sovereign disposal of God's resources that is both hidden and, for Jonah, objectionable.

4:1. "But this was very displeasing to Jonah" is literally "and it was evil to Jonah a great evil." Once again we have the keywords *rāʿâ*, here repeated in the author's favourite verb + cognate accusative construction (1:1, 16; 3:2), and "great." But *rāʿâ* is not necessarily "evil." It can take on several distinct nuances (Dohmen and Rick 2004), most of which are to be found in Jonah: (1) "evil," a moral evaluation of human behaviour (Jonah 1:2; 3:8, 10; Jer 3:5; 44:5). Golka suggests that the verse refers to the evil confrontational attitude of Jonah. But this is too harsh, for there is a distinction between attitude (where there is considerable freedom of expression) and behaviour (over which there can be no compromise). (2) "harm," "calamity," "misfortune," the effect of harmful outside circumstances (Jonah 1:7–8; Jer 17:17–18). (3) "punishment," a real or intended action by God (Jonah 3:10; Jer 18:8). (4) "distress," a subjective reaction to an unfavourable situation. Though rare, the translations and versions are probably right in finding this meaning here (and in v. 6), and it is found in a similar construction (Neh 2:10; 13:8; Davies 1977b, 105–10). "very" reflects how the doubled use of the root intensifies its meaning ("absolutely furious," Limburg 1993). What, though, is "this"? The wording at the end of Jonah's prayer (v. 2b) makes it likely that it is God's change of mind narrated in 3:10b. God's relenting of his *rāʿâ* (in the sense of punishment) leads not to Jonah being happy but to his *rāʿâ* (in the sense of displeasure). The use of the same word sharpens the disagreement between God and Jonah. Similarly God's turning from his hot anger (3:9) leads to Jonah becoming angry (*ḥrh*, the same "burning" root as 3:9). Sasson (1990) prefers a weaker "was distressed" (cf. NJPS's "grieved"), partly because angry people do not pray. It is true that human anger at God is never expressed directly (Freedman and Lundbom 1986, 176), but this may be because it would transgress fundamental biblical assumptions about God's sovereignty and justice. There is no need to soften the anger idea, and examples of angry people praying may be found (Num 16:15; Ps 39:3[4]), and the personal engagement in anger makes a good transition to the strong complaint in the next verse.

4:2. Jonah's prayer in vv. 2–3 is, like that of the sailors in 1:14, in three main parts. The opening is an invocation "O LORD." The body consists of a rebuke ("Is not this…"), a justification of his past action ("That is why…") and a rationale based on a traditional formulation of God's attributes ("for I knew that…"). The conclusion is marked by another address to God ("And now, O LORD") followed by another rationale, this time oriented to Jonah ("for it is better for me…"). Introducing the invocation is a strong particle of entreaty (*ʾānnâ*) that is often found in contexts of need or lament (Jonah 1:14; Neh 1:5; Ps 116:16). It could be more forcefully translated "I pray thee" (AV) or "Alas" (Exod 32:31 NRSV; NJB's "Please" is too weak). "what I said" is literally "my word," but Jonah's previous silence means that this was what he said to himself, or thought (Gen 20:11). The complaint sets Jonah's word against Yhwh's word (1:1; 3:1; the verb in 3:10). The content of "this" is again 3:10. Yhwh's word had implied first of all the destruction of Nineveh, but Jonah's word of response indicates that he had seen beyond this to the city's sparing. "while I was still in my own country" fills in the crucial gap left between 1:2 and 1:3. It is unlikely that this is a reference to the message of temporary forgiveness to the wicked Israelite king Jeroboam II in 2 Kgs 14:25–27 (Bolin 1997, 151). Some have doubted that Jonah is here being truthful. A character's speech is less trustworthy than the narrator's comments (Alter 1981, 116–17). Perhaps at the beginning he was simply frightened of the dangers of the journey or his treatment in Nineveh. However, these suggestions trivialise the issues raised in the book and undermine any sense of revelation and climax. "I fled … at the beginning" is more literally "I was in front to flee." The first verb (piel of *qdm*) is usually found in a spatial sense ("come before," "meet"), but other forms of the root can take on a chronological nuance. There is no easy way to understand its meaning in this context and several interpretations have been proposed: (1) "I tried to escape" (REB) has little lexical support. (2) "the first time" (Wolff 1986; cf. NJB; *HALOT* 999) would be a unique nuance (Kronholm 2003, 512). (3) "at the beginning" or "beforehand" (NJPS), so that the verb takes on an adverbial meaning. However, this would be a redundant repetition of the time note of the previous verse. (4) "I planned to flee" (Sasson 1990) is near to the LXX ("I anticipated fleeing") and the Vulgate ("I was concerned to flee"), but a reference to the speaker's intention stretches the meaning. (5) "I hastened to flee" (RSV; Simon 1999; "quick to flee," NIV) may be the most likely interpretation. Although this also highlights intention, the idea of being in front is a reasonably transparent image for making something a priority.

"for I knew that" introduces a traditional formulation of God's grace known primarily from exilic or postexilic texts, but with deep roots in Israel's earlier traditions (Spieckermann 1990). "Jonah is a specialist in credal confessions" (Allen 1976, 228; cf. 1:9). However, what elsewhere was a source of hope is for Jonah a matter of disagreement of despair. "gracious" and "merciful" cover similar ground and are the first of four linked pairs of words. The first three occur in Exod 34:6–7 (with "merciful" and "gracious" reversed); Pss 86:15; 103:8; 111:4; 145:8; Neh 9:17. Only in Joel 2:13 are all four found, and it is disputed who borrowed from whom (Magonet 1983, 77–79; Dozemann 1989). This "credo of adjectives" (Brueggemann 1997, 215) is a general positive statement of God's character. There is a negative side. "slow to anger" does not imply never being angry, but in prayer the certainty of God's eventual punishment of the wicked (Exod 34:7b) is generally left out. Here the accent is on those aspects of God's character that Nineveh has just experienced. Indeed, some have suggested that Jonah was largely written to illustrate this very confession. "gracious" (*hannûn*) describes active, unselfish action on behalf of the needy or helpless (Exod 22:27). merciful or compassionate (*raḥûm*) is related to the word for womb and suggests the passionate, protective love that comes to the fore when a mother sees her child endangered. Applied to God these attributes gain an effective edge since they are backed up by his sovereign power. "slow to anger" is literally "long of nostril" (cf. "short tempered"; see further on 3:9). God has endured Nineveh's evil for many years before sending Jonah. Prayer to the God of wrath and mercy often concerns the timing of his action or non-action, which in the rhetoric of prayer is often regarded as being dangerously precipitate (Deut 9:18–20) or tragically delayed ("how long," Ps 13:2; Isa 6:11). "abounding" (*rab*, "much," "great") intensifies the quality of Yhwh's steadfast love (*ḥeseḏ*), his kindness and love for Israel and indeed the whole universe. The fourth and final attribute, "ready to relent from punishing," is the same phrase as occurred in 3:10, except that "ready to relent" is the generalizing participle (*niḥām*). It is the prevailing character to which specific examples such as 3:10 testify. God has indeed relented from punishing Nineveh, and Jonah is not pleased.

4:3. The prayer concludes with Jonah's death wish. "And now" often introduces the practical conclusion from what has been stated (BDB 774), but the logic is hard to follow and on first reading Jonah's death wish "seems stunningly incongruous" (Sasson 1990, 283), for the affirmations concern a God whose first concern is all that grants and enhances fullness of life (John 10:10). Others had expressed a desire to die, but on account of grief (Job 3), failure (1 Kgs 19:4), frustration (Num 11:15), pain (Gen 25:22), fear or calamity (Exod 32:11; Num 11:15).

Jonah's plea "please take my life from me" has particularly close links to Elijah's similar death wish ("now, O LORD, take my life, for I am no better than my ancestors," 1 Kgs 19:4). As in that story, we find a despondent prophet, sitting under a tree, praying for death, but finding a debate with God instead.

However, there is also an ironic contrast: Jonah wants to die for too much success, Elijah for lack of success. However, the parallel may also suggest that there is a substantive reason for the despair, even though it is expressed in a way that challenges the sovereign wisdom of God. Elijah's pain over Israel's apostasy is equivalent to Jonah's pain over Nineveh's unrequited evil.

In asserting that "it is better for me to die than to live," Jonah's despair exceeds even that of the people of Israel, who expressed a preference for slavery in Egypt over death in the desert (Exod 14:12). The petition adds four more first person suffixes to the four at the beginning. The result is to make us suspicious of the use to which Jonah is putting the central theological confession, just as we become suspicious of the way in which Job's friends apply to Job's particular case their generally orthodox affirmations.

4:4. Yhwh speaks for the first time since 1:2: "Is it right for you to be angry?" There are other possible translations: (1) "You are really angry" (JM 161b). The initial *ha* can be exclamatory, but it normally indicates a question. (2) "Are you that deeply grieved?" (NJPS; Sasson 1990). The first verb can act as an adverb qualifying the next verb with the nuance "to do well/thoroughly" (GKC 113k; 3:9; 4:1). But in these cases it follows the verb (Deut 9:21; 2 Kgs 11:18). Intensification of the anger idea could have been achieved by using the infinitive absolute of the angry verb (as in 1 Sam 20:7). (3) "Is it right for you to be angry?" is thus probably the best translation, but what is its tone? In comparison to Jonah's extended prayer its brevity is striking (contrast Job 38–41). This suggests that God is indeed gracious and merciful, displaying "a positively tender kindness, which sets about bringing the sulky Jonah to a proper self-examination" (Wolff 1986, 169). It is not wrong to be angry, but it is the extent of Jonah's anger that is the problem. God's attempt to open a discussion fails, for Jonah remains silent, and God has to take more drastic action.

Jonah's Action and Yhwh's Response (4:5–10)
Jonah does not answer God by speech but with action. He goes out and makes a booth. God responds equally by action, an acted parable of destruction. God's compassion for Jonah extends even to the tragic death of a wondrous plant. Each verse of 7–9 has a similar structure. First, God appoints (a plant, a worm, a wind). Second, there is a consequence (the plant grows, the plant dies, the sun attacks Jonah). Third (though not in the middle verse), the reaction of Jonah is described. This then leads on to the first and only recorded conversation between Jonah and God. Jonah begins, but God ends it, not with a command (as at the beginning of the book) but with a question.

4:5. Jonah is indeed angry, but God's answer has shown him that he continues to fail to change God's mind. In a combination of heroism and foolishness he continues to assert his point of view, even while surely knowing that he will be no more successful than previously. He goes out of the city and sits down to the east. Why east? Proposals include: (1) Jonah had entered the city from the west and wandered it until he found himself leaving through a gate in the east (Stuart 1987). (2) It reflects the Israelite preference for the east (Sasson 1990). (3) He refuses to go home (in the west) until he dies or God changes his mind. It is as dramatic a geographical expression of disagreement with God as his original flight, but now in the opposite direction. "east" (*qeḏem*) is also cognate with "beforehand" (*qiddamtî*) in v. 2. The assonance may relate Jonah's two disobediences, opposite in direction but equal in intent (Simon 1999). In ch. 1, Jonah slept, here he sat down. Perhaps in both cases he knew he could not escape Yhwh, but made a symbolic gesture of protest

He makes for himself a booth ("shelter," NIV, REB, NJB), the *sukkâ* familiar to us from the festival of booths (Lev 23:42–43). Ezra told the people to "bring branches of olive, wild olive, myrtle, palm, and other leafy trees to make booths" (Neh 8:15). It was a temporary shelter for cattle (Gen 33:17) and people (1 Kgs 20:12). The flimsy character of the shelter suggests limited resources, for the repetition of "sat" suggests that Jonah is preparing for an extensive stay. The heat of the sun would make full exposure dangerous and cut short the argument with God prematurely. However, Jonah is not prepared to argue with God, unlike Abraham when he interceded on behalf of Sodom and Gomorrah (Gen 18:22–23). Instead he is "waiting to see what would happen to the city." The impression is that Jonah is stubborn enough to wait for as long as it takes for a change to happen, whether forty days or forty years. "to the city" is more literally "in the city," implying that Jonah is hoping for a reversal of behaviour by the Ninevites so that the original oracle of doom can be reinstated.

4:6. "LORD God" is used only here in Jonah, and is found mainly in Gen 2–3. A bewildering variety of names for God is used in ch. 4: Yhwh (vv. 2–4, 8, 10), God (*ʾēl*, v. 2), "the God" (*hāʾᵉlōhîm*, v. 7; cf. 3:10) and God (*ʾᵉlōhîm*, v. 9). The phrase is unlikely to be merely transitional (Golka 1988). The traditional distinction is between "God" as a title for the God of the whole world, and "Yhwh," the specific name of the God of Israel. This distinction works relatively well up until this point, and in this verse we could say that the creator God is at work in this miracle of nature on behalf of someone who worships Yhwh (1:9). Yet the rationale does not make straightforward sense of the remaining references in this chapter, and any solution must remain speculative.

Yhwh appointed a great fish in 1:17[2:1], and now the same word (piel of *mnh*) occurs in each of vv. 6–8. Unfortunately the NRSV translates with "prepared" in v. 8 (GNB uses three different words!). "Provided" (NIV, NJPS) is weak, for a king assigns a person or situation for the fulfilment of a task (Dan 1:5, 10, 11; cf. Ps 61:7[8]). "bush" is the unique *qîqāyôn* which has been variously identified (Robinson 1985). (1) It recalls "spewed" of 2:10[11] (*qyʾ*), hence "vomit-plant" (Halpern and Friedman 1980), but that verse is a long way away and there is no evident association of meaning. (2) The same objections apply to the suggestion that it is a code for "innocent blood" in 1:14 (Youngblood, quoted by Christensen 1985, 133–40). (3) Biological identifications include gourd (AV; "climbing gourd," REB; cf. LXX, Old Latin, Augustine), ivy or vine

("vine," NIV; Sym.; Vulg.) and the castor-oil plant (NJB; *ricinus communis*; the Egyptian *kiki* and Talmudic *qîq*). Much has been made of the castor-oil's great plate-like leaves (good for shade), its rapid growth and propensity to die easily. But its growth and demise in Jonah is by divine appointment and cannot provide hints for biological identification. (4) Ibn Ezra among others suggested we had no way of knowing its identity. This is probably why some translations chose a very general term, such as "bush" (NRSV) or "plant" (RSV, GNB). (5) The unique name suggests a unique plant, and this is best captured simply by transliterating (Targ.; Aq.; Th.). This leaves the *qîqāyôn* to do its mysterious divine work unhampered by dubious associations or identifications. Of course, this also needs to be explained to a puzzled reader!

The *qîqāyôn* has a crucial role in an acted parable of growth and destruction (cf. Mark 11:12–14, 19–21). In order to protect Jonah from the sun God "made it come up over Jonah." The NRSV takes the verb (*ʿlh*) as a causative hiphil, but it could also be the simple qal ("which grew up over Jonah," NJPS), although this lessens the force of the urgent miraculous involvement of God. A double purpose is indicated by two similar infinitive constructs. First it is to give shade (*ṣēl*) over his head, a physical symbol of God's grace (Isa 25:4; Ps 91:1). But why is this necessary if Jonah's booth of the previous verse also gave shade? A textual solution assumes that the shade is the same and one or other must be removed as a gloss or misplacement. However, Hebrew narrative often uses the same word with different nuances, and it is possible that we are to understand the shade of the booth as inferior to that of the *qîqāyôn*. Rather than a sturdy hut, the booth could have been a makeshift DIY structure of stone or wood, with branches overhead. The leafy cover could well have been inadequate, especially once the leaves began to shrivel in the heat. There is a characteristic wordplay between "to be a shade" (*lihyôṯ ṣēl*) and "to save him" (*lᵉhaṣṣîl lô*). The same consonants could be read "to shade" (*lᵉhāṣēl*), but this is a rare verb. The LXX has "shade," but this could be a contextual interpretation rather than an indication of a different underlying Hebrew text or reading tradition. "save" or "deliver" is an important theological word, suggesting at a secondary level rather more than mere relief from "discomfort" ("relieve," REB), especially since "discomfort" is the familiar *rāʿâ* (see on v. 1). This first of all describes Jonah's physical state, but it is difficult to avoid the implication that God wants to address Jonah's displeasure at his actions. "Wickedness" would be too extreme, but it is part of the continuing irony that God finds it easier to deliver Nineveh from its full-blown *rāʿâ* than Jonah. Jonah, however, is as yet oblivious to this deeper purpose, and we are simply told that "Jonah was very happy about the bush. This can be read literally as "and Jonah joyed (*śmḥ*) over the *qîqāyôn* with a great joy (*simḥâ gᵉḏôlâ*)," thus displaying two characteristic stylistic features: the keyword "great" and the verb + cognate accusative construction. Rudolph (1971) further suggests that he was happy because he deduced from God's miraculous care that he had also decided to look favourably on his desire for Nineveh's doom. If this is the case, then it emphasizes the importance of the appropriate interpretation of an ambiguous symbolic action.

4:7. The story proceeds at breakneck speed. Jonah has hardly had time to appreciate the plant when it is taken away from him by dawn the next day, probably while he is still asleep (cf. Ruth 3:14). God appointed a "worm" (*tôlaʿat*), or is it a maggot, weevil, beetle, centipede or caterpillar? The ancient Israelites appear to have had little interest in such distinctions, but our horror of this small yet deadly creature is intensified if we are aware that the *tôlaʿat* can be the agent of God's wrath (Deut 28:39) and consumes corpses (Isa 66:24; cf. 14:11). It did not merely eat the *qîqāyôn*, it "attacked" it. The verb (hiphil of *nkh*) is used to describe a person struck down by a sword (Jer 20:4) or with disease (Deut 28:27). Here it gnaws through the stem so that the water supply was cut, and so it withered. It may be significant that God directly engages with nature in its life-enhancing role (the fish, the *qîqāyôn*), whereas the worm (and later the wind) mediates between God and suffering or death (cf. the role of the Satan in Job 1–2). The author guards against a dualism that states that God is for death as much as he is for life (Deut 30:19; Ezek 18:23).

4:8. When the sun rose, perhaps less than an hour after dawn (Wolff 1986), Jonah finds out that this is not going to be his day, for "God prepared a sultry east wind." "sultry" (*ḥᵃrîšît*) indicates that the wind is hot, oppressive and enervating. The derivation of the adjective is uncertain, and older commentators suggested numerous emendations (e.g. from roots meaning "to be sharp" or "to burn"). Elsewhere the adjective is only found in 1QH 7:5: "a ship in the rage of a powerful/violent (?) [wind/storm]." The MT root (*ḥrš*) can also mean "to plough" (a cutting wind?), or "to be silent" (Targ.; "quiet," Simon 1999, 44). The context suggests "scorching" (most EVV; Vulg.; "scorching heat," LXX). The east wind is sometimes described as powerful (Exod 14:21; Ezek 27:26), as well as a wind that withers vines (Ezek 17:10; 19:12). Many assume the wind to be the sirocco, which Stuart (1987) describes as "constant hot air so full of positive ions that it affects the levels of serotonin and other brain neurotransmitters, causing exhaustion, depression, feelings of unreality, and, occasionally, bizarre behaviour." Do both the wind and the sun contribute to Jonah's faintness (i.e. the clauses are parallel; Isa 49:10), or does the wind mediate in such a way that the sun can attack with full force (i.e. the clauses are sequential, as in v. 7)? If the latter is the case, perhaps we can imagine a scorching wind that shrivels yet more of the roof of Jonah's booth. Sasson (1990) cites an imaginative but speculative suggestion of Joseph Kara that the wind knocked down the hut he had built. However, it is more likely that the wind reinforces the effect of the sun, which beat down on the head of Jonah. The ancients were well aware of the danger of sunstroke (Ps 121:6; 2 Kgs 4:18–20). "beat down" is "attacked" (as in v. 7). The sun, like the ship (1:5) and the worm, is given a personality and is hostile to Jonah. We sympathize with Jonah as he suffers from one attack after another, all the more bitter for being such a dramatic contrast from the care and attention he had received the previous day. The physical result was that "he was faint" (Isa 51:20; Amos 8:13), but this also conveys his spiritual and mental state, reflected in his second request to die. The forcefulness of his request is conveyed by its repetition, first as indirect speech and then as direct. Jonah asked (*šʾl*), that is, "prayed" (REB) or even "begged" (NJB, NJPS), that he might die. His request to die is an exact repetition of the first request in v. 4, but the context is now quite different, for it derives from physical suffering rather than a complaint about God's pity for Nineveh. God's agents of death have prevailed against Jonah's earlier resolve to see what would happen to the city. He is faced not with the destruction of Nineveh in the abstract, but with his own suffering and imminent demise.

4:9. God has another go at a conversation by repeating the question of v. 4, though now applying it specifically to the *qîqāyôn*, "Is it right for you to be angry about the bush." This is no doubt partly self-pity (Blank 1955), but the context charges the question with wider implications. Does Jonah's anger at the death of the *qîqāyôn* undermine his anger at God not bringing death to Nineveh? But Jonah refuses to engage with the implicit criticism and merely responds: "Yes, angry enough to die." "Yes" in fact repeats God's first word (*hêṭēḇ* from the root for "good"), except not as a question but as an emphatic assertion, "It is right" ("I have every right," NJB). "to die" is literally "until death" (cf. Matt 26:38). Some think this is merely hyperbole, "mortally afraid" (REB; NJB; cf. the idiom "sick to death"; Thomas 1953, 220), but the context suggests another repetition of his death wish. Jonah's strong affirmation here can be taken to be an implicit acceptance of God's point of view, once he works out the logic of God's closing argument.

4:10–11. The concluding verses of Jonah are a vital pointer to the theme of the book, especially since the author has only gradually revealed his concerns. At least, this is what is normally assumed; recent writers have been less sure that the analogy makes sense. Wolff (1986) regards v. 10 as irony, the exact opposite of what is said. Jonah does not pity the plant; rather, he is concerned merely for his own welfare. Others also suggest the argument is strictly utilitarian. The Assyrians are saved because they will be useful to God (to punish Israel?), just as Jonah finds the plant useful. Another way of reversing the traditional view is to take v. 11 as a statement, not a question: God does not pity Nineveh. The contradiction between this attitude and the actual fact of Yhwh's forgiveness emphasizes the absolute freedom of divine mercy that is unmotivated and unknowable (Cooper 1993; Bolin 1997, 163–64). Only in this way can Israel find hope beyond the unavoidable righteousness of God's judgment on the nation.

However, these revisionist readings are all too modern (or postmodern) and ill fit the prevailing seriousness with which the Bible affirms the goodness and compassion of God as summed up in v. 2. If God was not passionately concerned about the people of Nineveh, then there would be no reason for him to go to all the trouble of ensuring Jonah preaches to them. It is preferable to look for a more subtle logic behind these verses. Trible (1994, 221–23) points to the lack of recorded response by Jonah to the destruction of the plant in v. 7. She argues that we can deduce this reaction from God's authoritative statement in v. 10. Jonah did indeed pity the plant, but characteristically the author delayed the information until it was needed. God's challenge is to the integrity and consistency of Jonah's attitudes. Jonah's behaviour has been ambivalent throughout the story. Now God brings the issue to a head and questions Jonah's underlying motives.

God employs an *a fortiori* argument or, to use the rabbinic equivalent, *qal waḥōmer* ("from light to heavy"; e.g. Gen 44:8; 2 Kgs 5:13), a strategy conveyed also by the greater length of v. 11 in comparison to v. 10 (Trible 1996). The two halves of the argument correspond grammatically: (1) the assertion opens with a pronoun ("you/I") followed by the "concerned" verb and the object of concern ("about the bush"/"Nineveh"); (2) the object is then qualified by two relative clauses ("which"; the second relative in v. 10 before "it came into being" is omitted by NRSV). The argument depends on equivalence between the two parts. However, interpretation is made more difficult by the way in which quite different things are said first about the plant, and then about Nineveh. The plant (a) grew without Jonah's labour or nurture and (b) grew and perished quickly. Nineveh (c) contains many people (d) who are ignorant, and (e) it also contains many animals. It is not clear how many features of the bush apply to Nineveh, and vice versa. Potentially we can set up a number of relationships that are equivalent, opposite or a matter of degree.

The difference in number is certainly significant. Jonah's concern for one bush is far less than what God felt for the many people of Nineveh, a city that also contains many animals. The contrast is reinforced by a difference of kind. Genesis 1 sets out a hierarchy of being where plants are lower than animals, which are themselves lower than persons. Nineveh is also a "great city," whereas the plant (for all its uniqueness) is not in the same league. Further analogies can be made, but in a more tentative way. Plants are hardly ignorant, but there may be a hint that the people of Nineveh are more worthy of concern because they are able to learn and change, and so avoid the coming judgment on their evil. The bush, on the other hand, can only follow its biological blueprint and runs no danger of incurring guilt.

It is more difficult to move from the bush to Nineveh. God did not labour over Nineveh in any physical sense, although he did enable its growth in a general providential way. As the creator God, he is more intimately involved in his world than Jonah. The slow growth of humans and cities may also suggest that God has developed a deep concern for Nineveh over an extended time. The different forms of the verb employed in the two parts may also be significant (Sasson 1990). Jonah was concerned (the perfective), suggesting a completed action, and indeed he will soon become angry. God is concerned (the imperfective), implying a continuous and ongoing attitude. The argument is thus sustained by general equivalence, reinforced by difference and heightened by contrast.

4:10. "concerned" (*ḥûs*) can be translated in several different ways: (1) "concerned about" (NRSV, NIV, NJB) or "care about" (NJPS), which fits Gen 45:20, but is too bland for most occurrences. (2) "sorry about" (REB; Vulg.; Golka 1988, 124), which would again be a weak finale for the powerful drama of the book. (3) "spare" (cf. v. 11 Vulg.), though this does not fit here, for Jonah does not have the power to ensure that the act of sparing follows the attitude of pitying. (4) A more psychological emphasis is suggested by the normal subject of the verb, the eye (Deut 7:16; Ezek 7:4). We should then retain "pity" (AV, RSV) or "have compassion" (Tyndale 1992). *ḥûs* is often synonymous with other verbs of compassion (Jer 13:14; 21:7). In legal contexts it stresses that no pity should be shown on the guilty (Deut 13:8; 19:21). In Ezek 5:11 Yhwh's eyes have no pity on sinful Israel. However, the king has pity on the weak and needy in Ps 72:13 and prayer is offered to God to have pity on his people (Neh 13:22; Joel 2:17). Following Trible, we can speculate that Jonah was moved by the rapid death of such a fine, useful and possibly unique plant. For a brief moment he was faced with a tragedy in the created world that jarred him out of his preoccupied thoughts. It is this moment that God seizes and explores. His pity has led him to be angry, for the plant did not deserve to be destroyed (v. 9). On the other hand, if he had said that it was not right to be angry, then he would have contradicted his own attitude to Nineveh (Wolff 1986).

"labour" (*ʿml*) is a keyword in Ecclesiastes (1:3 and seven times more), and the lack of any contribution by Jonah emphasizes the character of the *qîqāyôn* as pure gift. "grow" (piel of *gdl*) is related to the "great" keyword. It is often used of children ("rear," "bring up," Isa 1:2; 49:21) but also of plants (Isa 44:14; Ezek 31:4). "it came into being in a night and perished in a night" uses the same idiom twice, "son of a night." The first time is with the verb "to be" ("it came to be") and the second with the keyword "perish," which elsewhere is used of human beings (Jonah 1:6, 14; 3:9) and so reinforces the analogy to a human person. In his usual way the author supplies after the event information we did not have. We might have thought the bush grew during the day, but its secret, mysterious, divine character is emphasized by the way "it appeared overnight" (NJPS), and died before Jonah awoke in the morning (v. 7).

4:11. The "I" is a separate emphatic pronoun: "and as for me" (*waʾᵃnî*, 2:4[5], 9[10]; Mic 7:7), setting up the strong contrast of the entire sentence. The interrogative particle is not used here, but it is often omitted if the context is sufficient to indicate a question (GK §150a). "that great city" is the final occurrence of the keyword "great." The numerical greatness of Nineveh and its inhabitants is conveyed by a threefold repetition of the *r* and *b* consonants in "more than" (*harbê*), 10,000 (*ribbô*) and "many" (*rabbâ*). The implication is that Yhwh cares greatly for so many persons. "a hundred and twenty thousand" is literally "twelve myriads" where myriad in arithmetical contexts counts as ten thousand. The Mesopotamian numerical system was based around the number 60, so that 12 was a round number ("dozen") similar to our ten. Although the Bible mainly adopts ten as the basic unit, from time to time twelve is important

(Josh 7:5). "persons" (a collective singular *ʾāḏām*) indicates that this is a count of the entire population, but is this a realistic or a hyperbolic figure? Historical interpreters draw attention to various counts for similar cities. Wiseman (1979, 39–42) suggests 18,000 for Calah/Nimrud, which is about half the size. He takes the much larger figure here as evidence for the district interpretation of Nineveh (see on 3:3), but others consider a count of 300,000 as realistic (Wolff 1986; Sasson 1990). However, ancient readers were more sensitive to symbolic quality than numerical quantity. If it is accepted that 3:3 is exaggeration, then 120,000 is most likely to be a vast number. Bolin (1997, 159) takes the twelve to hint at an explicit comparison with Israel: "Nineveh is larger than Israel to the nth degree."

"know" translates "know between," that is, to discriminate ("discern," AV; 2 Sam 19:36; Job 34:4). Not turning to the right or the left is used to describe how people travel on a road (Deut 2:27; 1 Sam 6:12) and metaphorically of whole-hearted obedient behaviour in the journey of life along the road of the law (Deut 5:32), as exemplified by David (2 Kgs 22:2). But elsewhere the right has a priority over the left (Gen 48:13–14). How does the phrase apply to pagan Nineveh? Suggestions include: (1) it refers to the density of Nineveh where there are so many people that people do not know who their neighbours are (Sasson 1990)—this would be a unique nuance and so unlikely; (2) it refers to the Ninevites' inability to choose between the good (= the right hand) and the bad (= the left hand; Eccl 10:2)—Nineveh's repentance tells against this; (3) their general moral knowledge is inadequate, so like children they need to develop a sharper moral discernment (1 Kgs 3:5–9; Isa 7:15–16)—but nothing is said about the Ninevites needing to do more than repent; (4) it refers to children (GNB "innocent children") or the mentally deficient (Deut 1:39; Isa 7:15–16)— but the reference is to citizens not children; (5) it might refer to a relative lack of knowledge of God and his law—they are thus worthy of compassion in com- parison to Israel, which has all the benefits of the Torah (Deut 4:6). Indeed, God's compassion for Israel is often related to their human mortality (Pss 78:39; 103:14–16). On this interpretation, then, it neatly reverses Jonah's contrary argument that Israel is more worthy of compassion than Nineveh. For the mention of animals, see on 3:7–8.

Jonah's answer, if he had one, is not recorded. We are left to speculate how he would have responded. Simon (1999) interprets the silence as a humble acknowledgment of God's righteousness (Ps 65:2). Most others prefer to leave the conclusion open as the author invites the reader to take on Jonah's role and respond appropriately (Luke 15:29–32).

MICAH

A. *Micah and His Time*

Our knowledge of the prophet Micah has to be drawn from what we read in the book of Micah, except for a unique and impressive mention in Jer 26:18, a century or so after Micah prophesied in the days of Hezekiah, king of Judah. The priests and prophets have accused Jeremiah for prophesying falsely against Jerusalem. In his defence, the officials and the people cite the words of Micah of Moresheth found in 3:12, also predicting Jerusalem's destruction. Ironically, Jerusalem was not destroyed, and the implication is that this was averted by Hezekiah's repentance. Jeremiah would not find a similar response from the kings of his day, but the precedent was sufficient to save him. This single quotation does not mean that Micah was solely a prophet of doom, but the book shows ample evidence that this was a key aspect of his proclamation.

Both the book of Micah and Jer 26:18 affirm that Micah was from Moresheth, south of Jerusalem (see on 1:1, 14). Unlike the well-connected Isaiah, he was from the country, and attacked the social and political policies that caused such hardship outside the "Establishment." Various attempts have been made to specify his social location more precisely. We can guess from the quality and character of his writing that he was more than a mere labourer or farm worker. Nor is it likely that he belonged to the official prophetic circles, whom he criticized for their collusion with the authorities (3:5–7; cf. Amos 7:14).

Wolff's theory (1978, 6–8; 1990, 5–9) is that Micah functioned as a local elder or head of a clan, and so may have been one of the elders of the land in Jerusalem (1 Kgs 8:3; 20:7). These elders preserved his prophecies, and identified him by his location rather than (as was usual) his father's name. The specific concern of Micah for "my people" (2:8) could also reflect the traditional role of elders in attaining justice for their village. However, we know too little about this class, and characteristic prophetic motifs are sufficient to explain the language and themes of the book (Carreira 1981). The same objections apply to Hillers' proposal (1984, 4–8) that Micah is a prophet of a new age, similar to the millenarian enthusiasts of other ages. Like them, he rages against the economic oppression of his group, and speaks of the need to remove foreign elements (5:10–15), the coming time of troubles (4:9–10), the reversal of the social classes (4:6–7), a future righteous, peaceable ruler (5:2–5[1–4]) and the coming golden age (4:1–4). However, all these features are also aspects of the general prophetic understanding of how God relates to Israel and the nations.

The title of Micah indicates that Micah the prophet prophesied in the eighth century, in the reigns of Jotham (759–43 B.C.E.), Ahaz (or Jehoahaz; 743–27 B.C.E.), and Hezekiah (727–698/9). During this period the Neo-Assyrian empire was rising to power, especially under Tiglath-pileser III (745–727 B.C.E.). His successor, Shalmaneser V (726–22 B.C.E.), attacked Samaria and after a three-year siege it fell to him or his successor, Sargon II (722–705 B.C.E.), who deported its inhabitants to Assyria (1:6). The Assyrians invaded Syria-Palestine several times in subsequent years, above all in 701 B.C.E., when Sennacherib (704–681 B.C.E.) attacked Judah and reached Jerusalem (2 Kgs 18–19; Isa 37–38). It is this invasion that seems the most likely setting for 1:10–16, but as with other parts of Micah, the general nature of the language and the poetic allusive-ness makes determining the setting tentative.

Reconstructing the history of the time is fraught with uncertainty and is both the focus of continuing scholarly investigation (Shaw 1993) as well as scepti-cism (Ben Zvi 2000). What is perhaps most important for understanding Micah is to recognize the general state of insecurity and danger. God's judgment on a sinful people at the hand of an Assyrian army was a possibility that anyone could understand. This warning of immanent judgment is one of the many paral-lels with the message of Isaiah of Jerusalem, and the similarities and differences between Micah and Isaiah have continued to intrigue scholars (Stansell 1988). The verbal overlap between Isa 2:2–5 and Mic 4:1–4 is particularly striking, and discussion continues about who said what first.

B. *The Structure and Integrity of Micah*

The difficulty of discerning the structure of the book is illustrated by the number of books and articles devoted to the issue (Willis 1969c; Hagstrom 1988). The breaks between significant sections (generally the English chapter divisions) are broadly agreed, but there is disagreement over which of these should be com-bined into larger divisions. Scholars have variously proposed two, three, four or six main divisions (Jacobs 2001, 62). One important dispute is whether ch. 3 is more closely related to chs. 1–2 or to chs. 4–5. One key indicator of the begin-ning of a new section is the summons to "hear," which comes in 1:2; 3:1; 6:1. This might suggest a threefold division (chs. 1–2; 3–4; 6–7). Others however point to the definite change of mood from ch. 3 to ch. 4, where the dominant note of judgment becomes one of hope.

Jacobs (2001) argues for two main divisions (1–5; 6–7) that display a similar structure. After an introductory dispute (1:2–16; 6:1–8), there is a discussion of Israel's present plight and God's judgment (2:1–3:12; 6:9–7:6), followed by an announcement of hope for the future (4:1–5:15[14]; 7:7–20). The main question is whether an author or reader would be aware of the long-range parallels between two parts of the book that are unequal in size. My own view is that broader considerations of mood, form and content should take priority over repetition of words. Such repetitions usually indicate significant subdivisions, but not necessarily the major sections of the book. I follow those who find three approximately equal divisions: 1–3; 4–5; 6–7 (Kessler 1999, 36–37; Andersen and Freedman 2000, 23–24). Each of these divisions includes both light and dark, with an overall shift from a dominant note of judgment in chs. 1–3 to a concluding hymn of praise in 7:7–20.

A particular view is often influenced by the approach taken to the growth and editing of the book. Jeppesen (1979) has surveyed the early study of Micah and how it gradually lost its integrity in the eyes of scholars, reflecting a more general scepticism towards the unity and integrity of biblical books. Jacobs (2006) reviews more recent literature and highlights the methodological tensions between historical, literary and reader-oriented approaches. Many continue to hold the view that was proposed by Stade in a famous article published in 1881. The only authentic texts going back to Micah the prophet are chs. 1–3, with the exception of 2:12–13. This historical-critical proposal has encouraged many to regard this as the first part of the book. If chs. 4–5 are held to be later than chs. 1–3, then it is less likely that chs. 1–5 are regarded as a unity. If 7:8–20 is later than 6:1–7:7, another commonly held view, then this too would be an argument for taking this as a distinct part of the book.

Nevertheless a wide range of views continues to be held, as may be illustrated by a selective survey of scholars. On the conservative wing lies Waltke (1993; 1988, 145–49; 2007), who maintains that there is no convincing reason why the superscription attributing the book to Micah cannot cover the whole book. The grammar and language are not evidently exilic, and Micah could have influenced Jeremiah (2:12; Jer 23:1–6). An unusual, if not eccentric, discussion of Micah that attributes the entire book to him is by Shaw (1993), who explains the varied features of Micah by detailed reference to the history of the eighth century. Micah 1:2–16 dates to the reign of Jotham before the death of Jeroboam II (747 B.C.E.); 2:1–13 to the time of Menahem's coup; 3:1–4:8 to the time of Pekah's takeover in Samaria; 4:9–5:15[14] to the Syro-Ephraimite siege of Jerusalem; 6:1–7:7 to the reign of Hoseah before 725 B.C.E., and 7:8–20 is addressed to the inhabitants of Samaria after the first capture of the city in 722–21 B.C.E. Although few, if any, have adopted his proposals, it is a reminder how far the interpretation of texts depends on underlying critical and historical assumptions.

Allen (1976, 251) is more open to later dating, and concludes that it is possible to defend Micah as the origin of the whole book except 4:1–4 (which is probably even earlier), 4:6–8 and 7:8–20, which is postexilic. He rightly points out that it is dangerous to date oracles on the basis of theology. There is no reason why Micah should not have announced salvation as well as judgment, or have introduced concepts of the remnant or the coming king. Rudolph (1971, 25) has a similar evaluation of the book, although he emphasizes that 4:1–4; 5:6–8[7–9] and 7:8–20 are later texts that further reinforce the tendency of the book, whereas this is not so for the later additions of 4:5 and 5:5b–6a[6b–7a].

The views of those who see a far greater contribution by authors and redactors from a later time are more difficult to summarize simply. Wolff (1990, 26) assigns to Micah most of 1:6, 7b–13, 14–16; 2:1–4, 6–11; 3:1–12. The other verses are later comments from a Deuteronomistic point of view. Chapters 4–5 are a collection of sayings from 587 B.C.E. to the early postexilic period. A postexilic move was to edit all of chs. 1–5 and to add the criticism of early postexilic abuses found in 6:2–7:7. A final level of redaction adapted the book for liturgical use, mainly through adding the psalm-like texts of 7:8–20.

Kessler (1999, 44–47) proposes a similar process of growth in five main stages, though with less assurance than Wolff (1990). The voice of the original Micah is found mainly in 1:10–16; 2:1–3, 6–11; 3:1–12. The destruction of Jerusalem motivated 4:8–5:4[3]. A third stage of redaction in the early Persian period saw 1:2–9; 2:4–5, 12–13; 4:1–7; 5:6–7[7–8], 9–14[10–15]. Further experience under the Persians led to 6:1–7:7. A fifth and final stage at the end of the Persian period or the beginning of the Hellenistic era is the origin of a few further additions (4:5; 5:5–6[6–7], 8[9]) and 7:8–20.

More detailed analyses of the development of the book of Micah are available (Metzner 1998; Wagenaar 2001), but two distinctive alternatives to the historical-critical approach should be mentioned. Ben Zvi (2000, 4–11) argues that more attention should be paid to the reading community that the book in its final form was intended to address. This was the learned readership of the late postexilic period. The purpose of the book is to explain Yhwh's punishment of Israel in the past and to communicate hope for the ideal future. This shift of focus allows Ben Zvi to accept a wide range of possible interpretations for the text of Micah. The problem with this approach is that we are so ignorant about these readers that it is difficult to set up controls on the limits of interpretation, and the decision to make this stage of the book decisive in interpretation is somewhat arbitrary.

The second alternative is that of the canonical approach of Childs (1979, 428–39), who emphasizes that it was the final form of the book that is primary for believing readers because this is what is received as holy scripture by the church and the synagogue. For Childs, the "purpose of the book is not to provide sources for the recovery of the 'historical Micah' but rather to incorporate Micah's witness within a larger theological framework" (1979, 437). The final addition of 7:8–20 interprets theologically how the readers of the book stand between God's judgment and salvation, between memory of the past and anticipation of the future.

The value of this approach is that it acknowledges the speculative nature of many of the answers to the traditional questions asked by historical critics. Certainty is impossible because of our general ignorance about how Micah (and other books) were written, edited and transmitted. This is not surprising, since the biblical books were not written to provide us with such information. Arguments about whether a particular idea fits within Micah's time or a later one are particularly difficult to evaluate, since the book of Micah comes to us from a distant time, an alien culture and with a weight of supercommentary that affects our interpretation more than we are aware. The general critical consensus is that it gradually attained its present form in postexilic times, although conservative scholars are still able to argue for a major contribution by Micah the prophet. But it is characteristic of a canonical book that its message was relevant to many different eras, in the era of its early growth and transmission from the eighth century to postexilic times, and to Jews and Christians in subsequent periods.

A commentary of this size cannot deal in detail with issues of the text of Micah. The version printed in the standard critical edition, *Biblia Hebraica Stuttgartensia* (*BHS*), is that of the Leningrad Codex from 1008 C.E. There are numerous difficulties in making sense of the text, but we are often unsure whether this is because the Hebrew text is corrupt, or because we have not sufficiently understand the compressed and allusive poetic style of Micah. The early translations often differ markedly, but this is more likely to be testimony to early interpretive creativity than evidence of a different underlying text. In recent years there has been less confidence in proposing emendations, and in many cases it is possible to make some sense of the traditional MT. A number of fragments of Micah have been discovered among the Dead Sea Scrolls, but these have not shown significant variations from the MT (Sinclair 1983).

C. *The Message of the Book of Micah*

The following overview sets aside questions of dating and authorship in order to sketch the message of the book of Micah (Mays 1977; Marrs 1999; contrast Mosala 1993). However many hands were in the composition, the canonical status of the book encourages the assumption that there is sufficient continuity for such theological reflection to be valid. This assumption guides how different parts of the book are integrated even when connections are not explicitly made.

The two most fundamental assumptions of the book are that Yhwh is the sovereign God over all the earth (4:13), yet also that Israel is his covenant people (2:8; 6:2, 3 5) whom he rescued from Egypt and preserved through the generations (6:4–5). The contingent interplay between the universal God and the particular people whom he has chosen is the reason why the language, the form and the theology of Micah is so complex. The nations of the world are present, but in a secondary role. They are agents of Yhwh's purposes (1:6–7), but their ultimate fate depends on how they relate to him and his people. Positively, they can acknowledge Yhwh as the source of all wisdom and knowledge (4:2) and receive the blessings of justice, peace and prosperity (4:3–4). Yet they can also foolishly set themselves up against Yhwh, his city and his people (4:11–12) and so suffer the consequences (4:13; 5:5–9[4–8]; 7:16–17).

The theological structure that underlies the way in which Yhwh's sovereignty is worked out is a sequence of sin, judgment and restoration (Miller 1982). God's judgment on sin is first of all regarded as his direct will and action. The "I" of the prophetic divine speech is unequivocal (2:3; 5:10–15[9–14]). In the theophany of 1:3–4, he descends in person to judge the transgressions of both the Northern and the Southern Kingdoms (1:3–5). Samaria's judgment at the hands of the Assyrians is proof of the truth of Micah's words (1:6–7), but is quickly passed over in order to concentrate on the Southern Kingdom, which still has time to hear and repent. The agents of his judgment are the nations, and this is presupposed by the portrayal of invasion (1:10–16), siege (5:1[4:14]) and exile (4:10).

Sin and judgment dominate the first three chapters. The focus of the opening accusation is the religious sin of the two kingdoms (1:5), but this gives way to a fierce condemnation of injustices arising from the economic and social policies of the privileged classes in Israel. Religion and ethics are inseparably linked in Israel's traditions (Exod 20:1–17) and are emphasized in a powerful and creative way in 6:1–8. Those with most responsibility, the leaders of the people (2:1–5), bear the brunt of his denunciations, but Micah makes sure he includes those who by their actions and words support them—the priests, the prophets and the judges (3:5, 11). Throughout it is assumed that they know that such behaviour is wrong, and that justice, not selfish gain, is the primary responsibility of those with power and influence (3:1, 8–9). Micah is not an innovator in the realms of ethics, for the prophets have no distinctive ethic of their own. Rather, they recall their hearers to the standards of behaviour they are committed to through their membership of God's covenant people (6:8; Janzen 1994).

A key feature of Micah's criticism relates to the unjust use of power to seize the land of the poor and the weak (2:2; Allen 1973). The importance of land as God's gift to his covenant people cannot be underestimated (Brueggemann 2003), and the laws were designed to prevent the accumulation of wealth that was characteristic of other nations (Lev 25; Deut 15; 1 Sam 8). Coveting the property of others was forbidden by the tenth commandment (Exod 20:17; Mic 2:2). The result of the abuse of inheritance rights will be the invasion of the land and the destruction of its chief city, Jerusalem (3:12). This is just one example of a key principle of justice that Micah works out in a number of places, the *lex talionis*, the principle that the punishment fits the crime (1:7; 2:4, 10:3–4, 7; see Obadiah, Section E).

The specific condemnations of the wealthy and privileged classes in chs. 2–3 gives way to oracles addressed to the people as a whole in 4–7. Although this might reflect a different time and situation, it could also be a matter of context and audience. The leaders may be singled out because of their special responsibility, but it is quite likely that the general population was not significantly more righteous. They would typically follow the behaviour and practices of the influential, limited only by opportunity. The possibility of general social breakdown through self-serving and distrust of even the closest relations is vividly portrayed in 7:1–7.

Yet not all is gloom. The purpose of God's judgment is not annihilation but restoration. Micah's language and message is intended to evoke a response. Yhwh's spirit inspires the prophet not only through the content of his proclamation (3:8) but also through the powerful rhetoric of his style. The play of sounds and words, the repetition with variation, the use of multiple genres, the alternation of voices and perspectives, all serve to reinforce the message (Peytrotten 1991). We should not make too much of the absence of an explicit call to repentance in the early chapters (contrast Wolff 1990, 14–17). The proclamation of a future gathering of a scattered people in 2:12–13 reflects the authentic prophetic hope that beyond judgment lies salvation. Only then will God's promises to Abraham and the ancestors of old be fulfilled through the exercise of his compassion and forgiveness (7:19–20).

Before this, though, the nation must endure many tribulations. It is unlikely that the central chs. 4–5 bear any simple relationship to the history of Israel, but the implication is that the prophet was well aware of the depths of the people's sinfulness, and that Yhwh's turning from wrath to mercy would only come through an acceptance of God's harsh judgment (4:10–5:1[4:14]; 7:8–10). This is the message of the famous royal passage in 5:1–5[4:14–5:4]. The ruler of Israel is humiliated (5:1[4:14]), but a new David will arise who will be the shepherd king all desire, the ultimate contrast to the present rulers of the people. The shepherd image returns in 7:14, this time describing God himself. The king can be at most an under-shepherd, mediating Yhwh's justice and blessing. The result of salvation is an exhilarating vision of a restored city, people, land and earth. Jerusalem may be destroyed (3:12), but the restored Zion will be the source of justice and the true knowledge of God (4:1–2). This will be the key to peace and prosperity for all (4:3–4). The mythology of God's dwelling on the highest mountain is evoked (4:1), as well as memories of the distant golden age of blessing that accompanied the conquest (7:14–15).

Even if Hezekiah's Jerusalem resisted the Assyrian onslaught, there was to be no essential reconfiguring of the pattern in the transmission of the text. Sooner or later the kings of Judah would be struck down and taken away, the city destroyed, and the people uprooted from their land. Equally, Micah's vision of suffering and restoration would remain a precious source of hope and inspiration to later generations. All this will be a satisfactory fulfilment of the promises given to Abraham of old (7:21).

The difficulty in determining the historical setting of many passages in Micah strongly suggests that the canonical text has been modified in the course of transmission to become a more general vehicle of prophetic insight and theology. A number of its themes are appropriate for the postexilic period (Mays 1976, 26–33; Mason 1991, 43–53). As other postexilic texts show (Zech 1–8), there were plenty of opportunities for the rich and powerful to better themselves at the expense of others, and many retained their hope for God to come and fully restore the people and glorify Jerusalem among the nations. The hope of a new David is also to be found in exilic and postexilic texts (Ezek 34:24; Zech 9:9–10; 12:7–9).

A number of quotations and allusions in the Dead Sea Scrolls testify to the ongoing power of Micah's words (CD 4:12, 20; 16:15; 1QSb 5:26), and 1Q14 is a commentary on verses of Micah (also the badly preserved 4Q168). In the New Testament, the most famous quotation is of Mic 5:2[1] in Matthew (Matt 2:6).

D. *Outline Analysis of Micah*

Judgment and Doom for the Wicked: Chapters 1–3

Title	1:1
God's judgment on his people	1:2–9
Lament over the towns of Judah	1:10–16
Weep and Wail, You Rich!	2:1–13
Woe to the land-grabbers	2:1–5
The complacent refuted	2:6–11
Hope for the scattered sheep	2:12–13
Judgment on Israel's Corrupt Leaders	3:1–12
Judgment on the greedy	3:1–4
Judgment on the false prophets	3:5–8
Judgment on the establishment	3:9–12

Hope for the Future: Chapters 4–5

The joy of all the earth	4:1–5
From weakness to strength	4:6–8
Exile and rescue	4:9–10
Attack and defeat	4:11–13
Humiliation and hope	5:1–4
Victory over Assyria	5:5–6
The triumph of the remnant	5:7–9
The refining of the remnant	5:10–15

From Reproof to Praise: Chapters 6–7

What the lord requires	6:1–8
Judgment on the corrupt city	6:9–20
Lament, judgment and hope	7:1–7
Hope for the future	7:8–20

Judgment and Doom for the Wicked (Chapters 1–3)

Title (1:1)

The first and primary statement made by the title is a claim of divine inspiration for the prophecy of Micah, traditionally understood to embrace the entire canonical book. "came to" (literally "was to") implies movement and activity, thus emphasizing the divine initiative. Insight into the will of God is not attained through the manipulative techniques of a diviner (3:7; Andersen and Freedman 2000). Three qualifying phrases show how this word from God was mediated through a prophet to a people in a particular chronological and historical context. The phrases specify (a) the addressee ("to Micah"; cf. Hos 1:1; Joel 1:1;

Zeph 1:1), (b) the chronological context ("in the days of…"; cf. Isa 1:1; Hos 1:1; (c) the object ("concerning…"; cf. Isa 1:1; 2:1; Amos 1:1) of the vision ("saw"; cf. Isa 1:1; 2:1; Amos 1:1). Different titles of the prophetic books have variations on these elements, which were probably editorial introductions to collections of oracles. Wolff (1990, 33) suggests as an earlier form "Words of Micah, the Moreshite, which he saw concerning Samaria and Jerusalem," but it is impossible to trace the development with any certainty. The work of editing and transmitting that allows us to read the words today reflects a humble concern to allow the divine word to speak with power to future generations. Jeremiah 26:18–19 is an example where the word revealed through Micah in the past affected the politics of a later time.

"The word of Yhwh" is a technical term for divine revelation, reflecting a God who speaks critically into a particular situation. At the same time it is a human word, for it "came to Micah of Moresheth." The empowering of the prophets by God's spirit (3:8) explains why Micah is bold to address Israel and the nations of the world with divine authority. Micah is a common name, used by several different persons in the Old Testament and found in several different spellings. *mîkâ* is a shortened form of *mîkāyâh*, which is how Micah is named in the LXX here (*Michaias*) and in the written Hebrew text of Jer 26:18 (the vowels indicate the shorter form should be read). The name means "who [is] like Yah[weh]," an expression of the uniqueness and incomparability of the God of Israel, whose proper name is indicated by the consonants *y-h-w-h* (Yhwh).

"of Moresheth" is an adjective, so more literally "the Morashtite" (NJPS). He is identified as the Micah of his home village, reflecting an outsider's perspective (cf. "Jeremiah of Anathoth," Jer 29:27). Normally a person is identified in relation to his father (Isa 1:1; Hos 1:1). This was one of the reasons why Wolff (1978, 6–8) developed his theory about Micah's status and role as a head of his clan (see Section A, above). However, Micah's impact in Jerusalem as an outsider may well have been sufficient reason for this identification. In 1:14 the village is more specifically Moresheth-Gath ("possession of Gath") and is normally identified as Tel ej-Judeideh, 10 km northeast of Lachish and 35 km southwest of Jerusalem. If this is correct, then the full name probably indicates that it was a satellite village of Gath, the Philistine city which had fallen into Israelite hands. It is on the border of the Shephelah, the foothills to the east of Jerusalem and the Judean hills. It was a crucial military region, since it was the area through which armies had to come from the coastal plain to reach Jerusalem. Within a circle of 10 km there were five of the fortified cities that Rehoboam is reported to have built (2 Chr 11:5–12), four of which are mentioned in 1:8–16 (Adullam, Gath, Mareshah, Lachish). It is possible that Micah's prophecies dealt (at least in part) with specific injustices that derived from dealings that the soldiers and rulers of these cities had with Micah's home village. Moresheth was probably destroyed in Sennacherib's 701 B.C.E. campaign (2 Kgs 18:13–16).

Using M. Cogan's dates, Jotham ruled from 759–43 B.C.E., Ahaz (or Jehoahaz) from 743–27 B.C.E. and Hezekiah from 727–698 B.C.E. (Cogan 1992, 1002–1011). Jeremiah 26:18 mentions a prophecy by Micah during the days of

Hezekiah about Jerusalem's destruction (cf. 3:9–12), but this limits neither the scope of his prophecy nor the duration of his ministry. Most of the oracles in chs. 1–3 plausibly relate to the reign of Hezekiah. Significant events during the reigns of these kings are known not just from the Old Testament but also from the Assyrian annals of the kings (Na'aman 1979). In 734 B.C.E. there is a record of Ahaz paying tribute to Tiglath-pileser III (*ANET* 282), who in 732 B.C.E. responded to a plea for support (Isa 7) and captured a considerable portion of the Northern Kingdom, taking away many of its people into exile (2 Kgs 15:29–30). The fall of Samaria in 722 B.C.E. in the fifth year of Shalmaneser is described in various Assyrian records (e.g. *ANET* 284) as well as the Old Testament (2 Kgs 17:1–6). This was in Hezekiah's sixth year (2 Kgs 18:10), and during the following years Hezekiah captured territory from the north and from Philistia and took part in planning a major rebellion against Assyria. Sennacherib acted to quell the rebellion in the great campaign of 701 B.C.E. He advanced first down the coastal plain, defeating the Egyptian armies supporting the anti-Assyrian coalition at Eltekeh. He then moved across towards Jerusalem, besieging and taking several towns along the way, including Lachish. The Israelite perspective on his subsequent withdrew from Jerusalem and return home is given in 2 Kgs 18–19.

"saw" is the special "vision" verb *ḥāzâ* ("he received it in visions," REB; Isa 1:1; Amos 1:1; Hab 1:1). For the coalescence of the visual and the auditory, see on Obad 1. Alternatively "which" can be "who" and refer to Micah, as in NJB's "who prophesied." The subject of the vision is Samaria and Jerusalem, the capital cities standing by metonymy for the Northern and Southern Kingdoms (Israel and Judah). Samaria is the object of the oracle of judgment in 1:6–7, whereas Jerusalem is the main recipient of Micah's words in the rest of the book. Samaria comes first both because it was overthrown first and because Micah uses its sins as a foundation for his condemnation of Judah (compare Amos's strategy in Amos 1–2). Andersen and Freedman (2000) even suggest that chs. 1–3 were composed before the fall of Samaria, and that Micah's successful prediction of the fall of the Northern Kingdom was one incentive for Hezekiah's reforms

God's Judgment on His People (1:2–9)

Scholars have used the different elements of this chapter to find two (vv. 1–9, 10–16), three (vv. 1–7, 8–9, 10–16) or more sections. It seems best to see vv. 8–9 as a personal response to the general announcement of judgment (vv. 2–7) followed by a lamentation focusing more specifically on various towns (vv. 10–16). The use of several subgenres is deliberately designed to gain attention, intensify the impact of the words, and so break through the barriers the people and leaders have put up against receiving the prophet's hard message. There is a unified theme, namely, the certainty of God's judgment, communicated in various ways. It is prepared for by a universal summons to hear (v. 2) and the report of a theophany, namely, the awesome cosmic manifestation of God (vv. 3–4). An accusation (v. 5) explains the need for judgment on both the Northern and

Southern Kingdoms, represented by their capital cities. Together vv. 2–5 comprise the indictment that is the basis for the announcement of the destruction of Samaria (vv. 6–7). The fearful implications are drawn out by Micah's statement of his own mourning (v. 8). A transition verse (v. 9) moves the focus onto Judah and towards its capital Jerusalem. The prophet summons various cities to mourn, for they will be destroyed by an invading army on its way to Jerusalem (vv. 10–16). The fact that this pitiful catalogue of destruction does not yet include Jerusalem magnifies the terror of that event by making it the implicit climax, all the more terrible for being unstated.

The relation of the prophecy to historical events is unclear (Fohrer 1981). Assuming a close relation to Micah's ministry, the first part appears to refer to the fall of the Northern Kingdom in 722 B.C.E. The prophecy of destruction is future and not closely related to the actual events, so could be dated shortly before the fall of Samaria (de Moor 1988, 182). But the whole chapter is unified in various ways, by language, tone, and movement, and the references to the towns of Judah in the second part of the chapter, which fell to Sennacherib later in 701 B.C.E. One attractive proposal is that Micah incorporated an earlier prophecy against Samaria into one against Judah around 701 B.C.E. But it is also possible that the whole chapter was formulated around this date. While strictly anachronistic if this is the case, the reminder that earlier prophecies against Samaria had come to pass would have reinforced the inevitability of the coming punishment of Judah and the need to do something about it. The coalescence of the Northern and Southern Kingdoms could explain the general character of the opening (vv. 2–4) and the fluidity of the term "Israel," which refers to the Northern Kingdom in v. 5, but to Judah in vv. 14, 15.

The shifts of perspective during the first half of the chapter (e.g. the universal vv. 2–4, the specific vv. 5–7) have suggested to many critics the presence of Deuteronomistic and postexilic redactional additions (Wolff 1990, 52–53; McKane 1995). However, there are no clear anachronistic elements in the section and there seems no compelling reason why Micah cannot take the credit for the powerful rhetoric of the chapter. Later readers would in any case interpret the chapter (and the rest of the book) against an eighth-century background, however extensive the additions (Ben Zvi 1998).

1:2. The prophets often begin on the largest stage, before narrowing down to God's people (Amos 1–2; Zeph 1:2–6). This summons, "Hear, you peoples," has been understood to be part of a prophetic lawsuit, but there is relatively little resemblance to what might have occurred in a real court of law (Daniels 1987; see on 6:1–8). "all of you" is literally "all of them," but such grammatical incongruence is often found (GKC 135r; JM 146j), not least in the close parallel of 1 Kgs 22:28. In that text the prophet Micaiah addresses the peoples or tribes of Israel and Judah, but here the parallel line and the wider context implies that the perspective is global. The first phrase is plural, the second singular, but both refer to the whole world. "and all that is in it" is literally "and its fullness" (Ps 24:1). The double call to attention in the first phrase ("hear," "listen") is so that the nations pay close attention to the message that God is a "witness against you (pl.)." This could theoretically be read "among you" (REB), but it is more likely that it identifies the guilty party (Deut 31:26; Jer 42:5). Yhwh is prosecutor as well as judge ("accuser," NJPS; "intends to give evidence against you," NJB). The cosmic context suggests that the holy temple is God's heavenly dwelling-place (Ps 11:4; Hab 2:20), rather than the earthly temple, but the two were intimately connected. The holiness of the temple derives from God's presence in it, which thus distinguishes it from all other places. Because God is also the supreme king, the temple is at the same time his palace (1 Kgs 22:19–28; Isa 6). The localization of Yhwh in the temple recognizes that there are places outside where the nations and the gods do not acknowledge his rule. But the summons to judgment and the theophany (vv. 3–4) also show that there is only one final and legitimate power in heaven and on earth.

The relation between the lawsuit against the nations and the condemnation of Samaria and Judah is left undefined. Elsewhere the nations can be witnesses to the trial of God's people (Amos 3:9–11; Andersen and Freedman 2000), but interpreting "against you" as referring to Samaria and Judah is forced. It is more likely that the nations are being condemned for their transgressions (Isa 34), but this is not pursued because the focus is on the guilt of God's people. Judgment against the nations is sometimes a signal of hope for God's oppressed people, so Micah may be ironically imitating the triumphalist message of the popular prophets who preached what the people wanted to hear (3:5). Micah thus gained the attention of his hearers, before turning the tables on them by announcing that this same God will exercise his sovereign power to punish them (Rudolph 1971; Willis 1968b).

1:3. At the end of the previous verse attention was fixed on Yhwh in his temple. The next two verses begin there but move the image from a passive witness to an active event, a theophany, a majestic manifestation of God's presence. Theophanies usually contain three main elements: Yhwh's coming, the reaction of nature to his coming, and its effect on the human plane. The latter is generally judgment on God's enemies and so the salvation of those who call to him (Judg 5:4–5; Isa 64:1–3; Nah 1:2–8; *Ass. Moses* 10:3). The theophany thus explains ("For lo") why the nations are to stand and listen (Ps 46:10). God has pronounced his verdict and is now about to execute the sentence. However, as the hearers will soon realize, the prophets sometimes dramatically reverse this expectation, instead asserting that God comes to punish his people who have now become the enemy (Amos 1:2; 5:18–20). The cosmic and theological language of the theophany serves to interpret and deepen the significance of the historical events referred to in the rest of the chapter.

"lo" (*hinnê*, "behold," AV) completes the shift of attention begun in the previous phrase from the nations to Yhwh, whose journey from heaven to earth is then described. The starting point is his "place" (*māqôm*), perhaps short for his dwelling place ("home," NJB; cf. 1 Kgs 8:30) but it can also refer to God's sanctuary (Isa 26:21; Hag 2:9; Gamberoni and Ringgren 1997, 532–44) and so links to v. 2 ("his holy temple"). "coming out" is often a going forth to war

(Deut 20:1; Isa 42:13). The participle form indicates that this action is immanent (Isa 19:1; GKC §116p). It is the prelude to a descent, the usual language for spanning the ontological and spatial distance between God's realm and that of humans (John 6:36–51). In Ps 18:8–16[7–15], Yhwh rides on the clouds and is manifest in terrifying atmospheric phenomena. Here, he will even "tread upon the high places of the earth" (Amos 4:13; Hab 3:19). "walk" (REB) is too feeble a translation of the tread verb (*drk*), which can describe the trampling of grapes (Job 24:11) or the backs of enemies (Deut 33:29), and the crushing of serpents (Ps 91:13). The high places (*bāmôt*) are the mountainous backbone of earth (v. 3), the hardest route available for humans (Ps 18:33[34]), but convenient stepping-stones for God. Although the everlasting mountains stand the best chance of withstanding his coming (Ps 76:4[5]), the next verse shows that the weight and power of Yhwh overwhelms even them. The greatness of God is communicated by portraying a person of crushing weight and gigantic size (M.S. Smith 1988).

1:4. The highly metaphoric and anthropomorphic character of this verse makes interpretation difficult. The imagery is not simply that of a thunderstorm, an earthquake or a volcano, for it is the tread of God that causes the upheavals. It is possible that the two lines demonstrate external parallelism, that is, the first and third phrases refer to the same phenomenon (the mountains melt like wax), as do the second and fourth (the valleys burst open like waters). The REB prosaically rearranges the phrases accordingly. If so, then a unified picture can be constructed. The four parts of the verse are unified by liquid imagery (melted wax, the waters) and by a progressive geological movement (the crumbling of the mountains down into the valleys). Just as stone crumbles and flows like melting wax under too great a weight, so do the mountains under Yhwh's tread (Ps 97:5). The perspective then shifts down into the valleys. If these are still higher than the coastlands, then we may imagine these rapidly collapsing and so pouring down similar to the way waters pour down a steep place. The overall effect is of a levelling of high and low under God's irresistible tread.

This seems preferable to other interpretations. The third and fourth phrases may describe what happens to the mountains rather than the valleys (Achtemeier 1996), but this undermines the expected parallelism. Alternatively, it could be the valleys (the fertile, inhabited lowlands) that burst open along fault lines caused by his titanic tread (Mays 1976), but the water analogy is then forced. Whatever the precise imagery, the implications for the hearers is plain through an implicit *a fortiori* argument. If the strongest and most stable features of earth cannot stand before Yhwh, how can a nation? Nor is there any place to hide from such a God (Hos 10:8; Rev 6:16).

1:5. The first part of the rhetorical trap is sprung. "All this" will indicate that the reason for the coming of God is that the people of God, rather than the nations, will be judged. The verse is marked off from the previous three by having three phrases (a tricolon), a change that often indicates a climax or the end of a section.

Neither Jacob nor Israel has an unambiguous referent. As the names of the original ancestors they stand for all the tribes, particularly when used in parallelism. The ancient character of these terms evokes an ideal of the united and faithful people of God. After the division of the nation (1 Kgs 12), Jacob and Israel could also refer to the Northern Kingdom. Thus in 1:13 the transgressions of Israel (i.e. the Northern Kingdom) are found in Zion. Once the Northern Kingdom fades from view, Judah can be addressed as Jacob//Israel (3:1, 8, 9), since it is the only remaining representative of God's people, although it may also point to the future hope that God will restore all the tribes (5:2–3). In this verse we might expect "the house of Judah" instead of "house of Israel" in the first part of the verse, since the two kingdoms are indicated in the rest of the verse. However, such an emendation (*BHS*) is not supported by the versions and it is more likely that the opening refers to both, while the next two lines refer to the kingdoms separately. From a rhetorical point of view, it may be that Micah leaves the meaning of Jacob//house of Israel ambiguous so as to make the final phrase the climactic punchline. Only when Judah and Jerusalem are specified do the hearers begin to realize that this is not merely a condemnation of the Northern Kingdom. Micah acknowledges the realities of the political divisions, but at the same time activates terms that remind the people that such divisions were tragic results of oppression and not God's primary will.

A full and open declaration of judgment on Jerusalem is delayed until 1:8–16 and 3:12 (where some of the same language as in vv. 5–7 is used). As the centre of power and influence and displaying the highest degree of corruption, the two capitals bear primary responsibility and will not escape destruction. The questions is more properly "Who is to blame" (TEV, NLT) rather than "what," reflecting a personification of the cities (Shaw 1993, 33).

"sins" (*ḥaṭṭāʾt*) is the most common and general term for deliberate fault. "transgression" (*pešaʿ*) is appropriate in the context of Yhwh's charge against his people, for it is a word with strong legal overtones ("crime," REB, NJB). However, the political and religious context also implies rebellion (NLT; Isa 1:2) or even treachery. The transgression of Jacob is defined as Samaria, the capital city of the North founded by Omri (1 Kgs 16:24). After it was destroyed by the Assyrians (in 722 or 721 B.C.E.; 2 Kgs 17:6), it became the name of the region. Its sins and fate is expounded in the next two verses. Corresponding to Samaria is Jerusalem, which is condemned for its "high place," although in the Hebrew this is plural (*bāmôt*; cf. AV). It is a surprising parallel for transgression, and the versions have "the sin of Judah" (Syr., Targ.; followed by REB) or "sin of the house of Judah" (LXX; so RSV, NJB). However, the parallel is found in Hos 10:8 and we should retain the more difficult MT (supported by 1QpMic; Symm.; Vulg.). It also prepares for the talionic judgment of 3:12, where Jerusalem will become a "wooded height" (the same word). It describes a cultic installation ("shrines," NJPS), traditionally associated with the heights, although the evidence for this is disputed (Barrick 1992). By metonymy the word could then be used for places of worship wherever they might be situated. Though some of these locations are the scene for authentic worship of Yhwh (1 Sam 9:16–24), they were increasingly associated with the worship of Baal and other gods (2 Kgs 17:9–12; Jer 19:4–5). Micah was probably condemning syncretism, although he might also have been criticizing the failure to centralize worship in the temple, which would also allow closer control over who was being worshipped (though not necessarily Ezek 8).

1:6. In announcing the reason for judgment ("therefore") Micah adopts the divine first person voice (contrast the third person voice in Isa 28:1–4). Samaria will become a formless heap of rubble, a ruin (ʿî, Ps 79:1; this will also be Jerusalem's fate in Mic 3:12). Abandoned by its people, it is now part of the sparsely populated "open country" (*śādeh*, "the field," AV, NAB). Instead of defensive slopes leading up to impressive walls, there are terraces where vines can be planted. *śādeh* can also be translated "hillside" (Judg 5:18), thus making a parallel to the hill Samaria (1 Kgs 16:24): "I will make Samaria into a ruin, the hill(side) (into a place) for vineyard plantings" (Wagenaar 1996, 30). This also makes an even closer parallel between the fates of Samaria and Jerusalem (3:12). The second half of the verse is earlier chronologically and explains how this is to come about. The battering-rams of the conquering army will demolish the walls, so that their stones will be poured down (the same root as in v. 3) into the valley. While the rams demolish the walls, the sappers would uncover the foundations, so that the walls were also undermined. Samaria's doom is assured, through both visible and hidden forces of destruction.

This is the historical counterpart of the metaphoric language of vv. 3–4, but it is God's will that is decisive, so no particular agents of judgment are mentioned. Shalmaneser V of Assyria (727–722 B.C.E.) began to besiege Samaria, which fell after three years to his successor Sargon II (722–705 B.C.E.). He did not in fact destroy Samaria but deported the people and replaced them with foreigners (2 Kgs 17:23–24). It became the capital of the province of Samaria until captured by Alexander the Great, when it became a Greek city. It was destroyed by John Hercanus in 107 B.C.E. (Josephus, *Ant.* 13.10.3) but rebuilt and occupied since then. The lack of any precise historical fulfilment of this oracle was of little concern, partly because it is evidently rhetorical and partly because the mode of fulfilment depended on many factors. It was devastating enough that "its inhabitants, the living stones, were deported to Assyria and went into the valley of death, never again to return" (Alfaro 1989, 17).

1:7. Micah 1–3 primarily condemns the moral failings of God's people, although there are occasional references to religious practice (1:5; 3:11). Shaw (1993, 33, 48–50) translates the three main terms as hewn stones, riches and carvings, and finds here a condemnation of Samaria's costly building program. However, the Northern Kingdom was associated with various forms of idolatry, especially Baal worship (1 Kgs 16:32; 22:53), and the nouns and verbs used here are found in contexts of idolatry.

"All her images" introduces a condemnation of idolatry corresponding to Judah's shrines in v. 5. There Samaria's sins were described in general terms ("transgression"). Here, the triple "all" and the repetition of words belonging to the semantic field of idolatry gives the impression of a city full of idols. As a parallel to images (*pesel*) and idols (*ʿāṣāḇ*) we expect another of the dozen or so Hebrew terms for idols, but instead we find "wages." There is no textual support for omitting the second phrase (*BHS*) or replacing it with another word for "images" (REB; Watson 1984). Yet the parallelism can be maintained if it is shorthand for idols that Samaria has purchased by means of its wages. "wages" (*ʾetnan*, derived from *ntn*, "give") describes the payment made to a prostitute (Deut 23:18). It is also found in metaphorical passages referring to political and commercial allegiances with other nations (Isa 23:17–18) and the worship of other gods (Ezek 16:34, 41). Yhwh can be portrayed as Israel's husband (*baʿal*, Jer 3:14; Hos 2:16[18]). When Israel looks to other gods or nations for gain, it was equivalent to hiring itself out as a prostitute (Hos 9:1; cf. 2:12[14]; 8:9, 10; Goodfriend 1992; van der Toorn 1992). The national character of the oracles makes it less likely that this is a reference to cultic prostitution, where temples sponsored prostitutes, or at least benefited from their trade through votive offerings. Rather, commercial allegiances to other nations provided the incentive to include the worship of other gods, and the wealth with which to buy idols.

The message of the powerlessness of idols and the futility of Israel's trust in them is hammered home by repeated verbs of destruction: the passives "beaten to pieces," "burned with fire" (cf. v. 4), and the active "I will lay waste." In Deuteronomy the Israelites are commanded to burn (Deut 7:5) or hew (Deut 12:3) the images (*pᵉsîl*), idols made of wood, stone or metal. Since Samaria has failed to do this, God himself ensures that they are beaten to pieces, as was the golden calf (Deut 9:21), the bronze serpent (2 Kgs 18:4) and the idols of Josiah's time (2 Chr 34:4).

The final line uses "wages" twice more, and seems to refer to the "before" and "after" of destruction. The Northern Kingdom gathered the wages (i.e. used foreign trade to multiply idols) during its illusory days of peace. But those same idols will become spoils of war for the invading soldiers who will use them as wages in payment for the services of a prostitute. The circle would be complete if these were prostitutes who passed on their earnings to the Assyrian temples. The underlying principle is that of the *lex talionis*. The correspondence between crime and punishment is highlighted through the use of the same word.

1:8. "For this" links to the previous verses. God has been speaking in vv. 6–7, and is again the speaker in v. 9 ("my people"; cf. Beal 1994). However, this verse is distinct, and the extremely physical description of mourning seems to fit a human speaker rather than God, and the prophet is the most obvious candidate. Lament is Micah's response to the announcement of judgment. The reversion to his own prophetic persona ("I") invites us to share his reaction to God's judgment. The prophets weep for those they are called to condemn, however much they deserve punishment.

The vocal expression of grief ("lament and wail") is primary (Amos 5:16), but possibly accompanied by the beating of breasts (Isa 32:12) and tears (Ezek 24:16). Other mourning customs are found in vv. 10 and 16 (cf. Ezek 27:30–32). "wail" (*wᵉʾēlîlâ* from *yll*) is onomatopoeic, suggesting the special mourning technique of ululation, a long, oscillating, high-pitched sound. "Barefoot" is one translation of a difficult word (elsewhere only Job 12:17, 19; another word is used in 2 Sam 15:30; Isa 20:3). Others have "stripped" (AV, NJB) or "despoiled" (REB), the preliminary step to becoming naked. Normal mourning involves sackcloth (see on Jonah 3:5–6), so "naked" suggests that Micah, like Isaiah (Isa 20:2–4), uses the lack of clothing to symbolize the fate of the future Jewish deportees (1:16). We may imagine these prisoners as being without an outer garment (i.e. "stripped"), but Assyrian reliefs also portray prisoners who are completely naked (*ANEP* nos. 332, 373). The terrible hurt and intensity of mourning is evoked by the comparison to the howls of jackals and the screeches of ostriches (REB's "wolf" and "desert-owl" [cf. Driver 1955] is less likely). An association with creatures of the desert is fitting since the survivors of the destruction will share the same habitat.

1:9. The reason for lament is that the past judgment on Samaria (v. 9a, recalling vv. 6–7) anticipates the future judgment on Judah and Jerusalem (v. 9b, anticipating vv. 10–16). The first two phrases begin with *kî* (NRSV ignores the second), which can be either explanatory ("for…for," AV; LXX, Vulg.) or a particle of emphasis ("indeed…surely," Wolff 1990). A mixture of the two is less likely because of the parallelism. The first possibility gives two reasons for Micah's mourning: Samaria's destruction and Judah's immanent conquest. The second alternative stresses the terrible certainty of the judgment (GKC §159ee). Micah mourns for both kingdoms, since together Samaria and Judah constitute the people of God.

"her wound" is plural in the Hebrew ("her wounds," RV), so why is the verb singular? (a) *BHS* suggests that the feminine suffix is an abbreviation of the divine name (*yh*) should be read ("the wounds that Yahweh inflicts," NJB). But there is little evidence for this abbreviation. (b) A slight emendation reads the singular. (c) The plural could be an abstract plural (GKC §145k; Schibler 1989). "wound" (*makā*) can describe either a "blow" (often of a military nature, Josh 10:10) or its result, a wound (1 Kgs 22:35). A divinely inflicted wound (Deut 28:59, 61) is as inescapable as an arrow (Job 34:6) and incurable (2 Sam 12:15; Isa 17:11). Yhwh is ultimately responsible, even if his agent is the Assyrian army.

The larger context suggests that the invasion of Judah is future, in which case the past tenses in the verse are the prophetic perfect, reflecting the certainty that God's threats will come to pass. The successive phrases evoke the successive victories of the conqueror: the towns of Judah (anticipating vv. 10–16), then finally "Jerusalem, the gate of my people." The gate of a town was its strategic entrance and the heart of political and commercial life (Ruth 3:11). Possession of a city's gates meant that the city had fallen (Gen 22:17), and its fate was in the hands of victors (Jer 39:3). "my people" (see on Obad 13) suggests that the nation is being spoken of metaphorically as a town. Jerusalem is the heart (the gate) of the entire nation, and once it fell, the nation's independent existence was finished. "reached" (*nāgaʿ*) suggests that the judgment is immanent but not quite complete. The account in 2 Kgs 18–19 describes Jerusalem's near escape in 701 B.C.E., but the rhetorical effect of the oracle is to appeal to hearers to act before it is too late.

Lament Over the Towns of Judah (1:10–16)

This lament is the continuation and more detailed exposition of what was announced in v. 8, so that many regard vv. 8–16 as a main subsection of the chapter (both v. 8 and v. 16 also include allusions to animals). A significant difference in vv. 10–16 is that Micah addresses various towns directly in the lament. These towns include a number that were significant in the life of David (Gath in v. 10, Adullam in v. 15). In vv. 10–13, judgment is proclaimed as if the towns had already been destroyed. This is a powerful rhetorical way of communicating the certainty and inevitability of destruction (compare the comments on the prophetic perfect in v. 9). In vv. 14–16, imperfect verbs are mainly used, implying that the destruction is in the near future. Assyria is not named (contrast Isa 8:7) since the focus is on the certainty of the coming judgment. Since Jerusalem is the goal of the invasion (vv. 9, 12), it would be fitting if the oracle was proclaimed there first, but this can only be an attractive speculation.

The opening is a quotation of 2 Sam 1:20, a poem defined as a funeral lament, a *qînâ* (2 Sam 1:17; J. M. P. Smith 1911, 45). However, this is characteristically transformed from an individual to a national lament (Jer 9:10–22; Ezek 19:1–14; Isa 14). The prophet portrays the immanent death of the body corporate of Judah, with particular reference to those towns in the Shephelah on the likely path of an invading army approaching Jerusalem. Micah would know these well since they were neighbours to his own hometown Moresheth-Gath (v. 14). The first part of the lament lists (after Gath) five towns that are little-known, perhaps small settlements in the region of Moresheth (Wolff 1990). The mention of the gate of Jerusalem (v. 12b) is a false climax, for five other towns are then discussed (vv. 13–15), prolonging the anguished expectation. The fall of these is portentous, for they were probably major fortified cities crucial to the defence of Jerusalem. Adullam, Mareshah and Lachish (and Gath) were cities fortified by Rehoboam (2 Chr 11:5–10). The eleven individual towns mentioned are left behind in the concluding v. 16, probably because Micah now turns to the rulers of Judah living in Jerusalem, the target of the lament. The repeated disasters experienced by the other towns heightens the threat hanging over Jerusalem.

A significant stylistic feature of the lament is the wordplay between the name of the town and the threatened disaster. These are not merely to sustain interest and burn the message into the memories of those who listened. The linguistic link between city and coming disaster is not arbitrary, but is authorized and directed by the divine authority that lies behind the prophet's words, and so inevitable. The overall point is clear even if the interpretation of the details is difficult (Schwantes 1964; Collin 1971; van der Woude 1971; Shaw 1987; Na'aman 1995). Many of the allusions assume geographical and historical knowledge of which we are ignorant. Nor have the locations of several of the towns been securely identified (the locations of Beth-leaphra, Shaphir, Zaanan, Beth-ezel, Maroth remain uncertain). Even the date is disputed. Although it is likely that it refers to a time just before 701 B.C.E., there is little specific to confirm or deny this or alternative suggestions (e.g. 734–32 B.C.E., 712–11 B.C.E.; even earlier according to Shaw 1987; 1993, 61–67). The early versions differ significantly from the MT, and have motivated a good number of the innumerable emendations that bestrew the scholarly literature. Elliger (1934), who also had primary responsibility for the *BHS* text-critical notes, even made the eccentric proposal that the outer right hand of the page was damaged and words needed to be inserted accordingly.

The view adopted here is that, despite the difficulties, it is best to try and make sense of the traditional Hebrew text. The differences in the versions may well reflect their puzzlement rather than provide evidence of a better Hebrew text. The selectivity, brevity and allusiveness of the text may well be a deliberate evocation of the confusion and chaos of an invasion. The historical setting is probably just before the invasion of Sennacherib in 701 B.C.E., and Micah announces the immanent destruction of the cities and the exile of their inhabitants. The towns are in the general area where invasion will come, to the southwest of Jerusalem (see the map in Hillers 1984, 29), but they are not on a single route (contrast Isa 10:27–32). In the actual invasion, two or more towns were besieged at the same time (Na'aman 1979).

1:10. Gath, whose location is uncertain, was best known as one of the five major Philistine cities (1 Sam 6:17; Amos 6:2). It is probably mentioned in Sennacherib's "Letter to God" as being in Hezekiah's control (*COS* 2:304; Na'aman 1974, 34–35), but here it seems to have a historical rather than contemporary reference. There is no need to emend to another place (e.g. "Giloh," *BHS*). Gath represents Israel's traditional enemies and is thus distinct from the other Judean towns that were destroyed by Sennacherib (Waltke 1993, 627). Specifically, the phrase recalls the opening of David's lament over Saul and Jonathan in 2 Sam 1:20, although in Micah the town comes before the verb (as in v. 10b), perhaps to give the sequence of cities an emphatic opening. It evokes an overwhelming national disaster: in 2 Sam 1 it is the demise of the king, here the demise of the kingdom. The physical consequences of invasion were not the only issue. Shame at being abandoned by their God and being subject to the taunts of their enemies was just as important, if not moreso (Pss 74:10; 89:41[42]). This opening is an appeal to restrict the knowledge of disaster so that Israel's enemies are given no reason to mock, and its very indirectness is ominous. The REB attempts (without any firm evidence) to give many of the phrases in vv. 10–11 an opposite meaning by making them into questions (e.g. "Will you not tell it in Gath?").

"weep not at all" seems to contradict the command to mourn in vv. 10b, 16. The tension can be resolved by emendation ("weep your eyes out," NEB) or by an appeal to the contradictory behaviour of a grief-crazed person (Andersen and Freedman 2000). But the whole point is the opening dramatic contrast between behaviour in an enemy city and an Israelite one. Not to weep among the enemies would be to hide the extent of the disaster in the same way as not telling.

"in Beth-leaphrah (*bêt l^{ec}aprâ*) roll yourselves in the dust (*ʿāpār*)" is the first of a series of wordplays, emphasized by the two words being next to each other. It may be illustrated by a translation such as "In Dustville roll yourselves in the dust" (Wolff 1982, 30). Sitting in the dust or ashes on the ground (Lam 2:10), and sprinkling them on the head (2 Sam 13:19) were common mourning customs. Rolling in the dust is an extreme practice or possibly prophetic hyperbole (Jer 6:26; 25:34; Ezek 27:30), but it may be better to translate "sprinkle" (REB) or "strew" (NJPS; LXX, Vulg.).

1:11. The address to Shaphir plays both with sounds and sense to emphasize the theme of reversal. "inhabitants" (*yôšebet*) is a collective singular from a root meaning "dwell," echoing shame (*bōšet*). Ironically, Shaphir ("beautiful" or "Fairtown"; cf. LXX, Vulg.) will have to be abandoned (Naʾaman 1995, 519). NJB ("Sound the horn, inhabitants of Shaphir") arbitrarily adds "horn" (*šôpār*) to provide a wordplay, but irony is sufficient. The REB ("from their city") reflects an unnecessary emendation of the word for nakedness. The image is of a defeated population going into exile.

"Zaanan" (*ṣaʾᵃnā*) echoes "come forth" (*yāṣ^{eʾ}â*) or "go out," and may be the same town as Zenan in Josh 15:37, but with an added aleph to emphasize the assonance. The appropriate nuance that makes sense is coming forth to escape (Jer 11:11; BDB 422–23 1c, d; Wolff 1990). This is a more appropriate reason for lament than the sense that the city does not come forth to fight. Rather, the population has either been killed or is now so ashamed or grief-stricken that they remain hidden in mourning (Deut 21:13).

"Beth-ezel is wailing" is more literally "lamentation of (i.e. for) Beth-ezel," possibly an exclamation of sorrow with the next phrase specifying a reason for sorrow. However, the second phrase is a highly ambiguous ("he/one will take from you [masc. pl.] its/his standing place/support"). A number of proposals have been made. (a) NRSV takes Beth-ezel as the subject of the verb, so that the town "shall remove its support from you" (i.e. unable to give military or financial support to the nation). This would be an ironic comment on the meaning of Beth-ezel, probably "house by the side of." However, cities are feminine (GKC §122h). (b) It is hard to understand the sense of making the subject of the verb the lamentation (RSV). (c) The "he" could be Yhwh, or his agent (historically the Assyrian emperor), although the verb could also be impersonal, indicated by a passive translation ("is taken," NIV). In one way or another the town's support is destroyed. (d) "support" is from a verb meaning "to stand," and so the reference may be to the destruction of its walls or foundations (NJB, NLT). (e) "support" may instead be related to Akkadian *imdu*, "tax," "obligation to work" (the corresponding verb is found in Mishnaic Hebrew), hence "he [the invader] will take from you his tax (Na'aman 1995, 521; cf. 2 Kgs 23:34–35). But this is unlikely if the rest of the passage indicates destruction or exile. (f) "He [Yhwh] will take away from you [the inhabitants of Beth-Ezel] his [Yhwh's] protection" (Andersen and Freedman 2000, 224–25). The advantage of this interpretation is that it would parallel v. 12b. God will allow the city to fall by removing his protection from the people.

1:12. The same conjunction or particle (*kî*) begins each line (see on v. 9). The lack of connection with what comes before suggests that the first is emphatic, "surely" (often omitted e.g. REB, GNB). The strong contrast between good and disaster in the second line implies a negation ("instead," NJB; "but no!," Waltke 1993; cf. BDB 474 1e).

Maroth only occurs here and its location is unknown. "wait anxiously" (*ḥālâ*) derives the meaning from a root (*ḥûl*), meaning "to writhe" (Judg 3:25; Job 35:14). "hoped" (NJPS; Symm.) reflects an alternative root (*yḥl*), although this assumes that a letter has dropped out due to dittography. Both possibilities set a similar tone. The wordplay is a contrast of senses. Maroth has the meaning "bitter," and the polar opposites of taste (bitter/sweet) can be metaphorically equivalent to opposite historical fates (good vs. disaster; Job 21:25; Isa 5:20). "good" has the nuance of sweet in Song 1:2–3; Ps 34:8[9]. Many consider that Maroth hoped for good from the invaders, but it is also possible that they foolishly expected Yhwh to save them. But instead of the expected good comes disaster. Disaster (*rāʿ*) is a common opposite to good. Here both refer to physical events (calamity/benefits) rather than moral character (RSV's "evil" is misleading). "from the LORD" in the second line emphasizes the ultimate explanation for the disasters that are being announced and echoes v. 3b. "gate of Jerusalem" reprises v. 9b in a climax that turns out to be only provisional. Like v. 12a, there is an implied reversal of sense, for Jerusalem (*yᵉrûšālayim*) evokes peace (*šālôm*; Ps 122:6), the opposite of the disaster it will actually experience.

1:13. There is a play on the *rk* sounds between "chariots" (*merkābâ*) and "steeds" (*rekeš*). The normal order is also reversed (literally "harness the chariot to the steed") to highlight another wordplay, "to the steed" (*lārekeš*) and Lachish (*lākîš*). Chariots were the ultimate military hardware of the ancient world (Exod 15:4; Judg 4:15), and Solomon used Lachish as a base for his chariots (1 Kgs 9:19; 10:26). Chariots represented the military might of Lachish, which was one of Rehoboam's fortified cities (2 Chr 11:9) and had a double wall in the ninth and eighth centuries. However, the chariots here are not for battle but for desperate flight (1 Kgs 12:18) or deportation (Wolff 1990). Lachish is 40 km southwest of Jerusalem and 10 km southwest of Moresheth. Its fortifications, however impressive, were ineffective when Sennacherib captured it in 701 B.C.E. (2 Kgs 18:14, 17; 19:8; for Sennacherib's pictorial record, see *ANEP* 371–74).

The next line is literally "the beginning of sin it (fem.) [is]"), but what is the "it"? (1) If it were a reference to the city of Lachish, we would expect "you" (NIV, REB), but this is without textual support and Lachish hardly seems a good candidate for "the beginning of sin to daughter Zion." (2) "She" might be a goddess (Andersen and Freedman 2000; cf. v. 5), but there is no hint of such a figure. (3) A more abstract explanation would be that Micah is referring to military pride, illustrated by the completion of Lachish's fortifications under Solomon and Rehoboam. (4) On a shorter timeframe the leaders of Lachish may have been prominent in advocating a national policy of rebellion against Assyria that was dependent on military considerations rather than trust in Yhwh. A social consequence of such a military build-up may have been the diversion of resources leading to the impoverishment of many and the abuse of power (Alfaro 1989). It is this sin that has led to the corresponding divine judgment, the military defeat described in these verses.

"daughter Zion" is a better translation than "daughter of Zion" (RSV, NIV), understanding the genitive as appositional, indicating identity (similarly "land of Israel"; Williamson 2006, 67–71). Cities are feminine and Zion (along with other capital cities, *DCH* 1:284) is personified not as a daughter of a father, but simply as a young woman. "Daughter" may imply overtones of beauty ("Fair Zion," NJPS; cf. Jer 6:2), or possibly the idea of a stable, nurturing community (Follis 1987). However, the note of sin in this context may suggest the corruption of a pure, chaste daughter. Rather than trusting in Yhwh, the Northern Kingdom ("Israel"), Lachish and Jerusalem share a family resemblance in trusting in other things. This is thus another example of the long tradition of prophetic condemnation of Israel's reliance on military might rather than on Yhwh (Deut 17:16; 2 Sam 24:1–10; Isa 2:7; Hos 10:13–15; 14:4[3]).

1:14. "Therefore" often introduces the punishment following a prophetic accusation. "parting gifts" can also be the "dowry" (NJB) given by a father to a bride when she leaves home (1 Kgs 9:16). NRSV sees these as being given to Moresheth-gath, but the preposition (*ʿal*) usually means "on account of" rather than "to." A more likely interpretation is that this refers to the cities and lands that were Jerusalem's inheritance from God and that now have to be given to another husband/lord, the invading army. This accords with a wordplay between Moresheth-gath (Micah's home-town; 1:1), and the similarly sounding "betrothed" (*mᵊʾōrāśâ*, Deut 22:23, 25, 27). It does not necessarily imply that Jerusalem will be spared, since it may be a comment from the middle of the action. On account of the fall of Moresheth-gath, Jerusalem has had to give a dowry to the Assyrians. The "you" (fem.) is thus Daughter Zion of v. 13b, but now "she" has switched roles to become a father forced to lose a beloved daughter.

Demsky (1966) has made a good case that the "houses of Achzib" refers to pottery guilds. In 1 Chr 4:21–23 these guilds are found in Cozeba at work in the king's service. The workshops (or factories) may have been responsible for some of the many jars found with a seal marked *lmlk* ("to the king") that have been found in these towns (Naʾaman 1979). Achzib is probably the same as

Chezib (Gen 38:5) and Achzib (Josh 15:44) as well as Cozeba, and is normally identified as Tell el-Beida, 5 km east of Moresheth. Micah may well have chosen or invented this form of the town's name (cf. Zaanan, v. 11) to highlight the wordplay with "deception" (*'akzāb*, hence "Deceitville" in Wolff 1982, 30). This word comes in Jer 15:18, describing a brook whose waters fail (cf. Job 6:15–20), although NJPS ("like a spring that fails") adopts the similar metaphor of Isa 58:11. The "kings of Israel" may refer to the present and future kings of Judah, who now alone represent the people of God. Micah may imply that they are about to lose their lucrative income from these workshops. They have been deceived by their false expectations.

1:15. A first-person statement by Yhwh ("I will bring") is unexpected and the verb is written defectively. If the consonants are reversed (*'by* to *yb'*, *BHS*), it becomes a simple statement that the conqueror "will come" upon you (cf. NJB). The play of words is between the conqueror (*yōrēš*) and Mareshah (*mārēšâ*), which sounds similar (an army of occupation takes over "Occupationtown" in Wolff 1982, 30). Mareshah is identified as Tell Sandakhanna, 7 km southwest of Achzib and 5 km south of Moresheth. The verb underlying conqueror (*yrš*) means either "inherit" or "dispossess," implying that the town would be taken violently. The "glory (*kābōd*) of Israel" (i.e. Judah) could be its king (Wolff 1990; cf. 2 Sam 1:19, though a different word is used) or its nobility (Isa 5:13; Allen 1976). Adullam was a fortified town in the Shephelah (2 Chr 11:7), but David fled to the cave of Adullam in extreme need (1 Sam 22:1). The prophecy is that his latter-day descendants will have to flee Jerusalem and come to Adullam in similar affliction and despair.

1:16. Three imperatives with the same overall meaning and a statement of the ultimate judgment make this verse a fitting climax. A prominent feature of mourning in Israel and many other cultures is cutting off the hair (Job 1:20; Jer 7:29) and so making oneself bald (Jer 16:6; Ezek 27:31). Since the growth and care of hair is characteristic of living persons, the opposite allows the mourner to identify with the dead. Going into exile is the equivalent of death, for the necessary elements of a fulfilled life (land, city, temple) are removed. Better than "your pampered children" is "children of your delight" ("who were your joy," NJB), since the focus is on those who have been bereaved (in 2:9 the word is used of pleasant houses). "make yourselves as bald" is literally "widen your baldness," ensuring we picture not a half-hearted tonsure but a total loss of hair. The eagle (*nešer*) in the Bible is usually "vulture," which is most appropriate here (NJB, NJPS, REB; Kronholm 1999, 77–85). The griffon vulture has a white down-covered head and a neck that looks like a bald pate. The customary food of vultures (corpses and carrion) further reinforces the association with death.

The note about the exile of the towns need not be in the future (NIV, RSV) or a postexilic addition. If puppet kings could not keep a subjugated nation in line, Assyrian policy was exile and replacement of the population (2 Kgs 17). The fate of the other towns is a pledge that the inhabitants of Jerusalem will also be exiled. The implicit threat of the previous verses (cf. v. 8) is now made explicit.

"from you" (fem. sing.) is again a reference to Jerusalem, rather than the Shephelah or Judah or Lachish (Vargon 1994). Although historically Jerusalem was spared (2 Kgs 18–19), this is not the perspective adopted by Micah (3:12). Jerusalem is addressed as if it was experiencing the brief interval between the exile of the towns mentioned and the siege and fall of the capital (Achtemeier 1996). The rhetorical purpose was to force the people of Jerusalem to recognize the crisis and bring them to repentance and trust in Yhwh.

Weep and Wail, You Rich! (2:1–13)

From a statement about the external threat to Judah and especially Jerusalem, Micah turns to denounce a series of specific wrongs within the nation in chs. 2–3. They are primarily in the area of social justice, and are directed particularly against the prophets (2:6–11; 3:5–8) and the rulers (3:1–4, 9–12). These are therefore rather different from the sins against God of ch. 1, but the implication is that Micah is providing further illustrations of the sinfulness that was a significant cause of the judgment announced there.

An opening oracle of judgment (vv. 1–5) is followed by the objections of opponents (vv. 6–8), which are then refuted (vv. 8–11). A coda prevents the chapter from becoming unrelieved darkness, and puts the positive side of judgment (vv. 12–13). As was the case in ch. 1, various later glosses and additions have been proposed, but there are no decisive arguments against attributing all or most of the chapter to Micah. The most disputed passage is vv. 12–13, but although there are some close parallels in exilic literature, arguments against its authenticity are not decisive. The presence of vv. 12–13 reflects a central and original biblical affirmation that judgment must always be seen in relation to the hope of future salvation.

Woe to the Land-Grabbers (2:1–5)

The first five verses begin with a woe oracle (Amos 6:1–7; Isa 5:8–10; 30:1–3). It is the equivalent of an oracle of judgment in that a description of the injustice is followed by a corresponding announcement of punishment. The two parts are linked by a "therefore," and in v. 5 a second "therefore" reinforces and extends the judgment. The section is unified by the repetition in the two main parts of "fields" (vv. 2, 4) and "evil" (vv. 1, 3). In a paradigmatic exposition of the *lex talionis* (Willis 1967), those who seize fields will lose them, and those who seek evil against others less powerful will find that they are subject to "evil" from one more powerful than them, Yhwh. The significance of this opening accusation lies in its reference to the central role that land and inheritance play in defining Israel's identity, an affirmation that can be traced back to the original occupation of the land.

Micah's opponents have been variously identified, but it is most likely to be the wealthy businessmen and ruling classes. The interpretation below regards them as being consistently the subject of all five verses. However, the language of vv. 3–5 is general enough that they could refer to the people as a whole and is one of the reasons for regarding these verses as a later addition reflecting the fall of Judah. Wolff (1990) suggests a very specific setting. The oracle was given in Moresheth and aimed at the royal officials who occupied the fortified cities and used their powers to make life comfortable for themselves at the expense of citizens (see Section A, above). However, the third person reference in v. 3 ("this family") implies that the oracle was meant to be overheard by others, and it is difficult to reconstruct the original setting of the oracle. Certainly in its canonical written form it is intended to be read as a generalized condemnation of such evils (Ben Zvi 2000, 45–54). The underlying theological assumption is that Yhwh will assert his rule over his people. Through his prophets he makes known his concern for the weak and oppressed and condemns the wicked. Those who set themselves against the covenantal and legal principles laid down for the well-being of Israel will find death and destruction.

2:1. Originally "Alas" (*hôy*) was used in a funeral lament to express deep sorrow over the dead (1 Kgs 13:30; Jer 22:18; Clifford 1966). As such it links well to the previous passage, for now Micah sets out the reason for the events portrayed through lament in ch. 1. Yet in the majority of occurrence in the prophets *hôy* is more than a simple cry of sorrow, for it introduces a condemnation of sin and wickedness. A similar oracle against those who abuse the land is found in Isa 5:8. Translations of the cry suggest a range of nuances, from the sorrowful "how terrible" (GNB) to the more threatening "disaster for" (NJB) or "woe to" (AV). Because God's judgment is sure, the cry of lament anticipates what is sure to come to pass (vv. 3–5; Zobel 1978, 364; Janzen 1972, 64). The tone is ambiguous, because this could be a mocking taunt of those who thoroughly deserve punishment, but it might also genuinely reflect the prophet's deep sadness for his people (1:8). If this obituary, announced ahead of time, cannot change the attitude of the addressees, then nothing will.

The NRSV assumes that "devise" governs both "wickedness" and "evil deeds," but in the MT "deeds" is a participle, "doers of." The normal idiom is to "plan evil" (2:3; Hos 7:14) and "doers of wickedness" (Hos 6:8), but Micah switches the words. It is the devising rather than the doing that will be done "on their beds" (there is no need to translate with NJB, "planning mischief"). This is further indicated by assonance between "devise" (*ḥšb*) and "beds" (*mškb*). This is therefore not a reference to dreams (Willis 1967) but to the restless plotting that is the diametric opposite of godly meditation (Josh 1:8; Ps 1:2). "They do not dream; they calculate" (Wolff 1990, 77). The two lines of the verse vividly portray a typical night and day in the life of such a person. "wickedness" or iniquity (*ʾāwen*) often describes acts of violence (Isa 59:6; Hab 1:3) and deception (Isa 59:4) by those who abuse their power (Bernhardt 1974, 142–43). Both are appropriate nuances here. Wickedness so pervades the life of these people that they do not even take time off during their sleep and can hardly wait until light dawns (Amos 8:5).

"on their beds" provides a transition to "When the morning dawns" (lit. "in the light of the morning"). Frustrated planning can then become effective action. This may strike an ironical note, for morning was a time for justice (2 Sam

15:1–2; Jer 21:12; Waltke 1993). "because it is in their power" is literally "according to the god (*'ēl*) of their hand." *'ēl* is normally "God" but can occasionally mean "power" (*DCH* 1:259; cf. Gen 31:29; Deut 28:32), an idea often associated with the hand, the part of the body that enforces control (Ackroyd 1986). Its rarity implies that Micah is condemning those who find their source of legitimacy in their own strength rather than in the true God (Jer 17:5). The cameo portrait is of those who are rich and powerful enough to do whatever evil they desire, whoever the opposition, and whatever the laws that forbid it. Ordinary thieves work by night, but these people carry out their premeditated crimes by day (Alfaro 1989).

2:2. The emphasis in this verse shifts to a more detailed description of the actions that have been planned. The motivation for them is simultaneously analyzed and condemned using the keyword of the tenth commandment, "covet" (*ḥmd*, Exod 20:17; Deut 4:21), which governs both "fields" and "houses." "Greed becomes dangerous when it is linked with power... Power augments temptation and even gives birth to it" (Wolff 1990, 96). In rejection of the covenant and its basic demands these people set themselves against God as well as their victims. The result is that they seize fields, a closer specification of the wickedness of v. 1. The significance of fields cannot be overestimated, for the land was the source and marker of Israelite self-identity and many of the laws were designed to protect the free landholders and their children, for Yhwh had given them land in perpetuity (Num 26:52–56; 27:7; Lev 25:10). Now, however, the wealthy "seize them": "[The prophet] leaps over the intermediate steps between the birth of the desire and its fulfilment, such as extortionate rates of interest, foreclosure of mortgages, subornation and perjury of witnesses, bribery of judges" (J. M. P. Smith 1911, 57). The paradigmatic example of such abuse (along with indignant prophetic protest) is 1 Kgs 21 (Weil 1940). The rich use their powers to get richer, amassing great estates and leaving ordinary Israelites only the options of wage labourer or slave. They cannot literally "take away the houses," so perhaps this is a reference to forcibly removing the household, a frequent nuance of the word (Hoffner 1977, 113–15).

"householder" (*geḇer*) refers to a grown man with authority and strength (Kosmala 1977, 377), but here he is deprived of his legal rights. The law condemns those who oppress the poor (Deut 24:14), but in this society even a grown man is robbed and cheated in various ways (Hos 12:7[8]; Jer 21:12; Mal 3:5). The implication may be that this leads to the loss of his ancestral house, but (as with the previous line) it may refer to the wider household. The parallel word "inheritance" (*naḥᵃlâ*) can also sometimes include sons (Ps 127:3), but the emphasis here appears to be more on the inalienable character of the land given by Yhwh to the people.

2:3. The transition from accusation to sentence is provided by a "Therefore" and the messenger formula ("thus says Yhwh"). Micah's ironic lament turns into a divine first person statement of judgment, although both are authoritative. The theme of reversal is communicated both by word and imagery. The initial "Now I" (*hin'nî*, "behold," AV) emphasizes this shift in perspective (Berlin 1983, 62–64). The announcement of punishment echoes the language of v. 1, emphasizing the justice of the sentence. Yhwh is "devising evil" (*rā'â*), with "evil" gaining the overtone of "disaster" (see on Jonah 4:1). The logic of correspondence between accusation and punishment also implies that "this family is a reference to the "breed" (NJB) or "gang" (Hillers 1984, 33) of vv. 1–2, rather than a general reference to the nation (Amos 3:1–2). The word might be an ironic reference to those who had abandoned the ties that bind together members of a family or a nation. They are united only by their shared anti-social greed and crime.

The disaster is left undefined, but its inevitability and character is specified by the metaphor of a yoke (made explicit by REB) "from which you cannot remove your necks." This image often indicates political subjugation (Isa 10:27; Jer 27:8; 28), but the primary contrast here is with those who in their arrogance and wealth thought they could do what they wanted and used to "walk haughtily." "haughtily" is a good translation because in both English and Hebrew there is a transparent association with height, a common spatial metaphor of pride (Isa 2:11, 17). But now the proud will be brought low (Luke 1:51–52) and with necks bent under the yoke they are condemned to unceasing labour (Amos 5:5). Those who did not allow their victims to escape will now be unable to escape themselves.

The final phrase emphasizes the terror of the punishment by repeating the evil/disaster word. The context suggests that the initial particle is the emphatic "surely" rather than "for" (Waltke 1993). The behaviour of the few affects the fate of the many, for better or (as here) for worse.

2:4. "they shall take up" is more literally "one shall take up" and can be understood as a simple description ("there will be heard," REB). The closely related phrase, to lift up one's voice, is used to communicate an intense and formal expression of mood, sometimes joy (Isa 52:8) but often mourning (Gen 21:16; Job 2:12; Isa 24:14). But who is speaking—Micah, Yhwh, or the wealthy who have just been condemned? It most probably represents Micah's voice rather than God's (Mays 1976), although we cannot be sure. As authorized interpreter he utters a sorrowful lament about the entire people caught up in the catastrophe caused by the wickedness of the few. The preposition (*'al*) in "against you" can equally be read "about you" (REB). Verse 4 would be an aside before resuming the judgment in v. 5. It is directed against the wealthy wicked, filling out the punishment of v. 3 and leading on to v. 5. The taunt song consists of an ironic quotation of the bitter lamentation of those who had received their just punishment. The words of the lament show both their distorted values and the reversal of all that they had gained. "my people" would also be ironic and refer to cronies. This is an attractive contextual reading, although it is difficult to assess the persuasiveness of ironic readings (see on Jonah).

"taunt song" (*māšāl*) clarifies the character of what is being declaimed (Num 23:7; Hab 2:6). *māšāl* is usually translated "proverb" (cf. "parable," AV), though sometimes a simple "verse" (REB). However, it can also be a negative poem ("byword," 1 Kgs 9:7; Job 17:6) or a taunt song or "satire" (NAB, NJB; Isa 14:4) sung by triumphant enemies.

"wail with bitter lamentation" is full of alliteration and assonance (*wᵉnāhâ nᵉhî nihyâ*). Some have suspected an accidental repetition of one of the words (dittography), and others have associated the final word with the verb "to be." But Micah's love of wordplay suggests that this is a deliberate construction. The phrase intensifies the depth of the lament by repeating an onomatopoeic word for lamentation in three different forms (the verb, then the masculine and feminine forms of the cognate noun). The ingenious NEB translates "a lament thrice told." "We are utterly ruined" translates a double occurrence of the verb (absolute infinitive + verb). It is an emphatic construction indicating the certainty and forcefulness of the judgment (GKC §113n).

"inheritance" (*ḥēleq*) is a different word from that in v. 2, but the two are frequently found in parallel or linked (Gen 31:14; Deut 10:9). It comes from a verb meaning "divide" and the reference is to the portion of land that belongs to an individual or family or tribe by law or custom (Josh 15:13; 19:9; Tsevat 1980, 448). "parcels out" translates the corresponding verb. Instead of "change," many read (following the LXX) a similar verb meaning measure ("are measured out," NAB). However, Ezek 48:14 uses the verb in the similar sense of exchanging land, and the construction can be understood either with Yhwh as the implied subject (NRSV) or as an impersonal passive ("changes hands," REB, NJPS). The shift of form to an exclamation, "how he removes it from me" (or an impersonal "How it slips away from me!," NJPS) highlights the emotional impact of these events.

"Among (more literally 'to') our captors" assumes an emendation to a verb meaning "take captive," and so could refer to the Assyrians (on the national interpretation). REB's "renegades" ("traitors" NIV) associates the word with a verb meaning "bring back" or "turn back." In context this can take on a nuance of faithlessness (Jer 3:14) or apostasy (Jer 50:6). On the wealthy wicked interpretation this would then be an ironic reference to the poor to whom the fields have been returned (Hillers 1984, 32).

2:5. This verse extends the promised reversal of v. 3 to all future time. Those who had removed inheritance rights would themselves find no heirs who could be apportioned their land, as in the original distribution after the conquest. The line appears to be in prose, which Shaw (1993, 73) regards as a signal of the oracle's closure rather than a gloss or addition. The "line" was originally a rope that was cast to measure a length (2 Sam 8:2) or an area (Zech 2:1[5]; "mark out boundaries," NAB). By extension it described a portion of land, particularly those assigned to the tribes as recorded in Josh 14–21 (Josh 17:5; 19:9). The method of division was to cast a lot (Josh 17:14; cf. Jonah 1:7), an action often performed by a priest. Since God controlled the result of the lot, it was another way of acknowledging his ownership of the land and its nature as a gift to his people (Pss 16:6; 78:55). The "assembly of Yhwh" is the legal gathering of God's people (Num 20:4; Deut 23:1–3), but the wicked have forfeited their right of representation. The imagery here is of an eschatological repetition of the primeval division of land, from which the wicked are excluded in a "full and final excommunication" (Allen 1976, 291; Ps 1:5; Amos 7:17). The uncaring wealthy are denied the Old Testament equivalent of eternal life (Luke 6:24; 12:21; John 3:36; 1 Tim 6:10).

The Complacent Refuted (2:6–11)

References to preaching in v. 6 and v. 11 indicate the boundaries of the next section. Those attacked by Micah in vv. 1–5 attempt to silence Micah, but instead merely provoke another set of accusations. The verses raise a number of interpretive and textual questions. In particular it is not easy to determine what is quotation and what are the authentic words of Micah, especially for v. 7. On one understanding vv. 6–7 are largely the words of Micah's opponents, with his response in vv. 8–11, but Micah could begin his reply already in v. 7a or v. 7b. Verse 6 consists of brief, parallel sentences, communicating an indignant and defensive response. Verse 7 has a series of questions that could expand on v. 6, or it could begin Micah's refutation. However, his voice is clearly found in vv. 8–9, which describe the crimes of the landgrabbers in more detail. These verses lead up to an announcement of judgment in v. 10, where once again the punishment fits the crime. His opponents have demanded his silence in v. 6, and Micah concludes in v. 11 with an ironic comment on the kind of sermon they would really like.

Who were these opponents? It is often assumed that they were false prophets who opposed the canonical prophets (Amos 5:10; 7:10–17) and represented the political and religious establishment (van der Woude 1969). But prophets do not have a monopoly on speaking and the landgrabbers we meet in the first section are the obvious candidates. The prophets offended all sections of society and were in turn criticized by them (Jer 11:21; 26:8; 36; Amos 7:10–17). Prophets are named specifically in 3:5–8 and so may be in mind here, but the lack of explicit naming emphasizes that they were the agents and tools of these land-owners.

The emphasis on land rights suggests that Micah is not speaking about ordinary thieves and murderers. His opponents are the rulers and merchants who control the economics of the nation and know their way around the law. They make use of any means at their disposal to increase their wealth. Their methods may even have been within the letter of the law, but whatever the legalities, they are rejecting the vision of a just society that was at the heart of the original formation of God's covenant people. Through his language and rhetoric, his threats and metaphors, his irony and sarcasm, Micah attempts to alert these people to the plight of the oppressed, and warns them that God's point of view will one day prevail.

2:6. Some limit the words of Micah's opponents simply to "Do not preach," but the three parallel negatives imply a unified viewpoint and a more extensive quotation (Willis 1970, 76–77). "preach" is a neutral translation of a verb (hiphil of *ntp*) that is a synonym of "prophecy" in other occurrences (Ezek 20:46[21:2]; Amos 7:16). However, its basic physical meaning is "drop, trickle, flow" (Amos 9:13). In this context it might well have pejorative overtones, suggesting a zealous and verbose style in which plenty of spittle is sprayed out ("drivel," NJB; 1 Sam 21:13–15). The verb is plural (Amos 2:12), implying that its target is a group of prophets that included Micah and also possibly Isaiah.

"thus they preach" signals that the first words are a quotation. It is an ironic comment on the attitude of those who set themselves up as on the same level as the prophets, but who by their behaviour show how little they understand the moral and religious basis of authentic prophecy. Truth and justice, not rhetoric and forcefulness, are the ultimate judge of speech. "one should not preach" is more literally "they should not preach," suggesting general disapproval. It is unnecessary to turn the phrase into a question (REB) or a command (NIV). The content of this unwelcome preaching is the condemnations of vv. 1–2 and the threatened punishment of vv. 3–5.

"disgrace will not overtake us" has spawned a host of speculative emendations. In the Hebrew "overtake" is singular (*yissag*) and normally means "turn back," while "disgrace" is plural (*kᵉlimmôt*) and there is no "us." Various solutions have been offered. (1) NRSV emends the verb to the plural and understands as object "us." The landgrabbers make a defiant statement that judgment will never overtake them (Isa 59:9; Hos 10:9; Zech 1:6), just as Pharaoh's chariots were not able to overtake the Israelites (Exod 15:9). (2) If it is Micah's comment then it could be a prophecy of punishment. Waltke (1993, 642) translates: "[so their] shame will not depart." "disgrace" is often parallel to "shame" (Jer 20:11; Ezek 16:63), and by metonymy it can also refer to the disaster that is the cause of shame and that allows others to mock and insult its victims (Wagner 1995, 186, 195). Lack of shame for their sinful deeds was one of Jeremiah's criticisms of the false prophets opposing him (Jer 6:15; 8:11–12).

2:7. The parallel structure of this verse (four questions, 7a–d) responds to the parallel statements in v. 6, but do they come from Micah (Haak 1982) or his opponents or both? It is possible to interpret the verse in a way that is consistent with each of these possibilities, but the most straightforward reading is to take v. 7a–c as coming from the opponents, d from Micah. It is less likely that a and d are from Micah, b and c from his opponents (Neiderhiser 1981).

This form of "said" (*ʾāmûr*) occurs only here. *BHS* proposes an emendation to a verb meaning "curse" (*ʾārûr*; cf. "Can the house of Jacob be accursed," NJB), an appropriate comment by Micah's adversaries. However, it seems best to take it as an introduction to the next pair of questions. "house of Jacob" may hint at a complacent dependence on traditional covenant theology (Ps 114:1). It is often parallel to Israel (Exod 19:3) and here refers to the Southern Kingdom (as in Isa 2:5–6). An unreflective dependence on a theology of grace and election characterizes the following two questions, which expect the answer "no." Those asking the questions ignore the moral and religious dimensions of the covenant. Israel's memories and traditions set salvation and blessing firmly in the context of obedience, generosity and stewardship of the land. Although texts such as Exod 1–15 and Isa 37–39 demonstrate the positive value of these affirmations, it is essential for there to be the right attitude adopted by the people or the king. This is what these people were ignoring by their indignant assertions. "Theirs was a word for the wrong people at the wrong time" (Allen 1976, 196).

"Is the LORD's patience exhausted" is more literally "has the breath (*rûah*) of Yhwh become short?" The idiom usually indicates impatience (Prov 14:29) and this would then be a refutation of Micah's claim in vv. 1–5 that Yhwh is about to judge them. Instead, the landowners appeal to the traditional confession that Yhwh was patient and slow to anger (lit. "long of nose," Exod 34:6; see on Jonah 4:2). This would imply some admission of guilt, but one that was relatively trivial. The next question would suggest that the threatened events are not what Yhwh really intends. "Doings" (*maʿalālîm*) in the prophets often refers to evil human deeds (see on Mic 3:4). This would then be an indignant rejection of Micah's prediction.

We hear Micah's response in the final words. He adds a crucial qualification that his opponents have ignored, the issue of walking uprightly. God's attitude to his people depends on the quality of their lives. Whether he will do good to them or does harm (Josh 24:20; Isa 41:23; Zeph 1:12) matches whether they walk in evil (v. 1) or walk uprightly. Walking in a straight line rather than crookedly becomes a metaphor for good behaviour (see on 3:9; Alonso Schökel 1990, 466). The choice of paths is set sharply before the hearer in Proverbs (2:13; 8:8–9; 14:2; 15:21). It is unnecessary to aim for complete consistency, as when REB (with the help of a slight emendation to "his words," with LXX) assigns this line to Micah's opponents.

2:8. This might be the most obscure verse in the entire book and it is possible only to hint at the scholarly ingenuity that has been applied to making sense of it. A possible literal translation of the first two lines is:

> and yesterday/formerly my people to an enemy he/one raises up
> from in front of a garment a robe/glory you strip off

NRSV makes the following assumption. (1) The consonants of the MT (*wʾtmwl ʿmy*) are sensibly redivided to get "But you" (*wʾtm lʿmy*). This provides a shift to clear criticism, similar to other uses of the personal pronoun (4:8; 5:1; 6:12; Williamson 1997, 361). (2) However, this then requires the singular "rise up" to be emended to the plural. (3) "against" is an awkward reading of a preposition (*l*) that normally means "to" (Innes 1969, 13). (4) "garment" (*śalmāh*) is emended to "peaceful" (*śālēm*). (5) "in front of" is ignored. The REB reads instead:

> But you are not my people;
> you rise up as my enemy to my face, to strip the cloaks

Here "to" has been emended to "not," "from in front of" to "my face" and "garment" has been omitted as a gloss.

Perhaps the best attempt to interpret the MT is by Willis (1970, 84; cf. NIV):

> but recently my people rise up as an enemy:
> you strip the robe off the garment
> from those who pass by trustingly, returning from war.

"recently" ("lately," NIV) is one possible nuance of "yesterday" (2 Sam 5:2; Isa 30:33). It could be an ironic reference to Israel's persistent rebellion that has required God's patience over many generations. Willis retains both words for garments in v. 8b. The "garment" is the basic item of clothing that the laws prohibit from taking as a pledge (Exod 22:9[8]; Deut 24:13). "robe" (*'eder*) can also mean "majesty" or "splendour," suggesting a more elaborate and expensive covering (Josh 7:21; Jonah 3:6). Ahlström (1967, 6) alternatively suggests the reference is to some kind of buckle or fibula that is on the front of the garment. NJPS multiplies the injustice by having these people rob the "mantle with the cloak," but we would expect some kind of preposition.

The next line seems to indicate a more specific injustice (Shaw 1993, 80–81). "those who pass by" could be travellers in general, but this translation of v. 8c implies that these people are refugees fleeing from war, perhaps from the north, or survivors of the 701 B.C.E. invasion. They expected safety in Jerusalem and help from their fellows, but instead found themselves being robbed of the clothes off their back. NRSV instead interprets the phrase (more literally "returned/turned back of war") as "no thought of war" ("averse to war," Shaw 1993, 70; cf. AV). REB finds two different classes ("from travellers who felt safe or from men returning from the battle"), but the MT lacks the expected connective (*waw*). "trustingly" (*betah*) normally means "in safety" (Deut 12:10), but here it describes the subjective perception rather than the reality, that is, "who felt safe" (REB; "unsuspecting," NJPS; cf. "off guard" in Judg 8:11). Why are "my people" condemned and not the landowners (cf. v. 9)? We could adopt the "against" meaning of the preposition, or regard this as another ironic reference to "my people" (cf. v. 4). However, irony can always be used to reverse what may be the plain meaning of the text. Any interpretation of the verse must remain tentative.

2:9. Keeping a specific reference to robes in v. 8 would mean that there was a progressive intensification as those with less and less power are defrauded: from the rich robes of men (v. 8b) to the luxurious homes of women (v. 9a) to the splendid inheritance of children (v. 9b). The language is extravagant, but the hyperbole communicates God's outrage at such callous behaviour. It is possible to read the lines as a sequential and composite portrait of the typical family. First we see the husbands robbed and removed from their families (perhaps by slavery or forced labour), then wives are evicted, and finally their children are disinherited.

The parallelism with "their young children" means that the women here are not necessarily widows, although they would be particularly vulnerable and protected by covenant law (Exod 22:22[21]; Deut 24:17–18). "drive out" (*grš*) is a military term (Num 22:6), implying that the action of the landgrabbers is as pitiless as a military enemy. "pleasant" (*taᶜanûg*) elsewhere has overtones of luxury or great delight (Prov 19:10; Song 7:7; cf. Mic 1:16). For these women, especially if their husbands had died, their houses would be the primary source of joy, security and comfort (cf. Mark 12:40). "their houses" is singular ("her house" and similarly "her young children"), evoking the tragedy of each household. Even the young children are not spared, for "my glory" is taken away. The criticism is obscure, for glory (*hāḏār*—often "splendour") is primarily an attribute of Yhwh. He bestows it on his people (Ezek 16:14), the king (Ps 21:5[6]) or a land (Isa 35:2). It might be the gift of freedom, rather than the servitude that follows dispossession, but in this context implies it may refer to the splendid land that is God's gift to his people (cf. Jer 3:19). The portion of land due an orphaned child would be the only hope of escape from poverty and slavery. But the landgrabbers remove forever the possibility of farming or working the land, even when the child grows up.

2:10. Some think that v. 10a quotes the words of the landgrabbers, perhaps to the women of v. 9 (NJB adds "saying"), but it is more likely that Micah remains the speaker and here moves from accusation to an announcement of judgment. In line with the principle of the *lex talionis*, Micah may be using the same words the landgrabbers would have used to their victims. They had given others marching orders ("Arise and go"; see on Jonah 1:2), but now they have to be on the move. "place to rest" (*menûḥâ*) is used to describe God's gift of the Promised Land to Israel (Deut 12:9), but its continued possession was not guaranteed (Ps 95:11; contrast the attitude of v. 7). Unless the people were obedient, homelessness and exile would follow (Deut 28:65). Those who had denied others a secure home were themselves going to find themselves with nowhere to rest in exile (cf. Ruth 1:9). The threat to the land is also present in the explanation in the next line, "because of uncleanness." Although uncleanness is a priestly ritual term, it is also used to describe the result of certain kinds of unethical behaviour ("moral filth," Allen 1976, 293; cf. Lev 18:24–28; Num 35:33; Deut 21:23). This seems to fit the context better than other prophetic texts, where it is a cultic metaphor for sin (Ps 51) or a term for idolatry (Jer 19:13; Ezek 22:4). The next verb (piel of *ḥbl*) has several possible meanings, including "take in pledge" (cf. NJB), but "destroy" is more likely. "destruction" (*ḥebel*) is from the same root and reinforces the threat. "grievous" is from a root meaning "to be sick," here meaning "strong" (Jer 14:17; cf. English "sickening" in the sense of terrible).

2:11. This verse concludes the section by returning to its opening theme. The word for "preach" found in v. 6 is used twice more. Micah's opponents had told him to stop preaching. Here he sarcastically draws up a pen portrait of what he would have to say to be become a popular and successful preacher for this people. The first line is literally: "If a man going about wind/spirit (*rûaḥ*) and deception (*šeqer*) lied." "empty falsehoods" assumes that the two nouns make up one idea (hendiadys), and this is more likely than separating the words into two phrases (NJB). The words of false prophets were windy (Isa 41:29; Jer 5:13; cf. Job 6:26) and deceptive (Jer 14:14). Micaiah speaks of the "lying spirit" (*rûaḥ šeqer*) in the mouth of the king of Israel's false prophets. Such preachers were the compliant tail that was wagged by those in power (Isa 9:15[14]).

"wine" (*yayin*) is grape wine, and "strong drink" (*šēḵār*) usually barley beer, though also used to describe other alcoholic beverages. Together they describe any and every intoxicating drink. Micah echoes others (Isa 5:11–12; Amos 4:1) in this condemnation of those who misused God's good gifts (Lev 26:5; Deut 14:26) and saw themselves as exploiters rather than stewards. Possession and consumption of large amounts of alcohol is a powerful symbol of ill-gotten material wealth, selfish indulgence, and loss of a moral and religious vision (contrast 3:5).

Hope for the Scattered Sheep (2:12–13)

The traditional understanding of these verses is that they express a hope of salvation for the remnant of Israel following the judgment promised in the preceding chapters. Very different interpretations have also been proposed. Perhaps they are Micah's quotations of the words of optimistic false prophets, but there is little to indicate this, and what these prophets denied (the exile) is presupposed. Another revisionist solution would be if the promises have an ominous implication (e.g. gathering for judgment, Jer 8:13–14; sheep for the slaughter, Ps 44:22[23]; Brin 1989). However, the reinterpretation required is excessive and unpersuasive (e.g. translating "before them" as "against them" is a desperate measure).

The presence of a "salvation" strand in these three chapters should not be surprising, since each main section of the book contains both judgment and salvation, though in varying proportions. This conjunction reflects a historical and theological pattern that is pervasive in scripture (Exod 32–34; Isa 6). Worked out in terms of land, the pattern is disobedience, exile and gathering from exile (Deut 4:25–31; 29:17–30:5). Sin against the land leads to judgment (vv. 1–11), but beyond judgment lies a word of salvation that gives hope to the despairing and strength to the faint-hearted (vv. 12–13). Although oracles of salvation come later in the book, Micah (or a redactor) may well have felt that it was important to assert the balance at an earlier point (Shaw 1993, 88).

The openness and ambiguity of these verses makes it difficult to determine their authorship and date with certainty. The language is found mostly in later exilic texts dealing with exile, but this may be due to the subject matter (return from exile) and does not decide the question of date. Assigning it to an exilic author allows us to find a word of hope to those who have suffered the great judgment of the Babylonian exile, but the message would have been equally relevant in earlier times, including in Micah's day.

If the verses do stem from Micah, on the surface they seem to assume that Jerusalem will be destroyed, thus superficially contradicting the miraculous salvation of Jerusalem in 701 B.C.E. as recorded in 2 Kgs 18–20 (= Isa 37–39). But prophecy is always related to a specific situation where the attitude and behaviour of those involved affects the course of a prophetic judgment (see on Jonah 3–4; Mic 5:2). The main difference between Isaiah (who prophesied the salvation of Jerusalem) and Micah (who prophesied its doom) is that only Isaiah describes the changes brought about by Hezekiah's godly behaviour. Micah mentions only corrupt political and religious authorities, although Jer 26:18–19 records that his prophecies also influenced Hezekiah. Both prophets demand moral righteousness and dependence on Yhwh. Micah's recorded prophecies are closer to the uncompromising stance of Jeremiah, who does not promise salvation even to a king who asks what would happen if he obeyed the prophet (Jer 38:14–28).

2:12. Two parallel phrases, "I will surely gather...I will gather," use two different verbs (ʾsp, the piel of qbṣ) for Yhwh's promise to gather or assemble of Israel (Isa 11:12; Mic 4:6). Each verb is doubled in a characteristic emphatic construction (absolute infinitive + imperfect), and the synonyms further reinforce the certainty of the promise. The assurance is a fittingly dramatic contrast to the long section of judgment that precedes it. The divine promise affirms God's intention to reunite his people, who have been scattered by exile and flight. These verbs are often used in the promises of salvation and return addressed to the Babylonian exiles (Isa 40:11; Jer 23:3; Ezek 11:17). "survivors" (šᵉʾērît) is elsewhere translated "remnant" (Mic 4:7; Amos 5:15). God's promises to his covenant people will not be overthrown completely, even though judgment is inevitable. But through judgment comes the possibility of survival and hope.

The second part of the verse expounds the well-known sheep metaphor (cf. 5:8[7]; 7:14; Bosetti 1993), one that is particularly important in exile (Ezek 34). The shepherd is Yhwh (Ps 23:1) or his appointed king/leaders (2 Sam 5:2), his people the sheep and their military enemies are predatory animals who scatter them over the mountains (1 Kgs 22:17), from where the good shepherd will gather them (Jer 23:1–4; Ezek 34:12–13). "like sheep in a fold" is literally "sheep of Bozrah" (AV). Bozrah, the capital of Edom, may have been a well-known centre for shearing sheep (Andersen and Freedman 2000; cf. "flocks of Kedar," Isa 60:7), but this seems unlikely. Most of the ancient versions support a slight emendation to "in a fold." A closely related form of the word means "encampment" (Gen 25:16), perhaps used to emphasize the human target of the metaphor. "fold" makes a good parallel to "in its pasture (Isa 5:17). "resound" (hwm) comes from a verb meaning "to make a noise, confuse." "with people" understands the preposition (min) as causal, so that the noise comes from a great multitude (1 Sam 4:5). The same root is significant in explaining the change of Abram's name to Abraham (Gen 17:4–5). The verb may then hint at a fulfilment of the Abrahamic promise of blessing and progeny. The cities, of which the fold is a picture, will be full of people (cf. Gen 16:10; Zech 2:4[8]; Rev 19:6). The preposition could also be spatial, "from," and the NJB highlights the secure isolation of the pasture by translating "they will bleat far away from anyone."

2:13. If the setting for this verse is 701 B.C.E., the gate would be that of besieged Jerusalem (cf. 1:9, 12). But "break through" (*prṣ*) usually describes breaking through or down walls (Neh 1:3; Prov 25:28), and this is unnecessary for defenders. The text is also silent about the major problem of 701 B.C.E., the invading army. Instead, the picture may precede v. 12 and explain how the people have been regathered. Yhwh is "the one who breaks out" (2 Sam 5:20), because he has to lead the people out from their present confinement. The language used is that of the Exodus and highlights that Israel's hope lies in the character of the God who brought them up from Egypt. The Israelites go up (*ʿālâ*) from Egypt (Exod 13:18) because God goes before his people (Exod 13:21; Num 27:17; cf. Isa 52:12) and passes over before them (Deut 31:3). The escape from oppression at the Exodus is a powerful paradigm of the return from exile (Hos 11; Isa 11:16).

The gate is then that of a prison or city that holds the Israelites captive (Isa 45:1). It is the negative counterpart of the place of plenty and peace which in v. 12 is portrayed by the sheepfold metaphor. It may therefore metaphorically refer to the place of exile, rather than a literal city. With Yhwh in charge, they are able to overcome the guards, break through the gate, pass through it and so go out of the city by it (i.e. the gate). The final two parallel phrases describe the most important feature of the triumphal procession, "the LORD at their head." The parallelism suggests that the reference to "their king at their head" is another way of describing God, rather than any messianic figure (Isa 33:22; Zeph 3:15). However, the overlap of attributes of God and Messiah meant that later interpreters were not so exclusive (e.g. Targ). Although the pastoral imagery of v. 12 gives way to the military language of v. 13, the theme of kingship links the two verses. The shepherd-king is a well-known biblical figure (2 Sam 5:2; Ezek 34), and the care and compassion of a shepherd qualifies and complements the awesome power and justice of the king (Brueggemann 1997, 259–61). The New Testament asserts that both aspects inform the person and work of Jesus Christ (John 10; Heb 13:20; Rev 7:17).

Judgment on Israel's Corrupt Leaders (3:1–12)

The condemnation of evil deeds in ch. 2 leads to accusations that highlight the office of those who should have known how to behave in accordance with Israel's covenant law. In ch. 3 we find a well-constructed set of three oracles of judgment of roughly equal length (vv. 1–4, 5–8, 9–12). The third brings to a climax the previous two by addressing the target of the first oracle (Israel's leaders, vv. 1, 9) and the second (the prophets, vv. 5–6, 11a). It also adds the third pillar of Israelite society, the priests (v. 11a). The final accusation reprises the content of the first (perversion of justice) and the second (bribery and corruption), but emphasizes the underlying theological fault, a mistaken presumption about their relationship with God (v. 11b). Although justice is a key theme that comes in every section (vv. 1, 8, 9), social behaviour cannot be separated from the content and quality of faith in God.

The oracles have a similar form: (1) introduction (summons to listen, vv. 1, 9; messenger formula, v. 5); (2) general accusation (participles characterize the offending party) (3) exposition of accusation (4) announcement of punishment ("then," v. 4; "therefore," vv. 6, 12). The setting and date of the oracles is (as usual) disputed because of the lack of specific historical references. Most take them as addressing Israel shortly before 701 B.C.E. (see the commentary on v. 12). Wolff (1990, 96–97) speculates that the setting is the outer court of the temple in Jerusalem (cf. Jer 26), where those addressed would have gathered.

At the heart of the first oracle against the leaders is the accusation of their behaviour, expounded by means of a complex, extended metaphor that likens them to wild beasts and butchers (vv. 2–3). The second oracle against the prophets emphasizes instead the fitting judgment upon their claims to know the will of God, worked out in an extended promise of punishment (vv. 6–7). The third oracle begins with an almost exact repetition of v. 1, but the scope of the earlier accusation appears to be broadened beyond the judges and the law court as it moves towards the general accusation of v. 10. The judgment is on all those who run the city (cf. the leaders listed in Isa 3:2–3). Three specific accusations follow: (1) the leaders oppress others (v. 10); (2) they make money the dominant value (v. 11a); (3) they presume upon God's favour (v. 11b). The result is a comprehensive announcement of judgment on Jerusalem (v. 12). The poetry as well as the content brings the section to a stirring close. The balanced parallel phrases of vv. 9 and 10 give way in vv. 11a, 11b and 12 to three sets of three parallel phrases.

Such oracles of judgment are not necessarily irrevocable decrees (cf. 2 Kgs 20 = Isa 38). Depending on the response by their hearers, they can function as desperate warnings. Their ultimate purpose is thus to encourage repentance and radical trust in Yhwh's mercy.

Judgment on the Greedy (3:1–4)

3:1. The initial "And I said" has troubled commentators (Willis 1968a), since it usually appears in the middle of a narrative (Hos 3:3; Isa 6:5) rather than at the beginning of a prophetic oracle. Some think that it is a remnant of an autobiographical section, but it is difficult to see why it would have been retained. If it were Micah's response to the false prophets mentioned in 2:11, we would expect it to be more specific. Its function in the present context seems to be to resume Micah's accusations, since this section of oracles (3:1–12), while distinct, contains a number of words found in 2:1–11.

"Listen" (*šmᶜ*) marks the opening of another section of the book (cf. 1:2; 6:1; but also 3:9). The parallel pair Jacob//Israel comes in 2:12, but there the context is positive. In addressing the "heads of Jacob and rulers of the house of Israel" Micah draws a sharp contrast between the future salvation of the people of God and their suffering under the present political leadership. The "heads" (*rōʾš*) were originally clan or tribal leaders with military or judicial responsibilities (Exod 18:25; Josh 14:1), but they were always to be subject to Yhwh, the true head (Mic 2:13). "rulers" (*qāṣîn*) can describe a military commander (Josh 10:24), or someone who holds power (Isa 3:6–7). Both words in parallel refer to those who held power in Jerusalem. The king is not mentioned, perhaps because the main offences take place lower down the official hierarchy. Nevertheless, the king can be included in the accusation, for he has the ultimate responsibility to maintain justice, the keenest test for the corruption of power.

Micah's accusation starts with a rhetorical question ("Should you not know justice?") that takes as a premise (GKC §150e) that these leaders do know their responsibilities. Justice (*mišpāṭ*) is central to Israel's theology (Gen 18:25; Ps 89:14[15]; Jer 9:24) and its covenantal traditions (Lev 19:15). The administration of justice is the primary requirement for Israel's leaders, who took on the role of judge when necessary (Deut 16:18–20) and who were required to know the law (cf. Deut 17:19). Justice establishes the norms that are to guide the relations between members of the covenant community, preventing exploitation of the weak and innocent by the strong and ruthless (Exod 23:1–9). The authentic prophetic voice is found in calling the powerful to account for their perversion of justice (1 Kgs 21:17–29; 2 Sam 12; Hab 1:4). In this chapter Micah passionately seeks to communicate God's desire for justice. He warns too of the measures that will be taken if it is not established, for Yhwh is the ultimate guardian of justice (Ps 140:12[13]) and he will act to ensure that it is maintained and the unjust punished.

3:2a. As in the other oracles (3:5, 9) the general accusation is expounded by means of a relative participle ("you who"). The perversion of justice is defined as a double inversion of basic values (Isa 5:20): "hate the good and love the evil." In the legal context, "good" (*ṭôb*) and "evil" (*rāʿâ*) might be translated "right" and "wrong" (Hillers 1984), but "hate" (*śnʾ*) and "love" (*ʾhb*) emphasizes that behaviour in law and society reflects the deepest personal passions. Both pairs of opposites are found in wisdom texts, suggesting that justice embodies fundamental and universal values (for good/evil, see Prov 11:27; 12:2; Ps 34:14[15]; for love/hate, see Prov 1:22; 8:36; Ps 45:7[8]). These are so intertwined in Israel's covenantal commitment that it is impossible to isolate the moral, legal and religious components. To do so would undermine the coherence and scope of Micah's accusation. The law court is a paradigm and metaphor for the entire range of human values and relationships. These people have not only overturned the required legal standards, they have also rejected the fundamental moral basis for their society, which in turn is a rejection of the God who stands behind Israel's law and who ensures that it is obeyed. Micah joins the other prophets who vigorously advocated the proper ordering of basic values (Amos 5:15; Isa 1:16–17).

3:2b–3. The images that follow are probably metaphoric rather than literal (for people as food, see Ps 14:4; Prov 30:14), but the cannibalistic overtones sharpen the accusation and heighten the offensiveness. The Old Testament does know of cannibalism, but only in extreme situations of siege (Deut 28:52–57; 2 Kgs 6:26–29). The source of the metaphor in v. 2b appears to be of wild animals preying on sheep or other defenceless animals (Judg 14:6; Ezek 34:5). Like carnivores, the leaders are violent and lack any concern for the victim. Micah attacks head-on the impersonal and indirect character of injustice that is possible in a corrupt law court (1 Kgs 21). In v. 3 the verbs change from participles to perfects and a chiastic pattern (skin–flesh–flesh–skin) maintains continuity while replaying the metaphor in the human realm of cooking. In the modern world these people would be butchers, a fitting term for such ruthless murderers. In a traditional society the person who prepares the meat is usually the same person who eats it (1 Sam 2:13–15), but the wealthy and unjust would be able to afford to sacrifice more often. The style of the section matches its content. The slow, systematic, complete destruction of innocent life for selfish purposes is communicated by the inexorable progression of brief phrases. The passage is a recipe intended to shock and horrify. These people care as little for their neighbours as a lion for its prey, or a greedy person for what he is eating. The leaders and judges should have been watchdogs; they turn out to be ravenous lions or wolves (Zeph 3:3). The "like" of the two final phrases acknowledges the metaphoric character of the passage, bringing it to an end and preparing us for a further announcement of judgment on the targets of the oracle.

In the prophets "tear" (*gzl*, as in 2:2) describes those who snatch away what belongs to the defenceless and the poor (Isa 10:2; Ezek 18:12). The sequence skin–flesh–bones describes the progressive consumption of the entire animal. Two phrases describe the preparation of the food (dealing with the skin and bones), and two the cooking (the cutting up of the meat, then the cooking in a cauldron). "flay" (hiphil of *pšṭ*) is the verb used in 2:8 for stripping off clothing, but it is also a technical term for skinning a sacrificial animal (Lev 1:6). In English its use is reflected in the idiom of skinning someone alive (cf. GNB, NJB). "kettle" is better translated as "pot" (REB), but to know how it differs from "cauldron" would need an eighth-century B.C.E. kitchen catalogue. The only other occurrence of cauldron in the Old Testament is 1 Sam 2:14, where it is the third of four terms for cooking pots.

. Almost all translations accept an emendation of the Hebrew "as into" (*kᵉšr*; so NJPS) to "like flesh" (*kšᵉr*; so LXX). NRSV confusingly translates it "like meat," despite this being the flesh of vv. 2b, 3a. This then makes a good parallel to the final "flesh," which is a synonym (*bāśār*) that can be a collective for humanity (Isa 40:5). This brings the passage to a fitting close by coalescing the source (animal flesh) and the target (human beings) of the metaphor.

3:4. "Then" (*ʾāz*) projects us forward to the future, when the evil deeds mentioned in the accusation will be punished. It carries the logic of the oracle of judgment and is the equivalent of the normal "therefore." The chronological order of the phrases appears to be the reverse of the written order. The final phrase alludes to the initial provocation ("they acted wickedly"), then comes the hiding of God's face, which results in punishment. This punishment is not specified, but is so terrible that the sufferers "cry to the LORD"—there is, however, no response. The disordered chronology highlights the shock of reversal. The helplessness indicated by the cry is a dramatic contrast to the previous verses, where they are in complete control. By informing us only of their response, Micah leaves it to our unconstrained imaginations to picture the horrifying details of the punishment that has caused such self-confident and ungodly people to appeal to God. Putting the cry first means that their plight remains with us through the following phrases. "cry" (z^cq) describes the desperate appeal of those in acute distress to someone who can answer (i.e. save) them. God answered his people when they cried to him at the Exodus (Exod 5:8, 15) and promises to answer those who cry out to him in repentance (Isa 58:9). But these people have abandoned their obligations as God's covenant people, so they have no claim when they cry to him (cf. Jer 11:11). The verb also occurs as an aspect of a legal appeal (2 Kgs 6:26; 8:5), so there may be another illustration of the *lex talionis*. Those who refused to answer the cry of those whom they had defrauded and robbed in court will find themselves equally helpless when they appear in the divine court (Prov 21:13; Jas 2:13). The shining of God's face leads to blessing (Num 6:26), but sin causes him to hide his face and the result is disaster (Deut 31:17–18; Jer 33:5). All who suffer can share the psalmist's hope and trust that God will answer and not hide his face (Ps 27:7–9). But this last resort is excluded for these people, who are utterly God-forsaken (2 Thess 1:9). "If God be against us, who can be for us?" (Achtemeier 1996, 318). The final phrase rounds off the oracle by returning to the accusation: "because" emphasizes once again the justice of God in punishing these people who "acted wickedly" (r^{cc}; recalling the evil $r\bar{a}^c\hat{a}$ of v. 2) and rejected justice (v. 1). It can also be translated "in accordance with" (NJPS), highlighting the *lex talionis*, the correspondence of their evil deeds (2:7; 7:13) with the consequences that follow. Those who imposed on others misery without relief will in turn suffer unrelieved distress.

Judgment on the False Prophets (3:5–8)

3:5. The second oracle begins with the second (and final) messenger formula ("Thus says the LORD," 2:3) in Micah, perhaps to emphasize the contrast between Micah's genuine oracles and those false prophets who gave a very different message. These prophets "lead my people astray" (hiphil of t^ch), letting them wander without direction like Hagar in the desert (Gen 21:14) or an ownerless ox (Exod 23:4). The implied norm is the moral and religious path that the prophets should have been helping the people to follow (Jer 23:13, 32). "when they have something to eat" is literally "who bite with their teeth" (cf. AV). The verb describes the bite of poisonous snakes (Jer 8:17; Amos 5:19), thus echoing the vicious image of vv. 2–3. But the root is also used for the extortion of interest (Hab 2:7). Though not intended literally, the implication is that these people are "greedy snakes" (Andersen and Freedman 2000) and that allowing them to feed is potentially lethal. Early prophets were indeed paid for their services (1 Sam 9:7; 1 Kgs 14:3), but that should not have affected their message. Later on the independence of the prophets was compromised by their financial dependence on the king or wealthy patrons. The result was that they overlooked or even sanctioned abuses of the covenant such as those described by Micah. Rather than warning about the judgment to come, they "cry 'Peace'." "cry" (*qrᵓ*) is better translated "proclaim" (NIV) or "announce" (see on Jonah 1:2), suggesting an official and authoritative announcement about the present state of the nation or an individual. Conveniently ignoring behaviour, they promise "peace" (*šālôm*), perhaps the Old Testament's richest word to indicate the blessings of salvation (Deut 28:1–14). The term *šālôm* included bodily health, social harmony, economic plenty, and political security. The prophets promised such peace, but without its essential ethical and religious foundations (Jer 6:14; Ezek 13:10). The corruption of the prophetic office may explain why Micah, like Amos (7:14), does not describe himself as a prophet. The existence of prophets (or at least men of God) saying contradictory things about the divine will raises the question of how the people were to discern which prophets were true and which were false. The discussion is complex, partly because the canonical prophets have given us only one side of the debate and we must deduce the other side from their criticisms. Further, not everything the false prophets do or say is illegitimate (Matt 23:2–3). Micah denounces the false prophets for their motives and how they worked out their calling, rather than the institution of prophecy as such. Nevertheless, certain basic differences between true and false prophets stand out. From the ethical point of view, the canonical prophets stood up for the weak and recalled the powerful to the fundamental demands of the covenant. The message of the false prophets was less conditional on behaviour. On the personal level, the true prophet had to be prepared to be unpopular and stand against the powerful, risking rejection, mockery, imprisonment and isolation (1 Kgs 22:6–13; Jer 28). The false prophets were concerned primarily for themselves, and so were happy to cater to those with wealth and power. Nor is it just members of the ancient Israel religious establishment that find a prosperity theology oriented to wealth preferable to social action.

"declare war" is literally "sanctify war" or "consecrate war." The verb includes the "holy" root (piel of *qdš*; cf. Josh 7:13; Jer 6:4; Isa 13:3) and probably indicates a verbal declaration of war (Joel 3:9[4:9]). A war so sanctified was one waged specifically on behalf of Yhwh, although it was never called a "holy war" (Jones 1978). Here it ironically describes the behaviour that has aroused Yhwh's enmity. They declare war against those who refuse to feed them. "those who put nothing in their mouths" is more literally "those who do not give/put/pay (*ntn*) upon their mouth." "mouth" (*peh*) may stand (by metonymy) for what comes from their mouth, namely, demands or wishes. The phrase would then describe someone (the verb is singular) who does not give what these prophets demand (Waltke 1993) or desire (Wolff 1990). The situation in mind might be an honest person seeking a prophet's guidance for a legitimate reason, but finding that he demanded too much money. The prophet then employs the threat of God's enmity to get what he wants, a form of religious extortion.

3:6–7. "Therefore" (*lāḵēn*) is the classical transition from accusation to punishment in a prophetic oracle of judgment, indicating that the terrible consequences are completely just and fitting. The nature of the judgment is driven home in eight brief phrases. The first two address the prophets directly ("to you"), but later references are in the third person ("the prophets"), perhaps indicating that they had no more choice in the matter. The first two phrases of v. 6 echo the first two in v. 7, although NRSV unhelpfully uses different translations. "revelation" ("divination," REB, NJB, NIV) has the same root as "diviners" (*qsm*; cf. v. 11a), and "vision" the same as "seers" (*ḥzh*; see on Obad 1). Divination usually implies the exercise of various techniques to discover the divine will (Jer 27:9; Ezek 21:21[26]) and is fiercely condemned (Deut 18:10, 14; 1 Sam 15:23; 2 Kgs 17:17). Yet Micah uses in parallel other words (vision, seer) that reflect legitimate Israelite ways of discovering God's will (Prov 16:10 even has a positive reference to divination). One possibility is that Micah accepts the legitimacy of divination and merely criticizes the motives, not the message or methods (perhaps why NRSV translates "revelation"). But Micah may be interpreting rather than describing the work of these prophets. Their techniques may have been perfectly orthodox, but the content and result of their prophetic work was as empty and abhorrent to God as if divination had been used.

Sight is the surest source of knowledge and is a prominent metaphoric feature of the vocabulary of revelation and prophecy. But these prophets have misused their authority and office, so judgment will instead bring night and darkness (v. 6). The fourth phrase includes a verb, and the parallelism also suggests a more dynamic translation such as "the day will go black" (NJB). In apocalyptic passages this imagery frequently conveys the onset of disaster, death and exclusion from God's presence (Amos 5:18; Isa 8:22; Rev 16:10). As in v. 4, the chronological order of the metaphor seems to be inverted, for night falls after the sun goes down.

The status as well as the subsistence of these prophets depended on public belief that they had genuine access to God. When their punishment makes it clear that they are charlatans, they will be disgraced and put to shame (Zech 13:3–4). Even in the modern world, the success or wealth of a person counts for little without the respect and affirmation of others. Micah here states that those who had previously looked to them for guidance will spurn them. Their spiritual bankruptcy will be evident to all at the time of crisis, when guidance was most needed (1 Kgs 22:5; 2 Kgs 19:2). Judgment in the Bible has a prominent social dimension.

"cover their lips" refers to a mourning custom (Ezek 22:17, 22; cf. Lev 13:45), indicating the depth of the grief resulting from loss of contact with God. "cover" (*ʿṭh*) is used of wrapping round clothes, so the reference is probably to veiling (rather than "hands over their mouths," REB). "lips" (*śāpām*) is a rare word that NRSV elsewhere translate "upper lip" (Lev 13:45). In 2 Sam 19:24[25] it is a beard or moustache (LXX *mustax*; so BDB 974; *HALOT* 1348). Andersen and Freedman (2000) suggest that a robe is wrapped round right up to the moustache. The origin of such mourning customs is obscure, but they may symbolize solidarity with the dead through the symbolic temporary covering of essential signs of life (smell, speech, growth of hair). A conjunction ("for") sets off the final phrase from the others, indicating that it is a summary and climactic restatement of the essence of the judgment (vv. 4, 6), the absence of communication with God and any hope of his help. This is again an outworking of the *lex talionis*. Those who served themselves when requested for an answer from God will find in the end that God refuses to answer them under any circumstances (cf. 1 Kgs 18:29).

3:8. The end of the oracle stands somewhat apart, but its affirmation of Micah's status as a true prophet is a dramatic contrast to the opening criticism of the false prophets in v. 5. There is no call narrative in Micah, but it is implicit in this verse, which reflects Micah's confidence that he has the authentic prophetic gifting (v. 8a) that will enable him to declare the authentic prophetic message (v. 8b). The rare autobiographical declaration is provoked by the false spirituality and message of the false prophets. "But as for me" (using the long form of the independent personal pronoun *'ānōkî*) is the strongest possible antithesis, often found in the middle of a speech (Num 14:21; 1 Kgs 20:23). The false prophets have plenty to say but they are windbags, full of their own words. In contrast, it is God who has made Micah an overflowing container, so filled with divine passion and indignation that he must pour out his message (for the same metaphor, see Jer 6:11; 15:17). The three nouns (power, justice, might) are interrupted by "with the spirit of the LORD," which is introduced (unlike the others) by a preposition. Many think this is a later redactional gloss, because of the interrupted sequence and because of the later association of prophecy with the spirit (Joel 2:28[3:1]). However, the general association of prophets with the spirit of Yhwh is an early one (1 Sam 10:6; 1 Kgs 22:24). The verses shares several elements of the royal gifting of Isa 11:2–5 (spirit of Yhwh, might, the justice root; Crook 1954). Whatever its origin, the phrase is a polemical refutation of the false prophets and an affirmation of the divine source of Micah's power (Ringgren 1982, 124–26). Human power is frequently inadequate (1 Sam 2:9) and easily countered (Hos 7:9), but power given by God is sufficient for every need (Isa 40:29, 31; Eph 6:10; 1 Pet 4:11). Such power is in the service of justice, the heart of Micah's preaching (see on v. 1). "might" (*gᵉbûrâ*) is related to the word for "mighty warrior" (*gibbôr*, e.g. Gen 10:8), and suggests the physical bravery and courage that Micah will need in his war against the prophets and leaders. The prophets (along with the king) represent the people and provide the ethical and religious lead. Therefore Micah must declare to the nation (Jacob//Israel) its transgression and sin (see on 1:5).

Judgment on the Establishment (3:9–12)
3:9. "abhor" (*t°b*) is a strong expression of ethical (Amos 5:10), religious (Deut 7:26) and ritual (Isa 14:19) rejection, and the cognate noun (*tô°ēbâ*) is often translated "abomination." These English translations suggest a strong emotional reaction. This may also be true for the original Hebrew, but if so then it is also based on a general recognition that there are certain actions that are completely incompatible with the judge of all the earth (Gen 18:25). "pervert all equity" is more literally "make crooked all that is straight" (NJPS). Those who walk in a straight path (Isa 40:3; Ezek 1:7) are not tempted to the right or left (2 Kgs 22:2) and demonstrate upright and blameless behaviour (1 Kgs 22:43; Hos 14:10). The heads and rulers (the same pair as in v. 1), on the other hand, bend the rules and so undermine the norms and limits that are essential for a just society. They not only take crooked and twisted paths themselves (Prov 28:18), they also ensure that others are not able to make honest progress on the journey of life (Isa 59:8).

3:10. Amos (3:15; 5:11), echoed by his successors (Jer 22:13–17; Hab 2:12), condemned the wealthy of Samaria for building luxury houses while the foundations of society, justice and compassion for the poor, were neglected. However, the mention of "Zion" and "Jerusalem" in parallel suggests that a public building program is in mind. The expansion of building in Hezekiah's time is reflected in 2 Chr 32:27–29, which mentions the Siloam tunnel, one of the great engineering feats of the time. But Micah is not an admiring tourist. Instead, he forthrightly condemns the motives and methods of those responsible for the building. Although the king is ultimately responsible, Micah does not mention him (see on v. 11). No doubt the builders defended their architectural masterpieces by the way they expressed the capital's wealth and status, enhanced national pride and provided international respectability. But what matters to Micah is the living stones of the city, its people (1 Pet 2:5). "Micah, like Jesus contemplating Jerusalem (cf. Mark 13:1–2), has an 'X-ray vision' that penetrates below the surface" (Alfaro 1989, 38). "blood" (*dām*) stands by metonymy for the death that comes from the shedding of blood ("bloodshed," REB, NIV; "murder," NLT). The plural form may suggest a multitude of deaths. It is uncertain whether the reference is to innocent victims whose land had been seized, to those who suffered building accidents, or to general hardship due to the necessary forced labour and taxes. While not necessarily fatal, all of these could result in poverty, starvation and eventually death, particularly for the old and the very young. "wrong" (*°awlâ*) may describe the corruption of the legal process by the judges (Zeph 3:5; Isa 61:8; Lev 19:15). In extreme cases this could result in death (1 Kgs 21). "blood" has ritual and legal overtones of bloodguilt. Those who shed innocent blood are guilty before God and incur punishment (Gen 4:10; Deut 19:10).

3:11a. Micah condemns in turn the legal, ritual and religious leaders who were responsible for maintaining the social fabric of Jerusalem. The divine authorization of their offices made such actions all the more heinous. The verbs are in the imperfect, suggesting persistent behaviour. "give judgment" (*špt*) may refer not just to judicial verdicts, but also to decisions on various aspects of city life. The prohibition of judges not accepting a bribe was an important demand of the law (Exod 23:8; Deut 16:19) as well as the Wisdom Literature (Prov 17:8). The canonical prophets were aware that integrity in the administration of justice was an essential basis for the right ordering and continuation of the covenant community (Isa 1:23; 5:23). When money and not justice becomes the decisive factor, then trust and unity evaporates, division grows and the downfall of the nation became inevitable. The task of priests was to teach (hiphil of *yrh*, the same root as Torah/law) general ethical and religious duties (Lev 10:11; Deut 33:10; Hos 4:6), but they also rendered verdicts on disputed ritual issues, such as the presence of a blemish or impurity (Lev 14:57; 22:20). Since maintaining the laws of purity and sacrifice could be a costly business, a price paid to the priest could be a profitable transaction for both parties (e.g. the acceptance of a blind animal for sacrifice, Mal 1:8). But it also destroyed the integrity of those who should have most fully reflected God's holiness and righteousness. Micah's third accusation sets out what has been implied in v. 5, the avarice of the prophets, who give oracles ("divine" as in vv. 6–7) for money (*kesep*; lit. "silver," the most common medium of exchange). The difference between a gift for the services of a prophet (Num 22:18; 1 Kgs 13:7–8; 2 Kgs 5:15) and bribery was easily blurred. When payment comes from those who may need to hear awkward truths, there is a strong temptation to compromise the truth or simply remain silent.

It is striking that Micah mentions rulers, priests, prophets, but not the king. His absence in Mic 1–3 is puzzling, for the king was ultimately responsible for the exercise and establishment of justice (2 Sam 15:1–6; 1 Kgs 3:28; Ps 72:2) and a just king was an important element in Israel's messianic hope (Isa 9:7; Jer 23:5). Of course, as the nation grew the responsibility had to be delegated for most of the day-to-day legal work and 2 Chr 19:8 states that Jehoshaphat appointed Levites, priests and heads of families to judge cases. Yet this would diminish but not remove the responsibility. Perhaps the role of the king in the law courts had by this time greatly decreased. Perhaps Micah knew that Hezekiah did not deserve the same outright condemnation as the other leaders. Perhaps he was such an unknown and distant figure to Micah, who would not have had the same access as Isaiah had, that he was regarded as practically irrelevant and simply omitted. The messianic portrait of 5:2 recalls the earlier, simpler times of the books of Samuel, rather than the more complex, delegated and dispersed set of authorities that grew as the nation developed.

Why do the leaders behave in such a way? Micah traces the lack of social conscience to a theological error, a foolish and one-sided doctrine of election that takes no account of behaviour and Israel's covenant traditions. Micah uses another vivid spatial metaphor (cf. v. 9), that of leaning against an object (2 Sam 1:6) or person (2 Kgs 7:2) and being supported. To "lean upon Yhwh" is synonymous with trusting him (Isa 30:12; Prov 3:5). It is an attitude that is linked to salvation (2 Chr 16:8), but these people had forgotten that moral integrity is a necessary precondition of this trust. When this happens the result will be judgment not salvation (Isa 30:12; 31:1).

"Surely the LORD is with us!" sets out the central premise in the argument. "with us" is more literally "in our midst" (*beqirbēnû*; REB, NJB), reflecting a strong presumption of God's favourable presence. Israel's early accounts of war affirmed that when Yhwh was with this people, victory was assured (Deut 7:21). With Yhwh in the midst of Jerusalem, the city was guaranteed safety and salvation (Ps 46:5[6]). Yet Israel's traditions also warned that the nation could not presume upon his presence, and if it did, then defeat would follow (Num 14:42; Deut 1:42). Micah's leaders had ignored this principle and the fatal conclusion of their one-sided interpretation of the tradition was that "No harm shall come upon us" (cf. Amos 9:10). "harm" (*rāʿâ*) is the same word as v. 2 and the opposite of the peace of v. 5. The link between theology and ethics is foundational to Israel's being, witnessed to by all of Israel's varied literature, whether story, law or prophecy (Janzen 1994). The attitude of God to his people depends on how they behave, particularly in ensuring that the weak and the powerless find justice (Exod 22:22[21]; 23:6; 2 Sam 12). The blessings and curses set out with uncompromising clarity that good or harm pursue and overtake Israel depending on their behaviour (Deut 28:2, 45).

3:12. "Therefore," as in v. 6, asserts that the punishment fits the crime of Israel's leaders. The buildings that were a source of pride and evil in v. 10 will be utterly demolished. Those who trusted Yhwh to protect its walls (v. 11b) will find only "a heap of ruins." Jerusalem will follow Samaria (1:6–7) in experiencing the judgment of God. "The prophecy stands as a declaration of Yhwh's freedom from any institutionalization of his presence, a freedom manifest in readiness to judge even those who believe in him" (Mays 1976, 92). God will abandon what has become merely a monument to covenant infidelity (Allen 1976) and Jerusalem will become as vulnerable as a house built of straw (1 Cor 3:11–17).

This prophecy is unique in its severity and comprehensiveness (compare the more limited punishment of Isa 1:21–26; 5:14). A testimony to its explosive impact is its lively presence a century later. After Jeremiah had predicted the destruction of the temple in a similar way to Micah (Jer 7), those discussing what to do with him quote this verse almost verbatim. There it is introduced by the messenger formula ("Thus says the LORD of hosts"). Here the divine "I" is not used, although divine agency is made perfectly clear by the use of passive and impersonal verbs. The following verse (Jer 26:19) attributes the repentance of Hezekiah to Micah's message, even though in 2 Kgs 19 it is Isaiah and not Micah who is the key figure. The prophecy may appear irrevocable, but the story shows that Yhwh remained free to forgive and allow Jerusalem to stand. Yet the prophecy is suspended rather than revoked. It remained an authoritative pronouncement preserved by Israel's canonical traditions and waiting to be triggered at the right moment. The unrepentant response to Jeremiah's message led to its tragic fulfilment: "O God, the nations have come into your inheritance; they have defiled your holy temple; they have laid Jerusalem in ruins" (Ps 79:1).

Such prophecies remain potent for later generations, ready to be recycled at an appropriate time. So it is that Jesus of Nazareth sorrowfully promises another ruination when the leaders of Jerusalem reject his warnings against presumption and pride (Matt 23; Mark 13).

Rather than "ploughed as a field," the parallel phrases suggest a process of transformation, "ploughed into a field." The image is not of farmers cultivating land, but enemies making a thorough job of destruction. Even the foundations will be ploughed up, leaving uninhabited open country, fit only for animals (Gen 27:3). The "heap of ruins" (the same word as in 1:6; cf. Ps 79:1) probably describes a tel, the overgrown remains of what was once a city but whose very name may well have been forgotten. Zion and Jerusalem are synonymous terms for the city, mirroring their pairing in the accusation of v. 10. Finally, Micah refers to "the mountain of the house," an abbreviation of "the mountain of the house of the LORD" (Isa 2:2 = Mic 4:1). Wolff (1990) suggests that Micah deliberately avoided using the divine name, for by this time he had abandoned his dwelling place (cf. Ezek 10:9; 11:23). But this is a threat rather than a description. The "house of Yhwh" was a common name for the temple, so what is being described is the "Temple Mount" (REB, NJPS, NJB; cf. Vulg., Targ.). The Temple Mount was located on the height where the ancient Jebusite city Zion had stood (2 Sam 5:7). This was to the southeast, and with the growth of the state Jerusalem had been extended to the south-western hill. It is lower than the surrounding hills, and the claim that it was built on a mountain is a mythological rather than a geographical description, reflecting the majestic presence of the God who dwelt there (see on 4:1). But God has abandoned it and so it will become a wooded height, literally "the heights (*bāmôṯ*) of the forest." "heights" is an unusual construct form so some have read a singular (with LXX, Vulg.). It is also the word used to describe shrines (cf. NJPS), but the parallel ("heap of ruins") implies a more secular meaning. Forest (*yaʿar*) can describe a range of habitats, from regions of lofty trees to low shrubland ("rough moorland," REB; Mulder 1990, 208–10). Whichever habitat we imagine, the threat is that what was regarded as the centre of the Israelite political and religious universe will become a place of desolation, forsaken by God and people.

Hope for the Future (Chapters 4–5)

The structure of this section is disputed, since there are complex interrelationships between the subsections with regard to language, theme and setting. The distinct sections are generally identified by key opening words or phrases, such as "In that day, says " (4:6; 5:10), "now" (4:9, 11; 5:1) "and shall be" (5:5, 7, 10). Other keywords unite sections (e.g. "daughter Zion," 4:8, 10, 13). When combined with other signs of the opening and close of sections, up to ten subsections have been detected (Andersen and Freedman 2000): 4:1–5; 4:6–7; 4:8; 4:9–10; 4:11–13; 5:1; 5:2–4; 5:5–6; 5:7–9; 5:10–15. Different analyses relate these various subjections to each other in various ways and with different levels of hierarchy (Jacobs 2001).

Others explore chiastic relationships between various sections (Nielsen 1954). This is the common biblical technique in which outer and inner subsections correspond to each other). Renaud (1977, 281), for example, has the following overall chiastic structure (my summary of his lengthy titles):

A	4:1–5		In the last days: pilgrimage of the nations
B		4:6–7	The remnant transformed into a strong nation
	C	4:8–13	To Jerusalem: promise of victory
	C′	5:1–3	To Bethlehem: establishment of the messianic era
B′		5:4–9	The remnant supreme in the messianic era
A′	5:10–15		In the last days: purification of the nations and destruction of idols

Although this helpfully highlights a number of echoes and parallels, it also illustrates problems typical of such complex structures. The themes do not correspond as closely as we would like, and some sections identified by significant repetitions are not accounted for (e.g. 5:5–15).

Hagstrom (1988, 45–87) proposes a simpler threefold structure: 4:1–7; 4:8–5:3; 5:4–15. This takes into account most of the verbal repetitions mentioned above, and suggests a logical (but not chronological) relation between the main sections. The first section portrays the ultimate future that is the result of the following verses. The second is characterized by a contrast between the present era of distress and the coming era of salvation. The third focuses on the positive implications of the coming of the messianic era for Israel. Jacobs (2001) distinguishes the opening statement of Yhwh's future reign (4:1–5) and its actualization (4:6–7; 4:8–5:9; 5:10–15). Innumerable other proposals could be listed. Perhaps more significant than the precise structure is the overall tone of this section. The orientation is primarily to God's actions in the future rather than Israel's sins in the past. The mood is one of hope in God's salvation rather than dismay at his judgment on Israel's sins.

For reasons of simplicity the following commentary discusses in turn the ten sections identified by Andersen and Freedman (2000), tracing their connections with the other sections. Since the verse numbers in Mic 5 are one more than the Hebrew from 5:1[Heb 4:14] to the end of the chapter, only the English numbering will be used in this section to avoid cumbersome referencing.

The Joy of All the Earth (4:1–5)

The future orientation of this section links it to 3:9–12, but the portrayal is positive rather than negative and sets the tone for chs. 4–5. The vision begins with the establishment of the Temple Mount (v. 1), which thereby becomes a centre of pilgrimage for the nations as they seek instruction from Yhwh (vv. 1b–2). It is also the place where they receive his justice, with the result that conflicts cease (v. 3a) and peace reigns (v. 3b). The consequence for individuals is prosperity and security (v. 4a). The sequence ends with an affirmation of the divine word that lies behind this incredible promise (v. 4b). An appendix (v. 5) is a response to the vision, a confession of commitment to Yhwh, the God of Israel.

This great promise of salvation for city and nation stands in dramatic contrast to the devastating announcement of Jerusalem's destruction in 3:12, and indeed to the general tenor of chs. 1–3. There the nations were the scourges of Israel, unwitting agents of God's judgment. Here, they humbly acknowledge the rule of the God of Jacob. Jerusalem in Micah's time contained many who hypocritically perverted the law (3:11). Now Zion becomes a centre for instruction (4:2). The city of blood (3:10) that Yhwh had abandoned (3:12) becomes a city of peace (4:3b) where he reigns (4:1). The city divided against itself (3:9–10) becomes the centre of international justice and peace (4:2–3).

Yet the vision also far transcends Judah and its internal concerns. The comparison of the Temple Mount to the mountains and hills (v. 1) introduces a cosmic dimension. Zion dwarfs all other mountains. Rudolph (1975) suggests that its height makes it visible from the ends of the earth so that it draws the peoples and nations (vv. 2–3) to it like a magnet. Cosmic change goes along with a revolution in international relations. The promise of universal justice and peace (v. 3) is a startling reversal of the war and conflict that dominates the normal course of human history. All this takes place without compromising Israel's particularistic faith centring on the God of Jacob (v. 2), his distinctive instruction (Torah, v. 2), the chosen city (Zion, v. 2) and the people of Yhwh (v. 5). The fate of Jerusalem and the world may look bleak in the immediate future, but God is unwilling to abandon his covenant people and promises a future for the city where he has put his name.

Difficult questions about the origin, date and purpose of this section are raised by the way in which vv. 1–3 are almost (but not quite) the same as Isa 2:2–4. In addition to various minor differences, there is no equivalent in Isaiah to v. 4, and only a partial overlap between v. 5 and Isa 2:5. Many explanations have been offered (see the surveys by Wildberger 1991, 85–87; Andersen and Freedman 2000, 413–27). Any proposal must take into account a range of issues, including style, vocabulary, meter, theme, context and a general understanding of the nature of prophecy and the formation of prophetic books.

The main alternatives are: (1) Isaiah is the author—the cosmic and international significance of Zion comes more frequently from Isaiah than Micah (Isa 6; 28–29; Wildberger 1957), but this is a precarious argument from silence. (2) Micah is the author (there are verbal and thematic links with 3:9–12 and the fitting 4:4 appears only in Micah)—but the links could be tighter, and we may simply be looking at good adaptation to the context by Micah or a redactor. (3) Isaiah and Micah adopted an oracle from elsewhere—it could have been composed by a prophet, or have been a liturgical fragment (its vocabulary and content echoes various psalms). (4) These and other verses (2:12–13; 4:1–9, 11–13; 5:4–5) are the words of Micah's prophetic opponents (van der Woude 1973; cf. Strydom 1989)—but this is speculative and the consequent diminishment of elements of hope makes Micah's message one-sided in comparison to other prophets. (5) The majority of scholars consider this to be an exilic or postexilic composition (Williamson 2006, 175–79)—the vocabulary often parallels that found in later texts, although the piecemeal nature of the comparisons and the uncertain direction of influence (did the oracle influence later writers?) weakens this argument (Schibler 1989; cf. van der Woude 1973, 397; Gosse 1993). The approach adopted here is that it is possible to make good sense of the passage in its present context in the book of Micah, and there is no overwhelming reason not to read it as from the prophet Micah.

One argument that has properly had little influence in recent discussions is the idea that Micah could not have written this oracle because its message contradicts the judgment announced against Jerusalem in 3:12. There are several possible explanations for this common prophetic phenomenon (Kapelrud 1961). Of most interest is that the contradictions point to fundamental theological tensions. God relates to his people as both judge and saviour, righteous and merciful. This is not so much a contradiction as a dialectic or polarity that is resolved or explored in various ways (Goldingay 1987; Brueggemann 1997). For example, judgment is often the necessary prelude to salvation. The introduction to 4:1 ("In days to come") suggests events in an indeterminate future, in contrast to the immanent future of 3:12. Those who survive the judgment are the remnant, a concept found in 2:12 (4:7; 5:6–7; 7:18; Isa 4; 6:11–13 etc.). It is the leaders of the nation rather than the common people who are criticised by Micah, and it is they who would be expected to bear the brunt of the threatened punishment. Others, such as those invited to join in the confession of v. 5, are encouraged by the oracle to remain faithful and trust in a better future (Heb 11).

4:1. "In days to come" refers to a time after a dramatic turning point (Num 24:14; Jer 48:47; Hos 3:5). Scholars have made a helpful distinction between prophetic and apocalyptic eschatology, although sometimes the boundaries are blurred and texts are often ambiguous. Prophetic eschatology is more characteristic of pre-exilic biblical writings. It looks towards an end that is substantially continuous with the present world. Ignorance and sin are rife, but they can be corrected (v. 2). Disputes occur, but they can be resolved (v. 3). The later apocalyptic eschatology, on the other hand, sees the future in more catastrophic and dualistic terms. The present world is irretrievably fallen, so that the world to come must exhibit a different order of being from this age. It will only come about as the result of a catastrophic, supernatural intervention by Yhwh (Hag 2:6; Zech 14). If the oracle is pre-exilic, then we should not import (at least to begin with) views characteristic of apocalyptic eschatology (this view might be implied by the translation "In the last days" of AV and NIV). A consideration of the date and viewpoint of the oracle affects the exegesis of the assertion that the Temple is "established as the highest of the mountains." As apocalyptic eschatology, this could be taken literally as the consequence of a supernatural cosmic and geographical upheaval. However, this is not necessarily the case if it is dated earlier, for Israel expounded its view of the significance of the Temple ("the LORD's house") and the City of God in terms that were drawn from a Canaanite and Mesopotamian mythology (see the summary in Talmon 1977, 441–47). The geographical reality was that the temple, built on Mount Zion, was relatively low and surrounded by higher hills (such as the Mount of Olives). But because Yhwh dwelt there, Israel asserted the supremacy of Yahweh by invoking the mythological idea that the gods dwelt on mountains in houses that were a heavenly reflection of the earthly sanctuary. The psalms thus assert that Zion was incomparable in height (Pss 48:1–2[2–3]; 78:69; cf. 68:15–18[16–19]), for the God who dwelt there was incomparable. As prophetic eschatology, then, the geographical reference is a political and religious metaphor communicating the prestige and authority of the God who dwelt in the Temple. It is the strongest possible reversal of the abandonment and destruction described in 3:12. Metaphorical geography continues to be an important theological resource in the New Testament (Acts 1:9; Rev 21–22). Later interpreters, however, could easily read it in accord with a more radical apocalyptic program.

NRSV correctly reads as parallel lines the last phrase of v. 1 and the first of v. 2. "stream" (*nhr*, the same root as "river") implies a continuous and substantial river of pilgrims coming to Zion to marvel and learn from the God who is there. The verb may hint at a reversal of the normal order, since rivers flow down a mountain, not up it. The parallel "come" makes it unlikely that it is a homonym meaning "to shine" (Isa 60:5; cf. "The peoples shall gaze on it with joy," NJPS). The previous threats were that the exiles would flow into exile (cf. Jer 51:44), but now the political order has been reoriented around the Temple. This is now the hub of a communications centre, with nations coming and instruction going out (v. 2).

4:2. The portrait of the pilgrimage of the nations to Jerusalem echoes Israel's own pilgrimages ("let us go up," 1 Kgs 12:28; Jer 31:6). That which Israel prizes is now desired by the whole world. We overhear the conversation at the foot of the Temple Mount, with the excited visitors encouraging each other in preparation for the steep climb. They do not come as tourists to marvel at the wonderful city and its exalted Temple. Rather, they come as pilgrims to learn from the God of Israel how to live in truth and peace. This is not quite the same as becoming Jews or proselytes, but marks a decisive change in reference point. No longer are the assorted shrines, moralities and customs of the ancient world a source of division and war. It is one resolution of the tension between unity and diversity. "Must mankind be condemned to choose between the Scylla of a sterile, colorless cosmopolitanism and the Charybdis of a mad, bloodthirsty nationalism?" (Gordis 1971, 274). The nations visit the house of God, not to stay and be absorbed, but to learn and to depart with a resolution of their grievances and a knowledge that will transform their behaviour. A similar variegated unity is implied by the concentric circles of the worshippers in Revelation (Rev 7).

The words of the nations illustrate several features of Hebrew poetry: parallelism, specification and narrativity (Alter 1985). The three parallel lines describe a story, providing us with three snapshots of the journey that is being undertaken. The first describes an inward and upward movement and the description of the temple in v. 1 is split between the phrases. They first ascend "the mountain of the LORD," then reach "the house of the God of Jacob." The third line reverses the movement of the first line, but now the nations return to their places informed by a knowledge of God's ways. The parallel phrases of the first line move from the general to the specific. The "mountain" includes the bottom (where the nations meet) as well as the top, the specific location of the temple (house). The second line displays complementary parallelism in that the first phrase focuses on God's "ways" and the second the corresponding "paths" (*ʾōraḥ*; cf. Koch 1978, 281) of human obedience. "ways" (*derek*) refers to a knowledge about how God acts and judges, the essential foundations for guiding how the nations will live in the future (Exod 33:13; Deut 11:22). The third line is chiastic (Zion–instruction–word–Jerusalem).

"instruction" (*tôrâ*) can refer to comprehensive "teaching" (GNB, NLT; "the law," NIV, NJB), but may also refer to specific decisions or verdicts (cf. v. 3). "the word of the Lord" can similarly refer both to general revelation and a more specific word (1:1; Jonah 3:1). Sweeney (1996) argues that an analogy is being drawn between the revelation of the first Torah at Mount Sinai, and this revelation of Torah on Mound Zion is the result of a new Exodus and establishes the norms of conduct between Israel and the nations under the sovereignty of Yhwh.

"God of Jacob" occurs only here in the prophets, but there are parallels in the Psalms (Pss 20:1[2]; 46:7[8]). Here it may emphasize that, while the imagery is Canaanite, the theology must be Israelite (Wildberger 1991, 92). The goal of the journey is an encounter with this specific God, who alone is able to instruct the peoples how to live together in peace. "teach" (*yrh*, the same root as Torah) is what the priests do in 3:11, but here it is implied that Yhwh teaches directly without intermediaries who might corrupt the instruction or demand a price (Isa 55:1). "his ways" is preceded by the preposition *min* ("of his ways," AV) and the verbs are imperfect (continuous), suggesting that instruction is unlimited, so that the nations need to undertake a regular, repeated pilgrimage rather than a one-off visit. Zion is more Grand Central Station than Mecca. There needs to be an ongoing hearing and interpretation of the inexhaustible Torah (Deut 6:7; 31:11–12; Ps 1:2).

4:3. The previous verse has set out the positive ideal. Here the prophet speaks of how Yhwh deals with the material and motivational barriers to such a vision. War is often the result of an escalation of disputes between nations, but now Yhwh himself will ensure that the competing claims are weighed fairly. A just judge needs both the authority and the insight to reprove those in the wrong, but no one qualifies for that post in the international arena, then or now. Yhwh alone, as the King of Kings, has the power and the will to establish universal justice and peace, however strong or far away the nations are. There will then be no need for destructive instruments of war (represented by swords and spears, 1 Sam 17:47), and so they will be transformed into fruitful tools of production (plowshares and pruning hooks). It may reverse a call to war, for Joel 3:10[4:10] uses this imagery in summoning the nations to war. In other texts Yhwh shatters the weapons of war prior to the final reign of peace (Pss 46:9[10]; 76:3[4]; Ezek 39:9; Hos 2:18[20]), but here the vision is transformative and gradual, enacted willingly by the nations. Following enforced disarmament, the political will to "lift up sword" will fade away, and then even the potential to wage war will be lost, for they shall not "learn war any more." However naive in formulation, the program reflects a shrewd realism: "Peace followed by arms control or disarmament has never worked in the past" (Alfaro 1989, 48). Since only soft iron was available, blacksmiths would be able to beat or hammer a sword or spear into the blade of an agricultural tool. "plowshares" (*ʾittîm*) comes in the list of items to be sharpened in 1 Sam 13:19–21, but there NRSV translates another word as plowshare and for this has "mattock." It appears that the most likely reference is to a single-bladed hoe (Byington 1949; *IDB* 3:315, 828 has pictures of hoes and adzes and ploughs). This filled in early times the role of the plowshare, breaking up the soil in preparation for sowing. The common function may explain why early translations (LXX, Vulg.) understood it to be a plough-share. "pruning hooks" (*mazmērôt*) were knives used to remove the extra leaves and young shoots from vines, and could be made by adapting a javelin or spear.

4:4. This verse is not found in Isaiah, but it is the logical result of the cessation of war announced in the previous verse. Perhaps it reflects Micah's rural roots in contrast to Isaiah's Jerusalem orientation, but the Assyrian spokesman promises the same to the people of Jerusalem (2 Kgs 18:31). The verse highlights the economic implications of what has taken place in the theological and political realm. Both for the nations and for Israel, freedom from the crippling economic burden of war leads to a vision of paradise in the language of an agrarian econ-omy. "What usurps vines and fig trees is not just invading armies but the tax structure and the profit system that are both cause and effect of military dan-gers" (Brueggemann 1981, 97). Vines and fig trees produce the most important fruit and provide shade for the sun. Vines are often trained to grow up fig trees, so it was perfectly possible to sit under both at once. Yet the pairing is first of all a proverbial symbol for wealth and leisure, especially as characterizing Solomon's reign (1 Kgs 4:25). They convey in concrete terms the larger bless-ings of having one's own family estate, having plenty to eat, not being depend-ent on others and being able to offer hospitality (Zech 3:10). Peace also means that "no one shall make them afraid." "make afraid" (hiphil of *ḥrd*) is probably better translated "terrify" or "panic," since it suggests a bodily physical reaction (1 Sam 14:15; Hos 11:11). There is no need to remain alert and ready to flee to a fortified city at news of invaders, who would then eat the fruits of a family's labour (Jer 5:17).

"for the mouth of the LORD of hosts has spoken" concludes the section, emphasizing that the words of the prophet have divine authority (Isa 1:20; 40:5; 58:14). "Yhwh of hosts" occurs only here in Micah. It can refer to Israel's earthly hosts (1 Sam 17:45) and was taken as an abstract plural of majesty by the LXX (*kyrios pantokratōr*, "Lord almighty"), but in most texts it refers to the heavenly hosts who are at God's royal command (Josh 5:14; Ps 89:5–8[6–9]). The phrase draws on this traditional affirmation of Yhwh's power and authority and so makes the fulfilment of the oracle all the more sure.

4:5. There are verbal overlaps with the previous verses (peoples, vv. 1, 3; walk, v. 2), but this is not mere random association. After travelling from immanent future (3:12) to distant future (4:1–4), the appendix brings us back to the abiding present. The nations have never been greatly interested in abandoning their gods or giving up their faith in war as a solution to difficult problems. Here Micah speaks for all those who confess that this future hope depends on faith in Yhwh. Because the verse complements rather than explains the previous verses, "For" (*kî*) is better translated "though" (NJPS), or it may possibly be an emphatic particle (which REB and NIV omit). The contrast is reinforced by the "we" of the second line, which represents an emphatic independent personal pronoun (*waᵃnaḥnû*; "but as for us, we…"). The two lines set out a radical choice, for Israel must choose which god they believe rules the world, and who is worthy of obedience (Gen 17:1; Deut 11:26–32). The mood is neither exhortatory (Isa 2:5) nor celebratory (as in vv. 1–4) but a sober confession of commitment, whether matters turn out for better or for worse (Amos 3:18; Hab 3:17–19). The corporate character of this confession and the psalmic "forever and ever" (Pss 9:5[6]; 45:17[18]; cf. Exod 15:18) gives it a liturgical ring, and some have speculated it was a traditional affirmation of the Jerusalem community. Present realities are acknowledged, but this does not affect a basic commitment to "the LORD our God" and the behaviour that is consistent with his character ("walk in the name of"; cf. Ps 86:11). The repetition and internalization of this commitment will guard against the apostasy and disaster that followed Solomon, when he turned from walking in God's ways to walking after other gods (1 Kgs 3:14; 11:33).

From Weakness to Strength (4:6–8)

This promise of hope for those injured or scattered by God's judgment is closely linked to vv. 1–5 by an opening reference to the future and the theme of Yhwh's reign on Mount Zion. The metaphor of the gathering of the flock and the kingship theme makes it parallel to 2:12–13, and the interpretive challenges are similar. Many scholars date the section (or various parts of it) to the exilic period or even later. But there is no clear reference to exile, only of dispersal. Even if exile is being described, this was a common punishment in the ancient world (as the Southern Kingdom knew all too well from Samaria's example), and so a general allusion to exile does not absolutely determine the date of an oracle. The metaphor and language is general enough to have come from a variety of authors or redactors, including Micah. If it does come from Micah, then it could refer to those who had gone into exile from Samaria (1:6–7), those who have suffered in the invasion of Judah (1:8–16) and, in anticipation, those who will be scattered or exiled following the destruction of Jerusalem (3:12). Since the latter did not happen in Micah's time, then the oracle would naturally be read by later generations as a promise for those exiled to Babylonia in the seventh century. The promise of return from exile (however and whenever experienced) remained a vital element of both the Jewish and the Christian hope for the future (Heb 12:22; 1 Pet 1:1).

4:6. "In that day" echoes "the days to come" of v. 1 and implies that this too is a feature of Israel's future hope. Chronologically, the gathering of the people and the establishment of Zion precede vv. 1–4. "says the LORD" (*neʾum yhwh*) is a characteristic prophetic assertion of divine authority (cf. v. 4b). The verse begins with a great promise to those in exile: "I will assemble...and gather." "lame" (participle of *ṣlʿ*) occurs elsewhere only in Gen 32:32 (describing the limping Jacob) and Zeph 3:19 (a similar promise of salvation). Some have found an allusion to the Jacob tradition, for Jacob too was exiled, lamed by God and then brought back home. But here it is more likely another aspect of a sheep metaphor. Filling in the gaps in a maximal way, we can imagine Yhwh bringing calamity upon his people (the flock) by giving them over to the wild beasts (Assyria or other nations). In the resulting flight those who were not killed became lame or were "driven away" (NIV's "exiles" makes the target explicit at the expense of dissolving the metaphor). If the poetry exhibits narrativity as well as parallelism, then we can imagine Yhwh finding first of all the lame, who have not been able to flee far, and then those who were not injured and so "have been driven away." "driven away" in the sheep metaphor simply means "outcast" (NJPS), but the historical reference is probably to exile (cf. TEV, NLT). "and those whom I have afflicted" is a general statement that probably sums up those spoken of in the preceding clauses, rather than a separate class ("and" with the sense of "that is"). It alludes to the calamity that resulted in the scattering of the flock (3:12). "afflicted" (hiphil of *rʿʿ*) echoes other occurrences of the "evil/calamity" root (2:3; 3:4, 11).

4:7. The same group is addressed, but the promise is enlarged. "lame" is repeated for continuity, but those "driven away" are replaced by "cast off." This verb occurs only here and is probably derived from an adverb meaning "far off." "remnant" (*šeʾērît*) emphasizes the gracious preservation of a few (cf. 2:12), but in the parallel they become a strong nation. "strong nations" occurred in v. 3, but the singular here suggests a superlative. By Yhwh's action Israel will become the strongest nation. The final line forms an *inclusio* with v. 1. In both verses, though expressed in different ways, the primacy of Zion and the reign of Yhwh are affirmed. The shift from the first ("I") to the third person ("the LORD") may reflect a liturgical tradition, for the psalms frequently affirm that he reigns (Pss 47:8[9]; 93:1; cf. Exod 15:18). "now and forevermore" is also found mostly in the psalms (Pss 125:2; 131:3). Over against the variable fortunes of Israel's historical experience, the kingdom that these verses announce will stand forever. In accord with the biblical and ancient Near Eastern ideal of the shepherd king (see on 5:3[4]), the caring shepherd of vv. 6–7a is one with the sovereign king of v. 7b. The long final line (cf. v. 5b) brings the promise to a fitting close.

4:8. The triumphant mood and the sheep metaphor suggest that this verse concludes vv. 6–7. Others, however, find this verse the start of a section, linked by "daughter Zion" (4:8, 10, 13). The association of city and king is found in both 4:8 and 5:1, and the positive 4:8 and 5:2–4 (both beginning with "and you") frame the oracles in-between. The sheep metaphor also returns in 5:5. It is perhaps best to take v. 8 as transitional as well as opening a new section. It is a prophecy of the restoration of Davidic rule over a united kingdom, portraying the human and earthly counterpart or externalization of the divine rule affirmed in v. 7. The reference of v. 8b is to a Davidic ruler. Since v. 9 can be read as reflecting the demise of Davidic sovereignty (though see the commentary), this verse is often dated late. But if Micah is able to speak of the restoration of Zion, then he can also prophesy the restoration of a Davidic monarchy, whose power and effective presence would inevitably be destroyed along with the capital city.

"And you" introduces a *casus pendens*, where the emphasized term (*w^{e}attâ*; the independent personal pronoun) is put outside the structure of the sentence ("And as for you…") and is then resumed ("to you"). The reference is to Jerusalem, but is a ruined or a restored city being described? Wolff (1990) suggests that a postexilic redactor is describing a herd of sheep grazing around a tower among the ruins of Jerusalem, but the positive mood of the verse favours a positive interpretation. "tower of the flock" ("Migdal-eder," NJPS, NAB) was the name of a small town near Jerusalem (Gen 35:21), but here the sheep metaphor is predominant. A watch-tower next to the sheepfold allowed the shepherd to guard against attack by wild animals or thieves (2 Chr 26:10). In the same way, the towering Mount Zion (v. 1) will provide protection for the people of God who will enjoy living in Jerusalem as a safe, fortified environment. A second description of the city is as a "hill" (*^{c}ōpel*), a mound or bulge (2 Kgs 5:24). This is also the name of an area in Jerusalem ("Ophel," NJB), the ridge to the south of the Temple linking it with the City of David. Its use for fortifications is mentioned in 2 Chr 27:3 and 33:14, and Neh 3:25–27 refers to a great tower in the vicinity of the wall of Ophel (cf. Isa 32:14). However, the parallelism suggests again a wider reference to the temple mount or all Jerusalem. The third image is "daughter Zion" (see on 1:13).

Two synonyms for "come" occur together in the middle of the verse, dividing it into two, the first referring back to the city and the second looking forward to the coming Davidic kingship. This is indicated through two closely related nouns: "dominion" (*memšālâ*) and "sovereignty" (*mamleket*; normally "kingdom," RSV). The corresponding verb to "dominion" comes in the messianic promise of 5:1 ("ruler"), and "former" refers to the rule of David and Solomon over the united kingdom. The second term also comes frequently in the story of the early monarchy before the split (1 Sam 24:20; 2 Sam 5:12; 7:12). The implication is that Yhwh will bring back the scattered inhabitants of both Samaria and Judea and appoint over them a Davidic ruler, thus a promise anticipating 5:2–5.

Exile and Rescue (4:9–10)

This is the first of three similar oracles beginning with "now" (4:9, 11; 5:1). The first two oracles include a command addressed to "daughter Zion" (4:10, 13), while the third has the mysterious "daughter of a troop" (5:1). The oracles are marked off from the preceding by the depiction of the nations as hostile, and by a movement from a situation of distress to one of salvation. The logical presumption is that this reversal was a necessary preliminary for the salvation portrayed in 4:1–8 and 5:2–4.

The relation of the oracles to each other and to historical events is obscure. The first seems to indicate defeat and exile before redemption, while the second implies an immediate and decisive victory. The movement of the third is similar to the first, but the focus shifts from Zion to a royal, messianic figure. What then might be their historical context? (1) An eighth-century setting: the oracles all come from Micah. The prophecy of exile reflects the similar prophecy following Hezekiah's favourable response to Merodach-Baladan's embassy (2 Kgs 20:12–19; Isa 39; Willis 1965). Or v. 10 might be taken as a hypothetical question, "if now you go forth from the city…" (Shaw 1993, 128). The second oracle reflects the successful resistance by Jerusalem to the Assyrian assault on Jerusalem. The third is similar, but has a royal, messianic focus. (2) A sixth-century setting: the oracles are prophecies of consolation, reflecting the Babylonian assault on Jerusalem in 587 B.C.E. (2 Kgs 25). The positive 4:11–13 could be a general eschatological statement of Yhwh's grand design (Wolff 1990), or (less likely) it could be taken as a speech by the false prophets (van der Woude 1969). (3) No specific historical setting: the oracles are too general to relate to historical events (Schibler 1989, 99–100). The "now" emphasizes an immanent reversal of fortunes that addresses the reader as much as the original hearers. "In its own times of crisis, the church, together with Israel, will have to search these prophetic words for the kind of encouragement and direction they can impart to her" (Wolff 1990, 149). The following commentary will emphasize the third of these possibilities.

Turning to 4:9–10, the situation presupposed is of great anguish suffered by daughter Zion ("you" is feminine singular). The context indicates that the cause of distress is military invasion. The tone of v. 9 appears to be mocking, but it then turns into a call to accept the allotted punishment, for only afterwards will Yhwh rescue them from exile. The explicit mention in v. 10 of Babylon as the goal of exile has led to most scholars dating it to the time of the Babylonian exile. There are close links with Jeremiah, who also describes invasion of daughter Zion through birth imagery (Jer 4:31; 6:23–24) and recommends submission to God's punishment (Jer 21:8–10). However, some propose that the oracle originally read Assyria, which was then changed by a later redactor to Babylon (Kaufmann 1960, 352; Alfaro 1989). Others have found even this minimal redaction unnecessary. People from Babylon replaced Israelites in the Northern Kingdom in 2 Kgs 17:24, so that Babylon could be a distant place of exile rather than the exiling power (Rudolph 1971). The language used is not normally that of exile (Shaw 1993, 134–35). Which king the oracle has in mind is as uncertain as its dating. Suggestions include Ahaz (2 Kgs 16; Isa 7), Hoshea (2 Kgs 17:1–18:12), Hezekiah (2 Kgs 18–20), Manasseh (2 Chr 33), Jehoiachin (2 Kgs 24:6–12) and Zedekiah (2 Kgs 24:17–25:11). A particularly fitting background would be Hezekiah's flirting with the Babylonian kings who were seeking to arrange a rebellion against Assyria (1 Kgs 20:12–13), but the generality of the oracle makes certainty impossible. Even if it did originally refer to Hezekiah, whose action managed to save Jerusalem, the threat remained alive for each generation and was eventually fulfilled in 587 B.C.E.

4:9. "Now" introduces a new future development, seen as present and inevitable according to the vision of the prophet. The verse has a chiastic structure (suffering–leader–leader–suffering). "why do you cry aloud" implies a situation of anguish that is given a specific and powerful emotional charge by the metaphor in the fourth phrase ("like a woman in labour"). Different answers have been proposed for the two central questions. One possibility is that the answer "no" is expected, so that the text refers to a time when there is no king in Jerusalem. But the questions seem to undermine the value rather than the presence of a king. They might then have a mocking tone, expressing surprise that the people feel distress, given that they are guided by a king. The answer to the riddle is that the leaders have departed even further from God's ways than the people and so cannot be a source of hope or rescue (cf. ch. 3). "cry aloud" is a rather weak translation of an emphatic construction (*tārîʿ rēaʿ*; verb and cognate noun). The NLT has "why are you now screaming in terror?" "king" might refer to Yhwh (v. 7; Jer 8:19), but the reference to perishing in the next parallel phrase makes it more likely to refer to a Davidic descendant. "your counselor" probably refers to the same person. The wise counsel of the king (Isa 9:6[5]; 11:2; Ps 20:4[5]) should guide the people and keep them from disaster. There is a sharp contrast between the implications of this verse and the role that King Hezekiah played in the biblical account of the 701 B.C.E. invasion, where the people also demonstrated trust and obedience to God and king (2 Kgs 18:36). However, the uncertainty of the dating and the poetic rhetoric of Micah, and the idealized character of the narrative in 2 Kgs 18–20//Isa 36–39, make proposals for both harmonization and contradiction a dangerous exercise. The metaphor of a "woman in labour" is frequently applied to those overcome by fear and dread, and the description of the people of Jerusalem as "daughter Zion" (vv. 8, 10) makes it particularly appropriate. "pangs" implies an extreme psychosomatic pain initiated by the nearness of the enemy. "seized" suggests the sudden onset of a long-dreaded event that was on the horizon but has now drawn near.

4:10. The childbirth metaphor is developed further in the next verse. "a woman in labour" is more accurately "a woman about to bear a child." A woman will endure the pain of labour in the knowledge that it is the prelude to the joy of bearing a child. In the same way the people of Jerusalem are commanded to "writhe and groan," for only through enduring the agony of exile will there come future joy.

The three phrases of the punishment can be interpreted as three stages of a journey: departure from the city, camping in the open country, travel to Babylon. The first indicates the abandonment of all held dear and the basis for Israel's national and political identity. The second implies danger, insecurity and dependence (Jer 6:25). The third eliminates the possibility of escape and seals an irrevocable punishment. However, "camp" is rather "dwell" (*šākan*, RSV, NJPS), a more permanent mode of existence. It is possible that the fall of the city is not regarded as a distinct journey into exile, but a general scattering. The people have to dwell in the open land (*śādeh*), and this might be "as far as" (the more usual nuance of the preposition *ʿad*) rather than all the way "to" Babylon.

Wherever the people end up, the decisive promise is that from there (repeated twice for emphasis) they will be rescued (*nṣl*; cf. 2 Kgs 19:11) and redeemed (*gʾl*). When fields or persons belonging to a family were sold to someone else, a kinsman-redeemer (*gōʾēl*) could buy them back (Lev 25:25, 47–49; Jer 32:6–15; Ruth 4). This schema of liberation is a fitting metaphor for Yhwh's rescue from captivity of those who belonged to his family, the people of Israel. A possible further implication is that the exiles will gain again the use of that which had been lost (i.e. the land). The selective character of metaphor makes it unnecessary to find an equivalent for the price of redemption. "from the hands of your enemies" asserts with a powerful personal note that Yhwh has the authority and power to act in this way, even against the wishes of the greatest empire of the day. In the midst of defeat and the triumph of the enemy arises a ray of hope that will not be extinguished (John 1:5).

Attack and Defeat (4:11–13)

Whereas the focus of 4:9–10 was on Israel, here the nations are in view. They gather to crush Israel, but they pose no threat because they do not know the real controller of events, Yhwh. Instead they will receive a devastating defeat at the hands of Israel. If it is read as subsequent to the return of vv. 9–10, then the nations attack the newly re-established kingdom. But v. 11 might also refer to the present plight, while v. 13 looks to the far future following deliverance of v. 10. Kessler (1999, 215) describes it as a fantasy of revenge evoked by the trauma of the conquest of Jerusalem in 587 B.C.E. But once again this has to remain speculative. The lack of historical references and the metaphorical language makes it difficult, and perhaps inappropriate, to apply the passage to any specific historical period. Rather, in tension with the more reconciliatory vision of 4:1–5, it contributes to the wider biblical hope for a future reversal of the situation of God's threatened people (cf. Rev 18–21).

4:11. In contrast to 4:2, the "many nations" are hostile. The great imperial armies included detachments from their vassal armies (Isa 22:6; 2 Kgs 24:2), but the enemy in view need not be limited to one empire. The oracle is general enough to evoke the standard motif of enemy attack on the city of God (Ps 2; Zech 12:1–9). From an Israelite point of view, their intention is that Jerusalem and its temple is "profaned" (*ḥnp*) or "desecrated" (NJB). The verb is not the usual one for profanation or defilement, and is used elsewhere to describe ungodliness and wickedness (Isa 9:17[16]; 10:6). Those who set themselves against the God of Israel care nothing for his holiness and righteousness. In the ancient world military and political victory was also the triumph of the gods of the victors, who would enter the temple and carry away the statues of the gods (Isa 46:1). "gaze" may seem a rather innocuous parallel, but the overtone may be to gloat (REB, NJB, NIV; Obad 12), or to look victoriously with joy (cf. 7:9–10; Hillers 1984). It is also possible that the two verbs describe one and the same action ("Let our eye Obscenely gaze on Zion," NJPS).

4:12–13. "But they" ($w^e h\bar{e}mm\hat{a}$; the emphatic independent pronoun) introduces a strong motif of reversal and irony. "The supposed self-will of the nations is really the sovereign work of all" (Achtemeier 1996, 336). The violence of the attack arises from the will to power. Its failure is inevitable because the nations are ignorant of the "thoughts of the LORD." This in part refers to Yhwh's general bias for the weak and helpless (2 Sam 14:14; Kessler 1999), but here sharpened by the object of concern being his covenant people (Jer 29:11). Those who think to take advantage of the weakness of Jerusalem will themselves be humbled (Isa 14:24–27). The second line repeats the thought with the synonym "plan" ($^c\bar{e}s\hat{a}$) and introduces an extended harvesting analogy for the unexpected and over-whelming military reversal. In the metaphor Yhwh is the owner of the harvest, the sheaves are the nations, the threshing floor is the field of battle and the thresher is the army of Jerusalem (daughter Zion). The metaphor comes through also in the promise to "make your horn iron." The "horn" is a stock symbol of strength, indicating that Yhwh will strengthen the Israelite army for their task. A wild ox uses its horns to gore its opponents (Deut 33:17), and lifts them in victory. Defeat and powerlessness occurs when the horn is cut off (Ps 75:4[5]), but this is impossible if it is iron (1 Kgs 22:11). The evocation of animal strength leads naturally to the next stage of the harvest process, the threshing. With hard, unbreakable "bronze hoofs" (Deut 25:4) Jerusalem treads down and destroys its enemies. "you shall beat in pieces" translates a verb associated with making fine (dqq). The violent and thorough separation of the wheat into kernel and chaff made it a stock image for complete and utter defeat (Isa 41:15; Jer 51:33; Amos 1:3). Extending the metaphor yet further, the valuable kernel is the gain that can then be devoted to Yhwh. What remains is the chaff, light and useless, and so rapidly dispersed or burnt without remainder (Ps 1:4; Matt 3:12). "devote" (hrm) is the verb associated with the ancient "ban," and describes the transfer of objects or people to the realm of the holy, resulting either in destruction (Deut 7:26) or in permanent storage in the temple treasury (Josh 6:17–24). This cultic word is appropriate because the banks of the ancient world were the temples of the gods (1 Kgs 14:26). But now the never-ending cycle of plundering and being plundered is brought to a decisive end. Jerusalem was a city too far, and its besiegers are themselves despoiled of the "ill-gotten gain" (REB) that they had acquired by violence (Prov 28:16; Jer 6:13). In accord with the rules of the "Yahweh war" (see on 3:5), Israel obediently devotes both the spoils of war and its own wealth ($hayil$) to the only true owner of these things, "the Lord of the whole earth." In doing this they acknowledge the source of their victory, and deconstruct the profit motive that is so often a central issue in waging war (Vargon 1994).

Humiliation and Hope (5:1–4)

Because there are no clear links to the context, there is a longstanding debate whether 5:1 belongs to the previous section (the MT includes it in the previous paragraph as 4:14), whether it is an isolated fragment or whether it links to the following verses (LXX, followed by EVV). Although it begins with the "now" that has introduced the previous two sections, without 5:2–3 it would be the only one not linking a state of need in the past with a future restoration by God. It seems best to take it as a further comment on the same situation of distress as the previous two oracles, but also as a fitting introduction to the following verses of promise by including a royal theme. A restatement of distress for both city and king (5:1) is followed by the promise of a messianic saviour (5:2–3).

The language and content of this section is so compressed and obscure that it has inspired a kaleidoscope of datings, redactional theories and interpretations. The humiliation has been variously associated with the towns lost by Hezekiah to Sennecharib, the insults dealt him by the Assyrian spokesman (2 Kgs 18:13–27), the siege and exile of Jehoiachin in 597 B.C.E. (2 Kgs 24:10–12) and the terrible fate of Zedekiah in 587 B.C.E. (2 Kgs 25:5–7). The many emendations and interpretations of this passage are discussed by the major monographs and commentaries, and so will not be covered in detail here. Instead, I shall follow Willis (1968) and others in assuming that sense should be made of the section as a whole, and that it may be located first of all within the context of Micah and the Assyrian threat of 701 B.C.E. In the biblical accounts of Sennacherib's siege there was indeed a marvellous reversal (2 Kgs 18–19; Isa 36–37). Even this falls short of the mysterious and ambitious character of the text. In expounding the implications of the Davidic promise, the prophet overreaches the immediate historical events. The poetic character of the oracles encouraged this surplus of meaning. Parallel lines often display intensification, a strategy that encourages hyperbolic statements and which contributed to Israel's eschatological and cosmological hope (Alter 1985, 146–62). In a generalizing move, Mays (1976, 119) suggests that Assyria "is probably a code-name for any great power which may threaten Israel in the future." As such, it can be a word of encouragement and hope for the downhearted in many different eras and circumstances.

5:1. According to the MT, the first phrase includes a verb (*gdd*) followed by "daughter of a *gᵉdûd*." The root *gdd*, however, can be translated in two different ways, and there is in addition some textual uncertainty.

(1) "Now you are walled around with a wall" (cf. NJB, REB). Following the LXX, this assumes a small change in one consonant (*d* to *r*) so that the original root is *gdr* ("wall"). This could refer to a defensive wall erected by the invaders that would protect them and prevent the escape of defenders. Or it might be an ironic reference to the walls of Jerusalem, which now comprise a prison rather than a refuge. However, if it is possible to make good sense of the MT, we should avoid emendation.

(2) "Marshal your troops, city of troops" (NIV; cf. Schwantes 1963). Both occurrences are related to *gdd* I, "to band together" (Jer 5:7). The verb occurs only rarely in the Old Testament, but the noun *gᵉdûd* is a common one usually

meaning a band of raiders (Gen 49:14), here being a term for the besieging army (Jer 18:22). Later occurrences were more neutral ("sons of a troop," 2 Chr 25:13) so it is also possible that it refers to the troops that Jerusalem is attempting to gather to defend itself ("troop-like daughter," Waltke 1993). The city is now defined by its military character rather than by the presence of Yhwh (contrast 4:1–3).

(3) "Inflict on yourselves wounds of mourning, you that are full of wounds of mourning" (cf. NJPS; Hillers 1984; Michel 1996). Most occurrences of the verb are from *gdd* II, "to cut," usually in the context of lamentation (Deut 14:1; 1 Kgs 18:28; Jer 41:5). The shedding of blood identifies the mourner with the dead and portrays physically the emotional anguish of the besieged. However, there is no other occurrence of *gᵉdûd* as a collective referring to the cuts made for mourning (although Jer 48:37 has a related word).

(4) "Now you gash yourself with marks of mourning, daughter of a troop" (cf. Rudolph 1971; Allen 1976; Mays 1976). This combines the strong points of the previous two translations, finding the usual but different meanings for the verb and the noun, and avoiding mere repetition. The presence of such wordplay is made more likely by the similar wordplay in "rod" and "ruler" (see below), and it is a feature of Micah's style. The second half of the line, referring to Jerusalem's hopeless military situation, thus gives the reason for the command in the first half.

"siege is laid against us" repeats and clarifies the reason for the command to mourn. "they strike" further specifies the reason for the mourning, or perhaps threatens further disaster ("they will strike," NIV). The victim is the king, the likely reference of "ruler" (*šōpēṭ*). The underlying verb means "to judge," and can describe the king through reference to one of his main functions (2 Sam 15:4; Ps 2:10; Isa 16:5). The choice of this word allows a wordplay with "rod" (*šēbeṭ*), often used for the royal sceptre (Esth 4:11; Ps 2:9). Striking on the cheek is a deadly insult, only possible if the victim is defeated and powerless (1 Kgs 22:24; Amos 3:30; cf. Matt 5:39).

5:2. The opening of the verse is the same as 4:8 (*wᵉʿattâ*), although the translations find the adversative "but you" from the context. It sets up both a parallel and a progression. Both 4:8 and 5:2 promise future rule, but 5:2 states that the new ruler who arrive in a surprising and unexpected way, from a lowly town rather than the capital. A king of promise will take the place of the present humiliated ruler. The shift of address from besieged Zion to Bethlehem (vividly addressed as a person) hints that Zion is doomed, and the restoration of the capital and the country requires a new David, born and nurtured in David's original hometown. All who hear or read these words are encouraged to endure their sufferings in the hope that the future will bring a new era overseen by a worthy successor to Israel's greatest king.

Bethlehem was a country village 9 km south of Jerusalem. Ephrathah could be used as a parallel for the town (Ruth 4:11) since it was the district in which it was located (1 Sam 17:20), and also the name of the Judahite clan that lived there (Ruth 1:2; 1 Chr 2:50). Elsewhere it is called Bethlehem of Judah (Judg 17:7; 1 Sam 17:12), to distinguish it from a Bethlehem in Zebulun (Josh 9:15). It is "one of the little clans of Judah." The syntax of the phrase is difficult (literally "little to be among the tribes of Judah"). It is unnecessary to translate as "too little" (Fitzmeyer 1956), and there is no article to indicate a superlative ("the least," LXX). The contrast is simply between little Bethlehem and great Jerusalem. "little" (*ṣāʿîr*) often means young, implying inferior strength and stature (Judg 6:15; Job 32:6). Yet from Bethlehem came David (1 Sam 16:1–13), the archetypal king of Israel who defeated all his enemies and introduced (at least according to Israel's more idealized memories) a golden age for Israel. Yet the powerful Davidic dynasty in Jerusalem had proved a deep disappointment. Nathan's founding oracle remains valid (2 Sam 7:8–16), but the timing and target had to be revised. David's family was a large one and some branch of the family from the ancestral home rather than the present ruling dynasty could provide a fresh start (Isa 11:1). Indeed, this is precisely the story of the exaltation of the youngest son that is found in Samuel's anointing of David (1 Sam 16:1–13). The story of David's origin and destiny becomes an historical parable of the way that God works (Allen 1976), and the prophetic poetry appeals to the believing imagination rather than the pedantic genealogist. The reversal of worldly expectation is a characteristic biblical motif, showing how God can choose those who are accounted little from a material or political point of view (Judg 6:15; 1 Sam 9:21; John 1:46; 1 Cor 1:27–29). They in turn have nothing to boast about, for God alone lifts up the lowly and vindicates the suffering (Luke 1:52; 19:16–18). The generality of the thought leaves the precise outworking open to all kinds of possible fulfilments, including for Christians the story related in the infancy narratives of Matthew and Luke.

"clans" (*ʾelep*) recalls the premonarchic organization of Israel, perhaps implying that the clock will be put back to before the disastrous shift in social structures that monarchy brought with it, associated with the crimes that Micah criticized so vigorously. The promise is more literally "from you to/for me shall go out (*yṣʾ*) [one who is] to be ruler in Israel." There are echoes of the Nathan oracle: David is "to be prince over my people Israel" (2 Sam 7:8), and God will give him offspring who will "come forth (also *yṣʾ*) from your body" (2 Sam 7:12; 1 Kgs 8:19). The promise affirms that, just like David, this person will go out "from you" (Bethlehem) and end up in Jerusalem as ruler "for me" (i.e. on behalf of Yhwh and obedient to him; cf. Jer 22:30; 33:26; Willis 1967–68). "rule" (*mšl*) is not the "royal" verb (*mlk*) usually used to describe kingship. Micah uses this verb only with reference to Yhwh (2:13; 4:7), and perhaps avoids it here to indicate a new quality of royal rule (Gross 1998, 70). "from of old, from ancient days" refers historically to the days of David (Neh 12:46; Amos 9:11), and emphasizes the faithfulness of Yhwh's promises to the Davidic dynasty as recorded in the Nathan oracle.

This verse is a classic "messianic" text, but care must be taken to recognize that the concept of the messiah developed over many centuries. In texts like this the promise of a coming ruler is continuous with the Davidic dynasty. He is one of a line rather than one of a kind. It is perhaps best to reserve "messiah" for the later more developed hope. The best known messianic interpretation of the verse is by Matthew in the infancy narrative of Jesus: "And you, Bethlehem, in the land of Judah, are by no means least among the rulers of Judah; for from you shall come a ruler who is to shepherd my people Israel" (Matt 2:4). Matthew's citation of Mic 5:1 integrates interpretation and translation. The unnecessary Ephrathah is omitted, and instead the Davidic character of Bethlehem is empha-sized by linking it with the location of David's tribe, Judea (as is already done in the Old Testament). "by no means least" heightens the original, which also asserts a contrast between the two towns. "rulers" is not the common word found in most LXX manuscripts (*ʾarchōn*), but a less common word found mainly in Genesis to describe the chiefs of tribes (*hēgemōn*). This may reinforce the idea of a return to old tribal roots, although the LXX also uses it of David (2 Sam 5:2; 6:21; 7:8). The final phrase in Matthew is original, but sums up the idea of the shepherd-king that is found in Mic 5:4 and that described the career as well as the royal role of David (2 Sam 5:2; Ezek 37:22). Matthew thus reinforces the Davidic overtones of the original, in line with his characteristic stress on the Davidic character of Jesus' person and ministry (Matt 1:1, 17, 20; 15:22). Later Christian interpreters perceived hints of the pre-existence of Christ in the last part of Mic 5:2, but this is an interpretation inspired by a developing Christology.

5:3. Before the vision of v. 2 can be accomplished, a time of punishment is necessary ("therefore"). The one who will "give them up" is Yhwh. Israel's suffering is no accident but a necessary part of his sovereign plan. But why "them" when the previous verse has just described an individual, the coming Davidic king? Although the woman could be a metaphor for the whole people (Calvin), the royal context implies rather a specific reference to a future time when a woman will give birth to the royal son. The phrase repeats the verb twice in different forms (*yôlēdâ yālādâ*, "she who is bearing bears forth"), and it is the same one that is found in Isa 7:14 (which also has "therefore" and the "give" verb). There it probably refers to someone who is already pregnant, but here it is more likely to refer to an indeterminate future and an unknown mother originat-ing from Bethlehem. It may be an early interpretation of the Isaiah text (Werlitz 1996). A royal interpretation is encouraged by the next phrase. "The rest of his kindred" might refer to David's family, to the Northern Kingdom that had been scattered and exiled, or to the whole people. Those who have been scattered will rejoin those who managed to stay in the land. It was David who finally suc-ceeded in uniting the different tribes after the death of Saul (2 Sam 2:26; 19:12), and here the new David will accomplish the same miracle. The people of Israel (literally "sons of Israel") normatively refers to all Israel, North and South (Zobel 1990, 414–16), ideally united under a Davidic king (cf. the ruler of Israel in v. 1). Here the rise of the king will encourage the survivors of the destruction of the Northern Kingdom to return (cf. 2 Chr 30:6; Schibler 1989). The prophecy refers to an individual but is intended to encourage a suffering people: "[Micah] wished then here to prepare the minds of the godly to bear evils, that they might not despair in great troubles, nor be depressed by extreme fear" (Calvin). The hope expressed in the verse had physical, political and theological implications that encouraged later readers to expand the scope of its fulfilment.

5:4. The description of the future ruler shifts from his birth and saving work to the character of his enduring reign. The metaphor of king as shepherd is a commonplace in the ancient Near East, but it also evokes another aspect of the Davidic ideal (2 Sam 7:7; Ps 78:70–72). Without a shepherd the people are defenceless and easily scattered and destroyed (1 Kgs 22:17; Zech 13:7). The verse looks forward in hope to a shepherd-king who could gather those who had been scattered (2:12; 4:6) and lead, protect and provide for his people/flock (Jer 23:1–4; Ezek 34). This coming ruler will first stand, possibly a reference to his accession to the throne (Wolff 1990; cf. 2 Kgs 11:14; Dan 8:23; 11:2–3) but the verb implies even more an undefeated and enduring reign. He will ensure that his people's essential material needs are provided. This will be "in the strength of the LORD," since he is "an expression, not a replacement of YHWH's kingship" (Mays 1976, 117). The priority of the divine dimension is emphasized in the next phrase, since the king's achievements are carried out "in the majesty of the name of the LORD his God." The name of Yhwh sums up his power and character, which includes the "majestic authority" (Allen 1976) that the king shares and enjoys. It echoes the promise of a great name given to David (2 Sam 7:9). Mention of "Yhwh his God" may well evoke the unique covenant relationships between the Davidic king and Yhwh (1 Sam 30:6; 1 Kgs 15:3–4). "And they shall live secure" translates a verb usually meaning "dwell" (*yšb*), but the nuance of security is evident in passages such as Deut 12:10; Ezek 34:28 (Görg 1990, 426–29). Such peaceful contentment is possible because God has gathered his people (4:10) and given them a Davidic king who will be great to the ends of the earth. This is not yet world dominion, but rather a great name (i.e. reputation; 2 Sam 7:9; cf. Gen 12:2) that has spread even to the most isolated nations.

Victory Over Assyria (5:5–6)

This brief section is often linked to the previous section, but is distinguished by a shift to the "we" form and the appearance of enemies. It may well be an exposition of "live secure" (v. 4). The hypothetical case of an invasion by Assyria is explored (it is better to take the conjunction *kî* as "if" rather than "when"). But the rapid defeat of the greatest empire of the day emphasizes how even they cannot triumph against the might of the coming king. Perhaps already here Assyria has become a symbolic codename for the enemies of God (Amos 5:6; Ezra 6:22) whose defeat is the final proof of the coming of the kingdom of God (Ezek 38–39; Rev 20:7–10).

5:5. The first five words of this verse are literally "and he/it will be—this (*zeh*)—peace (*šālôm*)—Assyrians—if/for/when." The first three words may be linked either to the following or the preceding lines. The phrase might also do

double duty, pointing both forwards and backwards and linking the sections, but
the meanings are so different that this seems to be overinterpretation. If this is
so, then the main options are: (1) "and he shall be the one of peace" (NRSV). The
phrase is linked to the previous verses and there is a break before the next word,
"Assyria." "the one of peace" is understood to be a messianic title. Yhwh is
called *zeh sînay* in Judg 5:5 and Cathcart (1968) argues that *zeh* can mean "the
one of." However, this is a rare meaning of the word, and the opening verb
marks the beginning of a section in vv. 7, 10 and is likely to do so here. (2) "And
this one shall be salvation from Assyria" (Mays 1976; cf. McKane 1998). But
the "from" has to be either inserted or understood. (3) "And this shall be peace,
when the Assyrians…" (RSV). The best solution may be to regard the phrase as a
summary of the following hypothetical scenario, in accord with the traditional
verse division (Cathcart 1978). "Assyria" may have been put before the conjunction for the sake of emphasis (a *casus pendens*; BDB 473): "As for the
Assyrians, if/when…"

The two verses are unified by repetitions at the beginning and end ("come
into our land," "tread," Willis 1968c, 543). NRSV's "upon our soil" reads "in our
land" (*bᵊʾadmāṭēnû*; cf. LXX) instead of the MT *bᵊʾarmᵊnōṭenû*, referring to
strongholds (REB) or fortresses (NJPS). This is unnecessary, since the parallel
phrases exhibit both narrativity (entry, then possession) and intensification (not
just ordinary land, but even the fortified castles; cf. Amos 2:2, 5). The terror of
invasion is matched and countered by a further pair of phrases that display
numerical intensification: seven shepherds (*rōʿîm*) and eight rulers (*nᵊsîkê ʾādām*;
"princes of men," RSV). The contrast between this plurality and the singularity
of the one future ruler has been resolved in various ways: (1) it describes Israel's
allies or vassals; (2) it is a quotation from a national war-song, now reused by
Micah to apply to the coming king (Allen 1976); (3) it is a mathematical representation of the sufficient and adequate leadership of the king (Willis 1968c,
541–42); (4) it is perhaps most likely to refer to Israelite princes and rulers, perhaps tribal or clan chiefs. The several incursions of the Assyrians are necessarily
dealt with by the king's generals and subordinates. The unity of the king and his
commanders is emphasized by reusing the shepherd image, although the chiefs
would need to be regarded as under-shepherds (1 Pet 5:4) and their commander
receives the glory of the eventual victory. The seven/eight sequence is more
common in extra-biblical texts than in the Bible (it appears elsewhere only in
Eccl 11:2 in the Bible), but here implies an indefinite but sufficient number of
generals required for the necessary military action.

5:6. The crisis of v. 5 is reversed with breathtaking speed and assurance. The
rulers raised up to respond to invasion turn the tables and invade the invaders.
The poet expects us to fill in the gaps imaginatively with a rapid defeat of the
Assyrian armies, a punitive expedition into the heart of Mesopotamia and the
complete capitulation of the region. Continuity is maintained by the reuse of the
"shepherding" verb (*rāʿâh*), which NRSV translates "rule" ("shepherd," NJB,
NJPS). In this vision irresistible military force is not inconsistent with benevolent

rule. "with the sword" recognizes that those who live by the sword must be controlled by it (cf. Matt 26:52), but the shepherding imagery implies that this forcefulness is only necessary for the establishment of peace and justice.

"land of Assyria" is parallel to "the land of Nimrod." Nimrod is the pre-Israelite hero of Gen 10:8–12 who is named as the founder of the chief cities of Babylonia and Assyria. He is thus a suitable poetic synonym for Assyria, but the earlier occurrence suggests a wider scope, perhaps including Babylonia. A possible further nuance is that even Mesopotamia's legendary antiquity and prestige will not prevent its subjugation. "with the drawn sword" is a slight emendation of the MT's "in its gates" (NJPS), but a better parallel to "sword" (Williamson 1997). "they shall rescue us" unnecessarily translates a singular verb ("he will deliver us," NJPS, NIV; cf. 4:10), since the king is ultimately behind the victory. Through his generals the king removes not only the immediate danger, but also the possibility that it will recur (cf. 4:3). The lightly sketched story told in these two verses illustrates the power that lies behind the king's worldwide reputation (v. 4).

The Triumph of the Remnant (5:7–9)

These verses introduce the theme of the remnant (2:12), whose role among the nations is portrayed first positively as dew and then negatively as a lion. The contrast is emphasized by the almost identical repetition of the first lines in v. 7 and v. 8. It is possible that the blessing of v. 7 is not intended to extend to the "many peoples" (Mays 1976), but it is more likely that the two verses present complementary views of the relation between Israel and the nations (similar double perspectives are found in Isa 25:6–11; 60:10–12; cf. Prov 19:12). The Abrahamic blessing (Gen 12:3) was universal in scope, and Jerusalem had a positive role in the midst of many peoples in 4:1–4. Further, dew and showers do something; they are not there for their own sake (Ben Zvi 2000). Nations that acknowledge Yhwh and his people (4:1–4) will be blessed; those who do not will be punished (4:11–13).

5:7. The "remnant of Jacob" are those who will have survived the testing times to come and will be the foundation for the renewed and victorious people of God. "surrounded by" (*beqereb*) is literally "in the midst of" (RSV). The image could be of the exiles "dispersed among many peoples" (REB), and this is certainly appropriate for those reading this after the exile in 587 B.C.E. However, if it is from Micah then it is more likely to refer to those gathered around Jerusalem, the centre of the nation. The reversal of fortunes is similar to that in vv. 5–6, but now with the addition of an element of blessing. "dew" (*ṭal*) is linked to blessing and fertility (Gen 27:28; Hos 14:5). "showers" (*rebîbîm*) normally refer to the light rain or drizzle in mid-October to early November that prepares the soil for ploughing and planting (Jer 3:3; 14:22; Ps 65:10[11]). It is a metaphor for the positive effect of divine teaching or the king's presence (Deut 32:2; Ps 72:6). "grass" refers generally to any herb or plant (Gen 1:11–12; Maiberger

2001, 410–13). The movement from "dew" to "showers" would be an intensification both of quantity and significance in relation to the seasonal cycle. The curse of drought, often associated with judgment, is the opposite side of this promise of blessing (Deut 28:24; 1 Kgs 18). Unlike water drawn from rivers or directed through irrigation channels, this source of water is independent of "human agency" (NJB) and is entirely "from Yhwh." Israel is totally dependent on God's grace for life and blessing.

5:8. The first line is the same as that of v. 7, except with the addition of "among the nations." The metaphor developed in this verse is that of a marauding lion. Gods and kings are often compared with lions in the ancient Near East, since their fierceness, deadliness, power and untameability are fitting attributes of a war leader. "At the beginning of a battle, Sargon II becomes furious 'like a lion,' and stalks through the lands of his enemies 'like a raging lion which strikes terror'" (Botterweck 1971, 380). But here it is Israel that is metamorphosed from a defenceless and cowering sheep to a raging lion. The parallel term for lion may be a synonym ("fierce lion," NJB, NJPS), but it may shift the image from an adult male to a "young lion" (Ezek 19:1–6). A full-grown lion is able to deal with any of "the animals of the forest," while a young lion can deal adequately with the flocks of sheep and goats (the term includes both). Though in one sense a step down, the image may suggest the boundless appetite of the young and highlight the powerlessness of the nations that are now being attacked by Israel. The four verbs of the final line may reflect a narrative development of the lion metaphor (Alter 1985, 39). The first stage of the kill is when the lion goes through the land and finds its pray. It then seizes it, drags it down and so treads it down underfoot. The next step is when the lion tears it to pieces for the meat. There is ample time to finish the meal, for the lion is the incomparable and uncontested king of the beasts, so there is "no one to deliver" (contrast the assurance to Israel in v. 6).

5:9. "Your hand shall be lifted up" continues the promise of triumph of v. 8 and so is more likely to refer to the remnant of Israel than the coming king ("your enemies" are also Israel's in 4:10). However, the MT is literally "let your hand be lifted up" (cf. RV). Addressed to God, it would be a concluding prayer that emphasizes that God is ultimately responsible for Israel's triumph in v. 8 (Rudolph 1971). It is less likely to be an exhortation to Israel (Allen 1976), since the context of present distress suggests that the promise is for the more distant future.

The meaning of hand gestures depends on context (Ackroyd 1986, 416–17). Here the hand that is lifted up seems to imply the kind of power and triumph represented by Moses' raised hands of Exod 17:11 (aggressive overtones are also present in Num 33:3; 1 Kgs 11:26–27). Warriors are often represented in the iconography of the ancient Near East with a weapon in their raised right hand (Keel 1978, 219–20, 291–97). The first line may portray God ready to strike, while the second describes the consequences of the blow, namely, "all your enemies shall be cut off." The verb (*krt*) is found frequently in the prophetic oracles against the nations (Isa 14:22; Amos 1:5; Obad 9, 10, 14) and implies total destruction. Whether as a promise or a prayer, it reflects a firm faith in the one who one day will prove that he is the Lord of history.

The Refining of the Remnant (5:10–15)

The opening of v. 10, "And it shall come to pass" (AV; vv. 5, 7), links the subsection with the previous two. The next phrase ("In that day, says the LORD") is found in 4:6. The implication is that this also looks towards the establishment of the future kingdom. Who is being addressed? It might be the nations, the target of v. 15 (and Targ. adds "of the peoples" to vv. 10, 11, 13, 14). But it is more likely that the singular "your" refers to Israel, and the language implies a Canaanite religious context (cf. the sacred poles of v. 14) that then broadens out in v. 15. The linking of universal and specific statements of judgment are found elsewhere (Zeph 1:2–6). As usual, the generality of the language makes dating very difficult, but Willis (1969a) argues for an original Mican setting, and the critique is very similar to that of Isa 2:6–8. It might reflect the extensive military preparations that would have been made by Hezekiah in preparation for his revolt against Assyria (2 Kgs 18:7), as well as to his religious reforms (2 Kgs 18:4). The oracle would warn against excessive trust in the former, and encourage a thorough implementation of the latter. Its basic message would, of course, be very appropriate at later times, particularly just before the Babylonian exile.

The first four verses begin with the same verb in the same form (*waw* consecutive), "I will cut off." In v. 13b the syntax and subject changes to a positive virtue (no more idolatry). Kessler compares this to a ritardando, with the pace resumed and even increased in the next line, which has two different verbs yet the same construction as before. The overall effect of the repetition is to emphasize God's determination to remove from Israel everything that might lead it to trust in something or someone other than him. It is a radical implementation of the first and second commandments (Exod 20:3–4; Rudolph 1971). We might compare the ninefold "smash" of Jer 51:20–23. The various statements are synthetic and comprehensive rather than sequential. The various pairs of words found in the parallel phrases embrace all possible elements of the category. The oracle is a promise or threat that God would destroy all military (vv. 10–11) and religious (vv. 12–14) sources of temptation and apostasy. The final verse expands the scope of this critique to include the nations. The remnant that comes through this judgment can only be a purified and obedient Israel.

The subsection is a fitting conclusion to both Mic 4–5 and Mic 1–5. God finally deals with the sins of Israel described and judged in Mic 1–3. In 1:2 the peoples are summoned to hear/obey, and in 5:15 the consequences of refusing to hear/obey are set out (Schibler 1989). The relation between Israel and the nations was introduced positively in 4:1–5, but is here concluded in a minor key both for Israel and the nations. Both the formal repetitions in vv. 10–14 and the final prose verse indicate a distinctive closure to this part of Micah.

5:10. In priestly texts "I will cut off" refers to the excommunication of those who violate the holy (Lev 17:10; Ezek 14:8), but the context here is more political (v. 9). It occurs in v. 9 in the passive, but there it refers to the nations rather than Israel. The parallelism of horses and chariots may suggest they are to be understood as one, that is, they are horse-drawn chariots. These were the epitome of military power and so the foremost object of fear (Deut 20:1; 2 Kgs 7:6) and pride (Ps 20:7[8]). Dependence on them was heartily condemned by the prophets, who exhorted the people to believe in Yhwh alone (Isa 2:7; 31:1). The Exodus had shown that against his might even such fearsome weapons were useless (Exod 15:19) and would one day be destroyed (Zech 9:10).

5:11. The oracle moves from offence to defence. As in the previous verse, the move from "cities" to "strongholds" is a poetic intensification, but also suggests the synthetic "fortified cities" (Num 32:17). These generally had buttressed walls, strongly built gates and high watchtowers. The invasion of both Sennacherib (2 Kgs 18:8) and Nebuchadnezzar (2 Kgs 25:4, 10) emphasized how fragile faith in these measures was (Jer 5:17) and how easily the unwitting agents of Yhwh could throw them down (cf. Ezek 26:4, 12). Here God removes all human sources of security, perhaps opening up a negative space in which to imagine the good life of perfect trust in him (4:4).

5:12. From military we turn to religious resources. "sorceries" (*kᵉšāpîm*) may indicate magical techniques ("spells," NJB; "witchcraft," NLT), while "soothsayers" (*mᵉʿônᵉnîm*) practice the arts of divination and so have access to the future ("fortune-telling," NLT; cf. Jer 27:9). It is also possible that "sorceries" is a general term for all approaches to other gods and spirits, including divination (André 1995, 365–66). It is often difficult to provide precise definitions, for these words come mainly in lists of prohibited activities (Deut 18:10; Jer 27:9). What they have in common is that they are regarded as totally inimical to the life of trust in Yhwh. Obedience to him and his will (revealed in the law) is the only path to present success and future blessing. Isaiah 2:6–8 uses several of the same words and suggests that the eighth century was one era when recourse to such means was a strong temptation. Several references imply a foreign origin for such practices (Exod 7:11; 2 Kgs 9:22).

5:13. The next verse moves from people to the material representations of worship. The images (*pᵉsîlîm*) of Samaria have already been condemned (1:7) and here it is the turn of Judah. They are paired with "pillars" (*maṣṣēḇôt*), and both were probably features of Canaanite local sanctuaries (2 Kgs 17:10). Although they may have been allowed or tolerated earlier, increasingly (along with the Asherim) they were condemned, and this is the dominant note in the canonical literature (Deut 7:5; 12:3; 1 Kgs 14:23). Hezekiah is praised for removing them (2 Kgs 18:4; cf. 23:14) and Hosea reflects the same uncompromising stance (Hos 3:4; 10:1). The prohibition of such objects was one implication of the second commandment (Exod 20:4–5). Yhwh could not be represented materially, but only through word and deed. They were not to "bow down to the work of your hands" (cf. Isa 2:8; Hos 14:3), and the symbols of cloud and fire emphasize his elusive presence and nonmaterial essence (Deut 4:12, 15). Their destruction will enable God re-establish his original relationship with Israel (Wolff 1990).

5:14. The "sacred poles" or Asherim are often mentioned alongside pillars as objects to be destroyed (Exod 34:13; 2 Kgs 18:4). Asherah was the Canaanite mother-goddess, associated with fertility. In the Ugaritic texts she is the consort of El, the high god. References to Asherah are sometimes to the goddess (Judg 3:7; 1 Kgs 18:19; 2 Kgs 23:4), but more usually to the cult objects (sacred poles) representing her. Whereas the pillars were of stone and so should be broken (Exod 23:14), the sacred poles were of wood (Judg 6:26) and were to be cut down and burned (1 Kgs 15:13; 2 Kgs 23:14). Although only here is there a threat to "uproot" them, the verb is very appropriate for an upright wooden object like a tree (Deut 16:21). Some aspects of popular or peripheral Israelite religion may have linked Asherah to Yhwh as his consort, for in many ways Yhwh assumed the mantle of El. In Kuntillet Ajrud, a ninth-century B.C.E. site on the route to southern Sinai, several inscriptions were found, one of which referred to "Yhwh of Samaria and his Asherah." The Asherah here may well be a cult object rather than a proper name, but it implies worship of the goddess alongside Yhwh. The prophets fiercely condemned all such material representation and reference to other gods, for it compromised the first and second commandments (de Moor 1974, 444). A link with Asherah may also have implied a sexual aspect to Yhwh, a feature conspicuously absent from the canonical texts.

"your towns" does not seem to give a good parallel for "sacred poles," and numerous emendations (e.g. "idols," *BHS*) and reinterpretations (e.g. "blood-spattered altars," REB) have been proposed. The versions support the MT, and there is no hint that a more specific nuance of city is meant (e.g. "temple-quarter," Fisher 1963). Nor is there much evidence that Micah is condemning multiple local identities of Yhwh (Jeppesen 1984). Micah is concerned about the widespread existence of the sacred poles, not their ontological diversity. Andersen and Freedman (2000) propose that the verse summarizes the prohibitions of the previous verses (towns for vv. 10–12; sacred poles for vv. 12–14), but this is not evident from the terms chosen. Perhaps the relation between the terms is intensification rather than parallelism. The sacred poles are specific and localized in the temple, but the presence of idolatry in the midst of the towns spells their doom too (cf. "the cities where your idol temples stand," NLT). The growing scope and intensity could continue into the next verse as well, where an emotional charge is added ("in anger and wrath") and "the nations" included in the judgment.

5:15. This verse shifts the object of address (from "you" to "the nations"), genre (from poetry to prose) and content (from purification of Israel to vengeance on the nations). Perhaps it comes from a different source, but the surprising character of the verse may well be deliberate. It continues the series of first-person promises related to the future establishment of God's rule. The gap between vv. 9–14 and v. 15 can be bridged in various ways. The warning to Israel in v. 10–14 may be the specific case that is now generalized and applied to the nations. Wherever idolatry and immorality is found, God will execute vengeance (cf. Isa 11:4). Or the thought might be that the nations should learn from what Israel has undergone (cf. Deut 29:21–28). Willis (1969a, 356) suggests that, like 4:9–10, the oracle is a response to an attack by foreign nations. Israel is condemned for trusting in military might and idolatrous alternatives, but it is Yhwh alone who can and will destroy the nations (cf. 2 Kgs 18–19). Shaw (1993, 157) points to the similar double accusation of both Israel and the nations in Isa 7.

"vengeance" (*nāqām*) is to be understood against the general biblical and prophetic assumption of the justice of God's actions against evil and rebellion, whether of Israel (Deut 32:35, 41, 43) or the nations (Isa 59:17–18). Evil upsets the balance of the world and arouses God's emotional opposition, his righteous "anger and wrath." Vengeance re-establishes the balance by punishing the wicked and satisfying God's anger. "vengeance" may not in fact be the best translation in a modern world that interprets actions in terms of individual self-interest. The NJPS has "wreak retribution," and Peels (1994, 265) suggests "punishing, justified retribution." "It is not irrational personal revenge to satisfy a wounded ego, but the exercise of legitimate sovereignty in a punishment which must occur if the rule of God is to be maintained against the self-seeking power and lusts of men" (Mays 1976, 127). The nations, like Israel, have been given an opportunity to hear/obey, but have not done so (Jer 12:14–17). Further, just as there were implied positive results of the refining of Israel in vv. 10–14, so vengeance has an implicit positive function. The destruction of the nations that oppose God will allow the establishment of the future era of peace and harmony (4:2–4; cf. Rom 2:8; 2 Thess 1:5–8).

From Reproof to Praise (Chapters 6–7)

The "hear" of 6:1 opens the third major section of the book, chs. 6–7. It is distinguished from the previous sections in various ways. Where 1:2 addressed the nations (cf. 5:15[14]) and 3:1 the leaders of Israel, now the spotlight turns onto Israel as a whole (6:3, 5). The subsections tend to be longer and more unified than in previous chapters, and make use of genres that have not occurred to this point, including a dispute (6:1–8), a lament (7:1–7) and a conclusion with many hymnic elements (7:8–20). The section begins with God's reproof of a people who are ignorant, arrogant and sinful. It ends with a people who express faith, hope and praise.

What the Lord Requires (6:1–8)

This section describes an imaginary dispute between Yhwh and his people. In the introduction (vv. 1–2) Yhwh through the prophet summons the people (v. 1b) and the mountains (v. 2a). He first sets out his accusation (v. 3), ironically by asking what complaints the people have against him. A historical review of Yhwh's saving acts emphasizes how little basis Israel has for complaint (vv. 4–5). When Israel eventually answers (vv. 6–7), the third person references to Yhwh emphasize the lack of personal communication with him. This is also reflected in the content of the answer, which demonstrates a grotesque distortion and misunderstanding of God's demands. The prophet closes the section by giving an exemplary answer, a quintessential summary of the law and the prophets (v. 8).

Until recently the form has been understood to be a prophetic lawsuit, similar to that found in several other texts (Hos 5:1–6; Amos 3:3–8; cf. Deut 32:1–25; Ps 50:1–23) and based on secular legal process. However, these texts display little similarity in structure and content (Daniels 1987). Further, the keyword *ryb* ("controversy") need not indicate a formal legal process before a judge (deRoche 1983). The dispute is only between Yhwh and his people. Other backgrounds have been proposed for these texts. Huffmon (1959) argued that it is a covenant lawsuit, with a basis in international treaties, but this is to over-emphasize one feature of the text that can be understood in another way (see on v. 1). It is best to see this passage as an original and creative use of various genres and backgrounds and to use the more general term "dispute" rather than the narrower "lawsuit."

A number of scholars see a sharp distinction between the legal character of vv. 1–5, and the priestly character of vv. 6–8. McKane (1998, 177–79) argues that they are merely juxtaposed comments with no relation to one another. However, the appeal of v. 3 ("answer me") requires some sort of response, and the content of the people's implied complaint in vv. 1–5 can be found in vv. 6–8. The people had exhausted Yhwh's patience, not because of neglecting their sacrificial duties (v. 6–7), but because they had neglected the weightier matters of the law, the first and second commandments (v. 8; cf. Matt 22:36–40).

The coherence of the text lies not in its form, but in its vocabulary, theme and flow of argument. The dialogical character of the section is emphasized by "what," which comes seven times in all three subsections (vv. 3 [×2], 5 [×2], 6, 8 [×2]) and nowhere else in Micah. It takes on a mood of sad rebuke in v. 3, then an indignant and almost hysterical tone in the response (vv. 6–7). The prophetic catechetical "what" leads into the cool climactic catechism of v. 8. The move from creation (vv. 1b–2) to history (vv. 4–5) to cult (vv. 6–7) to ethics and theology (v. 8) ranges comprehensively and cumulatively over all the main areas of Israel's life. With characteristic creativity the prophet has combined diverse elements in a unique way to show what was at the heart of Israel's faith. The strong legal nuances of the vocabulary and form are essential because for Israel the law is the ultimate test of truth and integrity. The dispute is a personal one that goes to the heart of how God responds to his people when they seek to avoid and reject him.

6:1. The identification of who is speaking to whom in the opening verses is difficult. (1) The opening phrase leads us to expect Yhwh to speak throughout vv. 1–5. But then whose is "your case"? The first phrase may be redactional, in which case hearers are being summoned to pay heed and to distance themselves from those who are being accused. (2) Yhwh summons the prophet to plead the case in v. 1 ("rise" is in the masculine singular); Micah speaks in v. 2, and then Yhwh resumes in vv. 3–5. However, this is awkward and it is more appropriately Yhwh who addresses the mountains and hills (Job 38). (3) The prophet summons Yhwh in v. 1, who then responds in vv. 2–5 (Andersen and Freedman 2000). This is the simplest reading and there is no difficulty in Yhwh referring to himself in the third person (2:5; 4:7, 10), especially since this highlights the covenant relationship that has been spurned.

The dispute is with God's people as a whole, although no doubt the leaders are primarily responsible (3; 6:9–16). "Rise" probably refers to the custom of standing before speaking or presenting a case (Deut 19:15–16). "plead your case" (*ryb*) is the same root as "controversy" (v. 2) and is better translated "state your case" (REB), since the dispute is bilateral and not before a third party such as a judge or a jury. Yhwh is always open to reason and argument (Gen 18), but he will also ensure that the dispute is resolved and justice is established. The mountains and hills are not judge and jury, nor "a cipher for the nations" (Wolff 1990, 173) but witnesses. Huffmon (1959) suggests that they fulfil the same function as witnesses to the covenant as the cosmic entities that are mentioned in ancient Near Eastern treaties (e.g. "the mountains, the rivers, the springs, the great Sea, heaven and earth," *ANET* 205; cf. "Heaven and earth" in Deut 4:26; 30:19; 31:28). They would then witness to Israel's offences against the covenant. As enduring and all-seeing entities the mountains would be authoritative witnesses to Israel's past and present failures. Although, strictly speaking, Yhwh does not need them, they confirm the accuracy of the charges.

6:2. The parallel for "mountains" is now not "hills" (v. 1b) but "you enduring foundations of the earth." "enduring" (*hā'ētānîm*) is frequently emended to a verb meaning "give ear" (*ha'ăzînû*, NJB; cf. "listen," REB, NIV), which often parallels "hear" (Hos 5:1; Isa 1:2). However, this is "suspiciously easy" (Hillers 1984, 75) and the ancient versions support the MT. The word may describe an ever-flowing stream (Deut 21:4) or a perennial pasture (Jer 49:19). Here it emphasizes that the foundations of the earth are paradigms of permanence and stability. They are the ultimate buildings blocks of creation (Isa 48:13; Prov 8:29), and so are competent witnesses to the story of Israel's faults from the very beginning. "contend" or "argue" (*ykḥ*; Isa 1:18; Mic 4:3) is found in a unique form of the verb (the reflexive hithpael), emphasizing the characteristic dialogical character of the relationship between God and his people as mediated through the prophets. "The prophet's recourse is not to authority, nor to fanatical emotion, but to the self-evidencing power of truth and undeniable fact" (J. M. P. Smith 1911, 120).

6:3. We might expect an accusation or judgment, but the tone is that of sorrowful entreaty, reflecting the love of a father or husband. Covenantal overtones would give added emotional and historical depth to the appeal "O my people." Though formally a self-defence (cf. Isa 5:4), the purpose is to awaken Israel's awareness of their lack of any cause for complaint. The implication is that Israel has been complaining of undue burdens placed upon them by Yhwh. Commentators have pointed to various periods of Israel's history where dissatisfaction with Yhwh was evident, but the enduring power of the poetry is its openness to interpretation. "what have I done" is the aggrieved complaint of an injured and innocent party (Num 22:28; 1 Sam 26:18). There is still a little space before Israel is required to answer the accusation "what have you done?" (Gen 4:10; 1 Sam 13:11). The people only have an excuse for their behaviour if God had "wearied" them beyond what they can stand. The word (hiphil of *l'h*) has spiritual and mental rather than physical overtones (Jer 20:9; Ringgren 1995, 395–96). The question sets up the sharp contrast between the unnecessary demands of vv. 6–7 (which would indeed be burdensome) and the invitation of v. 8 (of potentially infinite scope but realistic in its limits). Reversing the accusation, it is remarkable testimony to the patience and long-suffering of Yhwh that, though wearied, he has not yet burst out in judgment (cf. Jer 6:11). "answer me!" or "testify against me" (NJPS) requests any evidence to the contrary to be set before the parties (1 Sam 12:3). This is ironic, since it is Yhwh who is innocent and the people who are guilty.

6:4. Between v. 3 and v. 4 Rudolph finds a significant pause of silence that testifies to the guilt and shame of the Israelites (cf. Isa 41:23). Instead, Yhwh continues to set forth his case in vv. 4–5 through a historical review of his gracious saving deeds for Israel from the birth of the nation. Rather than wearying them, they have every reason to be grateful and faithful. The four phrases recall in turn the Exodus as a whole (v. 4a): Israel's inspired leadership (v. 4b), salvation in the wilderness on the journey (v. 5a) and entry into the Promised Land (v. 5b). These flashes of God's saving deeds could be multiplied indefinitely (e.g. Neh 9), but the lesson is clear. Israel doubts whether Yhwh can be trusted, but his deeds show his constant love and care throughout the extended and hazardous birth of the nation.

"For" would indicate by ironic reversal a refutation of Israel's criticism. Alternatively, this could be an emphatic particle ("In fact," NJPS). The similarity of sound between "I brought you up" (*he^{ce}litîkā*) and "I wearied you" (*helʾētîkā*, v. 3) emphasizes the radical difference in content and attitude. Bringing up Israel from the land of Egypt is a paradigmatic statement of the identity of Israel's God (1 Kgs 12:28), defining him by deed rather than by attribute. Egypt is often further identified as "the house of slavery" (Exod 20:2; Deut 7:8), but here it has become the second line of the poetic couplet, intensified by the reference to redeeming from slavery (Deut 7:8). The following triple identification of God's gracious gift of leaders for the people is unusual. Normally Moses and Aaron are paired as those sent by God to deliver the people, with Moses named first as pre-eminent (Josh 24:5; 1 Sam 12:8; Ps 105:26). However, the addition of

Miriam, their sister according to 1 Chr 6:3, may suggest that Moses stands for the law, Aaron for the cult, and Miriam for prophecy (Exod 15:20–21; Num 12). The unity of their message was emphasized by Ibn Ezra: "The Torah was given by Moses and Aaron was his mouth. Miriam taught it to women" (cited by McKane 1998, 182).

6:5. The repetition of "O my people" (v. 3) reinforces the note of sorrow and concern. Yhwh wants them to "remember" (*zkr*), an activity applying to all of vv. 4–5. This is not a passive, intellectual appreciation, but a forceful application to the present of what is known from the past. In the face of Israel's forget-fulness, appeal to God's saving acts (*ṣidqôt*)is a common motivation in the attempt to change attitudes and behaviour (Deut 7:18; 15:15; Judg 8:34; Ps 106:7). The reference to King Balak of Moab and Balaam son of Beor assumes knowledge of Num 22–24, where Yhwh turns curse into blessing. The MT simply has "from Shittim to Gilgal." Some think this a fragment of a longer text now lost, but the NRSV's addition of "what happened" assumes that it is also governed by the opening "remember." Shittim was the site of Joshua's camp before the miraculous crossing of Jordan (Josh 3:1), and Gilgal the camp after it (Josh 4:19), so that together they evoke the gracious gift of the land to Israel. The final phrase clarifies the purpose of this review: "that you may know" again indicates a personal, ethical knowing that is authoritative for living. "the saving acts" (*ṣidqôt*) of Yhwh is a shorthand for all the deeds mentioned previously and more (Judg 5:11; 1 Sam 12:7). The root (*ṣdq*) is normally translated right-eousness ("righteous acts," RV, NIV). The REB's "victories" gives the term a militaristic overtone, but the translation "saving acts" emphasizes that Yhwh characteristically saves those in distress. *ṣdq* may well describe behaviour that is in accord with some standard (Reimer 1996, 746), and if so, then the people are to recognize that Yhwh's good will towards his people is a fundamental norm on which they may base their lives, whatever the circumstances.

6:6–7. Perhaps after an even longer pause (Rudolph 1971), a representative Israelite responds to Yhwh's complaint. The background appears to be the custom of a priest questioning those seeking to enter the sanctuary about their moral and cultic fitness (Ps 15). But here the speaker gives this genre a unique and bizarre twist. Initially we might think that the speaker was honestly seeking guidance, but the lack of closure and the development of the speaker's argument quickly make it evident that the tone is quite different. Further, if we assume that v. 8 reflects the content of the criticism (see above), choosing to discuss sacrifice shifts the ground of the debate in a significant way. It indicates that the accusations about behaviour have been ignored, sidestepped or rejected. If sacrifice is the only arena for debate (and Israel may indeed be blameless in this regard), the only response can be an increasingly extravagant and extreme extension of cultic practice. The *reductio ad absurdum* of the argument reflects the speaker's self-righteousness and his lack of insight. As with other prophetic critiques of sacrifice (Amos 5:21–24; Hos 6:1–6; Isa 1:10–17), it is not a matter of the rejecting the cult but maintaining the right priorities.

"With what" introduces the opening general question of how a person can draw near to God (cf. Exod 23:15). Three further questions (each beginning with the Hebrew interrogative particle *h^a*) introduce parallel phrases, the second of which intensifies the first. Beginning realistically and leisurely, the quantities rapidly become impossibly large. Then the almost humorous images of thousands of animals and rivers of oil give way to a dark vision of human sacrifice. Even if the proposal is hypothetical, honest enquiry would not bring up a pagan custom strictly prohibited by Israelite law and custom. It suggests a bankruptcy in the moral and theological realm, thus setting up the counterproposal of v. 8. Gifts or sacrifices could be a means of atonement or praise (2 Sam 21:3; Ps 54:6), but the prophetic critique of sacrifice emphasizes that far more than mere ritual performance is required.

The first two phrases demonstrate both parallelism and progression. To "come before" Yhwh at the sanctuary is necessary before a worshipper can bow down. The first act is horizontal and dynamic (the approach); the second is vertical and passive. But although bowing low might represent humility in a needy worshipper, it is also used of oppressive regimes (Pss 57:6[7]; 145:14). The implication may be that God is a tyrant as well as unreachable ("God on high"). The first sacrifices are burnt offerings (Lev 1), the most costly since the meat was completely consumed on the fire and the worshipper gained nothing from them. Here they probably refer to what the Priestly writings call the sin or purification offering (Lev 4), intended to deal with impurity or unintentional sin. But the validity of this sacrifice depended on the integrity of the whole system. Bringing a person into a right relationship with God was always more than offering the right sacrifice. They were meant to be a joyful response to God's saving actions (cf. vv. 4–5) and gift of the Torah. "calves a year old" would be more expensive than most private offerings, which would normally be a goat, a lamb or a bird (Lev 5:6–7). It was legitimate to sacrifice calves that had not had to be fed for a whole year (Lev 22:27), and costly yearling calves were usually a special sacrifice required when the party involved was a priest or the people as a whole (Lev 9:2–3).

6:7. "be pleased" (*rṣh*) is a priestly technical term for the acceptance of a sacrifice by God (Lev 1:4), but elsewhere it is used to emphasize that sacrifice is inseparable from the life that it represents (Jer 14:10). "pleased" catches the overtones of God's delight and approval in the honest sacrifice (Mal 1:10; Ps 51:18). The speaker's querulous tone reverses the intended assurance of acceptance, suggesting instead an impossible level of demand.

"thousands" followed by "ten thousands" is the highest form of numerical intensification (1 Sam 18:7; Dan 7:10; weakened by NJPS's "myriads"). Solomon offered a thousand burnt offerings (1 Kgs 3:4), although the number is probably hyperbolic (1 Kgs 8:63). Further escalation is from multiple but countable rams to immeasurable "rivers of oil." Some olive oil was included in the grain offering (Lev 2:1), and was used in anointing and various other rituals. Perhaps the point is a fantastic multiplication of even a relatively minor ingredient of sacrifice.

No further intensification is possible in allowed categories of sacrifice, so prohibited forms become the climax and conclusion of the complaint. To "give my firstborn" is to sacrifice the firstborn son, allowing him to be burned in the altar fire on which burnt offerings were consumed. This was within God's rights (Gen 22; Levenson 1993), but it is strictly prohibited in Israel (Deut 12:31; 18:10) and the firstborn had to be redeemed (Exod 13:2). Even among Israel's neighbours it was a rare practice used only in extreme circumstances. For them, a human sacrifice (especially the son of a king) could bring deliverance (2 Kgs 3:27) or overturn a curse (1 Kgs 16:34), but anyone who did this in Israel displayed conclusive evidence of apostasy and contempt for Yhwh and his law (2 Kgs 16:3; 21:6; 23:10; Jer 7:31). Far from being a costly evidence of devotion it violated the most fundamental moral and religious norms. The second phrase refers to the same action, but intensifies through the use of a minimal metaphor, "the fruit of my body" (cf. Deut 30:9).

6:8. The indignant and misguided "what" of the people (v. 6) is given a cool, authoritative and composed answer in the "what" of the prophet. Micah may be alluding ironically to priestly instruction regarding offerings ("mortal," Lev 1:2; "seek," Deut 23:21[22]), although moral integrity was a clear precondition for access to the temple (Ps 15). A general statement concerning the "good" is followed by two phrases that define it more closely in relation to others and to God (cf. Hos 12:6[7]). They thus mirror the double orientation evident in the ten commandments (Exod 20:1–17; cf. Mark 12:28–33), with the primary relationship with God coming first there and last here by reason of the climactic character of the second of a parallel pair of phrases. The first phrase consists of two qualities that establish and maintain a people in harmony with one another: "to do justice, and to love kindness" (paired in reverse order in Hos 12:6[7]). The second phrase moves from the ethical to the theological plane, "to walk humbly with your God." However, the three terms may also be seen as a sequence, "an ascending series that moves from the concrete to the general. The specific requirement is to do justice, which is a way of loving mercy, which in turn is a manifestation of walking humbly with God" (Mays 1976, 142).

Lescow (1966, 57) argues that "mortal" (*ʾādām*) refers to any human being, since the content of what follows is quite general, and reflects the universalism and individualism of postexilic texts such as Isa 40–55. But "kindness" (*ḥesed*) is usually a quality demanded of Israel, and the dialogue is with a representative Israelite. Although a general application of the verse is a legitimate extension of the implicit claims of the text (for the God of Israel is Lord of all), an acknowledgment of what is good for all humanity is too abstract. Being told the good requires a revelation of God and his will, which is a gift first of all to Israel (Ps 147:19–20) before it is accepted by the nations (Mic 4:2). Shaw (1993, 177) has a more specific interpretation, arguing that "mortal" refers to the king, who had a special responsibility to establish justice (Ps 72:2). Admittedly a king would come closest to offering the sacrifices of vv. 6–7 and represents the people most fully, but such a restriction is unnecessary. "mortal" brings with it overtones of creatureliness and fragility (Pss 66:5; 144:3–4). This nuances sets up an effective contrast with the presumptuous answer of the previous two verses, and is consistent with the stress on walking with God at the end of the verse.

The basis of the "good" (*ṭôḇ*) is the revelation of God's character ("He has told you"), which has been rejected by the leaders who should most pursue it (3:2). What follows is not new, but a summary of the will of God already set out in the commandments and freshly applied to Israel's life by the prophets (cf. 3:8). Such brief summaries are typical of the prophets (Isa 1:16–17; Amos 5:14–15) and essential for both pedagogue and preacher (in *b. Mak* 23b–24a it is the three-member paradigm of a number of summaries of the Torah). On the recognition and the pursuit of the good depends the health and the continued existence of the people (Hos 8:1–3). "seek" (*drš*) is often used of those seeking God (Deut 4:29; 1 Kgs 22:5), but vv. 6–7 have shown how this has been grossly misinterpreted. So here is a statement of what God seeks of his people, a gracious revelation of how to live as he desires. It is an attitude that is realistic as well as unlimited, a sober contrast to the hyperbole and caricature of vv. 6–7.

"to do justice" (*mišpāṭ*; see 3:1, 8–11; 7:3, 9) is to establish it, if necessary in the lawcourts. The prophets are particularly scathing when the rights of the poor and weak are neglected (Jer 7:5–6; 22:3; Mic 3:1) and it is far more important than cultic performance (Isa 1:12–17). But because God is the judge of all deeds and his will lies behind the specific work of the court, justice can take on broader nuances of all that is in accord with a well-ordered society (Johnson 1998, 92). The requirement to seek justice, though certainly universal, is given special force by the covenantal character of Israel, who knew what it was to be weak and oppressed (Deut 10:17–19).

"kindness" is the almost untranslatable *ḥeseḏ*—"mercy" (NIV), "loyalty" (REB, NJB), "goodness" (NJPS). In the past it has been understood as the mutual obligations of behaviour required of those in a covenant community (Deut 7:9, 12; 1 Sam 20:8). However, it is also used of the generous behaviour of a stronger or superior party to an other who is in need of salvation or help (Ps143:12). Like justice, *ḥeseḏ* is pre-eminently a quality of Yhwh (Ps 89:14[15]; see also on Mic 7:18), but it must also characterize Israel's internal communal life (Hos 4:1; Mic 7:2). The command is to "do justice" and "love kindness," but elsewhere it can be to "do kindness" (Exod 20:6; 2 Sam 9:1) and to "love justice" (Ps 99:4). There can be no divorce between the act and the intention, the inward and the outward, even if love and kindness highlight the attitude and the doing of justice the deed. In context we may see this demand as an appropriate response to the outworking of God's *ḥeseḏ* in passionate acts of salvation during Israel's history (vv. 4–5). The exercise of kindness and justice always take priority over sacrifice (Hos 6:6; Matt 5:24).

"to walk" (*hlk*) describes a quality of behaviour in terms of the fundamental metaphor: life is a journey. "humbly" (*haṣnēaʿ*) is technically a hiphil infinitive absolute, but the verb serves here as an adverb. It is hard to determine its meaning from the few times it occurs, as is illustrated by the wide variety of early

translations (McKane 1998). In Prov 11:2 it is the opposite of pride or arrogance. The meaning is ambivalent in its four occurrences in Ben Sira (Sir 16:23;
31:22; 32:3; 42:8) and the Dead Sea Scrolls (1QS 4:5; 5:4; 8:2—all dependent
on this verse). Scholars have suggested both passive and active nuances for the
word, ranging from "humbly" (NRSV, REB; Dawes 1988) and "modestly" (NJPS),
to "attentively" (Lescow 1966, 56), "wisely" (Hillers 1984, 75), and "prudently"
(Stoebe 1959). In this verse the contrast to "with your God" is consistent with
the traditional "humbly," while walking and the association with the preceding
phrases suggests a more active nuance. Perhaps we may need to acknowledge a
range of possibilities, in all of which it is fear and love of God that will sustain
and direct behaviour in the social and political sphere. The final phrase, "with
your God," resonates (despite having a different preposition) with one pole of
the traditional covenant formulation linking Yhwh with "my people" (vv. 3, 5):
"you shall be my people, and I will be your God" (Jer 30:22; cf. Exod 6:7; Hos
1:9).

Judgment on the Corrupt City (6:9–16)

After the general injunction of 6:8 comes specific instances of the city
(Jerusalem) whose people refuse to hear and obey. The oracle of judgment is
introduced in v. 9, which is then worked out twice in a typical act-consequence
movement. The accusation in vv. 10–12 (emphasizing commercial crimes) leads
on to an announcement of judgment in vv. 13–15 (a curse on the natural order of
life). The same pattern is found in brief in v. 16, where the imitation of the
crimes of the Northern king (v. 16a) is the basis for a promise of destruction and
shame (v. 16b). Because of the mention of Omri and Ahab in v. 16, some have
regarded this as a text from the northern kingdom of Samaria. But there is no
reason why these kings could not have been known in the South, and the
reference may echo the opening reference to Samaria in 1:5–7. Judah is about to
suffer the same fate as Samaria for replicating its sins. It is generally regarded as
a reflection on the reason why Jerusalem was destroyed, but (as with other texts)
the passage is general enough to fit many occasions when Judah was invaded
and under threat.

There are a number of textual difficulties, and some have suggested the
rearrangement of various lines. But the main content and structure is clear
enough, and good sense can usually be made of the MT.

6:9. "the voice of the LORD" replaces the usual messenger formula (2:3; 3:5).
"voice" (*qôl*) is used of the revelation of the Torah at Sinai (Deut 5:25), but
Israel's disobedience to that Torah foregrounds instead a reference to the
thunder of God's voice, indicating his authority and power (Ps 29:1–3). It
"cries" or "calls" (*qrʾ*, REB; see on Jonah 1:2) to the city, which represents the
nation and its people (Mic 1:1; 3:12), indicating how urgent it is to hear and
respond.

The second phrase interrupts the poetry and the flow, and most agree that this
is a later comment (hence the NRSV's brackets), although others defend it as a

reflection by the prophet (Utzschneider 2005; cf. 3:8). It is literally "wisdom will see your name," but many follow the early versions and accept a minor emendation of "see" (*yirʾeh*, AV) to "fear" (*yirʾē*). Whether we read "regard" (Waltke 1993) or "fear" the phrase probably urges a later readership to pay close attention to the lessons either of v. 8 or this oracle. The word translated "sound wisdom" (*tûšîâ*) is found in the Wisdom Literature, sometimes parallel to "advice" (Prov 8:14). It may also have a nuance of success (Job 5:12), hence REB's "the fear of his name brings success." "your name" refers specifically to Yhwh (v. 9a), whose character as judge is revealed in the following verses. It is therefore prudent and wise for both the righteous and the wicked "to fear your name" (cf. Ps 86:11).

The translation of the following line is difficult, since it is literally "hear (pl.) O tribe and who appointed her." Suggestions, none of which are persuasive, include: (1) "Hear, O tribe and assembly of the city!" The NRSV regards "tribe" (*maṭṭeh*) as those summoned by the prophet to hear (i.e. the tribe of Judah). The final phrase and the first word of v. 10 are then emended, arriving at "assembly of the city," a typical poetic movement towards greater precision. However, it is strange for city to come twice, and the emended word for "assembly" is more usually "meeting" (Rudolph 1971). (2) "Hear, O scepter; For who can direct her but you?" (NJPS). The rod here is understood to be the symbol of a ruler, and "her" refers to Jerusalem, but a different word (*šēbeṭ*) is normally used for a royal sceptre (Isa 14:5) and "direct" is mild in context. (3) "Hear the rod, and the One who appointed it" (NIV; cf. McKane 1998; Görg 1990, 142). *maṭṭeh* can also mean rod or staff, an instrument of oppression (Isa 30:32) or punishment (Isa 10:5). However, "it" (feminine) does not accord with "rod" (masculine).

6:10–11. These verses comprise two double rhetorical questions, expressing Yhwh's abhorrence at commercial cheating in measuring and weighing. This is strictly prohibited in the law (Lev 19:35–36; Deut 28:13–15), since it radically undermined the trust and justice that should characterize relationships between members of the covenant people. The underlying motive of coveting is condemned in the tenth and climactic commandment (Exod 20:17). Such behaviour would lead to bitter division between the powerful town merchants and country farmers. The terms used to describe the measures and weights are usually moral and personal qualities (e.g. wicked/righteous), since they partake of the character of those who employed them, and God sees them as one.

Instead of the literal "are there…?" (AV), the NRSV has emended to "Can I forget…?," (or "can I forgive…?," REB; "can I overlook…?," NJB, NJPS). The first line may be a general lament, describing the fruits of unscrupulous practice followed by specific types of fraud. "the treasuries of wickedness" would be the hoarded grain (cf. NJPS) that is as precious as silver and gold in royal treasuries. An attractive though uncertain emendation is for "house" (*bêt*) to be read "bath" (*bat*), a unit of liquid measurement (Isa 5:10), hence "false measure" (REB). Liquid measure would then be complemented by dry measure, followed by weights (cf. Isa 40:12; Ezek 45:10).

Three specific examples of bad practice follow, echoing many other condemnations in the Old Testament and the ancient Near East:

(1) The "measure" is literally an ephah (10–20 litres), which the merchant has doctored to make "scant" or "short" (Ps 106:15; "short bushel," REB, NJB). For example, the basket used for selling the grain could be smaller than the standard (Amos 8:5). Such a measure is "accursed" ($z^{ec}\hat{u}m\hat{a}$), a word usually applied to the cursing or denouncing of people (Num 23:7). Those defrauded would curse the merchants, and the curse would then be enacted by God as judge (vv. 13–15; Wiklander 1980, 110).

(2) Turning to weighing, small scales with two pans (the word is dual) were used for money (before coins were minted money was a weighed amount of metal). "Scales of wickedness ($re\check{s}a^c$)" or "rigged scales" (NJB) might have a heavier scale bowl or a bent crossbeam. The opposite are "righteous," that is, "accurate scales" (Job 31:6, NJB).

(3) Another way to cheat with scales was to use different weights (literally stones), which would be kept in a bag (Deut 25:13). Larger and heavier ones than the standard would be used for buying, while selling would be done using lighter ones from which pieces had been chipped off (contrast whole or complete weights in Prov 11:1). Yhwh cannot tolerate such dishonest or deceitful weights (Hos 12:7).

6:12. The first word ($^{\circ a}\check{s}er$) usually introduces a relative clause ("Whose rich men," NJPS), although Wolff (1990) argues that the first word is causal, "because" ("For," NJB), and introduces the announcement of judgment in v. 13 (the same sequence is found in Jer 13:25–26). "your rich men" is literally "her rich men" (NIV), the reference being to the (feminine) city of v. 9. From underhand fraud we turn to open aggression by deed and word. With typical hyperbole the rich are described as "full of violence ($h\bar{a}m\bar{a}s$)" (cf. Gen 6:13), "steeped" in it (REB) until it is their dominant characteristic. Trade and violence are linked in the paradigmatic cases of Tyre (Ezek 28:16) and Babylon/Rome (Rev 18:24), and Jerusalem joins these notorious cities. The lawcourt is probably where the inhabitants "speak lies" and exercise "tongues of deceit" on behalf of their patrons. Perhaps the wealthy have been accused of cheating (by a country farmer? cf. Allen 1976), but their wealth allows them to buy false witnesses and so corrupt the law (Exod 20:16). Thus the tables are turned and the lawcourt, instead of establishing justice, becomes the means for violence (cf. 1 Kgs 21).

6:13. The foundation has been solidly laid for the sentence of the judge ("I" is the emphatic independent pronoun $^{\circ a}n\hat{i}$) upon the body corporate ("you" is masculine singular) of the nation (cf. Isa 1:5–7). Instead of the normal "therefore" (Mic 2:3; 3:6), the particle here (*gam*, "also") emphasizes the correspondence between the crimes of the wicked and their own punishment ("I, in turn" NJPS). Violence provokes violence (Matt 26:52). The next phrase is literally "I have made sick the striking of you" (a prophetic perfect). Although NRSV emends the first verb to "I have begun" (reflected in LXX, Vulg., Syr. but not Symm., Targ), sickness and punishment are often related (e.g. Deut 28:59; Jer 10:19), so the MT may well make good idiomatic sense ("beaten you sore," NJPS; cf. "a sickening blow"). "making you desolate" might describe the subjective state of the people ("stunned," NJPS), but the context suggests the external situation, the devastation caused by military invasion and siege (the sword of v. 14; cf. Lev 26:31–32; Ezek 30:12). "Because of your sins" recapitulates the moral and religious grounds for the sentence (cf. 1:5).

6:14. There follow in vv. 14–15 five threats of woe against those who try and gain a living from the land (cf. Hag 1:6). The two in v. 14 are longer than the three in v. 15, perhaps because of expansion, but the increased pace in v. 15 is fittingly climactic. These "futility curses" (Hillers 1984) are similar to those from elsewhere (e.g. the Sefire treaty, *ANET* 659; cf. 300). They consist of a threat that the natural order of blessing and fertility (Gen 1) will be overturned, and is a central feature of the curses of the covenant (Lev 26:26; Deut 28:18, 30, 38–40; cf. Hos 2:8). The frustration of the natural order is a feature of the prophetic judgment on Israel and reflects punishment by the creator God (Hos 4:10; Zeph 1:13). However, here it is traced not so much to natural disaster as to the consequences of war.

The word translated "gnawing hunger" occurs only here and has inspired numerous suggestions (Cathcart and Jeppesen 1987). One is "excrement," hence the euphemistic "your food will lie heavy in your stomach" (REB), while "dysentery" (Waltke 1993) would provide another good parallel. "you shall put away" probably refers to an attempt to hide or evacuate wives or children, but no one can save or deliver them (Isa 5:29). Even if someone appears to succeed, it is only temporary, for God will "hand over to the sword." For similar multiple stage judgments allowing no hope of escape, see Isa 24:18; Hos 9:16; Amos 5:19. The REB reflects a quite different interpretative tradition, since the word translated "save" (*plṭ*) can also occasionally mean "deliver [a child]" (Job 21:10), hence "you will come to labour, but not bring forth." A curse on the womb (miscarriage, barrenness) is common (Deut 28:18; Hos 9:11), as is the loss of children to captivity or death (Deut 28:41; Hos 9:12–13). Williamson (1997, 368) suggests another interpretation of the phrase, leading to "though you plant a protective hedge, you will not make it secure," but the non-specific NRSV is probably to be preferred.

6:15. The previous verse painted a general landscape of catastrophe. Allen (1976, 381) now imagines Micah inspecting the farmers' marketplace in Jerusalem. "The fresh food displayed so lavishly on the market stalls among which Micah prophesied would soon be a mocking memory." All the hard work in preparing these basic essentials would be in vain. They would sow various crops in November/December, but hope in vain to harvest them in April/May. "tread" governs both the next two phrases although, strictly speaking, olives were beaten or pressed in a stone mortar or depression. It was grapes that were trodden to provide the grape juice or new wine. That at least was the expectation, but Micah announces that there would be no opportunity to anoint themselves with oil (Deut 28:40). Nor would there be time for the juice of the fresh grapes in the winepress (*HALOT* 1728) to be fermented into wine (Deut 28:39; Amos 5:11). "drink" fittingly ends a sequence that begin with "eat" (v. 14a), with the pair standing for all that sustains life.

6:16. The verbs in this verse shift awkwardly between singular and plural, second and third person, and a range of emendations have been proposed to ease the flow. Nevertheless the overall sense is clear. The people of Jerusalem and Judah are following after the standards and actions of infamous kings of the Northern Kingdom. Omri was the founder of Samaria (1 Kgs 16:24), the capital of the Northern Kingdom (1:5), but he was even more renowned for being a notorious sinner (1 Kgs 16:25). However, even he was outdone by his son Ahab (1 Kgs 16:30), whose deeds were the standard against which future kings were assessed (2 Kgs 8:18, 27). The "statutes of Omri" is an ironic perversion of the "statutes of Yhwh," a common term for the commandments of the Torah (Deut 4:6, 8). Statutes (*ḥuqqôt*) might refer to the idolatrous behaviour of Ahab, who encouraged the worship of Baal (1 Kgs 18; 2 Kgs 10:18), but the context suggests a moral nuance. "statutes" and "works" describe behaviour that undermined traditional Israelite standards of justice and morality. They might be the customs common to other nations (2 Kgs 17:8, 15), but Micah's assumption is that the people of God have a different and distinct morality. The paradigmatic case was the seizure of Naboth's vineyard and Naboth's legally sanctioned murder (1 Kgs 21). The "house of Ahab" includes other members of the family regarded as notorious for their evil, including his wife Jezebel (1 Kgs 16:31), and his sons Ahaziah (1 Kgs 22:51–53) and Joram (2 Kgs 3:1–3). Judgment and destruction came upon the entire dynasty (2 Kgs 9:7–9; 10:11), which was indeed eventually the fate of the entire Northern Kingdom (Mic 1:5–7). The clear message is that Judah is in similar danger because the people have "followed (literally 'walked in,' *hlk*) their counsels" or "policies" (REB; cf. Jer 7:24; Ps 81:12[13]).

"therefore" (more literally, "so that," *lᵉmaᶜan*) signals the shift from accusation to punishment, which is given a threefold exposition. First, they will become "a desolation," devoid of inhabitants and productive land (cf. Deut 28:37). Second, the inhabitants become "an object of hissing," a term that almost always refers to a city (Jerusalem in Jer 19:8; Babylon in Jer 51:37). When people see the ruins of the city, they will express their horror and shock with a sharp whistling or hissing intake of breath. Third, "you shall bear the scorn of my people." This might mean that the people bear the consequences of their own shameful behaviour. However, scorn is usually heaped on others, hence "you will endure the insults aimed at my people" (REB), or perhaps "of the peoples" (RSV), since LXX has the plural (cf. Ezek 36:15).

Lament, Judgment and Hope (7:1–7)

There are numerous analyses of ch. 7 (de Moor 2000, 154–55), but the shift from lament in vv. 1–6 to hope in vv. 8–20 is reasonably clear, with v. 7 as a transitional verse. Although many regard the chapter as a later addition, there are several characteristic features of Micah's style and there is nothing definitely late. Even if there is later editing, there is no clear shift of speaker and context, suggesting that the editor expects us to continue regarding Micah as the author. In the context of chs. 6–7, this section can be understood as a response to the judgment portrayed in 6:13–16. Whereas wealthy city dwellers were condemned in ch. 6, the critique is now widened to include all. Although the corruption of the officials and judges is specifically noted (7:3), the sketch of a total breakdown of family relationships confirms that this is a comprehensive indictment (vv. 5–6).

The passage begins in vv. 1–4a with a lamentation in the first person ("Woe is me!") describing through a metaphor (v. 1) and its interpretation (vv. 2–4) the moral bankruptcy of the people and its leadership. The speaker is most likely the prophet, who represents the faithful remnant that has completely disappeared (cf. 1 Kgs 19:14, 19). The cry of lament will eventually be answered in an act of judgment (v. 4b), but meanwhile there is a call to act circumspectly (cf. Amos 5:13) and endure to the end (cf. Mark 13:13). Micah commends the behaviour that will be necessary due to a complete breakdown of society (vv. 5–6). Yet the final verse (v. 7) refuses to let darkness reign and expresses a deep trust and an intense hope in God as saviour as well as judge.

7:1. "Woe is me!" expresses Micah's desolation at the state of society. His mood is expressed through an agricultural metaphor (cf. 6:15). The prophet adopts the persona of a poor person who searches for food after the pickers have finished. Harvesters were exhorted to leave some of the produce for the poor to glean (Lev 19:9–10; Deut 24:19–21), but, alas, the harvesting has been so ruthless that the fig trees and vines are utterly denuded. The metaphor evokes feelings of despair, for this is effectively a death sentence for a hungry person awaiting a barren winter.

"cluster" (*ʾeškôl*) is an unusual word for grapes, chosen because of the similar sound of "to eat" (*leʾekōl*). "summer fruit" is simply "summer" (*qayiṣ*), used metonymically to refer to the most important fruit of the summer, the fig. The fruits are stated chiastically: fig ("summer fruit")–grapes ("vintage")–grapes ("cluster")–fig ("first-ripe fig," Isa 28:4). The "I" in "for which I hunger" is *nepeš*, thus "my soul desires" (RSV), but its original physiological reference was the throat (Isa 5:14), which appropriately represented the appetite of the starving person. This final phrase reinforces the intense disappointment and desperation that is implied by the opening exclamation. Although the metaphor often refers to the devastation of the divine judgment (Isa 17:6; Jer 49:9), here the leaders themselves are responsible for the situation.

7:2. Israel is evidently the vineyard (Isa 5:1–7), but the metaphor of v. 1 is clarified and developed with significant social detail. The fruit are the "faithful" and the "upright" (see on 2:7), both singular representative figures, emphasizing that "there is no one left." But the prophet looks for any of them in vain, however much he hungers and thirsts for righteousness (Matt 5:6). The faithful (*ḥāsîd*) are those who live according to *ḥesed*, the kindness of 6:8. It might describe a God-ward orientation ("godly," NIV; "pious," NJPS), but the next phrase and the contrast in the second half of the verse suggests that the social dimension is primary (cf. Hos 4:1–2). The faithful behave loyally and generously to others in the covenant community. Of course, ultimately all faithfulness depends on the character of Yhwh (Ps 145:17). Robbers usually "lie in wait" for the unsuspecting and the helpless (Ps 10:9; Prov 1:11; 24:15), but if the righteous have disappeared, then the only alternative is to "hunt each other with nets." This is no longer a matter of relative gain but of "blood," of violence and murder (a stage beyond 6:10–12). Doing away with someone is simply equivalent to catching a fish (Ezek 26:5; Hab 1:15–17). "each other" (literally "his brother," NIV, NJB) refers not only to a blood brother but also a "kinsman" (REB) or even "fellow-countryman" (GNB). The law set out the responsibilities owed to the "brother" (Lev 19:17; Deut 22:1–4), but now the closest family ties mean nothing.

7:3. In this upside-down world the attributes of success are being "skilled to do evil." "skilled" (*hêṭîb*) is derived from the "good" root (*ṭôb*), and often means thoroughly, but here there may be an ironic reversal of the moral norms implied by the good. Their efforts are whole-hearted and they make use of both hands (the dual). The focus on a representative individual continues. The following three phrases use three different terms for leaders: the "official" (*śar*), the "judge" (*šōpēṭ*) and the "great one" (*gādôl*). The first two phrases are probably meant to be read together: "the official demands [recompense] and the judge [demands] recompense." It may also be an example of hendiadys, that is, the judging official. The word for "bribe" (*šillûm*) is not the usual one, and usually means retribution (Deut 32:35), but here it refers to some sort of payment for giving the required judgment—for those who can pay ("fee," NJPS). The third word, the powerful (literally "great one," paired with official in 2 Sam 3:38) can describe the rich and the influential, often the king's higher administrative officials (2 Kgs 10:6; Jonah 3:7). "dictate what they desire" interprets the more literal "speaks the desire of his throat/soul" (see on v. 1). "pervert justice" makes good sense in the context, but the meaning of the verb is uncertain and justice is a simple (feminine) "it." The closest reference is to "desire" ("they grant it," NJPS), but the RSV has "weave it together" (relating the verb to a noun meaning rope or twisted cord). Perhaps the image is that these leaders twist the situation to their advantage ("conspire together," NIV; "All three twist their offices," McKane 1998).

7:4. The total corruption of the nation is emphasized by taking "the best of them" and comparing him with the most useless and injurious of plants, a "brier" or a "thorn hedge." Perhaps the tangle of thorns continues the thought of the previous verse ("twisted like rank weeds," REB). The image anticipates the following announcement of judgment, since only fire allows thorns to give way to productive ground (Rudolph 1971; cf. Isa 9:18[17]; 10:17). The finely honed skills of v. 3 will count for nothing in an invasion. The "sentinels" or watchers (from *sph*, "watch") are God's servants, the prophets (Jer 6:17; Ezek 3:17; Hos 9:8). The day of punishment that the prophets warned about "has come" (cf. Isa 10:3; 37:3). This is the prophetic perfect: the judgment is so certain, vivid and imminent that it is portrayed as already enacted, even though it remains future. The Hebrew has a change to direct address in the first two "your sentinels…your punishment…their confusion" (cf. NIV, NJPS), perhaps highlighting the accusation. The correspondence between sin and punishment (*lex talionis*) is emphasized by a wordplay between "thorn hedge" (*mᵉsûkâ*) and "their confusion" (*mᵉbûkātām*), one of the consequences of defeat (Isa 22:5).

7:5–6. These verses echo the lament vv. 2–4, but also intensify it by moving from the public to the personal sphere. All are involved, not just the wealthy and powerful. The style is varied by shifting from third person description to direct address (anticipated in the "your" of v. 4b), but the warnings only reinforce the earlier lament over a total breakdown of society. For a people whose identity, security and happiness were found above all in relationships within the community, this is indeed a portrait of hell (Rudolph 1971). Such division and suspicion is the end result of sin and self-serving (Isa 3:5; Jer 9:4–5[3–4]), the polar opposite of the command to love the neighbour (Lev 19:18; Mic 6:8). Later apocalyptic writers saw such a breakdown of community as a sign of the chaos and distress before the end of all things (*1 En* 56:7; 100:2; *Jub* 23:16). Nor can the faithful escape, as Jesus warned his followers (Matt 10:35–38; Luke 12:53).

The verse contains three descriptions of ever more intimate relations, for even the closest cannot be trusted. The "friend" (*rēaᶜ*) is a "neighbour" (REB, NJB) or fellow member of the covenant community. The "loved one" (*ʾallûp*) is a close friend (Prov 16:28; 17:9), over whose betrayal the psalmist laments bitterly (Ps 55:13[14]). Nearest of all is the wife, "who lies in your embrace (*ḥêq*)." "embrace" ("bosom," AV) has sexual connotations ("shares your bed," NJPS; Gen 16:5; Deut 13:6[7]; 28:54; 1 Kgs 1:2). "guard the doors of your mouth" is a vivid metaphor, the lips being the double doors that allow words to emerge. The individual is portrayed as a guarded house in a dangerous town, full of those who are looking for hostages to seize and use to the harm of the owner. Whether it is worth leading such a life would no doubt be considered questionable.

7:6. Following relationships within the same generation, three further pairs of hostile relationships between the generations communicate an additional crescendo of intensification. The paradigmatic family unit has five significant members: father, mother, son, daughter, daughter-in-law (cf. Luke 12:52). As is common in a traditional society, the closest relationships are between the same members of the two sexes, who would spend most of their time together in their tasks, most of which usually differed significantly for men and women. A rebellious son deserves death according to the law (Deut 21:18–21), reflecting the honour and respect that children were to have for their parents (Exod 20:12; Lev 20:9). But now "the son treats the father with contempt." This may be the basic idea to the verb (*nbl*; Deut 32:15; Jer 14:21; Marböck 1998, 160–61), but it is also related to a noun meaning "fool" (*nābāl*; 1 Sam 25:25; Prov 17:21). If this nuance is active, then the son treated or spoke of his father as a fool in public, a powerful expression of contempt (Waltke 1993). There are a number of examples of sons turning against fathers (Gen 9:25; 2 Sam 15), but the close relationship between mother and daughter in a household would make insubordination an even more shocking matter. A daughter-in-law owed respect and obedience to her mother-in-law (cf. Ruth 1), whose authority would be reinforced by the status of the daughter-in-law as outsider. However, here too the natural order is turned upside down.

The final phrase is literally "the enemies of a man/person–men/persons of his house." The chiastic ABBA form conveys syntactically the opposition between the individuals. The "men" may be the slaves of the household (Rudolph 1971). However, only wealthy households had slaves (Gen 17:23, 27; 39:14), and it makes even better sense as a climactic summary of the two verses. In this case the NRSV's inclusive translation is appropriate: "your enemies are members of your own household." The breakdown of the basic family structure is both the result of a breakdown of society in general (vv. 2–4) and a cause of it.

7:7. "But as for me" first of all contrasts the prophet's attitude to those described in the previous verses. It brings to a close the subsection that began in v. 1 with another first person statement, although now the tone is significantly modified because the prophet is focusing on God. This shift is frequently found in the prophets (Jer 17:16; Hab 3:18) and the Psalms of Individual Lament (Pss 38:15[16]; 40:17[18]). But the verse also looks forward since the contrast between lament and hope links it to the expression of confidence in vv. 8–12. The failure of the foundational structures of family (v. 5) and nation (v. 2) means that there is only hope left. This hope can only be in a God who can save those near to death (v. 8). The movement of the verse thus parallels that in v. 8, in that the speaker's situation is dire, but he looks to the future salvation of his God. "look" and "wait" describe an active commitment of trust (Pss 71:14; 130:5), which only requires God to hear for him to act and to make all things well (Ps 5:3[4]).

Hope for the Future (7:8–20)

This passage conveys a significantly different tone to the previous verses. There are no complaints, accusations, threats or instructions. The passage includes at least four different genres, with the mood becomes increasingly more positive and assured, possible because the focus is intensely God-centred. A song of trust (vv. 8–10) leads to an oracle of salvation (vv. 11–13), and a prayer for God to shepherd his people (vv. 14–17) leads to a climactic hymn of praise (vv. 18–20). Whatever their date and authorship, the final three verses fittingly round off the entire book, which has several times followed descriptions of woe with promises of future joy. The book of Micah began with God coming in his wrath; it concludes with praise to the God who comes in grace.

Since all of these elements are found in psalms of lament, many have followed Gunkel's proposal that it was based on an early liturgy from Northern Israel (Gunkel 1928; Reicke 1967). The towns mentioned are all found in Northern Israel, and the problem for the author seems invasion rather than exile. However, there is no certainty that this text was meant to be performed, and elements of lament may occur in many different kinds of writing. Dating is, as usual, also disputed. For some, the reference to rebuilding walls (v. 11) has suggested a Persian date, but rebuilding was a regular feature of Israel's life and "Assyria" (v. 12) suggests an earlier rather than a later historical context.

7:8. The first person feminine address and the themes of light/darkness and salvation/vindication unite the first section (vv. 8–10). Since cities are feminine in Hebrew, it is probably Lady Zion or Daughter Jerusalem, representing the nation (so 1:16; 4:9–10; 6:9). She addresses her enemies and warns them "Do not rejoice" at the way she is suffering the consequences of her sin (v. 9). This kind of rhetorical address to an enemy who gloats (cf. NJB) over the speaker's humiliation is characteristic of laments (Ps 35:19, 24). The enemy (also feminine) is also likely to be a city such as Edom (Obad 12; Ps 137:7), Nineveh (the capital of Assyria) or Babylon (in an exilic context). It could also be a generalized evil city since no specific name is given (the Targ. identifies the city as "Rome"!).

"when" makes the affirmation a general one, but the two verbs are in the perfect and probably point to a specific reversal of the present situation of distress. Most therefore take the conjunction as "though" rather than "when." The contrast between fall and rise, and between light and darkness, may indicate the difference between disaster and prosperity. But a darker interpretation would see in these terms a reference to life and death. "fall" is often used of military defeat and the attendant slaughter (Isa 21:9), while "rise" evokes the hope of a miraculously restored nation (Hos 6:2). Darkness is supremely found in the grave, the realm of the dead (Ps 88:12[13]). Conversely, light implies salvation (v. 7; Ps 27:1), restoration (Isa 49:6) and (when understood in a later context) resurrection (Acts 26:23).

7:9. Until Yhwh acts Zion must "bear" or endure "the indignation of the LORD." "indignation" is rather weak for the Hebrew (*za'ap*), since it is the word used of the rage storm in Jonah 1:15, and in context refers to Yhwh's wrath against the evil that has been described in previous chapters. However, his anger is temporary and the path to forgiveness and redemption is opened when corporate

Israel acknowledges that "I have sinned against him" (cf. 2 Kgs 18:14; contrast Jer 2:35). "until" directs us to the future affirmed in v. 8b, which is recalled also through the repeated light imagery. "takes my side" uses the same root as the controversy in 6:1–2 (*rîḇ*), but this time the judge acts for the defence ("pleads my case," NIV). "executes judgment" echoes the "do justice" of 6:8, but the context here makes it clear that this is a specific vindication on Israel's behalf. "vindication" is the many-sided "righteousness" word (*ṣᵉḏāqâ*) and implies full salvation ("saving justice," NJB; Isa 45:8).

7:10. The verse continues the story further ("then," not a generalizing "when") and describes the reaction of the enemy when it sees Jerusalem's vindication (v. 10a). In turn Zion will (literally) "look upon her," that is, "see her downfall" (v. 10b). The consequence of seeing is as much emotional as physical. The enemy not only ceases to rejoice (v. 8), but "shame will cover her" like a cloak (cf. Obad 10). Whereas in v. 9 vindication is on behalf of Israel, here at stake is the reputation of Yhwh. "where is the LORD your God" mockingly belittles the presence and power of Yhwh, thereby asserting the superior power of some other god, for the fate of a god and his or her people was inseparable. But the coming reversal will reveal the true order of things. The REB's "gloat" for the second "see" suggests an unattractive personal vindictiveness, whereas the fundamental affirmation is the vindication of Yhwh's reputation. The opposite of rising in triumph (v. 8a) is being "trodden down," while the stock comparison to the "mire of the streets" adds nuances of degradation and powerlessness (cf. 2 Sam 22:43; Isa 10:6).

7:11. In vv. 11–13 the "I" becomes a "you," first feminine (v. 11), then masculine (v. 12). The new voice addressing Zion is perhaps the prophet or even God (Rudolph 1971) and expands on the reversal of fortunes indicated in vv. 8–10. The threefold day of vv. 11–12 evokes excitement and intensity in the readers as they contemplate the promised reconstruction (Mays 1976). Although some think of Nehemiah's rebuilding in Persian times, ancient city walls were in constant need of repair from the innumerable wars that punctuated Israel's history. But it is also possible that the city is unnamed because it represents the nation. "walls" (*gāḏēr*) is not the usual word for a fortified city wall, but one used, for example, of the dry stone wall enclosing a vineyard (Num 22:24; cf. Isa 5:5) or a flock of sheep (Num 32:16). In the blended metaphor (the city or people as Israel's vineyard or sheepfold) the breaching of these walls (plural because they are so extensive) represents defeat of the kingdom (Ps 80:12[13]). If the parallelism is synonymous, then "boundary" (*ḥōq*) refers to the city walls, which will be so enlarged that its population or prosperity will not be restricted (Isa 49:19–21; cf. Waltke 1993). On the other hand, there could be progression from city to nation, so that a secured city is the basis for outward expansion beyond the borders of the land (Isa 26:15).

7:12. The first phrase is literally "he/one will come to you (masculine)." In context it is probably the remnant that will come, hence "they" or "your people" (REB). A minor revocalization to feminine rather than masculine allows "to you" to refer to Zion. Alternatively, Williamson (1997, 371–72) suggests an emendation from the unusual "and to you" (*wᵉᶜādêkā*) to "and your flock" (*wᵉᶜedrᵉkā*), a standard symbol of God's people (v. 14; cf. Isa 40:11; Mic 2:12). The geographical logic of the rest of the verse is a puzzle because some of the prepositions are left out and some of the references are uncertain. The first pair is literally "from Assyria and the towns of Egypt" (NJPS), but most emend "towns" to "to." One symmetrical explanation of the four pairs of regions would find a reversal pattern according to whether the location was in the north or south (travelling to Mesopotamia required first a journey north, even though it was geographically east). Thus we have (1) from Assyria (north) (2) to Egypt (south); (3) from Egypt (south) (4) to the River (the Euphrates) (north/east?). The word for Egypt is an unusual one (*māṣôr*), although it could have been chosen because it can also mean "stronghold" (parallel to "towns" of the previous phrase). Some accept an emendation that removes the repetition and read "from Tyre" for its second appearance (LXX; NJB, NAB). The second pair would then be (3) Tyre (west) (4) Euphrates (east) (Rudolph 1971).

The third and fourth pairs only have one preposition (literally "and sea from sea, and mountain mountain"). This may encompass the entire world by a double reference to two extremes (merismus; cf. Ps 72:8; Zech 10:10). In ancient cosmogony an all-encompassing sea and cosmic mountains marked the outer limits of the world (Keel 1978, 21). A more mundane solution would be to identify the seas as (5) the Mediterranean (west) (6) the Persian Gulf (east), with the mountains as (7) the Lebanon range (north) and (8) Mount Sinai (south). Whatever the explanation, this is an impressive statement of universal pilgrimage (cf. 4:1–2).

7:13. Salvation for Israel is often the counterpart to the punishment of the rebellious nations (Joel 3:18–20[4:18–20]), a theme later developed in the Christian doctrine of the last judgment (Rev 19:15). These coexist with more positive visions of the role of the nations (e.g. 4:1–4), but here the emphasis is on their wicked behaviour, the usual implication of the noun translated "their doings" (2:7; 3:4). Ironically, the fruit of such behaviour is a lack of all fruitfulness or blessing, a desolate earth (cf. 1:7; 6:16). Israel was warned of just these consequences in the curses of the covenant, which have a strong ecological dimension (Lev 26:33; Deut 28:20). Now those who overturn the moral order will come to experience death and destruction (Isa 24:1–6), leaving Jerusalem "an oasis in the desert of the earth" (Wolff 1990, 225).

7:14. A new subsection (vv. 14–17) begins with a prayer by Micah (again representing the faithful) to Yhwh urging him to shepherd his people (vv. 14–15). This is followed by an oracle of salvation (vv. 16–17), a promise of vindication in the sight of the nations. An alternative analysis is to read the verbs in vv. 16–17 as jussives ("let…," REB, NJPS) rather than indicatives ("shall…"), thus continuing the prayer. One gain from this would be to make vv. 18–20 a more satisfying conclusion and answer, but it also requires emendation of a v. 15 indicative ("I will show," RSV, NJPS) to an imperative ("show").

The shepherd metaphor (2:12; 4:6–7; 5:4) pervades v. 14. God is the Shepherd who leads his people/flock with his staff ("crook," NJB) in order to feed ("graze," NJB). The appeal to God as shepherd expresses trust and hope (Ps 80:1[2]). The normal interpretation of the second couplet is that it portrays a situation of need. Israel is isolated and without protection or guidance. The "forest" (*ya'ar*) is generally a desolate woodland (3:12) that is ruled by wild animals (5:8[7]; Hos 2:12). However, other mentions of Israel living "alone" (*bādād*) are positive, emphasizing Israel's uniqueness and Yhwh's special care for them (Num 23:9; Deut 33:28). Van Hecke (2003) argues that the forest is shrubland, ideal for grazing cattle (Isa 10:18), and that the "garden land" (*karmel*) is the Carmel district (cf. AV), well known for its fertile slopes. "Shepherd" then has the same force as "let them feed," in that it assumes that the redeemed people is already living in a restored land, and asks Yhwh to continue his protection and provision. Bashan and Gilead were the paradigmatic grazing lands (Deut 32:14; Jer 50:19), situated on the other side of the Jordan and granted to three tribes "in the days of old," at the beginning of the nation's conquest of the land (Num 32; Josh 22). In Israel's recent history these regions had been under threat from the Aramaeans and were eventually captured by Assyria (2 Kgs 15:29).

7:15. The reference to "the days of old" leads further back to a reference to the Exodus, "when you came out of the land of Egypt" (more literally "the days of your Exodus" LXX). "show us" is an emendation of an original "I will show him" (NJPS). In adopting this reading the NRSV understands "you" as a reference to Yhwh and allows the section to be a consistent prayer. However, usually Israel is spoken of as coming out of Egypt (Ps 114:1), and the MT is supported by all the ancient versions (except LXX, which has "you will see"). The verse would then interrupt the prayer with a divine answer, or a quotation of one by the person praying. The underlying assumption is the continuity of God's faithfulness to his covenant people. Accordingly, they may expect him to perform "marvellous things" (*niplā'ôt*). These are the "miracles" (REB) that had enabled the Exodus to take place (Exod 3:20). God's original gracious rescue of his people remained the foundation of Israel's hope for a future reversal of fortunes. God's mighty acts during the Exodus are an important basis for the appeal to God in the laments of the Psalms (Pss 78:12; 81:10[11]; 106:7).

7:16–17. The forms of the verbs in these two verses may either be understood as an indicative ("they shall," a promise of salvation; so NRSV), or jussive ("let them," continuing the prayer for salvation; so REB, NJPS). The parallel with vv. 9–10 suggests the latter, in which case the mood of these verses is similar to that of vv. 18–20. The negative attitude of v. 13 is expanded. Salvation for God's people means shame (cf. v. 10) for the nations, who manifest their humiliation in a number of vivid body images. Rather than gloating (v. 8) and mocking Israel and its God, they shall "lay their hands on their mouths" (Job 40:4; Prov 30:32) and "their ears shall be deaf" (Ps 28:1). Having fallen from a position of might they shall know the powerlessness of having to "lick dust like a snake" (Ps 72:9), a sign of humiliation (Barré 1982) and possibly a reference to defeated enemies kissing the feet of their victor (Isa 49:23; Dommershausen and Fabry 1995, 520). There may also be an allusion to God's judgment in Gen 3:14, where the snake has to eat dust. The second half of the verse can be understood either as two or three phrases, depending on whether the final two verbs are taken together or not. If the verbs are split, then they become a concluding chiastic pair of phrases (Yhwh our God–they shall dread–they shall fear–before you). On the other hand, the verbs can be taken together, in which case the two lines set up a strong contrast and narrative movement: they shall tremble–out of fortresses–to Yhwh our God–they shall be in dread and fear (cf. NJPS, REB). "fortresses" are the refuges of last resort, but on this day of judgment there is no choice but to "come trembling out." The concluding "they shall stand in fear (*yirʾû*) of you" sets up a wordplay on the opening verb "see" of v. 16 (also *yirʾû*, but from a different root). Since fear before Yhwh is often a positive characteristic (Deut 6:13), this may hint that the nations have a future beyond judgment, but this is an element of hope drawn from other more positive texts.

7:18. The final verses of the book (vv. 18–20) move from setting out Israel's relationship with the nations to their future relationship with God. At the heart of Israel's understanding of God's character is the "creed" of Exod 34:6–7 (see on Jonah 4:2; Brueggemann 1997, 213–28), with which these verses have several significant parallels: pardoning, the three main words for sin ("iniquity," "transgression," "sin"), anger, clemency (*ḥesed*, "steadfast love," RSV; see on 6:8), the "compassion" root (v. 19), and the pair "faithfulness" and "unswerving loyalty" (*ḥesed* again, v. 20). This section may be a meditation on that theological formula as it applied to Israel's hopeless situation. The high degree of repetition ("forgiveness" is affirmed no less than seven times in vv. 18–19), the variation in language, and the vivid metaphors all help to affirm the hearers' faith in God and encourage them to put their trust and hope in him for the future.

"Who is a God like you" is a characteristic mode of praise, expecting the answer "no one" (explicit in Targ.; Syr.). This kind of rhetorical question (Labuscagne 1966) allows Yhwh's incomparability and uniqueness to be affirmed whether the hearers recognize the existence of other gods or not. Elsewhere the subject is usually the mighty deeds of Yhwh (Exod 15:11; Deut 3:24), but this is the only text focusing on God's supreme power to forgive. "pardoning iniquity" (*nōśēʾ ʿāwōn*) is more literally "bearing iniquities." The participle form recalls the "hymnic participle," a frequent feature of hymns of praise (e.g. Ps 136:1–10) that celebrate the consistent character of Yhwh. The phrase evokes the scapegoat ritual, in which a goat carries Israel's sins away into the desert (Lev 16:22), an image also used of the role of the Isaianic servant (Isa

53:4, 12; Matt 8:17). The parallel with "transgression" argues against the meaning "guilt" (REB). "passing over the transgression" (cf. Prov 19:11) may suggest
another movement metaphor, for the verb (*ᶜbr*) is the usual one for "to cross"
(e.g. 2 Sam 15:18). "transgression" (*pešaᶜ*) can have the more specific nuance of
revolt or rebellion (see on 1:5), but the juxtaposition of the other phrases implies
a more general meaning (e.g. "sins," REB). "remnant of your possession" recalls
the earlier threats of judgment on the whole people, as well as highlighting
Israel's present plight. It echoes promises of salvation for the faithful remnant
made earlier in the book (2:12; 4:6; 5:7–8[8–9]). "retain" (hiphil of *ḥzq*) is often
translated "seize" or "keep hold of," so that this is an assurance that God will let
his anger go. At some point God's attitude will change (Ps 30:5[6]; Isa 57:16),
and consequently Israel's situation will be transformed. His wrath is temporary,
a means to an end, not an essential attribute (Heschel 1962, 279–98). "because
he delights in showing clemency" emphasizes that the basis for forgiveness is
God's gracious action, not Israel's behaviour.

7:19. The verbs now shift from perfects and participles to imperfects. The more
general descriptive praise of God becomes the basis for a more specific
declarative praise of what he is about to do. This may be one reason for the shift
from the direct second person address in v. 18 to third person in v. 19a (such
variations are common, and there is no need to adopt a consistent second person,
as REB does). "He will again have compassion upon us" reflects the tender affec-
tion of a superior that motivates him or her ("womb" is derived from the same
root *rḥm*) to help the needy (Deut 13:17; 1 Kgs 8:50; Hos 2:23). "tread…under
foot" translates a verb (*kbš*) used usually used to describe the subjugation of
nations (2 Sam 8:11) or people (Jer 34:11; Esth 7:8). This may then be a
personification of sin as "the archenemy of the people of God" (Wolff 1990,
231). Although this is unique, there is no need to find a nuance of cleansing by
trampling on clothes ("wash away our guilt," REB). The next phrase probably
continues the military note, since it alludes to Yhwh's triumph over Pharaoh's
military forces, which sank "into the depths of the sea" (Exod 15:5; cf. Jonah
2:3[4]; cf. Rev 18:21). For God "to cast all our sins into the depths of the sea" is
to ensure that they can never be recovered. Without exception ("all"), they will
be completely forgotten and will not threaten the glorious future God will grant
to his people.

7:20. The final verse reaffirms the special and longstanding relationship of God
with his elect people. The pair "steadfast love" and "faithfulness," found in
Exod 34:6 and frequently elsewhere, are split between the first two phrases in
reversed order, "faithfulness" (*ᵓemet*) and "unswerving loyalty" (*ḥesed*). They
refer (by metonymy) to the promises given to the patriarchs of land, posterity
and a special relationship with God (Clines 1997b). Because of his faithful love
God will act on Israel's behalf to fulfil these promises. As previously in the book
(1:5; 2:7, 12), Jacob stands for the people who were the promised descendants of
the patriarch (Gen 28:13–15). The implication is that Abraham also represents

the people who regarded him as their first ancestor (Gen 12), even though elsewhere they are called the offspring of Abraham (Ps 105:6; Isa 41:8). However, the patriarchs and their descendents are inextricably interlinked by being the recipients of the promises "sworn to our ancestors." These continue to be active in guiding the exercise of God's wrath and mercy, so they are spoken as being "from days of old." The book ends with a reference to Israel's first beginnings with God, sealed by gracious promises that had never been fully realized and had so often been frustrated, not least in Micah's day. But God is faithful and true, so these promises now become the grounds of hope for a future day when they will finally become a wonderful and joyful reality, not just for Israel but also (if we take into account passages such as 4:1–5) for the nations as well (cf. Rom 4; Gal 3).

SELECT BIBLIOGRAPHY

COMMENTARIES

Achtemeier, E. 1996. *Minor Prophets*. Volume 1, *Hosea–Micah*. New International Bible Commentary 17. Peabody, Mass.: Hendrickson.

Alexander, D. 1988. "Jonah." Pages 45–131 in *Obadiah, Jonah, Micah*. Edited by B. Waltke. Tyndale Old Testament Commentaries. Leicester: Inter-Varsity Press.

Alfaro, J. I. 1989. *Justice and Loyalty: A Commentary on the Book of Micah*. International Theological Commentary. Grand Rapids: Eerdmans.

Allen, L. C. 1976. *The Books of Joel, Obadiah, Jonah, and Micah*. New International Commentary on the Old Testament. Grand Rapids: Eerdmans.

Andersen, F. I., and D. N. Freedman. 2000. *Micah: A New Translation with Introduction and Commentary*. Anchor Bible 24E. New York: Doubleday.

Baker, D. W. 1988. "Obadiah." Pages 17–44 in *Obadiah, Jonah, Micah*. Edited by B. Waltke. Tyndale Old Testament Commentaries. Leicester: Inter-Varsity Press.

Baldwin, J. 1993. "Jonah." Pages 543–90 in Volume 2 of *The Minor Prophets: An Exegetical and Expository Commentary*. Edited by T. E. McComiskey. Grand Rapids Mich.: Baker.

Barton, J. 2001. *Joel and Obadiah: A Commentary*. Old Testament Library. Louisville, Ky.: Westminster John Knox; London: SCM Press.

Ben Zvi, E. 2000. *Micah*. Forms of the Old Testament Literature 21B. Grand Rapids: Eerdmans.

Bewer, J. A. 1911. "Jonah." Pages 1–65 in *A Critical and Exegetical Commentary on Haggai, Zechariah, Malachi, and Jonah*. International Critical Commentary. Edinburgh: T. & T. Clark.

Calvin, J. 1979. *Commentaries on the Minor Prophets*. Translated by J. Owen. Grand Rapids: Baker Book House.

Clark, D. J., and N. Mundhenk. 1982. *A Translator's Handbook on the Books of Obadiah and Micah*. Helps for Translators. New York: United Bible Societies.

Clark, D. J., N. Mundhenk, E. A. Nida and B. F. Price. 1993. *A Handbook on the Books of Obadiah, Jonah, and Micah*. United Bible Society Handbook Series. New York: United Bible Societies.

Fretheim, T. E. 1977. *The Message of Jonah: A Theological Commentary*. Minneapolis: Augsburg.

Golka, F. W. 1988. "Jonah." Pages 65–136 in *Revelation of God: A Commentary on the Books of the Song of Songs and Jonah*. Edited by G. A. Knight and F. W. Golka. International Theological Commentary. Edinburgh: Handsel.

Hillers, D. R. 1984. *Micah*. Hermeneia. Philadelphia: Fortress.

Keil, C. F. 1871. *Minor Prophets*. Translated by J. Martin. Grand Rapids: Eerdmans.

Keller, C.-A. 1982. *Jonas*. Commentaire de l'Ancien Testament 11a. Geneva: Labor et Fides.

Kessler, R. 1999. *Micha*. Herders theologischer Kommentar zum Alten Testament. Freiburg: Herder.

Limburg, J. 1993. *Jonah: A Commentary*. Old Testament Library. London: SCM Press.

Mays, J. L. 1976. *Micah: A Commentary*. Old Testament Library. London: SCM Press.

McKane, W. 1998. *Micah: Introduction and Commentary.* Edinburgh: T. & T. Clark.

Niehaus, J. J. 1993. "Obadiah." Pages 495–541 in Volume 2 of *The Minor Prophets: An Exegetical and Expository Commentary.* Edited by T. E. McComiskey. Grand Rapids Mich.: Baker.

Price, B. F., and E. A. Nida. 1978. *A Translator's Handbook on the Book of Jonah.* Helps for Translators 21. Stuttgart: United Bible Societies.

Raabe, P. R. 1996. *Obadiah: A New Translation with Introduction, Commentary, and Interpretation.* Anchor Bible 24D. New York: Doubleday.

Renkema, J. 2003. *Obadiah.* Historical Commentary on the Old Testament. Leuven: Peeters.

Rudolph, W. 1971. *Joel, Amos, Obadja, Jona.* Kommentar zum Alten Testament 13/2. Gütersloh: Gerd Mohn.

———, 1975. *Micha, Nahum, Habakuk, Zephanja.* Kommentar zum Alten Testament 13/3. Gütersloh: Gerd Mohn.

Sasson, J. M. 1990. *Jonah: A New Translation with Introduction, Commentary, and Interpretation.* Anchor Bible 24B. New York: Doubleday.

Schibler, D. 1989. *Le livre de Michée.* Commentaire évangélique de la Bible. Vaux-aux-Seine: Commentaire évangélique de la Bible.

Simon, U. 1999. *Jonah: The Traditional Hebrew Text with the New JPS Translation.* Translated by L. J. Schramm. JPS Bible Commentary. Philadelphia: Jewish Publication Society of America.

Smith, B. K., and F. S. Page. 1995. *Amos, Obadiah, Jonah.* New American Commentary 19B. Nashville: Broadman & Holman.

Smith, J. M. P. 1911. "The Prophet Micah." Pages 3–156 in *A Critical and Exegetical Commentary on Micah, Zephaniah, Nahum, Habakkuk, Obadiah and Joel.* International Critical Commentary. Edinburgh: T. & T. Clark.

Smith, R. L. 1984. *Micah–Malachi.* Word Biblical Commentary 32. Waco, Tex.: Word.

Stuart, D. 1987. *Hosea–Jonah.* Word Biblical Commentary 31. Waco, Tex.: Word.

Thompson, J. A. 1956. "Obadiah." Pages 855–67 in Volume 6 of *The Interpreter's Bible.* New York: Abingdon.

Trible, P. 1996. "Jonah." Pages 463–529 in Volume 7 of *The New Interpreter's Bible.* Nashville: Abingdon.

Vargon, S. 1994. *The Book of Micah: A Study and Commentary* [Hebrew]. Ramat Gan: Bar-Ilan University Press.

Waltke, B. K. 1993. "Micah." Pages 591–764 in Volume 2 of *The Minor Prophets: An Exegetical and Expository Commentary.* Edited by T. E. McComiskey. Grand Rapids Mich.: Baker.

Watts, J. D. W. 1981 (1969). *Obadiah: A Critical and Exegetical Commentary.* Reprint. Grand Rapids: Eerdmans.

Wolff, H. W. 1986. *Obadiah and Jonah: A Commentary.* Translated by M. Knohl. Continental Commentaries. Philadelphia: Augsburg.

———, 1990. *Micah: A Commentary.* Translated by G. Stansell. Continental Commentaries. Philadelphia: Augsburg.

Zlotowitz, M. 1978. *Yonah/Jonah: A New Translation with a Commentary: Anthologized from Midrashic and Rabbinic Sources.* Brooklyn, N.Y.: Mesorah Publications.

Utzschneider, H. 2005. *Micha.* Zürcher Bibelkommentare. Alten Testament 24.1. Zurich: Theologischer Verlag.

OTHER MONOGRAPHS AND ARTICLES

Ackerman, J. S. 1981. "Satire and Symbolism in the Song of Jonah." Pages 213–46 in *Traditions in Transformation: Turning Points in Biblical Faith*. Edited by J. D. Levenson. Winona Lake, Ind.: Eisenbrauns.

Ackroyd, P. 1968. *Exile and Restoration*. London: SCM Press.

——, 1986. "yād." *Theological Dictionary of the Old Testament* 5:393–426.

Ahlström, G. W. 1967. "ēder." *Vetus Testamentum* 17: 1–7.

Alexander, T. D. 1985. "Jonah and Genre." *Tyndale Bulletin* 36: 35–59.

Allen, L. C. 1973. "Micah's Social Concern." *Vox Evangelica* 8: 22–32.

Alonso Schökel, L. 1990. "yāšar." *Theological Dictionary of the Old Testament* 6: 1–6.

Alter, R. 1981. *The Art of Biblical Narrative*. New York: Basic Books.

——, 1985. *The Art of Biblical Poetry*. New York: Basic Books.

André, G. 1995. "kāšap." *Theological Dictionary of the Old Testament* 7: 360–66.

Andrew, M. E. 1967. "Gattung and Intention of the Book of Jonah." *Orita* 1: 13–18, 78–85.

Augustine. 1972. *Concerning the City of God against the Pagans*. Harmondsworth: Penguin.

Band, A. J. 1990. "Swallowing Jonah: The Eclipse of Parody." *Prooftexts* 10: 177–95.

Bar-Efrat, S. 1989. *Narrative Art in the Bible*. Journal for the Study of the Old Testament: Supplement Series 70; Bible and Literature 17. Sheffield: Almond Press.

Barré, M. 1991. "Jonah 2:9 and the Structure of Jonah's Prayer." *Biblica* 72: 237–48.

Barrick, W. B. 1992. "High Places." *Anchor Bible Dictionary* 3: 196–200.

Bartlett, J. 1969. "The Land of Seir and the Brotherhood of Edom." *Journal of Theological Studies* NS 20: 1–20.

——, 1977. "The Brotherhood of Edom." *Journal for the Study of the Old Testament* 4: 2–27.

——, 1989. *Edom and the Edomites*. Journal for the Study of the Old Testament: Supplement Series 77. Sheffield: JSOT Press.

Barton, J. 1980. *Amos' Oracles against the Nations*. Society for Old Testament Study Monograph Series 6. Cambridge: Cambridge University Press.

——, 2007. *The Nature of Biblical Criticism*. Louisville; Ky./London: Westminster John Knox.

Bauckham, R. 2003. *Bible and Mission: Christian Witness in a Postmodern World*. Easneye Lectures. Carlisle: Paternoster.

Bauer, J. B. "Drei Tage." *Biblica* 39 (1958): 354–58.

Beal, T. K. 1994. "The System and the Speaking Subject in the Hebrew Bible: Reading for Divine Abjection." *Biblical Interpretation* 2: 171–89.

Ben Zvi, E. 1996a. *A Historical-Critical Study of the Book of Obadiah*. Beihefte zur Zeitschrift für die alttestamentliche Wissenschaft 242. Berlin: De Gruyter.

——, 1996b. "Twelve Prophetic Books or 'The Twelve': A Few Preliminary Considerations." Pages 125–56 in *Forming Prophetic Literature: Essays on Isaiah and the Twelve in Honor of John D. W. Watts*. Edited by J. W. Watts and P. R. House. Journal for the Study of the Old Testament: Supplement Series 235. Sheffield: Sheffield Academic Press.

——, 1998. "Micah 1.2–16: Observations and Possible Implications." *Journal for the Study of the Old Testament* 77: 103–20.

Ben-Josef, I. A. 1980. "Jonah and the Fish as a Folk Motif." *Semitics* 7: 102–17.

Berlin, A. 1976. "A Rejoinder to John A. Miles, Jr., With Some Observations on the Nature of Prophecy." *Jewish Quarterly Review* 66: 227–35.

——, 1983. *Poetics and Interpretation of Biblical Narrative*. Sheffield: Almond Press.

Bernhardt, K. H. "ʾāwen." *Theological Dictionary of the Old Testament* 1: 140–47.

Beyse, K.-M. 1995. "kᵉlî." *Theological Dictionary of the Old Testament* 7: 169–75.

Bic, M. 1953. "Zur Problematik des Buches Obadjah." Pages 11–25 in *Congress Volume, Copenhagen 1953*. Vetus Testamentum Supplements 1. Leiden: Brill.

Bickerman, E. J. 1967. *Four Strange Books of the Bible: Jonah, Daniel, Koheleth, Esther*. New York: Schocken Books.

Blank, S. H. 1955. "'Doest Thou Well to be Angry?' A Study in Self-Pity." *HUCA* 26: 29–41.

Bolin, T. R. 1997. *Freedom Beyond Forgiveness: The Book of Jonah Re-Examined*. Journal for the Study of the Old Testament: Supplement Series 236; Copenhagen International Seminar 3. Sheffield: Sheffield Academic Press.

Bonino, J. M. 1993. "Marxist Critical Tools: Are They Helpful in Breaking the Stranglehold of Idealist Hermeneutics?" Pages 107–15 in *The Bible and Liberation: Political and Social Hermeneutics*. Edited by R. A. Horsely. Maryknoll: Orbis.

Bonnard, W. 1972. "Abdias." *Dictionnaire de la Bible: Supplément* 8: 693–701.

Bosetti, E. 1993 (1992). *Yahweh Shepherd of the People: Pastoral Symbolism in the Old Testament*. Slough: St Pauls.

Botterweck, G. J. 1974. "ᵃrî." *Theological Dictionary of the Old Testament* 1: 374–88.

——, 1990. "yônâ." *Theological Dictionary of the Old Testament* 6: 32–40.

Brin, G. 1989. "Micah 2,12–13: A Textual and Ideological Study." *Zeitschrift für die alttestamentliche Wissenschaft* 101: 118–24.

Brueggemann, W. 1981. "Vine and Fig Tree: A Case Study in Imagination and Criticism." *Catholic Biblical Quarterly* 43: 188–204.

——, 1997. *Theology of the Old Testament: Testimony, Dispute, Advocacy*. Minneapolis: Fortress.

——, 2003. *The Land: Place as Gift, Promise, and Challenge in Biblical Faith*. Overtures to Biblical Theology. Minneapolis: Fortress Press.

Budde, K. 1892. "Vermutungen zum 'Midrasch des Buches der Könige'." *Zeitschrift für die alttestamentliche Wissenschaft* 12: 37–151.

Burrows, M. 1970. "The Literary Category of the Book of Jonah." Pages 80–107 in *Translating and Understanding the Old Testament: Essays in Honor of Herbert Gordon May*. Edited by W. L. Reed. Nashville: Abingdon.

Byington, S. T. 1949. "Plow and Pick." *Journal of Biblical Literature* 68: 49–54.

Carreira, J. N. 1981. "Micha-ein Ältester von Moreschet?" *Trierer theologische Zeitschrift* 90: 19–28.

Carroll, R. P. 1990. "Is Humour Also Among the Prophets?" Pages 169–89 in *On Humour and the Comic in the Hebrew Bible*. Edited by A. Brenner. Bible and Literature Series 23. Sheffield: Almond Press.

Cathcart, K. J. 1968. "Notes on Micah 5,4–5." *Biblica* 49: 511–14.

——, 1978. "Micah 5, 4–5 and Semitic Incantations." *Biblica* 59: 38–48.

Cathcart, K. J., and K. Jeppesen. 1987. "More Suggestions on Mic 6, 14." *Scandinavian Journal of the Old Testament* 1: 110–15.

Childs, B. S. 1979. *Introduction to the Old Testament as Scripture*. London: SCM Press.

Christensen, D. L. 1985. "Andrzej Panufnik and the Structure of the Book of Jonah: Icons, Music and Literary Art." *Journal of the Evangelical Theological Society* 28: 133–40.

——, 1986. "The Song of Jonah: A Metrical Analysis." *Journal of Biblical Literature* 104: 217–31.

Clark, D. J. 1991. "Obadiah Reconsidered." *Bible Translator* 42: 326–36.

Clements, R. E. 1974. "The Purpose of the Book of Jonah." Pages 16–28 in *Congress Volume, Edinburgh 1974*. Edited by J. A. Emerton. Vetus Testamentum Supplements 28. Leiden: Brill.

Clifford, R. J. 1966. "The Use of Hôy in the Prophets." *Catholic Biblical Quarterly* 28: 458–64.

Clines, D. J. A. 1997a. *The Bible and the Modern World*. Biblical Seminar 51. Sheffield: Sheffield Academic Press.

——, 1997b. *The Theme of the Pentateuch*. 2d ed. Journal for the Study of the Old Testament: Supplement Series 10. Sheffield: JSOT Press.

Cogan, M. 1992. "Chronology: Hebrew Bible." *Anchor Bible Dictionary* 1: 1002–11.

Cohn, G. H. 1969. *Das Buch Jona in Lichte der biblischen Erzählkunst*. Studia Semitica Neerlandica 12. Assen: Van Gorcum.

Collin, M. 1971. "Recherches sur L'histoire textuelle du Prophète Michée." *Vetus Testamentum* 21: 281–97.

Cooper, A. 1993. "In Praise of Divine Caprice: The Significance of the Book of Jonah." Pages 144–63 in *Among the Prophets: Language, Imagery and Structure in the Prophetic Writings*. Edited by D. J. A. Clines. Journal for the Study of the Old Testament: Supplement Series 144. Sheffield: JSOT Press.

Craig, K. M., Jr. 1993. *A Poetics of Jonah: Art in the Service of Ideology*. Columbia, S.C.: University of South Carolina.

Crenshaw, J. L. 1986. "The Expression mî yôde-aʾ in the Hebrew Bible." *Vetus Testamentum* 36: 274–88.

Cresson, B. C. 1972. "The Condemnation of Edom in Post-Exilic Judaism." Pages 125–48 in *The Use of the Old Testament in the New and Other Essays: Studies in Honor of William Franklin Stinespring*. Edited by J. M. Efird. Durham: Duke University.

Crook, M. B. 1954. "Did Amos and Micah Know Isaiah 9,2–7 and 11,1–9?" *Journal of Biblical Literature* 73: 144–51.

Cross, F. M. 1983. "Studies in the Structure of Hebrew Verse: The Prosody of the Psalm of Jonah." Pages 159–67 in *The Quest for the Kingdom of God: Studies in Honor of George E. Mendenhall*. Edited by F. Spina. Winona Lake, Ind.: Eisenbrauns.

Daniels, D. R. 1987. "Is There a 'Prophetic Lawsuit' Genre?" *Zeitschrift für die alttestamentliche Wissenschaft* 99: 339–60.

Davies, G. I. 1977a. "A New Solution to a Crux in Obadiah 7." *Vetus Testamentum* 27: 484–87.

——, 1977b. "The Use of rʾʾ Qal and the Meaning of Jonah IV 1." *Vetus Testamentum* 27: 105–10.

Davis, E. B. 1991. "A Whale of a Tale: Fundamentalist Fish Stories." *Perspectives on Science and Christian Faith* 43: 224–37.

Dawes, S. 1988. "Walking Humbly: Micah 6,8 Revisited." *Scottish Journal of Theology* 41: 331–39.

Day, J. 1990. "Problems in the Interpretation of the Book of Jonah." Pages 32–47 in *In Quest of the Past: Studies on Israelite Religion, Literature, and Prophetism*. Edited by A. S. van der Woude. Old Testament Studies 26. Kinderhook, NY: Brill (USA).

Dell, K. J. 1996. "Reinventing the Wheel: The Shaping of the Book of Jonah." Pages 85–101 in *After the Exile: Essays in Honour of Rex Mason*. Edited by D. J. Reimer. Macon: Mercer University Press.

Demsky, A. 1966. "The House of Achzib: A Critical Note on Micah 1:14b." *Israel Exploration Journal* 16: 212–15.

DeRoche, M. 1983. "Yahweh's rîb Against Israel: A Reassessment of the So-Called 'Prophetic Lawsuit' in the Preexilic Prophets." *Journal of Biblical Literature* 102: 563–74.

Dick, M. B. 1984. "A Syntactic Study of the Book of Obadiah." *Semitics* 9: 1–29.

Dicou, B. 1994. *Edom, Israel's Brother and Antagonist: The Role of Edom in Biblical Prophecy and Story*. Journal for the Study of the Old Testament: Supplement Series 169. Sheffield: JSOT Press.

Dohmen, C., and D. Rick. 2004. "rˁˁ." *Theological Dictionary of the Old Testament* 13: 560–88.

Dommershausen, W., and H.-J. Fabry. 1995. "leḥem." *Theological Dictionary of the Old Testament* 7: 521–29.

Dozemann, T. B. 1989. *God on the Mountain: A Study of Redaction, Theology and Canon in Exodus 19–24*. Society of Biblical Studies Monograph Series 37. Atlanta: Scholars Press.

Driver, G. R. 1955. "Birds in the Old Testament." *Palestine Exploration Quarterly* 87: 5–20, 129–40.

Elata-Alster, G., and R. Salmon. 1989. "The Deconstruction of Genre in the Book of Jonah: Toward a Theological Discourse." *Literature and Theology* 3: 40–60.

Elliger, K. 1934. "Die Heimat des Propheten Micha." *Zeitschrift des Deutschen Palästina Vereins* 57: 81–152.

Emmerson, G. I. 1976. "Another Look at the Book of Jonah." *Expository Times* 88: 86–88.

Feuillet, A. 1947. "Les sources du livre de Jonas." *Revue Biblique* 54: 161–86.

Fisher, L. R. 1963. "The Temple Quarter." *Journal of Semitic Studies* 8: 34–41.

Fitzmyer, J. 1956. "lê as a Preposition and a Particle in Micah 5,1 (5,2)." *Catholic Biblical Quarterly* 18: 10–13.

Fohrer, G. 1966. "Die Sprüche Obadjas." Pages 81–91 in *Studia Biblica et Semitica: Theodoro Christiano Vriezen qui munere Professoris Theologiae per XXV annos functus est, ab amicis, collegis, discipulis dedicata*. Wageningen: Veeman en Zonen.

——, 1981. "Micha 1." Pages 53–68 in *Studien zu alttestamentlichen Texten und Themen (1966–72)*. Beihefte zur Zeitschrift für die alttestamentliche Wissenschaft 155. Berlin: De Gruyter.

Fokkelman, J. P. 2001. *Reading Biblical Poetry: An Introductory Guide*. Louisville, Ky.: Westminster John Knox.

Follis, E. R. 1987. "The Holy City as Daughter." Pages 173–84 in *Directions in Biblical Hebrew Poetry*. Edited by E. R. Follis. Journal for the Study of the Old Testament: Supplement Series 40. Sheffield: JSOT Press.

Freedman, D. N. 1990. "Did God Play a Dirty Trick on Jonah at the End?" *Bible Review* 6: 26–31.

Freedman, D. N., and J. Lundbom. 1977. "beṭen." *Theological Dictionary of the Old Testament* 2: 94–99.

——, 1986. "ḥārâ, ḥārôn, ḥºrî." *Theological Dictionary of the Old Testament* 5: 171–76.

Fretheim, T. E. 1978. "Jonah and Theodicy." *Zeitschrift für die alttestamentliche Wissenschaft* 90: 227–37.

Fuhs, H. F. 1990. "yārēˀ." *Theological Dictionary of the Old Testament* 6: 290–315.

Fuller, R. 1996. "The Form and Formation of the Book of the Twelve: The Evidence from the Judaean Desert." Pages 96–101 in *Forming Prophetic Literature: Essays on Isaiah and the Twelve in Honor of John D. W. Watts*. Edited by J. W. Watts and P. R. House. Journal for the Study of the Old Testament: Supplement Series 235. Sheffield: Sheffield Academic Press.

Gamberoni, J., and H. Ringgren. 1997. "māqôm." *Theological Dictionary of the Old Testament* 8: 532–44.

Gibson, J. C. L. 1994. *Davidson's Introductory Hebrew Grammar Syntax*. 4th ed. Edinburgh: T. & T. Clark.

Goldingay, J. 1987. *Theological Diversity and the Authority of the Old Testament*. Leicester: Inter-Varsity Press.

Golka, F. W. 1986. "Jonaexegese und Antijudaismus." *Kirche und Israel* 1: 51–61.

Good, E. M. 1981. *Irony in the Old Testament*. 2nd ed. Sheffield: Sheffield Academic Press.

Goodfriend, E. A. 1992. "Prostitution." *Anchor Bible Dictionary* 5: 505–10.

Gordis, R. 1971. "Micah's Vision of the End-Time." Pages 268–79 in *Poets, Prophets and Sages: Essays in Biblical Interpretation*. Bloomington: Bloomington Indiana University Press.

Görg, M. 1990. "yāᶜad." *Theological Dictionary of the Old Testament* 6: 135–44.

Gosse, B. 1993. "Michée 4,1–5, Isaïe 2,1–5 et les rédacteurs du livre d'Isaïe." *Zeitschrift für die alttestamentliche Wissenschaft* 105: 98–102.

Gray, J. H. 1953. "The Diaspora of Israel and Judah in Obadiah 20." *Zeitschrift für die alttestamentliche Wissenschaft* 65: 53–59.

Gross, H. 1998. "māšal II." *Theological Dictionary of the Old Testament* 9: 68–71.

Gunkel, H. 1928. "The Close of Micah: A Prophetical Liturgy." Pages 115–49 in *What Remains of the Old Testament?* London: Allen & Unwin.

Haag, H. 1980. "ḥāmās." *Theological Dictionary of the Old Testament* 4: 478–87.

Haak, R. D. 1982. "A Study and New Interpretation of QṢR NPŠ." *Journal of Biblical Literature* 101: 161–67.

Hagstrom, D. G. 1988. *The Coherence of the Book of Micah*. Society of Biblical Literature Dissertation Series 89. Atlanta: Scholars Press.

Haller, E. 1958. "Die Erzählung von dem Propheten Jona." *Theologische Existenz heute* 65: 5–54.

Halpern, B., and R. E. Friedman. 1980. "Composition and Paronomasia in the Book of Jonah." *Hebrew Annual Review* 4: 79–92.

Hauser, A. 1985. "Jonah: In Pursuit of the Dove." *Journal of Biblical Literature* 104: 21–37.

Hayes, J. H. 1968. "The Usage of Oracles Against Foreign Nations in Ancient Israel." *Journal of Biblical Literature* 87: 81–92.

Hecke, P. J. P. van. "Living Alone in the Shrubs: Positive Pastoral Metaphors in Micah 7,14." *Zeitschrift für die alttestamentliche Wissenschaft* 115 (2003): 362–75.

Heschel, A. J. 1962. *The Prophets*. New York: Jewish Publication Society of America.

Hillers, D. R. 1969. *Covenant: The History of a Biblical Idea*. Baltimore: The Johns Hopkins University Press.

Hoffner, H. A. 1977. "bayit." *Theological Dictionary of the Old Testament* 2: 107–16.

Holbert, J. C. 1981. "'Deliverance Belongs to Yahweh!' Satire in the Book of Jonah." *Journal for the Study of the Old Testament* 21: 59–81.

Houk, C. B. 1998. "Linguistic Patterns in Jonah." *Journal for the Study of the Old Testament* 77: 81–102.

House, R. P. 1990. *The Unity of the Twelve*. Journal for the Study of the Old Testament: Supplement Series 97; Bible and Literature 27. Sheffield: JSOT Press.

Huffmon, H. B. 1959. "The Covenant Lawsuit in the Prophets." *Journal of Biblical Literature* 78: 285–95.

Innes, D. K. 1969. "Some Notes on Micah Chapter II." *Evangelical Quarterly* 41: 10–13.

Jacobs, M. R. 2001. *The Conceptual Coherence of the Book of Micah*. Journal for the Study of the Old Testament: Supplement Series 322. Sheffield: Sheffield Academic Press.

——, 2006. "Bridging the Times: Trends in Micah Studies Since 1985." *Currents in Biblical Research* 4: 293–329.

Janzen, W. 1972. *Mourning Cry and Woe Oracle*. Beihefte zur Zeitschrift für die alttestamentliche Wissenschaft 125. Berlin: De Gruyter.

——, 1994. *Old Testament Ethics: A Paradigmatic Approach*. Louisville, Ky.: Westminster John Knox.

Jenson, P. P. 1995. "Models of Prophetic Prediction and Matthew's Quotation of Micah 5:2." Pages 189–211 in *The Lord's Anointed: Interpretation of Old Testament Messianic Texts*. Edited by G. J. Wenham. Carlisle: Paternoster; Grand Rapids: Baker Books.

——, 2007. "Interpreting Jonah's God: Canon and Criticism." Pages 229–45 in *The God of Israel*. Edited by R. P. Gordon. University of Cambridge Oriental Publications 64. Cambridge: Cambridge University Press.

Jeppesen, K. 1979. "How the Book of Micah Lost Its Integrity: Outline of the History of the Criticism of the Book of Micah with Emphasis on the 19th Century." *Studia Theologica* 33: 101–31.

——, 1984. "Micah V 13 in the Light of Recent Archaeological Discovery." *Vetus Testamentum* 34: 462–66.

Jepsen, A. 1970. "Anmerkungen zum Buch Jona." Pages 297–305 in *Wort-Gebot-Glaube. Beiträge zur Theologie des Alten Testaments. Walter Eichrodt zum 80 Geburtstag*. Edited by H. J. Stoebe. Abhandlungen zur Theologie des Alten und Neuen Testaments 59. Zurich: Zwingli Verlag.

Jeremias, J. 1975. *Die Reue Gottes. Aspekte alttestamentliche Gottesvorstellung*. Biblische Studien 65. Neukirchen–Vluyn: Neukirchener.

Jerome. 1994. "The Letters of Jerome." Pages 1–295 in *The Nicene and Post-Nicene Fathers, Series 2*. Edited by Philip Schaff. Reprint. Peabody, Mass.: Hendrickson.

Johnson, E. 1974. "ʿānāp." *Theological Dictionary of the Old Testament* I: 349–60.

Johnston, P. 2002. *Shades of Sheol: Death and Afterlife in the Old Testament*. Leicester; Downers Grove: Apollos; InterVarsity.

Jones, G. H. 1978. "'Holy War' or 'Yahweh War'?" *Vetus Testamentum* 25: 642–58.

Kapelrud, A. S. 1961. "Eschatology in the Book of Micah." *Vetus Testamentum* 11: 392–405.

Kaufmann, Y. 1960. *The Religion of Israel*. Translated by M. Greenberg. Chicago: University of Chicago Press.

Keel, O. 1978. *The Symbolism of the Biblical World: Ancient Near East Iconography in the Book of the Psalms*. Translated by T. J. Hallett. London: SPCK.

Koch, K. 1978. "derek." *Theological Dictionary of the Old Testament* 3: 270–93.

Kornfeld, W. 1957. "Die jüdaische diaspora in Ab. 20." Pages 180–86 in *Melanges bibliques rédigés en l'honneur de Andre Robert*. Travaux de l'institut catholique de Paris 4. Paris: Bloud & Gay.

Kosmala, H. "geber." *Theological Dictionary of the Old Testament* 2: 367–82.

Kronholm, T. 1999. "nešer." *Theological Dictionary of the Old Testament* 10: 77–85.

——, 2003. "qādam." *Theological Dictionary of the Old Testament* 12: 511–15.

——, 2004. "śaq." *Theological Dictionary of the Old Testament* 14: 185–89.

Labuscagne, C. J. 1966. *The Incomparability of Yahweh in the Old Testament*. Leiden: Brill.

Landes, G. M. 1967. "The Kerygma of the Book of Jonah: The Contextual Interpretation of the Jonah Psalm." *Interpretation* 21: 3–31.

——, 1978. "Jonah: A Ma-ša-l?" Pages 137–58 in *Israelite Wisdom: Theological and Literary Essays in Honor of Samuel Terrien*. Edited by J. M. Ward. Missoula, Mont.: Scholars Press.

——, 1982. "Linguistic Criteria and the Date of the Book of Jonah." *Eretz Israel* 16: 147–70.

Lescow, T. 1966. *Micha 6:6–8. Studien zu Sprache, Form und Auslegung*. Stuttgart: Calwer Verlag.

Levenson, J. D. 1993. *The Death and Resurrection of the Beloved Son: The Transformation of Child Sacrifice in Judaism and Christianity*. New Haven: Yale University Press.

Levine, É. 1984. "Jonah as a Philosophical Book." *Zeitschrift für die alttestamentliche Wissenschaft* 96: 235–45.

Lillie, J. 1979. "Obadiah—A Celebration of God's Kingdom." *Currents in Theology and Mission* 6: 18–22.

Lipiński, E. 1973. "Obadiah 20." *Vetus Testamentum* 23: 368–70.

Lohfink, N. 1961. "Jona ging zur Stadt hinaus (Jon 4,5)." *Biblische Zeitschrift* 5: 185–203.

Long, V. P. 1994. *The Art of Biblical History*. Foundations of Contemporary Interpretation 5. Grand Rapids: Zondervan.

Loretz, O. 1960. "Herkunft und Sinn der Jonaerzählung." *Biblische Zeitschrift* 5: 18–29.

Lux, R. 1994. *Jona: Prophet zwischen »Verweigerung« und »Gehorsam«: Eine erzählanalytische Studie*. Forschungen zur Religion und Literatur des Alten und Neuen Testaments 102. Göttingen: Vandenhoeck & Ruprecht.

Magonet, J. 1983 (1976). *Form and Meaning: Studies in Literary Techniques in the Book of Jonah*. Bible and Literature 8. Sheffield: JSOT Press.

Maiberger, P., "ʿēśeb." *Theological Dictionary of the Old Testament* 11: 383–86.

Marböck, J. 1998. "nābāl." *Theological Dictionary of the Old Testament* 9: 151–71.

Marcus, D. 1995. *From Balaam to Jonah: Anti-prophetic Satire in the Hebrew Bible*. Brown Judaic Studies 301. Atlanta: Scholars Press.

Marrs, R. R. 1999. "Micah and a Theological Critique of Worship." Pages 184–203 in *Worship and the Hebrew Bible: Essays in Honour of John T. Willis*. Edited by S. L. McKenzie. Journal for the Study of the Old Testament: Supplement Series 284. Sheffield: Sheffield Academic Press.

Mason, R. 1991. *Micah, Nahum, Obadiah*. Old Testament Guides. Sheffield: JSOT Press.

Mays, J. L. 1977. "The Theological Purpose of the Book of Micah." Pages 276–87 in *Beiträge zur alttestamentlichen Theologie. Festschrift für W. Zimmerli zum 70. Geburtstag*. Edited by R. Smend. Göttingen: Vandenhoeck & Ruprecht.

McCarter, P. K. 1977. "Obadiah 7 and the Fall of Edom." *Bulletin of the American Schools of Oriental Research* 221: 484–87.

McKane, W. 1995. "Micah 1,2–7." *Zeitschrift für die alttestamentliche Wissenschaft* 107: 420–34.

Metzner, G. 1998. *Kompositionsgeschichte des Michabuches*. Europaisch Hochschulschriften Theologie 23. Frankfurt: Peter Lang.

Michel, D. 1996. "Das Ende der 'Tochter der Streifschar' (Mi 4,14)." *Zeitschrift für Althebräistik* 9: 196–98.

Miles, J. A., Jr. 1974–75. "Laughing at the Bible: Jonah as Parody." *Jewish Quarterly Review* 65: 168–81.

Miller, P. D. 1982. *Sin and Judgment in the Prophets*. Society of Biblical Studies Monograph Series 27. Chico, Calif.: Scholars Press.

Moberly, R. W. L. 2003. "Preaching for a Response? Jonah's Message to the Ninevites Reconsidered." *Vetus Testamentum* 53: 156–68.

Moor, J. C. de 1974. "ʾăšērâ." *Theological Dictionary of the Old Testament* I: 438–44.

——, 1988. "Micah 1." Pages 172–85 in *The Structural Analysis of Biblical and Canaanite Poetry*. Edited by J. C. Moor. Journal for the Study of the Old Testament: Supplement Series 74. Sheffield: JSOT Press.

——, 2000. "Micah 7:1–13: The Lament of a Disillusioned Prophet." Pages 149–96 in *Delimitation Criticism: A New Tool in Biblical Scholarship*. Edited by M. C. A. Korpel and J. M. Oesch. Pericope 1. Assen: Van Gorcum.

Mosala, I. J. 1993. "A Materialist Reading of Micah." Pages 164–95 in *The Bible and Liberation: Political and Social Hermeneutics*. Edited by R. A. Horsely. Maryknoll: Orbis.

Mulder, M. J. 1990. "ya'ar." *Theological Dictionary of the Old Testament* 6: 208–17.

Mulzer, M. 2002. "Die Buße der Tiere in Jona 3,7f. und Jdt 4,10." *Biblische Notizen* 111: 76–89.

Murray, D. F. 1987. "The Rhetoric of Disputation: Re-examination of a Prophetic Genre." *Journal for the Study of the Old Testament* 38: 95–121.

Na'aman, N. 1974. "Sennacherib's 'Letter to God' on His Campaign to Judah." *Bulletin of the American Schools of Oriental Research* 214: 25–39.

———, 1979. "Sennacherib's Campaign to Judah and the Date of the LMLK Stamps." *Vetus Testamentum* 29: 61–86.

———, 1995. "'The-house-of-no-shade shall take away its tax from you' (Micah i 11)." *Vetus Testamentum* 45: 516–27.

Neiderhiser, E. A. 1981. "Micah 2:6–11: Considerations on the Nature of the Discourse." *Biblical Theology Bulletin* 11: 104–107.

Neiman, D. 1963. "Sefarad: The Name of Spain." *Journal of Near Eastern Studies* 22: 128–32.

Nielsen, E. 1954. *Oral Tradition*. SBT 11. London: SCM Press.

———, 1979. "Le message primitif du livre de Jonas." *Revue d'histoire et de philosophie religieuses* 59: 499–507.

Nogalski, J. 1993. *Literary Precursors to the Book of the Twelve*. Beihefte zur Zeitschrift für die alttestamentliche Wissenschaft 217. Berlin: De Gruyter.

———, 1993. *Redactional Processes in the Book of the Twelve*. Beihefte zur Zeitschrift für die alttestamentliche Wissenschaft 218. Berlin: De Gruyter.

Ogden, G. 1982. "Prophetic Oracles Against Foreign Nations and Psalms of Communal Lament: The Relationship of Psalm 137 to Jeremiah 49:7–22 and Obadiah." *Journal for the Study of the Old Testament* 24: 89–97.

Orth, M. 1990. "Genre in Jonah: The Effects of Parody in the Book of Jonah." Pages 257–81 in *The Bible in the Light of Cuneiform Literature: Scripture in Context*, Volume 3. Edited by G. L. Mattingly. Lewiston, NY: Edwin Mellen.

Peels, H. G. L. 1994. *The Vengeance of God: The Meaning of the Root NQM and the Function of the NQM-Texts in the Context of Divine Revelation in the Old Testament*. Old Testament Studies 31. Leiden: Brill.

Person, R. F. 1996. *In Conversation with Jonah: Conversation Analysis, Literary Criticism, and the Book of Jonah*. Journal for the Study of the Old Testament: Supplement Series 220. Sheffield: Sheffield Academic Press.

Pesch, R. 1966. "Zur konzentrischen Struktur von Jona 1." *Biblica* 47: 577–81.

Petersen, D. L. 2000. "A Book of the Twelve?" Pages 3–10 in *Reading and Hearing the Book of the Twelve*. Edited by M. A. Sweeney. Society of Biblical Literature Symposium Series 15. Atlanta: Society of Biblical Literature.

Peytrottan, A. J. 1991. *Lexis Ludens: Wordplay and the Book of Micah*. American University Studies Series VII Theology and Religion 105. Frankfurt: Lang.

Pola, T. 1997. "Micha 6,7." *Biblische Notizen* 86: 57–59.

Raabe, P. R. 1995. "Why Prophetic Oracles Against the Nations?" Pages 236–57 in *Fortunate the Eyes That See: Essays in Honor of David Noel Freedman in Celebration of His Seventieth Birthday*. Edited by C. A. Franke. Grand Rapids: Eerdmans.

———, 2002. "The Particularizing of Universal Judgment in Prophetic Discourse." *Catholic Biblical Quarterly* 64: 652–74.

Rad, G., von. 1965. *Old Testament Theology*, Volume 2. Translated by D. M. G. Stalker. London: SCM Press.

Redditt, P. L. 2001. "Recent Research on the Book of the Twelve as One Book." *Currents in Research: Biblical Studies* 9: 47–80.

Reicke, B. 1967. "Liturgical Traditions in Micah 7 (Translated by J.T. Willis)." *Harvard Theological Review* 60: 349–67.

Reimer, D. J. 1996. "ṣdq." *NIDOTTE* 3: 744–69.

Renaud, B. 1977. *La formation du livre de Michée*. Études Bibliques. Paris: Gabalda.

Ringgren, H. 1995. "lāᵓā." *Theological Dictionary of the Old Testament* 7: 395–96.

Robinson, B. P. 1985. "Jonah's Qiqayon Plant." *Zeitschrift für die alttestamentliche Wissenschaft* 97: 390–403.

Robinson, R. B. 1988. "Levels of Naturalization in Obadiah." *Journal for the Study of the Old Testament* 40: 83–97.

Robinson, T. H. 1916. "The Structure of the Book of Obadiah." *Journal of Theological Studies* 17: 402–8.

Rowley, H. H. 1945. *The Missionary Message of the Old Testament*. London: Carey Press.

Salters, R. B. 1994. *Jonah and Lamentations*. Old Testament Guides. Sheffield: Sheffield Academic Press.

Sauer, G. "ᵓap Anger." *Theological Lexicon of the Old Testament* 1: 166–69.

Schart, A. 2000. "Reconstructing the Redaction History of the Twelve Prophets: Problems and Models." Pages 34–48 in *Reading and Hearing the Book of the Twelve*. Edited by M. A. Sweeney. Society of Biblical Literature Symposium Series 15. Atlanta: Society of Biblical Literature.

Schmidt, H. 1905. "Die Komposition des Buches Jona." *Zeitschrift für die alttestamentliche Wissenschaft* 25: 285–310.

Schwantes, S. J. 1964. "Critical Notes on Micah 1:10–16." *Vetus Testamentum* 14: 454–61.

Seybold, K. 1978. "hāpak." *Theological Dictionary of the Old Testament* 3: 423–27.

Shaw, C. S. 1987. "Micah 1:10–16 Reconsidered." *Journal of Biblical Literature* 106: 223–29.

——, 1993. *The Speeches of Micah: A Rhetorical-Historical Analysis*. Journal for the Study of the Old Testament: Supplement Series 145. Sheffield: JSOT Press.

Sherwood, Y. 1997. "Rocking the Boat: Jonah and the New Historicism." *Biblical Interpretation* 5: 364–403.

——, 1998. "Cross-Currents in the Book of Jonah: Some Jewish and Cultural Midrashim on a Traditional Text." *Biblical Interpretation* 6: 49–79.

——, 2000. *A Biblical Text and Its Afterlives: The Survival of Jonah in Western Culture*. Cambridge: Cambridge University Press.

Sinclair, L. A. 1983. "The Hebrew Text of the Qumran Micah Pesher and Textual Traditions of the Minor Prophets." *Revue de Qumrân* 11: 253–63.

Smith, M. S. 1988. "Divine Form and Size in Ugaritic and Pre-exilic Israelite Religion." *Zeitschrift für die alttestamentliche Wissenschaft* 100: 424–27.

Snyman, S. D. 1989. "Cohesion in the Book of Obadiah." *Zeitschrift für die alttestamentliche Wissenschaft* 101: 59–71.

——, 1992. "YOM (YHWH) in the Book of Obadiah." Pages 81–91 in *Goldene Äpfel in silbernen Schalen*. Edited by K.-D. Schunck. Beiträge zur Erforschung des Alten Testaments und des antiken Judentums 20. Frankfurt: Lang.

Spieckermann, H. 1990. "'Barmherzig und gnädig ist der Herr...'." *Zeitschrift für die alttestamentliche Wissenschaft* 102: 1–18.

Stade, B. 1881. "Bemerkungen über das Buch Micha." *Zeitschrift für die alttestamentliche Wissenschaft* 1: 161–72.

Stansell, G. 1988. *Micah and Isaiah: A Form and Tradition Historical Comparison*. Society of Biblical Literature Dissertation Series 88. Atlanta: Scholars Press.

Sternberg, M. 1985. *The Poetics of Biblical Narrative: Ideological Literature and the Drama of Reading*. Bloomington: Indiana University Press.

Stoebe, H. J. 1959. "Und demütig sein vor deinem Gott. Micah 6,8." *Wort und Dienst* NF 6: 180–94.

Strydom, J. G. 1989. "Micah 4:1–5 and Isaiah 2:2–5: Who Said it First? A Critical Discussion of A. S. van der Woude's View." *Old Testament Essays* 2, no. 2: 15–28.

Sweeney, M. A. 1996. "The Book of Isaiah as Prophetic Torah." Pages 50–67 in *New Visions of Isaiah*. Edited by R. F. Melugin and M. A. Sweeney. Journal for the Study of the Old Testament: Supplement Series 214. Sheffield: Sheffield Academic Press.

——, 2000. "Sequence and Interpretation in the Book of the Twelve." Pages 49–64 in *Reading and Hearing the Book of the Twelve*. Edited by M. A. Sweeney. Society of Biblical Literature Symposium Series 15. Atlanta: Society of Biblical Literature.

Talmon, S. 1977. "har." *Theological Dictionary of the Old Testament* 3: 427–47.

Tanghe, V. 1997. "Die Trinker in Obadja 16." *Revue Biblique* 104: 522–27.

Theis, J. 1917. *Die Weissagung des Abdias*. Trier: Paulinus-Druckerei.

Thomas, D. W. 1953. "A Consideration of Some Unusual Ways of Expressing the Superlative in Hebrew." *Vetus Testamentum* 3: 210–24.

Toorn, K., van der. 1992. "Cultic Prostitution." *Anchor Bible Dictionary* 5: 510–13.

Trible, P. 1994. *Rhetorical Criticism: Context, Method, and the Book of Jonah*. Guides to Biblical Scholarship. Philadelphia: Fortress.

Tsevat, M. 1980. "ḥālaq." *Theological Dictionary of the Old Testament* 4: 447–51.

Tyndale, W. 1992. *Tyndale's Old Testament: Being the Pentateuch of 1530; Joshua to 2 Chronicles of 1537; and Jonah*. Edited by D. Daniell. New Haven: Yale University Press.

Vawter, B. 1983. *Job and Jonah: Questioning the Hidden God*. New York: Paulist Press.

Wagenaar, J. A. 1996. "The Hillside of Samaria. Interpretation and Meaning of Micah 1:6." *Biblische Notizen* 85: 26–30.

——, 2001. *Judgement and Salvation: The Composition and Redaction of Micah 2–5*. Vetus Testamentum Supplements 85. Leiden: Brill.

Wagner, S. 1995. "klm." *Theological Dictionary of the Old Testament* 7: 185–96.

Walsh, J. T. 1982. "Jonah 2,3–10: A Rhetorical Critical Study." *Biblica* 63: 219–29.

Waltke, B. 1988. "Micah." Pages 133–207 in *Obadiah, Jonah, Micah*. Edited by B. Waltke. Tyndale Old Testament Commentaries. Leicester: Inter-Varsity Press.

——, 2007. *A Commentary on Micah*. Grand Rapids: Eerdmans.

Watson, W. G. E. 1984. "Allusion, Irony and Wordplay in Micah 1,7." *Biblica* 65: 103–5.

Watts, J. D. W. 1993. "'This Song.' Conspicuous Poetry in Hebrew Prose." Pages 345–58 in *Verse in Ancient Near Eastern Prose*. Edited by J. C. de Moor and W. G. E. Watson. Alter Orient und Altes Testament 42. Neukirchen–Vluyn: Neukirchener.

Wehrle, J. 1987. *Prophetie und Textanalyse. Die Komposition Obadja 1–21, interpretiert auf der Basis textlinguistischer und semiotischer Konzeptionen*. Arbeiten zu Text und Sprache im Alten Testament 28. St. Ottilien: Arbeiten zu Text und Sprache im Alten Testament 28.

Weil, H.-M. 1940. "Le chapitre 2 de Michée expliqué par Le Premier Livre des Rois, chapitres 20–22." *Revue de l'histoire des religions* 121: 146–61.

Weimar, P. 1982. "Beobachtungen zur Entstehung der Jonaerzaählung." *Biblische Notizen* 18: 86–109.

——, 1985. "Obadja, Eine redaktionskritische Analyse." *Biblische Notizen* 27: 35–99.

Wellhausen, J. 1892. *Skizzen und Arbeiten, fünftes Heft: Die kleinen Propheten übersetzt, mit Noten*. Berlin: Reimer.

Wendland, E. 1996. "Obadiah's Vision of 'The Day of the Lord': On the Importance of Rhetoric in the Biblical Text and in Bible Translation." *Journal of Translation and Textlinguistics* 7: 54–86.

——, 1996. "Obadiah's 'Day': On the Rhetorical Implications of Textual Form and Inter-textual Influence." *Journal of Translation and Textlinguistics* 8: 23–49.

Werlitz, J. 1996. "Noch einmal Immanuel—gliech zweimal! Rudolf Kilian in Dankbarkeit zugeeignet." *Biblische Zeitschrift* 40: 254–63.

Westermann, C. 1967. *Basic Forms of Prophetic Speech*. Translated by H. C. White. London: Lutterworth.

——, 1982. *Elements of Old Testament Theology*. Translated by D. W. Stott. Atlanta: John Knox.

Wiklander, B. 1980. "zāʿam." *Theological Dictionary of the Old Testament* 4: 106–11.

Wildberger, H. 1957. "Die Völkerfahrt zum Zion: Jes. 2:1–5." *Vetus Testamentum* 7: 62–81.

——, 1991. *Isaiah 1–12: A Commentary*. Translated by T. H. Trapp, Continental Commentaries. Philadelphia: Augsburg.

Williams, A. L. 1907. "A Modern Jonah?" *Expository Times* 18: 239.

Williamson, H. G. M. 1997. "Marginalia in Micah." *Vetus Testamentum* 47: 360–72.

——, 2006. *A Critical and Exegetical Commentary on Isaiah 1–27*. Volume 1 of *Isaiah 1–5*. International Critical Commentary. London: T&T Clark International.

Willis, J. T. 1965. "Review of B. Renaud, Structure et Attaches littéraires de Michée IV–V." *Vetus Testamentum* 15: 400–3.

——, 1967. "On the Text of Micah 2,1aα-B." *Biblica* 48: 534–41.

——, 1967–68. "mmk ly yṣʾ in Micah 5.1." *Jewish Quarterly Review* 58: 317–22.

——, 1968a. "A Note on wᵊmr in Micah 3:1." *Zeitschrift für die alttestamentliche Wissenschaft* 80: 50–54.

——, 1968b. "Some Suggestions on the Interpretation of Micah I:2." *Vetus Testamentum* 18: 372–79.

——, 1968c. "Micah 4:14–5:5—A Unit." *Vetus Testamentum* 18: 529–47.

——, 1969a. "The Authenticity and Meaning of Micah 5:9–14." *Zeitschrift für die alttestamentliche Wissenschaft* 81: 353–68.

——, 1969b. "The Structure of Micah 3–5 and the Function of Micah 5:9–14 in the Book." *Zeitschrift für die alttestamentliche Wissenschaft* 81: 191–214.

——, 1969c. "The Structure of the Book of Micah." *Svensk Exegetisk Årsbok* 34: 5–42.

——, 1970. "Micah 2:6–8 and the 'People of God' in Micah." *Biblische Zeitschrift* NF 14: 72–87.

Wiseman, D. J. 1979. "Jonah's Nineveh." *Tyndale Bulletin* 30: 29–51.

Wolff, H. W. 1974. *Anthropology of the Old Testament*. Translated by M. Kohl. London: SCM Press.

——, 1975. *Studien zum Jonabuch*. 2d. ed. Biblische Studien 47. Neukirchen–Vluyn: Neukirchener.

——, 1978. "Wie verstand Micha von Moreshet sein prophetisches Amt?" Pages 403–17 in *Congress Volume, Göttingen*. Vetus Testamentum Supplements 29. Leiden: Brill.

——, 1982. *Micah the Prophet*. Translated by R. D. Gehrke. Philadelphia: Fortress.

Woude, A. S., van der. 1969. "Micah in Dispute with the Pseudo-prophets." *Vetus Testamentum* 19: 244–60.

——, 1971. "Micah I 10–16." Pages 347–53 in *Hommages à André Dupont-Sommer*. Edited by M. Philonenko. Paris: Adrien-Maisonneuve.

——, 1973. "Micah IV 1–5: An Instance of the Pseudo-Prophets Quoting Isaiah." Pages 396–402 in *Symbolae biblicae et Mesopotamicae Francisco Mario Theodoro de Liagre Böhl dedicatae*. Edited by M. A. Beek et al. Studia Francisci Scholten memoriae dicata 4. Leiden: Brill.

——, 1983. "Nachholende Erzählung im Buche Jona." Pages 267–72 in *Essays on the Bible and the Ancient World (I.L. Seeligmann Volume)*, Volume 3. Edited by Y. Zakowitch. Jerusalem: E. Rubenstein.

Zobel, H.-J. 1978. "hôy." *Theological Dictionary of the Old Testament* 3: 359–64.

——, 1990. "yiśrāʾēl." *Theological Dictionary of the Old Testament* 6: 397–420.

INDEXES

INDEX OF REFERENCES

The biblical references listed in this index follow the versification used in English versions of the Bible.

INDEX OF AUTHORS